# SECURITY
## FOR YOU & YOUR HOME...
## A COMPLETE HANDBOOK
### BY CLARENCE M. KELLEY & CARL A. ROPER

**TAB** TAB BOOKS Inc.

BLUE RIDGE SUMMIT, PA. 17214

*Crime is clearly one of the most
serious problems we face today.
Crime—and the fear of crime—
affects the lives of most Americans.*

Ronald Reagan
President of the United States

FIRST EDITION

FIRST PRINTING

Library of Congress Cataloging in Publication Data

Kelley, Clarence M.
Security for you and your home - - : a complete handbook.

Includes index
1. Crime prevention.   2. Dwellings—Security measures.
3. Security systems.   4. Accidents—Prevention.
5. Self-defense.   I. Roper, C. A. (Carl A.)   II. Title.
HN7431.K44   1984      643′.16      83-18134
ISBN 0-8306-0680-7
ISBN 0-8306-1680-2 (pbk.)

# Contents

# Preface

I have been intensely interested and devoted to the crime prevention programs developed in the past few years. I started a program in this area while Director of the Federal Bureau of Investigation and assigned more than 100 agents to it and a considerable sum of money for its implementation.

Traditional methods to reduce crime are not enough. Every citizen should try to reduce his own vulnerability as much as he possibly can. No longer can we rely exclusively on the law enforcement officers to bring us to a satisfactory level of safety and security. Security is a precious inheritance of our nation, but that inheritance must be a shared responsibility of all of us. We must cooperate with our fellow citizens and our designated representatives of the law.

Crime probably cannot be eradicated entirely, but I am confident it can be lowered to at least a more acceptable level than the ravages we have undergone in the past three decades. The time is now to do something about this problem.

Clarence M. Kelley

# Acknowledgments

We would like to thank the numerous security professionals and individuals from many companies who provided advice, assistance, and information for this book. We certainly appreciate and thank Lynda K. Roper for typing and editing the manuscript from our questionable spellings and chicken scratches into something of which we are very proud.

# Introduction

The risk of crime against person and property is a growing concern among all citizens. Why? Personal and property protection against crime is inadequate. You must invest some time and money to reduce the threat of crime against yourself, your home, the family car, and also against other family members. Imagine a person who is robbed at gunpoint for a measly three packages of cigarettes, or take a woman walking down the street who is robbed and beaten, her purse stolen, and who must spend several days recuperating in the hospital—all for a crime that netted the thief less than $5. These types of crimes are typical of today's society.

We are extremely concerned about the continued increase in crime. We are dedicated to the premise that, by helping others in crime prevention, crime can be reduced. By reducing the potential for crime through public awareness and crime prevention techniques, the fear of crime that has swept across our nation will also be lessened.

We have spent many years studying crime, the methods and techniques available to reduce crime, and the various devices that are readily available to protect the individual and the home. This book covers the products and methods available to protect both your property and yourself.

Much has been written about protective measures, what products and devices are available, and what should be considered for individual and home protection. With the exception of a very few books, these sources are not all-encompassing. Many books present good information, but cover only limited subject areas. Others cover a wide variety of areas, but not with proper depth. This book will provide you with the detailed information and techniques to dramatically increase your security.

The various products selected for inclusion in this book are recommended by us. Remember them when selecting either individual security devices or complete security systems for your property or personal protection. The items work; that's why they are here.

We are committed to reducing crime in all its various forms, and we solicit your assistance. Support your local police efforts in crime prevention. Your support and assistance, in addition to taking steps to reduce crime through the techniques in this book, will make for a safer nation.

# Chapter 1

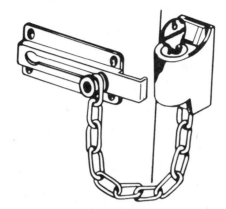

# The Need for Home and Personal Security and Safety

Home security and safety are concerns of everyone. All of us fear personal violence and/or the threat to the sanctity of our home and possessions.

The staggering crime statistics show that people will resort to crime "to succeed," even though the crime itself may be miniscule compared to a bank heist, drugs, prostitution, or murder. In 1970, there were more than 2 million burglaries. Experts thought that crime had reached its peak and would soon diminish. In the 1980s though, crime is more prevalent than ever. During 1983, you can expect the number of burglaries, street robberies, and thefts to top 6 million, and that figure will be only those crimes reported.

Everyone must work to prevent crime. Operation ID and the Neighborhood Crime Watch Program are available to help you and your neighbors reduce crime.

Someone may say, "Hey, I've got insurance; I don't have anything to worry about. As long as I'm covered, the company will pay me off." This is definitely the wrong attitude. It shows that the individual doesn't really know about home security and personal safety. Insurance money won't get back that family heirloom or picture of your great-great-grandfather. Neither will it heal the psychological wounds of a five-, six-, or seven-year-old child who woke up in the night, saw a burglar, and screamed for his or her life. Also, insurance will not bring back a young woman who was attacked on the street and killed when she refused to give up her purse to two young hoodlums.

Insurance coverage to replace items that may be stolen or destroyed is certainly a wise investment, but it is no reason for complacency. No policy from any insurance company guarantees security and safety.

Let's look at the need for security and safety in another perspective. Imagine that you are a corporate executive. You are moving up in society, so you and your family move into a larger home. You have two or three cars, several acres of ground, a large dog, fences (brick or wire), and

1

you feel that you have it made.

Your new job as vice-president in charge of overseas operations means that you are seen frequently in public, entertaining foreign visitors. You have visibility. You are now a target for criminals, terrorists, and kidnappers.

A member of your family could be kidnapped. Your home could be burglarized, ransacked, or vandalized while you are away. Because of your position, you hold numerous meetings concerning state-of-the-art technology in your home or your car. Your home or meeting area could be bugged to pick up your thoughts.

Crime takes various forms, and the threats against the individual are many. These generalties can't really set for the specifics of crime and safety.

## PROTECTION AGAINST CRIME

Some will be robbed and at least four homes will be burglarized every minute. At least two cars, bicycles, motorcycles or mopeds will be stolen. At least one home (a house, apartment, trailer, or condominium) will have a fire, possibly resulting in injury or death to the occupants.

Some owners will have insurance; others will not. Some with insurance will be fully covered, some moderately, and a few will have insurance that is wholly inadequate to meet their rebuilding needs.

Take an average community of 30,000 to 40,000 people. During a typical year, there will be at least 25 robberies, more than 500 burglaries, and more than 100 automobiles stolen. These losses will total well more than $350,000.

In a big city such as New York, Chicago, or Los Angeles, the crime rate statistics and cost figures are even greater. The larger the community, the larger the crime problem.

You may say, "I'm protected." You may be, but for how long? Your protection may be outdated. Your door lock that was installed new 20 years ago at the cost of $25-$30 is now well-worn, its pins are in poor shape, the key is worn down, and the springs have lost most of their original tension. A $9 lock on today's market

probably has as much if not more protection.

You wanted and purchased a door with panels because it looked nice. You installed it with your new lock. Those panels won't last too long against a good swift kick.

As for the items in your home, the silver set that cost $300 more than 25 years ago is now worth more than $1,000. Your stamp collection, stereo, television, video recorder, and color video camera are valuable possessions. If your home is not protected properly, a burglar may steal them.

A burglar knows that 95 percent of the time he will never see his victim. His crime is not against a person *per se*, but against property. He is more likely to succeed than to get caught.

Discourage burglars by using barriers, and by having a dog, an alarm system, good locks, and night lighting. Make sure that the alarm system is activated when you are not at home, the door lock is deadbolted, the garage is closed and locked, property is properly marked, and that there are no trees close to the house and no shrubbery near basement windows.

A good perimeter security alarm reacts to attempted entry through windows, doors and ventilation openings. At night, a photoelectric system spots a burglar when he is halfway across your lawn. The system turns on exterior lights that flood the entire area where the burglar is standing. Your alarm system reacts with a local alarm or a silent alarm to the local police station or to a neighbor's house.

## THE CHALLENGE OF CRIME IN A FREE SOCIETY

A report by the President's Commission on Law Enforcement and Administration of Justice, published in 1967 but still most applicable today, states that "crime is a response to a specific situation by a person with an infinitely complicated psychological and emotional makeup who is subject to infinitely complicated external pressures." Crime is an opportunity taken by a thief when he judges that the crime will benefit him. The reluctance or inability to take action against crime and public apathy and tolerance of certain

```
 9:15 A.M.   Strong-arm robbery, street, $2
10:00 A.M.   Armed robbery, liquor store, $1500
11:30 A.M.   Pocketbook snatched with force and violence, street, $3
12:30 P.M.   Holdup with revolver, roofing company, $2100
 2:40 P.M.   Holdup with gun, shoe store, $139
 3.20 P.M.   Holdup with gun, apartment, $92
 4:55 P.M.   Holdup with gun, bank, $8716
 6:25 P.M.   Mugging, street, $4
 6:50 P.M.   Holdup with revolver, tourist home, $30
 7:00 P.M.   Strong-arm robbery, street, $25
 7:05 P.M.   Holdup with gun, auto in parking lot, $61
 7:10 P.M.   Strong-arm robbery, apartment house, $3
 7:15 P.M.   Holdup with revolver, trunk rental company, $200
 7:25 P.M.   Mugging, street, $5
 7:50 P.M.   Holdup with gun, transfer company, $1400
 8:55 P.M.   Holdup with shotgun, newspaper substation, $100
10:10 P.M.   Holdup with gun, hotel, $289.50
10:15 P.M.   Strong-arm robbery, street, $120
10:30 P.M.   Holdup with gun, street, $59.50
10:53 P.M.   Strong-arm robbery, street, $175
11:05 P.M.   Holdup, tavern, $40
11:30 P.M.   Holdup with gun, street, $3
11:55 P.M.   Strong-arm robbery, street, $51
12:20 A.M.   Strong-arm robbery, street, $19
 1:10 A.M.   Strong-arm robbery, apartment house, $3
 3:25 A.M.   Strong-arm robbery, street, $25
 3:50 A.M.   Holdup with knife, street, $23
 3:55 A.M.   Holdup with gun, street, $25
 4:20 A.M.   Robbery with intent to rape, street, 75 cents
 4:20 A.M.   Holdup with gun, carryout shop, $80
 6:25 A.M.   Holdup and rape, street, $20
 6:25 A.M.   Holdup with gun, tourist home, no amount listed
 6:45 A.M.   Holdup, street, $5
 7:30 A.M.   Holdup with knife, cleaners, $300
 7:40 A.M.   Strong-arm robbery, street, $80
```

Source: *The Challenge of Crime in a Free Society*: A Report by the President's Commission on Law Enforcement and Administration of Justice

Fig. 1-1. Twenty-four hours of crime in our nation's capital (courtesy President's Commission on Law Enforcement and Administration of Justice).

types of activity directly promote crime.

As an example, slum residents in a large city feel they live in an area that is useless for them to defend. Many residents feel overwhelmed and thus do nothing about the crime problem. When the citizenry does not become involved crime flourishes.

Crime also flourishes in the more affluent areas of a city. The risk is greater, but the end result is also greater for the criminal. Where there is a potential for making money, anything goes—and crime rises.

Crime is everywhere: on the street, in the home, at a local hotel or motel, and in business. It knows no boundaries. Figure 1-1 lists crimes reported to the Metropolitan Police Department, Washington, D.C., during one 24-hour period. The "take" to the criminals was more than

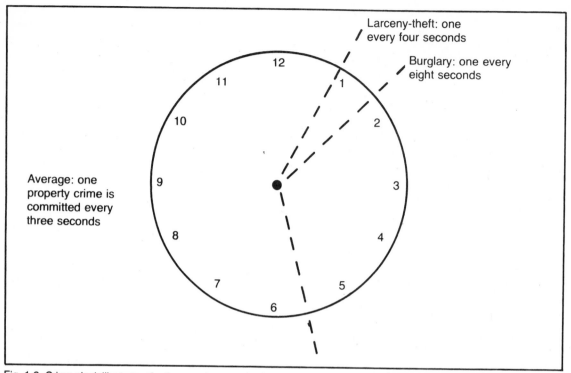

Fig. 1-2. Crime clock illustrates the three major property times in terms of one minute (source FBI Uniform Crime Reports).

$16,000. The anguish and terror to the individuals involved cannot be calculated in dollars.

Crime can be spontaneous, ruthless, systematic, or random. The crimes that concern people the most are those that will affect their safety. The most frequent and serious of these violent crimes are homocide, rape, assault, and robbery. Besides these crimes, the Federal Bureau of Investigation (FBI) also collects statistical information for the property crimes of burglary, larceny (more than $50 taken), and auto theft. Figure 1-2 shows the "crime clock" in terms of how often a crime is committed.

## ATTITUDES TOWARD CRIME

The widespread belief that the public is concerned and scared about crime is true. Crime is seen as one of the most serious domestic problems confronting the nation today.

The fear of crime also will make people want to move to other neighborhoods, cities, or even

Table 1-1. Americans Are Afraid (source U.S. Department of Justice Publications and President's Commission on Law Enforcement and Administration of Justice).

| Belief | Percentage |
|---|---|
| Will be a victim of a violent crime | 50% |
| Feel unsafe in everyday environment | 40% |
| Have a gun for protection | 50% |
| Fear of being raped | 55% |
| Fear in large cities | 52% |
| Fear in rural areas | 30% |
| Keep automobile door locked at all times | 70% |

states. In Boston and Chicago, a survey found that at least 20 percent of the citizens wanted to move because of the crime in their own neighborhoods. As many as 30 percent wanted to move out of high crime rate districts in Boston.

This survey found that people still felt better in their own neighborhood than in other areas, even though their neighborhood had a higher crime rate. Why? The answer is probably because they at least recognized some of the people in their neighborhood and knew roughly where and when crime would occur. In a new area they would know nothing about the fears and anxieties of the other residents, much less the types and numbers of crimes committed.

People interviewed in one study indicated they would stay home instead of going out for the evening. They feared for their safety.

A national survey showed that at least 82 percent of people asked normally keep doors locked at night. At least 25 percent keep doors locked during the day when everyone is at home.

In Boston and Chicago, 28 percent put new locks on their doors because they had previously been burglarized or were worried about the area's high crime rate. Another 10 percent put locks or bars on their windows, but this occurred mostly in areas with a high crime rate. Table 1-1 indicates concern of the citizenry.

## CRIME STATISTICS

In September, 1981, Attorney General William French Smith announced that the FBI's Crime Index of reported serious crimes increased 9 percent. This index was 18 percent higher than that of 1976.

During 1980, burglary, larceny, and motor vehicle theft rose 9 percent. Forcible rape increased 8 percent, burglary 14 percent larceny-theft 8 percent.

In 1976, crimes against property rose 16 percent. The figure was a staggering 54 percent increase during the 1970s. The police clearance rate (solving the crime) was only 19 percent for property crimes. Fourteen percent of burglary

cases, 18 percent of larceny-theft cases, and 14 percent of automobile theft cases were solved. Twenty-eight percent of these property crimes involved persons under 18 years of age.

Burglaries and other property crimes are anywhere from 1.5, 2, 3, or 4 million or more a year. The FBI Crime Index is based on *reported* crime to local police departments and jurisdictions across the nation. In burglaries occurring in the United States in 1980 alone, it represented 81 percent of all property crimes and 28 percent *of all crime reported*. This breaks down to 1,668 burglaries per 100,000 inhabitants and is an 11 percent increase over the previous year.

Residential property was the target in 67 percent of the reportable burglaries. Of this figure, 73 percent involved forcible entry and is a loss of more than $3 billion. That's an average of $882 per burglary.

Larceny-thefts amounted to 53 percent of all reported Crime Index crimes and 59 percent of property crimes. The theft rate was about 31,000 per 100,000 people. The average value of property stolen was $307, for an estimated total of some $2.2 billion. For miscellaneous thefts from buildings and vehicles, the averages work out to about 483 and 341 per 100,000, respectively.

There are around 500 car thefts per 100,000 people. In 1980, this meant that one out of every 143 registered vehicles was stolen. The average value of these cars was $2,879. The national total is $3.2 billion in automobiles stolen a year.

Fear of crime has led people rushing to arm themselves, often with weapons they don't know how to use. Other people have installed extremely elaborate and excessively expensive security systems to protect property and family. Many people haven't really done anything that will reduce crime.

FBI Director Judge William Webster, speaking in June 1982, referred to a national crime survey called *The Figgie Report on the Fear of Crime.* He stated that "virtually all of the leaders interviewed said their cities suffered from a 'marked increase in the public fear of crime.' [We are seeing] the precautions the public has taken: burglar alarms, security locks, watch dogs, and a proliferation of handguns to name just a few."

The fear of crime is being observed even at the highest levels of government. During the FBI's war on crime in the 1970s, task forces on crime were formed with the Police Foundation and the police departments in the United States. Crime Resistance Unit pilot programs were started to demonstrate that citizens, utilizing low-cost common sense measures, can effectively reduce crime. These task forces and the citizens of communities involved were largely responsible for reductions in targeted crimes ranging from 7 percent to 21 percent.

You can't run away from crime and you shouldn't have to adapt your life-style to that of the criminal element. Working together with your neighbors and your community, you can reduce and effectively stop crime.

# Chapter 2

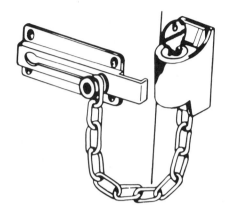

# Home Burglar Alarm Systems

The burglar alarm system is the central protection device(s) for the home. Unfortunately, many alarm systems are purchased solely on price — not on what they can or cannot do for the home's security.

## PERIMETER PROTECTION AND SPACE PROTECTION SYSTEMS

You must be aware of what types of systems are available and what they can and cannot do. Numerous independent studies, government studies, and some studies prepared by manufacturers are available. It's tough to totally understand the information and discern between fact and fiction.

We have selected a report by Massa Products Corporation, a major manufacturer of security intrusion detection systems, from which the following information has been excerpted. The excerpted material describes the anti-intrusion system products currently sold, their advantages, and disadvantages.

Systems for the home must meet several requirements:

☐ Simplicity and ease of installation.
☐ Moderate pricing.
☐ Attractive design to blend in with home decor.
☐ Self-contained system: a singular unit that will effectively perform the four basic functions of detecting, warning, reporting, and controlling.

These systems fall into two basic categories: perimeter protection systems and space protection systems.

### Perimeter Protector Systems

*Perimeter protection systems* are those in which only doors and windows of a home are protected. All entrances to the home must be equipped with sensors. If an intruder is able to gain entry into the home (such as through a broken window), no protection is provided internally.

**Hard-wired.** Required switches at each window and door throughout the home are interconnected by wire. Protection against broken windows as means of entry can only be obtained by installing conductive foil on each window pane.

**Wireless.** Very expensive rf (radio frequency) transmitters must be installed at the windows and doors for total protection. Radio frequency transmitters of this type typically cost $25-$35 each, and no protection against entry via broken windows is available.

**Line Carrier.** This type uses ac power lines in the home in place of the rf transmitter in the wireless system. Special transmitting modules are attached to each switch and then plugged into an ac receptacle.

Advantages of perimeter protection systems are:

—Wireless types are time-consuming, but they are relatively easy to install.

— Because of no internal protection, pets may roam freely throughout the home.

Disadvantages of perimeter protection systems are:

—There is no protection beyond the perimeter of the home. Not even the total perimeter is protected; only windows and doors are equipped with switches or sensors.

—The systems are expensive due to the need for transmitters at every window and door.

—Installation of hard-wired systems is time-consuming, messy, and unattractive, especially if foil is applied to each window. A hard-wired system, when installed in a home under construction, is about the only sure method to ensure that wires are concealed. After completion of the home, this is not always the case.

—Radio frequency transmitters are very prone to problems. Transmission can be erratic due to environmental conditions or interference from nearby metal objects or other rf transmissions; batteries used in every rf transmitter must be routinely checked. Most rf systems are non-coded, allowing for possible interference with neighboring units.

— Keys or switches are needed to disarm the system.

— Line carrier types require an electrician because a capacitor must be placed across the two phases of current in the fuse box.

## Space Protection Systems

*Space protection systems* are those in which the entire volume and perimeter of a room are protected. This protection is usually accomplished by motion detectors and interrupted beam detectors. Motion detectors fill a room with sound waves or microwaves. Movement of any object or person, such as an intruder, in the protected area will cause the frequency of the transmitted wave to change due to the *Doppler effect*. The processing electronics detects this frequency change and activates the alarm sequence. Interrupted beam detectors fill the protected space with a crisscross of beams. The interruption of any beam would indicate intrusion. Audio detectors that are activated by sound occurring in selected frequency bands are also used.

Interrupted beam and infrared detectors include:

**Active Infrared and Photoelectric.** Systems use an invisible beam or beams transmitted to a receiver in a line across a space from a transmitter.

**Pulsed Ultrasonic.** System transmits a short pulse of ultrasonic sound that bounces off a wall and returns to a receiver. An intruder blocks the echo and activates the system.

**Passive Infrared.** System senses the change in heat caused by an intruder.

An advantage of these systems is:

—Pulsed ultrasonic, active infrared, and photoelectric beams do not penetrate walls.

Disadvantages of these systems are:

—Active infrared, photoelectric, and pulsed ultrasonic systems only protect a one-dimensional line in a three-dimensional room.

—Active infrared and photoelectric systems are expensive. The typical cost is $175-$200 per beam. A control panel and sound devices are needed.

—Active infrared and photoelectric systems require constant critical adjustment.

— Passive infrared and pulsed ultrasonic systems are prone to false alarms due to changes in room temperature.

— Passive infrared systems have a limited angle of coverage.

*Audio detectors* are space protection systems with microphones that listen for audible sounds in selected frequency bands. Because of their lack of sophistication, sonic systems are very prone to false alarms. They do not discriminate between normal noise and the sounds of intrusion.

*Microwave motion detectors* are Doppler detection systems in which microwaves are utilized.

Advantages are:

—Total volume protection.

—Not affected by air turbulence.

Disadvantages are:

—Wall penetrability will change continuously with atmospheric conditions, such as changes in humidity.

—Microwaves penetrate walls including brick and cement. Without the knowledge of the consumer, the outside of this home or apartment is within the zone of detection. The mailman, pets, passing automobiles, or persons in adjacent apartments or hallways will activate the system. For this reason, microwave systems are prone to false alarms.

—Microwave radiation is a possible health hazard.

—Units contain gain controls that require user adjustment and cannot be accurately set without sophisticated equipment.

—Narrow angle of coverage is typically only in the range of 60°.

Ultrasonic motion detectors are Doppler detection systems in which sound waves above the range of human hearing are utilized.

Advantages are:

—Sound waves do not penetrate walls, windows, and doors. False alarms result from movement outside of desired protection zone.

—Total volume protection.

—Use harmless, ultrasonic energy.

Disadvantages are:

—The defectors are very prone to false alarms due to their inability to distinguish between moving targets and air turbulence caused by moving air or heating systems.

—Units contain gain controls that must be adjusted and cannot always be accurately set.

—Narrow angle of coverage is typically only about 60°.

## CONTROLLOR SYSTEMS CORPORATION ALARMS

A burglar generally makes breaking and pounding noises to gain entry. Thus, sound discrimination is a positive step in home (and business) security systems. A unit reacts to sounds and activates the alarm.

Sound discrimination is found in *wireless* home security systems. Because the system is wireless, it is easy to install and maintain. The heart of such a system is the control cabinet (Fig. 2-1). In this particular model, the control cabinet provides up to 2,500 square feet of protection by

Fig. 2-1. Control cabinet for a sound discrimination security systems (courtesy Controllor Systems Corporation).

Fig. 2-2. Various sensors used with the control cabinet for sound discrimination (courtesy Controllor Systems Corporation).

itself or with component sensors such as door/window sensors, vibrator sensors, and personal emergency transmitters (Fig. 2-2). These units are easy to install. Simply plug the unit into any standard ac outlet and adjust the sensitivity knob.

Let's look at the back of the console unit (Fig. 2-3). The on-delay-off switch is in the upper left-hand corner. In terms of alarm response, when you are home during the day and early evening, keep it turned to the off position, which allows you to move about freely. During the day or evening when you are away, you may want to position it in the delay position, thus allowing you a few moments to enter the home and turn off the system before it goes into the alarm mode. In the on position, the alarm would sound immediately when an intrusion is attempted. Without a delay mode every time you re-enter the home after being away for a short time, the alarm would immediately activate and start disturbing neighbors unnecessarily.

Immediately to the right is a power monitor. This indicates the unit is on and functioning. The sensitivity adjustment allows you to determine what level of sound discrimination you want to activate the system.

At the lower left is a standard ac outlet. From this you can plug in a lamp or radio. The unit, when going into an alarm mode, would activate the power, allowing the lamp to light or the radio to start playing. Because the activation would take place before the intrusion was completed, a burglar would logically assume that someone was home and had just turned on a light or the radio.

Such options as a 12-volt dc output, a normally open condition (NO), or an external speaker may be attached. Other features include:

☐ The detection of break-in sounds, such as glass or heavy pounding, while ignoring normal, everyday household sounds.
☐ Full sensitivity adjustment.
☐ LED (light-emitting diode) arming indicator
☐ Can turn on lights.

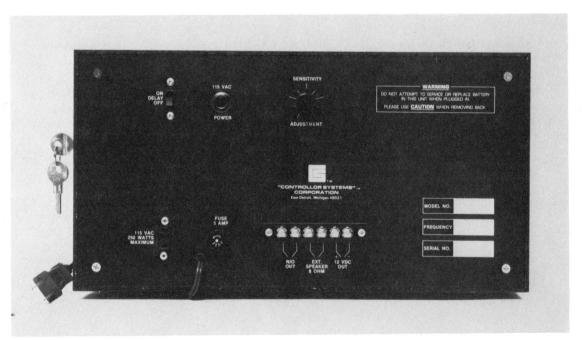

Fig. 2-3. Rear view of sound discrimination control cabinet (courtesy Controllor Systems Corporation).

Fig. 2-4. A sound discrimination unit module (courtesy Controllor Systems Corporation).

- ☐ Entry and exit delays (adjustable 0 to 60 seconds).
- ☐ Key switch on-off control (without a key, nobody can deactivate the system in your absence prior to the alarm sounding).
- ☐ Twelve-volt, 1½-amp gel cell standby battery (in case of power outage, the system continues to function).
- ☐ Two additional paging speakers can be added (can vary on specific models).
- ☐ Activation of a telephone dialer or leased line.
- ☐ Ac line fuse.
- ☐ Detection of high-impact and high-frequency sounds.
- ☐ Electronic siren.
- ☐ A normally open (NO attachment for hardware input to the system if desired).

Sound modules (Fig. 2-4) are available with most wireless systems. Like the control console, such units should be able to:

- ☐ Detect break-in sound while ingoring normal sounds.
- ☐ Have a full sensitivity adjustment.
- ☐ Have 6- or 12-volt operation.
- ☐ Have the potential to become part of a normally closed (NC) loop for a supervised circuit.
- ☐ Have an LED to show that the particular module was activated.
- ☐ Detect high-impact and high-frequency sounds.

The second variation of the unit, which looks exactly the same on the outside, is a sound discriminator with a line carrier transmitter. This model is not operated by a 9-volt battery internal to the unit, but it is plugged into any standard ac outlet. When this unit is triggered by hearing the proper combination of *intensity plus frequency*, it activates and sends a signal over the existing wiring of the building to a companion receiver. The signal can be sent from one building to another as long as the buildings share the same outside electrical transformer. Such a unit can be located in a garage or other outbuilding to provide additional protection while functioning off the same console unit. Thus, extra costs are not incurred by requiring a separate alarm system for one or more buildings.

### PASSIVE INFRARED IR SENSORS

The *passive infrared (PIR) sensor* has become one of the most used motion sensing devices in recent years. This is mostly due to its "forgiving" nature in regard to installation. The PIR unit (Fig. 2-5) is relatively easy to install as compared to Doppler motion sensors.

False alarms and nonsounding alarms have occurred with PIR sensors. Unit manufacturers blamed the sensor element manufacturers for these malfunctions, whereas the sensor element manufacturers pointed to the circuit design or application. Because of this continuing dispute, quality assurance has become a must.

Companies such as Pulnix devoted enormous time and effort into discovering the causes of the problems and the consequent solutions. The conclusions determined are the standards

Fig. 2-5. Typical passive infrared (PIR) alarm sensor used for motion detection (courtesy Pulnix America, Inc.).

by which any PIR unit must be rated to assure quality and performance in time of need. They include:

—An element test, which incorporates a 100 percent complete screening of the sensing elements at various environmental conditions. Findings indicate that even the best element man-

ufacturers have a 5 percent to 10 percent failure rate during this test.

—A 100 percent automatic PC board test conducted at various environmental conditions.

—A full-range sensitivity test. Manufacturers often establish only *minimum* sensitivity value and leave the maximum value untested.

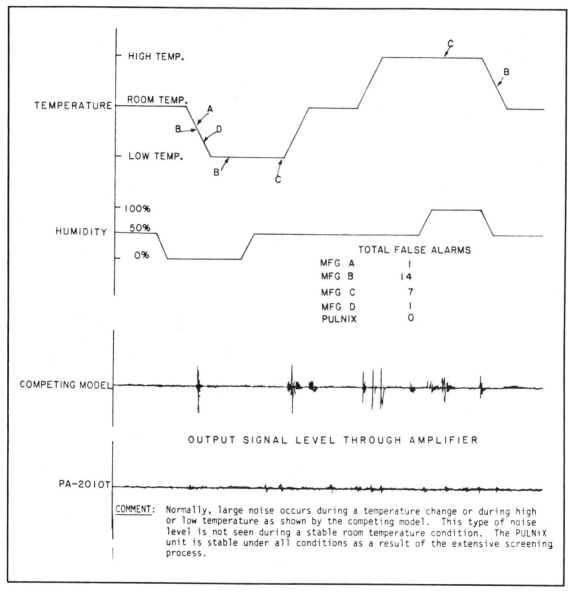

| TOTAL FALSE ALARMS | |
| --- | --- |
| MFG A | 1 |
| MFG B | 14 |
| MFG C | 7 |
| MFG D | 1 |
| PULNIX | 0 |

COMMENT: Normally, large noise occurs during a temperature change or during high or low temperature as shown by the competing model. This type of noise level is not seen during a stable room temperature condition. The PULNiX unit is stable under all conditions as a result of the extensive screening process.

Fig. 2-6. Chart illustrates false alarm occurrence during an environmental test of five different PIR sensors (courtesy Pulnix America, Inc.).

Fig. 2-7. The wide-angle PIR sensor can be used in a number of different applications (courtesy Pulnix America, Inc.).

The test developed by Pulnix uses a completely quantumized simulation value to keep each sensor within a tight tolerance range. The unit must be specified to detect a 25° centigrade temperature variation in a pure infrared radiation source, which is a more precise method than the simple human body test or its simulation.

—An induced noise susceptiveness test. Each PIR unit, when completed, should be subjected to this test. The test uses specially designed equipment to simulate noise from surge noise, induction noise, fluorescent light effects, and vibration during operation. A unit that causes an alarm if any individual noise or combination of noises sounds should be rejected.

—A temperature cycle test. Most PIR erratic false alarm activations occur mainly during temperature shifts, which are due either to higher or lower temperatures. A temperature variation test involves critical temperature variations. All PIR sensors should be able to pass this test.

Figure 2-6 illustrates the false alarm occurrence of five PIR units (made by five different manufacturers) during an environmental test. The false alarms occurred at the various points

indicated. Twenty-three false alarms occurred during testing. Of these, two PIRs had one false alarm each, one PIR had seven false alarms, one PIR had 14 false alarms and one PIR had no false alarms. The Pulnix unit was the only one to pass the environmental test with no false alarms.

Passive infrared sensors have various features and zone protection patterns. Each of these depends on your requirements. The following four units will adequately demonstrate the various zone, range, and applications for most units on the market.

The *wide-angle PIR sensor* (Fig. 2-7) is designed to fit many applications. The units can be either wall- or ceiling-mounted. A zone locator is built into each unit for installation convenience and state-of-the-art engineering, which results in high reliability. The metal-encased sensor element provides excellent immunity to interference. The unit can cover an area of 35' × 35" and has 28 zones built into the unit sensor system (Fig. 2-8). This unit is equipped with a zone locator that provides a visual check of the sensitive zones. An automatic return mechanism resets the unit to the protection mode. Angle adjustment for the unit allows it to be adjusted either vertically or horizontally. While the unit is set at a medium level of sensitivity at the factory, it can be decreased or increased depending on your own particular installation requirements.

Figure 2-9 shows a PIR unit used for spot

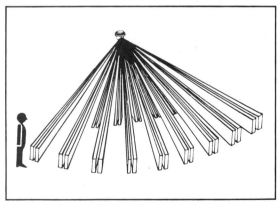

Fig. 2-8. Twenty-eight zones consist of 18 major distance zones and 10 shorter interior zones (courtesy Pulnix America, Inc.).

Fig. 2-9. A spot protection PIR sensor (courtesy Pulnix America, Inc.).

protection in the home. This can be for a window, specific entrance, or even items such as a valuable art object or a wall painting needing specialized protection. Figure 2-10 illustrates the specific types of pattern protection and distance of which the unit is capable.

Radial protection (360°) may be used to cover large rooms in corporate executive residences or even the entire basement of the average homeowner's residence. Units such as that in Fig. 2-11 ensure complete coverage of a 35' diameter area at an installation height of 9'. The sensor is ideal for protecting a large area. The unique design offers no suggestion of the protection to possible intruders. Within the unit, the zone shielding disk provides optimum adjustment of fields of view by allowing for the blockage

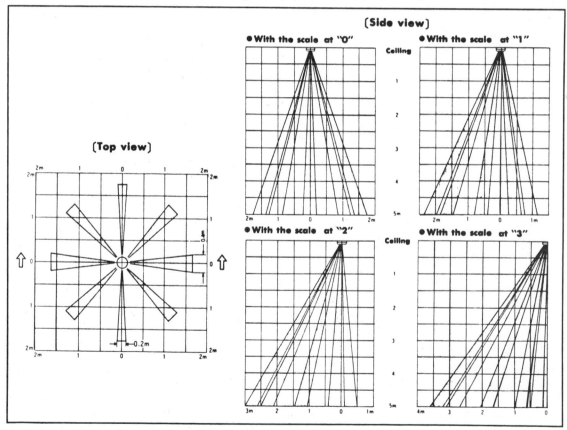

Fig. 2-10. A variety of coverage settings can be obtained for spot protection of different types of objects within the home (distances given in meters) (courtesy Pulnix America, Inc.).

Fig. 2-11. A PIR sensor providing 360° radial protection (courtesy Pulnix America, Inc.).

of any unwanted zones.

The *PIR bounce back sensor* (Fig. 2-12) is designed for protecting equipment, personal property, and valuable pictures. This compact transceiver responds to light reflected from a paper reflector strip. The reflector strip is attached to the area or item to be protected. The transceiver is mounted to a stable structure such as the wall. An alarm is initiated when the beam is interrupted by movement of the protected object. Anti-tampering and unobtrusive protection are the prime benefits of this sensor, because no wiring goes directly to the item being protected by the sensor.

The detecting distance of the PIR bounce back sensor is 2″ to 12″, and the response time requires a two-second minimum interception to

initiate the alarm. Figure 2-13 illustrates the sensor protecting two different items. Notice the size of the sensor; 3½″ × 1½″ × 2¼″ makes it extremely unobtrusive and practically unnoticeable.

Installation of PIR sensors is not really difficult (Fig. 2-14). You should remember:

☐ Do not install the sensor outdoors; install indoors to protect the building interior.
☐ Do not position the sensor facing a window. Avoid any place likely to receive headlight beams, direct sunlight, intense reflections, electric noise, etc. (they may needlessly activate the alarm).

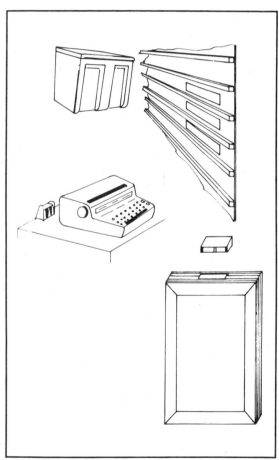

Fig. 2-13. Bounce back sensor protecting a home business office machine and a painting (courtesy Pulnix America, Inc.).

Fig. 2-12. A PIR bounce back sensor is excellent for protecting equipment, personal property, valuable pictures, etc. (courtesy Pulnix America, Inc.).

Fig. 2-14. Areas not to install a PIR sensor (refer to text for specific details of the illustrations) (courtesy Pulnix America, Inc.).

☐ Do not install a sensor in places where it may be affected by water splashes, steam, or oil.

☐ Avoid installation at sites within the reach of vandals.

☐ Avoid installation of the sensor where it may be sprayed by insecticides.

☐ Sensitive zones should be positioned away from the likely paths of small animals.

☐ Do not install the sensor in a site subject to rapid temperature fluctuations.

☐ Do not blind the sensor by placing any object in front of it.

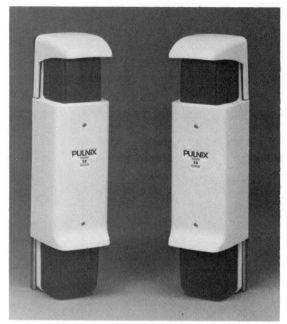

Fig. 2-15. Synchro-twin beam photoelectric beam detector for exterior protection (courtesy Pulnix America, Inc.).

☐ Install the sensor in such a direction that intruders are most likely to cross the sensitive zones.

For exterior protection, the next two units can meet most requirements. They are applicable for residences having a large yard of several acres and for large executive estates. First, the synchro-twin beam photoelectric beam detector (Fig. 2-15) uses twin beams that are synchro-

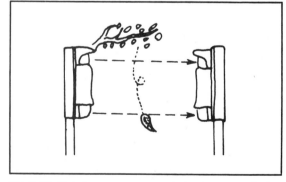

Fig. 2-16. Twin beams ensure against nuisance and other false alarms (courtesy Pulnix America, Inc.).

Fig. 2-17. Long-range outdoor photoelectric beam detector (courtesy Pulnix America, Inc.).

nized to work together to reinforce the range and tolerance in severe weather conditions. (Weather is the prime reason why many other beam detectors produce many false alarms.) The twin beams also eliminate nuisance alarms caused by birds, falling leaves (Fig. 2-11), and small animals because both beams most be broken to initiate the alarm. The system uses a rotary optical system for easy installation, and the unusual lens design will ensure proper alignment.

Another outdoor photoelectric beam is shown in Fig. 2-17. This long-range sensor is extraordinarily durable and resistant to various environmental conditions. A maximum arrival distance of the beam that is six times the length of the recommended operating distance ensures reliability in the worst of conditions. A standard operating distance of 600′ will allow for a maximum beam arrival distance of 3600′.

## SECURITY LIGHTING:
## SECOND LEVEL ALARM PROTECTION

Security lighting is an important adjunct to the home alarm system. It is a second level of protection, providing an exterior sensor. Some types of security lighting can tie into the alarm system, but most devices are not attached to the interior system.

### Automatic Light Control

The LightWatch is a versatile and innovative

Fig. 2-18. Outdoor automatic light control with one light head (courtesy Colorado Electro-Optics, Inc.).

automatic switching device that can provide reliable security, increased safety, energy savings, and lighting management to your home. Several models of this outdoor automatic light control are available: the LC1 /1 (Fig. 2-18), the LC 1 /2 (Fig. 2-19), and the LC II. These models deter crime and are energy efficient lighting mechanisms.

This passive infrared sensor uses a pyroelectric array technology to detect rapid changes in temperature when a hot or cold target moves through the detection pattern. This technology

Fig. 2-19. For versatility and covering more than one area, use a two-head exterior automatic light control (courtesy Colorado Electro-Optics, Inc.).

assures consistency and provides balance to minimize sensitivity to ambient temperature changes. The sensors do not emit or radiate energy; therefore, they are completely passive and harmless to humans, animals, and vegetation. In studying the features of the unit, we found that the utilization of integrated circuitry reduce the number of components. This enabled the control circuitry to provide maximum reliability.

The control is rated to handle 500 watts of incandescent (noninductive) lighting. Two external adjustments are provided: a sensitivity control that covers a five to one differential temperature range and a reset delay that is variable between approximately 10 seconds and 20 minutes. Within the LightWatch, a phototransistor disables the control during daylight hours.

The LightWatch unit can provide general area coverage at the side and rear of the home. Here are installation procedures.

This light control should only be installed by people with experience in standard ac household wiring. Consult your local building codes and make sure you understand all installation instructions before proceeding. Make sure your lighting load does not exceed 500 watts noninductive (incandescent). Also, do not connect this unit with more than one 120-volt, 60-Hz power source.

This automatic light control detects rapid changes in temperature (infrared energy) whenever a person, auto, etc., moves through its invisible detection pattern. It emits no radiation and is harmless to humans and animals. The unit is designed specifically to control up to 500 watts of lighting in one or more fixtures. It can also control other devices, but during normal operation it will occasionally activate due to rapid environmental changes, pets, etc. Do not connect the unit to any alarm system, siren, or loud audible device.

The light control should be located with the lens at the bottom center and aimed down at the area of traffic. The sensor is most sensitive to motion across the pattern and least sensitive to movement toward or away from the lens. Avoid aiming the detector at water pools or any object that may change temperature rapidly. Do not locate the unit over heating vents or air conditioners. Never allow direct sunlight to shine straight into the grille as it may damage the infrared sensor. This would include laying it on the ground during a midday installation.

Position the control to the side or below the lamp(s) so that heat from the lamp(s) will not pass in front of the lens. Do not let the control touch the lampholder or lamp(s). Do not mount the control above the lamp(s). Instability and /or irreparable damage may occur if this particular instruction is not followed.

Consider the accessibility and routing of the necessary wiring. The control should be mounted on a weatherproof surface (or recessed) junction box with a two-screw cover. The wire must be run from this box to the light fixture to be controlled, and power must be wired to this box.

Shut off the electricity to all affected circuits before beginning installation. (Note that the control unit can be mounted on the lower side of a rigidly constructed light fixture with a ½" conduit hole.) With the wiring, you are dealing with four wires.

Figure 2-20 shows the before-and-after wiring of the unit. Figure 2-21 shows the specific wiring that will be required. At this point when

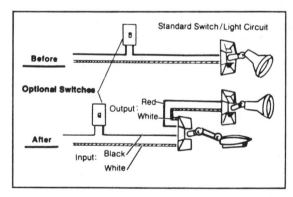

Fig. 2-20. Wiring installation for an automatic light control unit (courtesy Colorado Electro-Optics, Inc.).

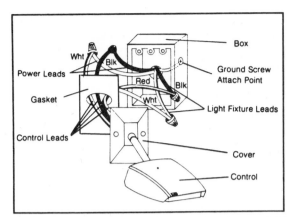

Fig. 2-21. Detail illustrating exact electrical hookup to a light outlet box (courtesy Colorado Electro-Optics, Inc.).

installing the unit, check again to ensure that the power to the affected light circuit is turned off.

The power lead and the light fixture leads are brought into the box. The ground wire(s) is attached to the box grounding screw. The gasket is then positioned on the wires.

All the wire leads should have ½" insulation stripped off. The power leads are then connected to the light control leads (black to black and white to white). The fixture leads are connected to the light control leads (black to red and white to white). The various connected wires are then covered with the protective wire nuts that come with the unit.

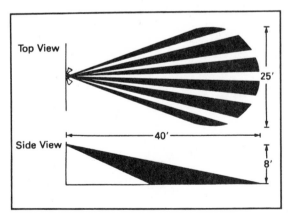

Fig. 2-22. Automatic light control detection pattern (courtesy Colorado Electro-Optics, Inc.).

The gasket is aligned to ensure a proper all-round seal. The cover is fastened to the box. The power is turned on and, if used, the light switch should be turned on.

The mounting arm of the unit should be adjusted so the unit is level, side to side, and looking out horizontally or somewhat downward. (Do not adjust the unit to look above horizontal.) Loosen the locking rings and elbow bolts to move the unit for proper positioning.

Make a "walk test." Figure 2-22 shows the detection pattern of the LightWatch unit. The walk test will allow you to determine your exact detection pattern and adjust the unit accordingly.

To allow the unit to activate during daylight hours, cover the daylight sensor tube with a small piece of electrical tape (Fig. 2-23). Adjust the reset to minimum. Walk around the perimeter of the detection pattern and observe the reaction of the light. When the pattern coverage is acceptable, tighten the locking rings and the elbow joints. Remove the daylight sensor tube covering and adjust the timing light to the desired level (Fig. 2-24).

Servicing of the unit is extremely minimal. The unit requires no maintenance with the possible exception of keeping the lens area and day-

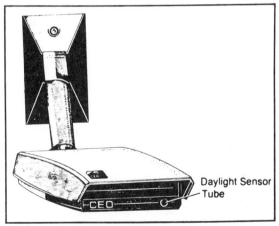

Fig. 2-23. A small piece of electrical tape over the sensor (arrow) and the unit operates during the day. Overlay with an arrow to sensor (right lower corner of sensor) (courtesy Colorado Electro-Optics, Inc.).

21

Fig. 2-24. Bottom view of the detector showing timing and sensitivity adjustments to allow proper sensor level (courtesy Colorado Electro-Optics, Inc.).

light sensor clear of obstructions. A tamperproof screw is used in the construction because there are no user serviceable parts.

### Security Light Control—Main Door Security Alert

With security protection at the sides and rear of the home, you may want to consider pinpoint security protection at your front door. A small unit to detect the approach of potential intruders near or up your front walk can be installed (Fig. 2-25). The automatic *Security Light Control (SLC)* turns on the home outdoor lights.

Please note that the unit is not a light. It is an automatic lighting control device using infrared radiation to detect the approach of a person (or vehicle) into its detection pattern. Figure 2-26 illustrates the infrared pattern area. Once detected, the SLC unit will automatically turn on your outside lights. As long as someone is moving within the sensitive area, your lights will remain on. Four minutes after the person leaves, the lights are automatically switched off. The unit is sophisticated but simple, and it provides the kind of exterior protection you and your family deserve. The detection range of the SLC is shown in Fig. 2-27. As you can see, it will

Fig. 2-25. The automatic Security Light Control is a compact unit mounted over the exterior door (courtesy Colorado Electro-Optics, Inc.).

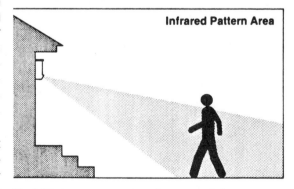

Fig. 2-26. Area coverage of the Security Light Control sensor unit (courtesy Colorado Electro-Optics, Inc.).

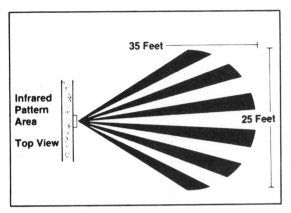

Fig. 2-27. The entire detection pattern protects the front area entrance to the home (courtesy Colorado Electro-Optics, Inc.).

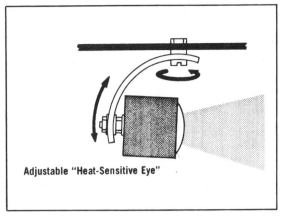

Fig. 2-28. The "eye" is adjustable to provide coverage for heavy traffic areas (courtesy Colorado Electro-Optics, Inc.).

adequately cover your front walk, the porch, and the surrounding area.

Even if no one ever tries to break into your home, you can still benefit from the added safety and convenience of this automatic lighting. You no longer will have to wish your lights were on when you return home on a dark night, with arms filled with packages and a long walkway to travel. Automatic lighting provides a warm welcome; the outside lights come on when you or a guest approaches the home.

Safety is assured with the SLC. Many accidents occur from tripping over an unseen object in the dark, slipping on a small patch of ice in the winter, or not noticing steps. With such a unit installed, the lights are on when really needed.

Consider energy savings. Everyone wastes energy by forgetting to turn off the lights. The SLC never forgets. The lights come on when someone enters the detection pattern and turn off after the person leaves.

The SLC on the outside of your home is an excellent unit for the do-it-yourselfer. The heat-sensitive eye on the SLC can be adjusted to achieve 35′ × 25′ coverage in areas of heavy traffic (Fig. 2-28). Wiring is relatively simple and can be done by anyone with a basic knowledge of electricity and local wiring codes.

Fig. 2-29. Alarm processor control unit (courtesy Linear Security Products Group).

23

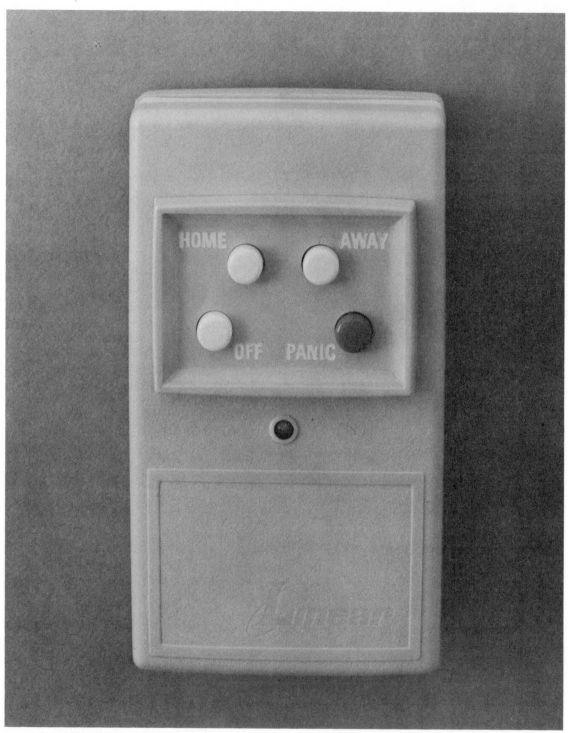

Fig. 2-30. Remote control hand-held four-button transmitter (courtesy Linear Security Products Group).

## LINEAR RADIO-CONTROLLED HOME SECURITY SYSTEM

The *P-65 alarm processor* (Fig. 2-29) is a multimode, multichannel, central control unit that receives security information from remotely located wireless transmitters. Digitally coded rf signals from these transmitters are processed to provide visual and audible annunciation, siren activation, and dialer outputs. The versatile unit combines the advantages of passive infrared technology with wireless rf operation.

Easy to use, yet sophisticated in its design and functional capability. The P-65 alarm processor is remotely controlled by a hand-held four-button transmitter (Fig. 2-30) or by a wall-mounted transmitter (Fig. 2-31).

The alarm processor features five input channels. Three channels are designed for security zone reporting, and two are dedicated solely to processing emergency alert signals. Each channel can be set to a separate code and can only be accessed by transmitters set to the same code.

Three programmable options add to the unit's versatility. The first option makes it possible to select between instant and delayed responses. The second dedicates channel number two to either perimeter or interior surveillance, while the third option modifies the off mode (where perimeter sensors do not activate alarms) to a "day" mode in which perimeter signals activate an annunciator (no sirens or other

Fig. 2-31. Wall-mounted transmitter control (courtesy Linear Security Products Group).

outputs are activated by the alarm processor).

The P-65 alarm processor has five input channels, three operating modes, and seven outputs. Typical applications for the five input channels include the following:

**Channel Number One.** *Perimeter protection* accepts signals from transmitters monitoring doors and windows. It functions in the home and away modes.

**Channel Number Two.** *Interior/perimeter (selectable)* responds to signals from transmitters monitoring doors and windows or from infrared zone protection devices. When set for perimeter protection, it functions in the home and away modes. Set for zone surveillance, it functions only in the away mode.

**Channel Number Three.** Dedicated interior infrared detectors activate this *space protection channel*. It is active only when the alarm processor is operating in the away mode.

**Channel Number Four.** *Emergency alert/panic* is active around the clock and receives signals from portable panic button transmitters.

**Channel Number Five.** *Emergency alert auxiliary* is also a 24-hour/day active channel. It is used for fire warning or medical alert responses.

The input/output capabilities are shown in Fig. 2-32. With five input channels available, the P-65 can receive and process signals from many detection devices. These devices include perimeter detection transmitters equipped with magnetic contacts, wireless infrared detectors for interior space protection, wireless smoke sensors, and emergency panic button transmitters.

Of the seven outputs, four are assigned to control signaling devices such as CATV (community antenna television) transponders, sirens (speakers), and telephone dialers. Two are dedicated to emergency reporting, and the seventh output is available to drive an annunciator.

The central processor unit has a key lock switch to control the master power. When the key is turned to the off position, the system is completely inoperative, including the 24-hour emergency channels. With the key safely in your pocket, you don't have to worry about someone turning off the alarm. Also, you may be concerned about power outages. The unit has a rechargeable standby battery to keep the console unit operating for a period when there is a power outage.

## DIGITALLY CODED ALARMS

The *Linear Alert P-61* is a digitally coded single-channel alarm (Fig. 2-33) that can operate with other digital security transmitters equipped with magnetic contacts or even motion sensors. This highly reliable unit is virtually immune to false alarms. There are 256 separate codes to allow for your selection of specific codes for the various sensors to be used with the control unit. Figure 2-34 illustrates the standard P-61 security system and the various sensor options. Note the remote alarm siren. This is separate from a warble tone siren that is built into the control console. As with the previous unit, you have battery standby in case of a power failure. The battery is rechargeable.

The *D-2C* is a two-channel receiver in a small and economical package (Fig. 2-35). Designed for use in wireless security systems, it makes available two separate control channels in one receiver. Any Linear Alert digital radio

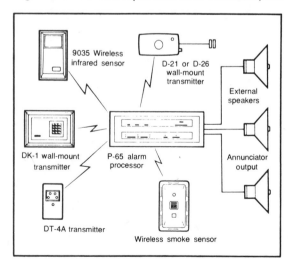

Fig. 2-32. Five channels allow the P-65 many detectors (courtesy Linear Security Products Group).

Fig. 2-33. Linear Alert's P-61 single channel alarm control unit (courtesy Linear Corporation).

transmitter can be coded to activate this receiver, and any number of transmitters may be used to operate each channel. Up to 64 independent two-channel security systems may be operated in adjacent areas, which means this receiver is excellent for apartment houses and individual residential dwellings.

Each of the two channels can perform various functions. Applications include fire warning, motion/intrusion detection, panic alarm response, and medical reporting. Alternatively, this receiver can provide for local annunciation or control alarms associated with up to two fire or intrusion zones.

## WIRELESS SECURITY SYSTEMS: INDIVIDUAL COMPONENT DEVICES

Let's examine some individual component parts that can increase a system's security potential. Figure 2-36 shows a two-channel, hand-held transmitter designed to initiate two separate functions. This lightweight transmitter contains two buttons, each activating a separate channel. When one of the buttons is depressed, it transmits continuously until the button is released. Also, the LED in front will show that a signal is being transmitted and that the transmitter battery is in good condition. The versatility of this two-channel transmitter means that it is possible to

27

control a variety of electrically-operated devices. Typical applications can include panic alarm activation, medical alert response, intrusion reporting, and arm/disarming of the system control. It can also be used for wireless light control, to activate telephone dialers, and even with video surveillance equipment.

The four-channel transmitter (Fig. 2-37) controls four different functions. Each button will activate a separate radio channel. Operating with four single-channel receivers or one multichannel receiver, the transmitter can perform many switching tasks. In addition to typical applications indicated above, this transmitter can also be used for entertainment and recreation devices. Sixty-four system codes are possible, and the code can be determined by you. It can be

changed as frequently as you wish, ensuring that your security control is never out-of-date and cannot be determined by someone else, as no one will know when you change your code or to what new code setting.

For window and door installations, a wireless transmitter can be used to provide perimeter sensing at various locations thoughout the home (Fig. 2-38). For example, this wall-mounted, battery-powered transmitter is installed adjacent to an entrance (door or window). A two-wire lead is connected from the internal terminals to a normally open (NO) magnetic switch. This switch is installed on the door or window. A magnet mounted next to the switch on the movable portion of the entrance holds the switch open. When the protected door or window is opened, the

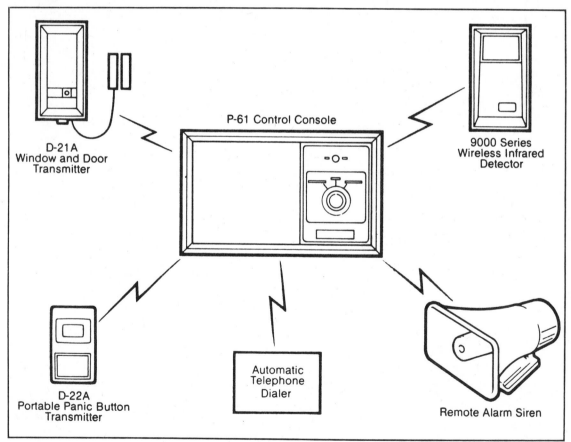

D-21A
Window and Door
Transmitter

P-61 Control Console

9000 Series
Wireless Infrared
Detector

D-22A
Portable Panic Button
Transmitter

Automatic
Telephone
Dialer

Remote Alarm Siren

Fig. 2-34. The P-61 security system and sensor options available (courtesy Linear Corporation).

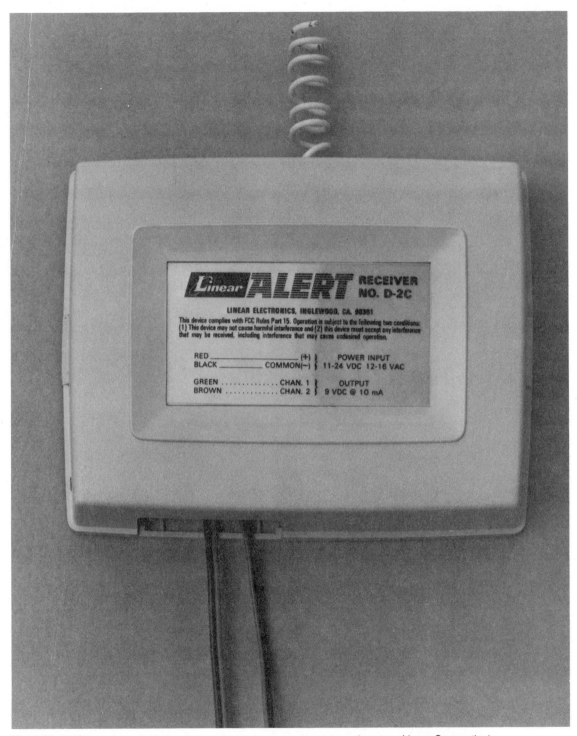

Fig. 2-35. D-2C two-channel receiver for use in wireless security systems (courtesy Linear Corporation).

Fig. 2-36. Two-channel, hand-held transmitter (courtesy Linear Corporation).

unit that can be located within the home to cover a small area, such as a specific door or window, or even to be pointed at a valuable object such as a painting or silver set. Like other sensors, when an object is detected within sensor range, the transmitter will alert the primary control panel, allowing an alarm to be audibly signaled.

### INFRARED SENSORS
Figures 2-41 and 2-42 show two sensor avail-

Fig. 2-37. A four-channel transmitter. Each channel operation is a separate radio channel (courtesy Linear Corporation).

magnet moves away and the switch closes. In doing so, the transmitter can now transmit a digital signal to its associated alarm system or control panel. The transmitter has an eight-key digital switch which, when set, can create up to 256 personal code settings per radio frequency.

Another door and window transmitter is shown in Fig. 2-39. Like the previously described transmitter, it is installed adjacent to an entrance and uses a magnet to hold the magnetic switch open.

Figure 2-40 shows an infrared transmitter

Fig. 2-38. Wireless transmitter for window, door, or other locations within the home (courtesy Linear Corporation).

simultaneously. An intruder must first enter one viewing area and then the other to obtain an alarm condition. The logic portion of the sensing circuit requires the activation of the two channels, within a specified time period, before the

able through local distributor/security system dealers. These two models feature an exclusive parallel detection system with A-B processing, plus a false alarm cancellation and logic circuit. These two sensors use an all-new design, enabling them to provide superior stability and performance that has not been seen before in passive infrared sensors. (In the past, PIR sensors have been subject to false alarms due to white light, rf, and lightning inductions.) These sensors use a two-channel system, requiring both amplifier channels to see hazardous signals

Fig. 2-39. Magnetic switch wireless transmitters for doors can also be used with Linear security systems (courtesy Linear Corporation).

Fig. 2-40. Infrared transmitter (courtesy Linear Corporation).

Figure 2-43 illustrates the sensing patterns for these two sensors. These sensors can be wall-mounted, flush-mounted, or corner-mounted. Figure 2-44 illustrates three mounting methods for the *R50 PIR* and wall and corner mounting for the *RW25 PIR*.

## SELF-CONTAINED ALARM
## FOR THE SMALL RESIDENCE

Figure 2-45 illustrates a self-contained burglar alarm. This compact unit requires no installation—simply plug it in and turn on the unit. It can

Fig. 2-41. The new design enables the passive infrared sensor to provide superior performance not available before in a PIR unit (courtesy Rossin Corporation).

circuit will be activated. Any simultaneous activation of both channels is canceled by the cancellation transistors, which essentially shunt the signal to ground. A single channel activation is also canceled by the logic circuit.

The sensors are powered by 15-year lithium batteries, thereby simplifying installation. When used in a closed circuit alarm system, the sensors employ a battery fail-safe system so that when the battery runs low, it will not allow the control panel to be armed. This system allows the sensor to tell you the battery is low at the time the control panel is armed rather than by reporting a false alarm.

Fig. 2-42. Another PIR with superior stability and performance. The two-channel system means the sensor is not subject to false alarms like other sensors (courtesy Rossin Corporation).

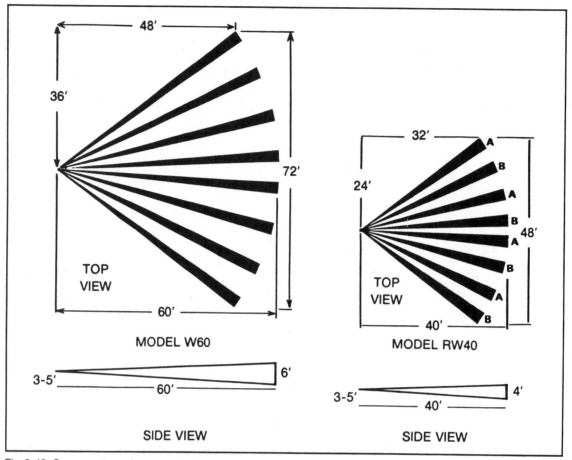

Fig. 2-43. Sensor patterns for sensors in Figs. 2-41 and 2-42 (courtesy Rossin Corporation).

protect up to 800 square feet of normal living space and offers a 150-watt (maximum) outlet that can be used to turn on a table or floor lamp. The alarm duration is approximately 1 minute with an automatic reset after the alarm is activated. This simple system can be used to protect individual rooms and apartments, and it can be used when staying in motels.

The *Audio Switch* (Fig. 2-46) from Blue Grass Electronics is designed to detect sounds such as shattering glass when a window is broken. It can be placed in an open area (not required to be adjacent to a window) and will provide protection for up to a 25′ radius.

The *Daisy Chain* is an Audio Switch system that allows the installation of up to 10 Audio Switches per installation. It uses a single pair of wires up to 1500′ long for multiple connections, and you can protect every window and room in your home (Fig. 2-47).

Like the individual Audio Switch, the Daisy Chain provides reliable break-in protection. It eliminates the costly installation of door contacts and tripping devices, and you don't have to use window tape or foil for protection. The unit consists of the master control that supplies the power to the Daisy Chain. Each remote unit is a separate sound discriminating switch. The switches are designed to detect glass breakage. Each remote audio switch covers 1200 square feet.

This system requires but a single two-wire

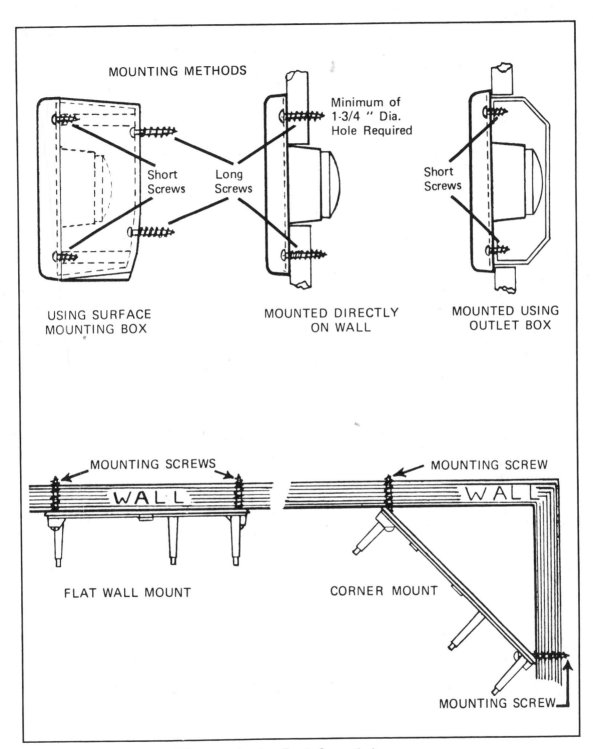

Fig. 2-44. Mounting methods for PIR sensors (courtesy Rossin Corporation).

Fig. 2-45. Self-contained burglar alarm system for a small home (one room) or a small apartment (courtesy Blue Grass Electronics).

Fig. 2-46. AS-7000 Audio Switch provides protection for up to a 25′ radius (courtesy Blue Grass Electronics).

circuit, with all of the remotes being paralleled across the loop. The fartherest remote unit can be located 1500′ from the master unit.

The Audio Switch in Fig. 2-48 has a built-in Linear transmitter, allowing it to work with any Linear receiver. It is powered by a 9-volt battery (life expectancy one year), has a low battery indicating LED, and can be flush- or surface-mounted.

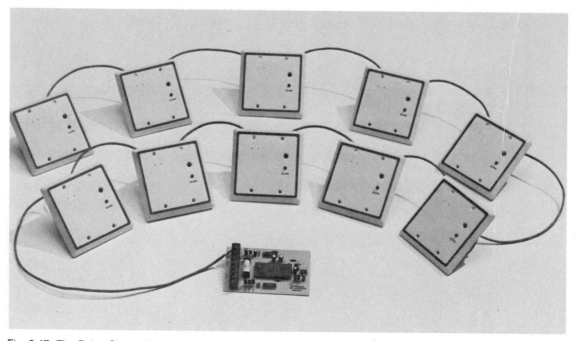

Fig. 2-47. The Daisy Chain allows for numerous Audio Switches in a continuous protection chain (courtesy Blue Grass Electronics).

36

Fig. 2-48. The Audio Switch can work with any Linear receiver (courtesy Blue Grass Electronics).

## THE SYSTEM 8

The SenDEC Corporation has developed the *System 8 security monitoring system* (Fig. 2-49). Devised to offer an innovative way to protect residential property, the system provides special features that enhance the effectiveness of electronic security.

The system can instantly locate and identify the nature of an alarm, thereby saving lengthy and often dangerous searches. It dramatically reduces false alarms with individually adjusted alarm delays. A specially computerized control panel enables you to arm and disarm the system by using an access code, thereby eliminating the need for cumbersome and sometimes risky conventional keys.

The system, built with state-of-the-art microelectronic circuitry (Fig. 2-50) has a flexibility that will accommodate several detection devices, no matter how they are electronically constructed. This makes it possible to use the best components on the market and to make conversions or modifications of old systems.

When installed in a home, the life-style of the residents and their security or protection needs are brought to bear on how the system will be customized. Considerations include the type of detection devices that will be employed and the establishment of alarm delays to suit the residents' living pattern.

The following security devices can be used: sound discriminators that detect breaking glass from sound frequency levels, motion detectors that pick up any unexpected movement with an

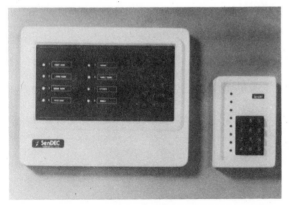

Fig. 2-49. SenDEC System 8 master control panel and miniature remote control. Up to four remote units may be operated from the master (courtesy SenDEC Corporation).

Fig. 2-50. The simple design and clean layout of the electronics for the System 8 make for easy installation and maintenance (courtesy SenDEC Corporation).

infrared beam or ultrasound pattern, surface-concealed sensors that note change of position in windows and doors, and pressure-sensitive floor mats that respond to body weight.

The System 8 also offers comprehensive monitoring of residential environmental conditions. Devices can be installed that detect abnormal heat, smoke, gas leaks, and low temperature. The system can also monitor functions such as sump pump operation, waterflow, and pressure, and any attempts to tamper with these functions or the system itself.

The selected protection and security devices are wired to create zones. Information regarding these scanned zones appear on a master control panel and other remote panels positioned around the house. The master control panel is distinct from the remote panels in one major way: on the master control panel, zones are labeled separately by name (i.e., front door), and easy to read backlighting makes it possible to see the location and the nature of the alarm immediately. The remote panels have the same control over the system and provide the same information. They are simply smaller, and the zones are unlabeled but are indicated by LEDs (Fig. 2-51).

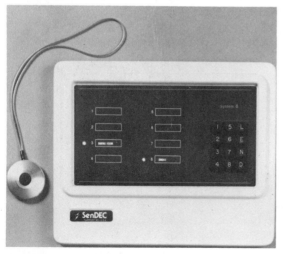

Fig. 2-51. Remote panels have the same control over the system and provide the homeowner with the same information (courtesy SenDEC Corporation).

Each control panel is comprised of a 12-character keyboard and scanning lights. When a scanning light does not move past each zone location on the board, that indicates a zone violation. The immobile light is accompanied by an audible sound that also indicates the nature of the alarm (a continuous tone, an intermittent one, a loud intermittent tone, or a warbeling sound). Within seconds, if the system has not been disarmed by the owner, an outside siren will also sound.

The alarm signal may be transferred, through the telephone lines, to a central monitoring station. A digital communicator in the home transmits the violation information to this center, including a readout of the nature of the violation and the customer's account number. From this information the center knows whether to contact the police, the fire department, or other appropriate parties.

In cases where the system has been set off and there is a question of the alarm's validity, the monitoring center calls the consumer's home telephone number and requests his account number. If the occupant cannot give this proper confidential number, the police are sent to the property immediately.

The master and remote panels are not exclusively for violation information. From the keyboards on these panels (Fig. 2-52), several functions can be performed. Through the *numbered* buttons, the consumer enters his four-digit access code that acts as the "key," which is frequently used to operate security systems. These numbers also enable him to select the zones that he would like to arm. The only exceptions are the zones that monitor environmental conditions or equipment functions. These are identified at the time of installation and are programmed to remain armed 24 hours a day automatically. This provision avoids any mistake that would leave a home unprotected against fire or gas leaks.

The lettered buttons (L-E-N-D) offer a selection of options for controlling the length of alarm delays. For instance, "L" (leave) allows exit and

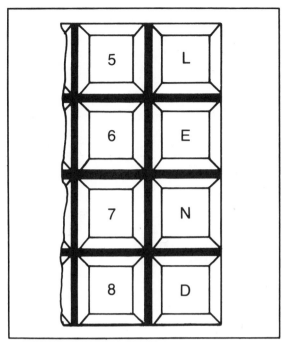

Fig. 2-52. Keyboard buttons used to enter the operating code, arm zones, initiate emergency call, and control accessory function (courtesy SenDEC Corporation).

enter with predetermined alarm delays. When this mode is adopted, it allows the consumer to set the system and have 2 minutes to walk through the house to leave. The length of re-entry time that is permitted is established by the consumer at the time of installation.

"E" (empty) is a mode that permits the same alarm delay for entry, but it has a further use. It assumes that no one will be in the house, so it can be programmed to interface with the home's heating system to turn down the thermostat on exit and to return it to the home's normal temperature on entry. Similarly, the "E" mode can be employed to turn on a telephone answering device on exit or turn it off on entry.

The "N" (night) mode fully arms the selected zones, allowing minimum time delay between violation and alarm. The immediacy of its response is based on the asumption that any change in the status of a selected zone is cause for alarm.

The "D" (day) mode can be employed when residents are on the premises. Zones can be separately selected, and a warning tone gives occupants time to disarm a violated zone, thereby preventing reporting of false alarms.

The System 8 has a panic signal mode that can be used by pressing a combination of two control panel buttons simultaneously. This can either be an audible alarm or a silent one. It is also possible to have simple single panic button locations placed elsewhere in the house.

Among the system's special features is a special memory capability that stores information pertaining to the last valid alarm that has taken place. By pressing a combination of buttons on the master control panel, the information will be recalled to the board. This is particularly important in some cases because the System 8 is programmed to rearm itself after an unaborted zone alarm. This eliminates the possibility of an undetected intrusion after an alarm has been sounded and the premises have been checked by the authorities (but the homeowner is not available to reset the system).

Another feature that adds to smooth operation is the system's ability to "supervise" itself. The System 8 can discriminate between a malfunction in the system and a genuine alarm. If there is a faulty wire, a power disruption, or a loose or nonfunctioning sensor in a fire detection zone, the system will advise the consumer with a special tone distinct from an alarm tone. In addition, the zone light will also blink on the master control panel until the necessary repair or adjustment is made. Even though the system may be supervising a problem, its ability to continue its other monitoring functions is not affected.

This sytem operates from a standard house electrical supply. If there is a power failure, standby power is provided by a 12-volt battery that is constantly charged by a special circuit in the system.

One of the greatest concerns of consumers is that the system may be tampered with before an attempted break-in occurs. The System 8 can monitor any improper interference with the tele-

Fig. 2-53. System 8 splice box. An accessory point for system component wiring, storage battery, and telephone communicator (courtesy SenDEC Corporation).

phones lines, the outside sirens, or the internal security control box. If tampering takes place, the information is immediately conveyed to the authorities.

It is customary to install a System 8 with one master control panel and one or two remote units. It is possible to have two master control panels, giving an extra readout capability. If circumstances dictate, up to four remote units can be positioned on a property. This might be done in cases where more than one door is frequently used, or the property is large enough to warrant the extra units for convenience. It can also be electronically expanded to accommodate more than eight zone areas.

The System 8 may also be customized to build a system that will scan up to eight additional inputs per zone and independently monitor those inputs. This may be desirable in an application where there are numerous functions to monitor. The system would be extremely useful on a small- or medium-sized executive mansion and in apartment buildings where the zoning system can identify the location and the nature of the alarm down to each specific hallway or staircase detector.

In the home, where there are special valuables to be protected, the system can "zone" such things as a gun closet or a safe. The control panels will reflect the status of those objects.

The System 8 has a splice box that provides an area for sensor wiring, the attachment and use of a digital communicator, telephone line monitor, and the backup battery supply (Fig. 2-53).

Figure 2-54 illustrates the System 8 master control unit in a typical hookup. Notice the potential for various sensor devices. Because of the ability to expand the system to meet current or future needs, the unit can easily qualify for a single dwelling, apartment, apartment building, or a larger estate where various functions must be monitored.

This system is easy to install. It is ideal for adaptation to old systems that are either outdated for present security needs or are inconvenient for the homeowner.

## MODULAR ULTRASONIC ALARM SYSTEMS

The *Massasonic ultrasonic intrusion alarm system* is a modular system that can be installed quickly and easily. Just plug it in and the system is operational. There are no complicated adjustment controls that may leave doubt as to how well the home is really protected. Plus, there is no wiring necessary.

Once plugged in, the entire volume of the room in front of the unit is protected without the need for wiring switches on every door or window. The unit will even catch an intruder entering through the floor or window. Figure 2-55 illustrates the area coverage of an ultrasonic intrusion alarm system.

The system is unique in that the fundamental acoustic analysis of other ultrasonic alarms resulted in a revolutionary breakthrough in the electronic processing of the alarm system. The system will increase your protection, privacy, and peace of mind.

Ultrasonic sound is used because it is of a frequency or pitch above the range of human hearing. Ultrasonic sound does not penetrate

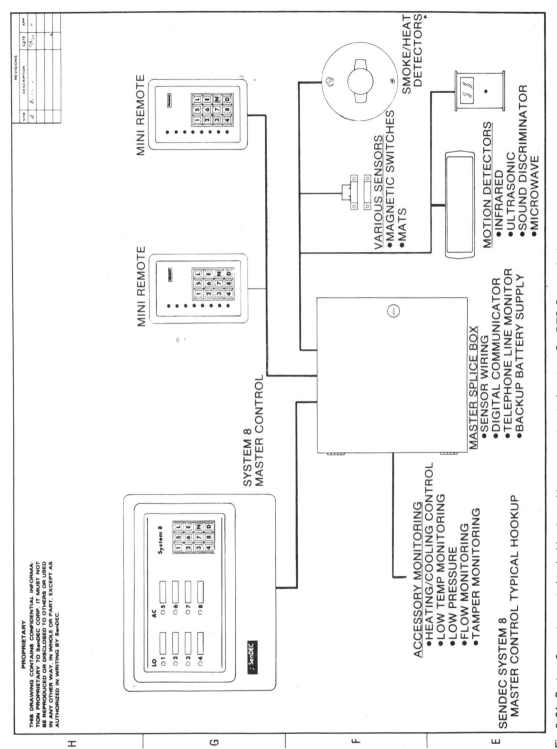

Fig. 2-54. System 8 master control typical hookup with component parts (courtesy SenDEC Corporation).

Fig. 2-55. The area coverage is a broad 120° cone of sound (courtesy Massa Products Corporation).

approximatel 2' to 5' from the floor (Fig. 2-56). This is because the ultrasonic transmitter sends out a broad 120° circle of sound, similar in theory to a spotlight. Acoustical reflections from nearby objects, such as a high-backed chair, large sofa, a shelf, or a large expanse of table surface positioned directly in front, close to the immediate side, or directly below the unit, will tend to overload the system. The area of coverage is reduced. To maximize unit coverage, the unit must be positioned and the area walk-tested to be assured of the total area to be protected (Fig. 2-57).

There is always a remote possibility of a near field thermocline condition affecting the unit. It is not recommended that the master unit be placed directly above a baseboard heater or radiator. Positioning the unit slightly in front of the heating element or even directly aiming the unit toward the heat source will not interfere with the alarm's operation.

Be sure that your ultrasonic alarm unit is pointed toward the areas of easiest intrusion, such as the windows and doors. If you have pets,

walls and unintentionally respond to movement outside the area being protected, which results in false alarms such as with microwave intrusion alarm systems. Instead, the sound is reflected off all the objects and walls of the room.

In the Massasonic system console, the microcomputer uses a patented signal processing system to sample the sound field 500 times a second. If the area of protection is ever violated by the opening of a door or by a person entering, the computer will immediately detect a change in frequency or pitch of the acoustic signal and activate the alarm. The system responds to a moving target and not to air turbulence caused by wind, air conditioning, or heating systems. These false alarms plague other ultrasonic systems.

The complete microcomputer burglar system actually consists of a master alarm unit, power supply unit, and a battery /siren unit. Their modular design allows these units to be placed inconspicuously in any room to provide total area coverage — up to 1,000 square feet. The master unit should be located on a horizontal surface (such as a shelf, mantle, table, desk, etc.) that is

Fig. 2-56. The master unit should be placed on a horizontal surface. It should be between 2' and 5' from the floor and pointed toward the areas you want to protect (courtesy Massa Products Corporation).

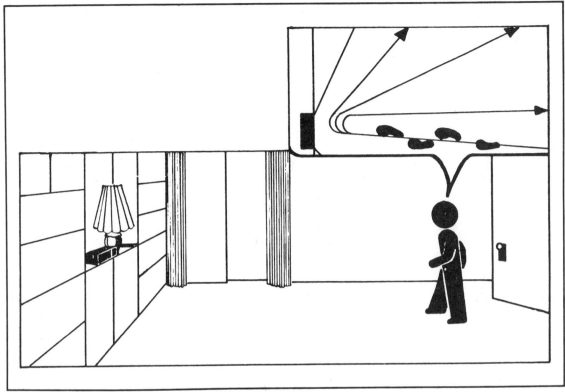

Fig. 2-57. A walk test assures the proper area is covered (courtesy Massa Products Corporation).

they should be restricted from the area of protection when the unit is programmed for alarm.

The battery/siren unit contains a battery pack that allows the ultrasonic system to continue operation in the event of a power failure. The backup battery provides continuous 48-hour protection. If you were to leave on a Friday evening, and the power went out in your neighborhood later that night, the system would still be operating Sunday evening when you returned. This is not true with many other systems; they usually offer anywhere from 4-12 hours of maximum backup battery protection.

### CHAMBERLAIN DUAL-CHANNEL ALARM

Figure 2-58 illustrates the *Chamberlain dual-channel home alarm system* that provides 24-hour burglar alert, plus fire or emergency alert capability. This is the master control unit that operates off your standard household current.

Several features are built right into the basic package of this expandable system:

—Automatic 4-minute alarm shutoff with system reset.
—Entry and exit delay.
—A powerful 86-decibel alarm built into the master control unit.
—Built-in emergency switch for instant manual activation.
—A key lock to protect the alarm controls.

You can customize your home alarm system to fit your own special needs. Figure 2-59 illustrates a typical home. The numbers refer to the various accessories available to protect your home.

1. The intrusion transmitter/sensor with an on-off battery test switch sends a radio signal to the alarm console at the instant of intrusion. One

Fig. 2-58. The Chamberlain dual-channel home alarm system (courtesy Chamberlain Manufacturing Corporation).

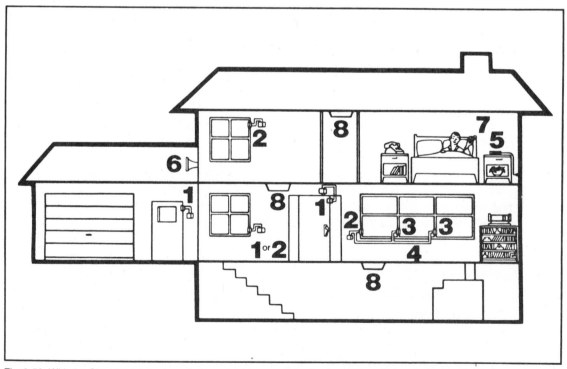

Fig. 2-59. With the Chamberlain system, the accessories can customize home security for maximum efficiency and coverage (courtesy Chamberlain Manufacturing Corporation).

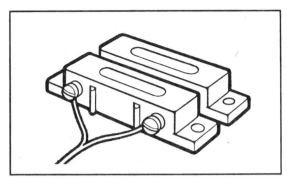

Fig. 2-60. Typical two-piece magnetic sensors for use with the Chamberlain security system (courtesy Chamberlain Manufacturing Corporation).

transmitter can serve multiple sets of sensors. The on-off test switch allows entry and exit without setting off the alarm.

2. It's the same as the first, except it does not have an on-off switch for entry or exiting without activating the alarm. It does have an LED indicator lamp to signal battery strength.

3. Magnetic sensors. Two-piece units protect every vulnerable door and window (Fig. 2-60). They send a signal to the transmitter when intrusion is detected. Multiple window situations can be covered with one transmitter, extra sensors, and extra hookup wire (Fig. 2-61).

4. Extra-strength, thin, and unobtrusive wire is used to hook up the various sensors employed in the system.

5. A portable smoke/fire alarm receiver plugs into an ac outlet. It sounds a piercing alarm when a signal is transmitted from a smoke detector anywhere in the house. This is essential for large homes where smoke detector or console alarms may be too far away to be heard.

6. An outdoor dual alarm with an extra-loud, 106-decibel constant alarm scares intruders and alerts neighbors and family. It sounds an intermittent alarm for fire or emergency alert and is weatherproofed (Fig. 2-62).

7. A remote emergency transmitter can be coded to instantly activate alarms from anywhere in the home at the touch of a button. It can be hand-held or clipped to clothing, which makes it valuable when working outside.

8. Remote signaling smoke and fire alarm modules (Fig. 2-63) add fire protection to the home. When smoke is detected, a loud alarm sounds, both in the alarm itself and also at the dual-channel master console unit.

For any alarm system to perform its intended tasks, the residents of the protected home must adjust their habits to the use of the system. For example, if one forgets to activate the alarm when leaving home, the alarm system

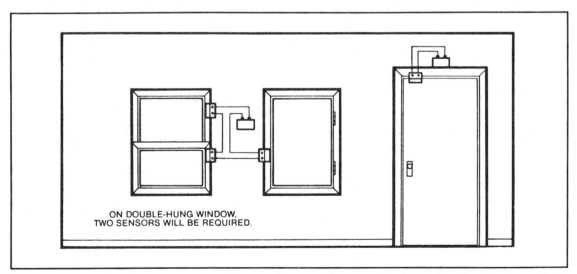

Fig. 2-61. Multiple window hookups are easy with magnetic sensors (courtesy Chamberlain Manufacturing Corporation).

ON DOUBLE-HUNG WINDOW, TWO SENSORS WILL BE REQUIRED.

Fig. 2-62. Exterior extra-loud alarm alerts neighbors and family to potential intruders or other trouble (courtesy Chamberlain Manufacturing Corporation).

cannot function. In a similar fashion, if someone forgets to inform another family member that the alarm has been activated, the alarm system will consider entry by that individual as an intrusion and activate the warning device. The Chamberlain system just described includes special features that greatly simplify living with an alarm system. Control settings let you adjust the system to different situations, such as normal household activity or sleeping hours. The master control receiver also blends well into the typical household and will probably attract no more attention than an ordinary table radio. This "wireless" system, in that intrusion· warnings are transmitted from small radio transmitters easily installed throughout the home, is designed for 24-hour protection and will continue to function in case of power failure through a backup battery unit.

### DIGITAL SECURITY CONTROL CONSOLE

Figure 2-64 shows the *Sescoa console control station*, which is an alternative to a standard control station. Used in single console systems with remote location of the alarm control panel, this model contains its own digital key logic. It can be wall-mounted or is available in a desk console model.

The system features a built-in speaker and tone generator that is used for a local alarm (siren), an audio listen-in, fire, and for prealarm early warning in time delay systems.

The 12-digit logic, a self-contained digital key, has more than 11,000 possible combinations that may be used. A keyboard audible feedback gives you an audible "chirp" each activation.

The digital key features or options include single digit arming of the system, a four-digit arm-disarm, hidden ambus, and panic. These are standard features. The instant delay switch can be used in entry-exit applications to make the entire system protection instant. When in an instant mode, the interior zone may be shunted, and the instant status LED is on.

A fire reset and test is a versatile switch to interrupt the power and reset smoke detectors. When in the reset position, the switch activates a trouble zone annunciation. It may also be used to send a system test code with a digital communicator. A ring-back beep verifies that the central station has received the test signal. There is a latching panic medical loop provision to install multiple panic or medical buttons, and these may be audible or silent.

Also, there is an auxiliary burglar loop (normally open and normally closed). This additional burglar zone over and above those provided by the alarm control is switched in and out of the system with the instant delay switch. Figure 2-65 illustrates a system layout.

Figure 2-66 shows a Sescoa local alarm

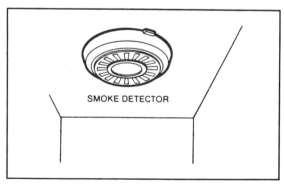

Fig. 2-63. Remote signaling smoke and fire alarm modules provide that extra minute of early warning (courtesy Chamberlain Manufacturing Corporation).

Fig. 2-64. Sescoa single console system (courtesy Sescoa).

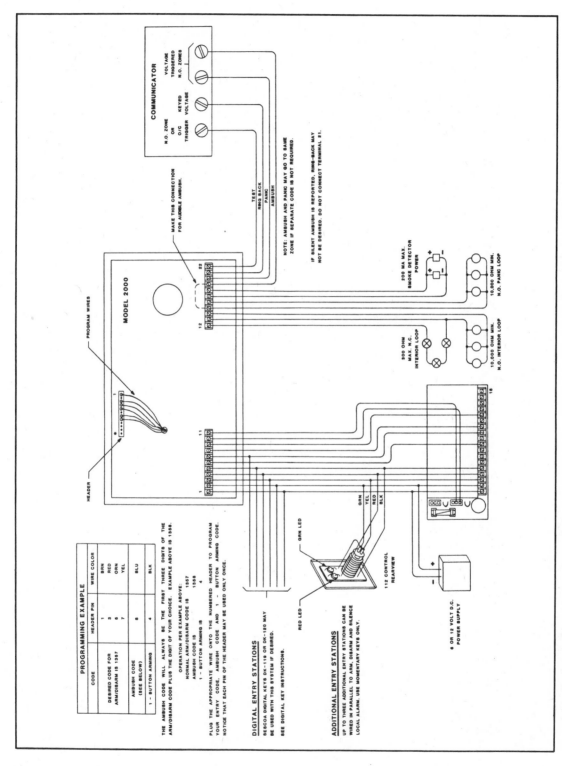

Fig. 2-65. System layout illustrates the number of optional devices available for residences of varying sizes (courtesy Sescoa).

Fig. 2-66. A decorator console with a plug-in communicator option (courtesy Sescoa).

Fig. 2-67. Residential burglar alarm control panel (courtesy Sescoa).

control decorator console with a plug-in communicator option designed for townhouses, condominiums, and apartments. It contains a complete burglar and fire control with a digital key, instant and delay switch, fire reset/test switch, and an internal speaker all in one package.

The plug-in communicator is used for reporting burglary, fire, panic, and auxiliary functions. A tremendous advantage, and one of the prime features that makes this particular alarm system interesting is that three telephone numbers can be programmed into the communicator when tied into a dialer system. This means that in an alarm mode, it will call, until reset, up to three phone numbers. It would be line one, line two, and then a backup if your station is busy or disabled.

Another important feature is the "line seizure" built into the communicator. The unit disconnects a subscriber phone to give an alarm priority when an emergency is registered with the system. Suppose that you were on the telephone in one part of the home, and the console registered an entry taking place in another part of the home. You definitely would want to know and to let authorities know as soon as possible. Instead of having to react to an alarm and then determine what the problem is, then return to the telephone to contact the authorities, the console communicator would disconnect the call you were on and automatically call a number already programmed into the communicator.

Figure 2-67 shows a very practical burglar alarm control panel available for residential security. The circuitry hookup of the panel provides for burglar inputs, an arm inhibit to avoid false alarms, time delay, multiple arming of stations, early warning, a built-in siren driver alarm cutoff and reset, and 24-hour panic. The panel is designed for easy conversion to a communicator compatible system.

### UPGRADING OLDER ALARM SYSTEMS

Most older alarm systems lack two devices: a prewarning entry and a low battery detector. The alarm system itself is still operational and pro-

Fig. 2-68. Prewarning entry alert, the Melo-Alert gives a reminder of somebody entering the door by playing a melody. The Melo-Alert can be hooked into an existing security system (courtesy Microtone).

vides an adequate level of security, but the alarm owner doesn't know when the batteries are running low or cannot be alerted to remember to turn off the alarm system on entering the home.

Low batteries can trigger a false alarm, or they will not have adequate power to trigger the alarm when an intrusion is detected. Forgetting to turn off the alarm on entry will trigger it. Either way, police may respond to check the situation. Sometimes a fine is the rule rather than the exception in many localities.

### Prewarning Entry

Figure 2-68 illustrates a prewarning entry device — the *Melo-Alert.* The Melo-Alert be-

comes a reminder to turn the system into the day mode before the alarm is activated. The unit works off the system's voltage (2 to 18 volts so it will fit all systems).

The Melo-Alert comes in two versions: one with two wires that requires no separate trigger input for play and two three-wire versions for either negative or positive Sonalert input. The three-wire versions require very little Sonalert input current to play—typically less than 1 milliampere. The three-wire version for a positive Sonalert input can replace the popular Ademco Mini-Howler, which has been around for many years. The two-wire version of the Melo-Alert requires full power in order to perform, and it is not recommended for some control panels that have low Sonalert current drive capability. It is, however, quite satisfactory for most control instruments and is the replacement for the original Melo-Alert.

Figure 2-69 illustrates instructions for the low current draw Melo-Alert hookup to your control panel. It is easy to hook up Melo-Alert.

### Low Battery Detector

The *low battery detector* is a subminiature, 100 percent solid-state device for maximum dependability that provides both positive and negative outputs in response to a low battery (Fig. 2-70). It is available for 6-, 12-, and 24-volt systems, but other voltage units can be obtained through a direct factory order.

The low battery detector provides both positive and negative outputs in response to a low battery. These voltage outputs are easily converted to switch closures by simply clipping a resister. The application examples in Fig. 2-71 best illustrate the ways in which this module can be configured to suit your specific needs.

In digital communicator systems, the device is very effective in the prevention of alarm system failures due to power interruption or charging circuit failure when connected. It also identifies false alarms caused by power fluctuations and temporary power outages.

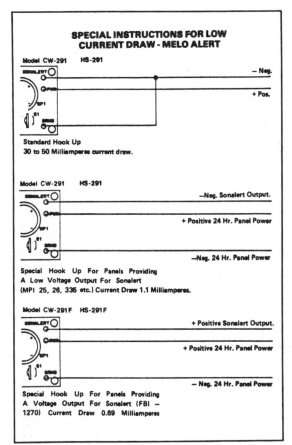

Fig. 2-69. Easy-to-follow instructions allow do-it-yourselfers to hook up the Melo-Alert (courtesy Microtone).

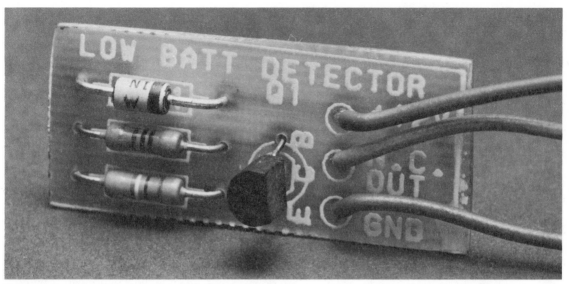

Fig. 2-70. The low battery detector should be hooked up to every home alarm system that uses backup batteries (courtesy Microtone).

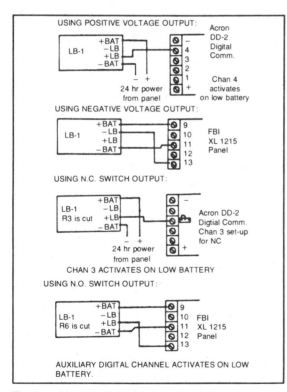

USING POSITIVE VOLTAGE OUTPUT:

Acron DD-2 Digital Comm.

Chan 4 activates on low battery

24 hr power from panel

USING NEGATIVE VOLTAGE OUTPUT:

FBI XL 1215 Panel

USING N.C. SWITCH OUTPUT:

Acron DD-2 Digtial Comm. Chan 3 set-up for NC

24 hr power from panel

CHAN 3 ACTIVATES ON LOW BATTERY

USING N.O. SWITCH OUTPUT:

FBI XL 1215 Panel

AUXILIARY DIGITAL CHANNEL ACTIVATES ON LOW BATTERY.

Fig. 2-71. Various applications for the low battery indicator module (courtesy Microtone).

## NUTONE SECURITY SYSTEM

Your security system must be designed to fit your needs. Some people will elect to determine the need and specific equipment themselves, while others will consult a professional installer trained in home security system design and installation.

The design starts by determining which areas are vulnerable to illegal entry and then selecting the intruder detection system that is most suitable. Naturally, all doors and windows are considered, and more specialized components may be necessary in key areas.

Let's examine a complete security system that can be used in the city (in a home, apartment, or condominium) and in suburban areas and on farms where there are numerous buildings. This system can also be used for larger mansions and estates.

This system is from NuTone and has 13 desirable intrusion alert features, plus optional fire detection. The entranceway to the home in Fig. 2-72 is protected by five security devices. All basic system components, various options, and accessories should be designed to blend in tastefully with your home surroundings. They

Fig. 2-72. Five items provide entranceway security. They are all concealed. Items are: (1) recessed magnetic detector, (2) glass-break detector, (3) ultrasonic motion detector, (4) concealed floor mat detector, and (5) infrared photelectric detector (courtesy NuTone).

must not stand out and should not be noticeable to casual visitors.

Proper security begins at your doors and windows. Doors are where the burglar looks first. Even the best locks won't stop a determined intruder.

Figure 2-73 illustrates a recessed magnetic detector installed in the door. Such detectors should be installed at all entries, including the front and back doors and even the garage doors. These detectors are wired to a closed protective circuit. When the door is opened, the circuit is broken and an alarm sounds. Magnetic and plunger detectors may also be installed on strategic interior doors within the home.

First-floor and basement windows should be equipped and heavily protected. Like doors, windows can be equipped with magnetic or plunger detectors if the window is opened. Surface-

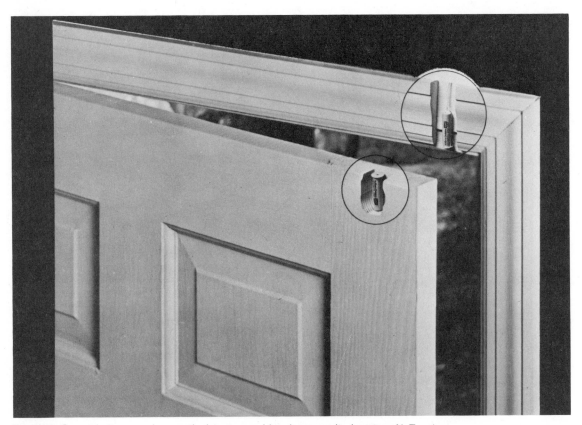

Fig. 2-73. Concealed recessed magnetic detector provides door security (courtesy NuTone).

Fig. 2-74. A pair of surface-mounted magnetic detectors (courtesy NuTone).

rupted, your system's alarm will be immediately activated.

Ultrasonic motion detectors (Fig. 2-80) are excellent for monitoring open spaces, especially large glass-walled rooms that might otherwise be difficult to protect. These units emit inaudible high-frequency sound waves in elliptical patterns that are adjustable from 12′ to 35′ by 5′ 20′. Movement within the secured area interrupts the waves and sounds the alarm.

Concealed floor mat detectors let you se-

mounted magnetic detectors (Fig. 2-74) may be installed at the side of windows (Fig. 2-75). If there are large areas of glass in the home, such as sliding glass doors, picture windows, etc., you should have a glass break detector installed (Fig. 2-76). These detectors respond only to breaks—not to shock or vibrations.

Another practical way to safeguard your windows or other glass areas is to use foil tape (Fig. 2-77). The breaking of the glass tears the tape and also breaks the electrical current running through it, triggering the alarm.

Sometimes wiring is difficult or impractical. If so, a digital radio transmitter and radio receiver are used to detect forced entry (Fig. 2-78). These are especially useful in linking outbuildings, including a garage, within a 150′ range.

Within the home, area surveillance provides you with that second line of security. Infrared photoelectric detectors (Fig. 2-79) are among the most popular means of protecting interior areas around entries, hallways, and even large open spaces. A transmitter projects an invisible pulsed infrared beam to a receiver across an unobstructed space (up to 75′). If the beam is inter-

Fig. 2-75. Magnetic switch attached to each window.

Fig. 2-76. A glass-break detector protects sliding glass doors and windows (courtesy NuTone).

cure strategic points along interior passageways, the top and bottom of stairways, doors, and anywhere else an intruder is likely to step. They can also be used beneath windows and along large glass walls.

An audio detector (Fig. 2-4) is designed to sense certain sounds created by forced entry, such as splintering wood, breaking glass, etc. They are especially good in seldom used areas. When the detector's miniature microphone "hears" these specific frequencies, it triggers your alarm.

Manual emergency push buttons (Fig. 2-81) (panic buttons) can be installed at any location through the home. You can manually activate the security system from anywhere within the house. Portable digital radio transmitters (Fig. 2-82) also allow manual activation of the alarm system through radio waves.

Remote controls, either key-operated or digital, operate the security system. Up to five indoor or outdoor remotes, including one master remote, can be used in convenient locations throughout the home. Figure 2-83 shows a key-operated outdoor remote, Fig. 2-84 illustrates a key-operated indoor remote, and Fig. 2-85 shows a digital indoor remote control.

Fig. 2-78. Digital transmitters can be used when wiring is difficult or impossible (courtesy NuTone).

Fig. 2-77. Foil tape can be used in areas when other sensors are not desired. The foil tape also provides complete protection (courtesy NuTone).

56

Fig. 2-79. Infrared photoelectric detectors are popular in many residences for protecting hallways and the like (courtesy NuTone).

Digital remote controls operate with a simple four-digit code. A code can be changed anytime. The indoor digital remotes control the perimeter and interior circuits independently. Thus, entry points can be protected 24 hours a day, and the family can move about freely within the home.

Optional entry/exit switches (Fig. 2-86) let you momentarily bypass a detector without disarming the rest of the system. The entry timer-switch gives you up to 60 seconds to pass, and it has a "hold" position so your entire family can go freely through one door while the rest of the home remains protected. The entrance key switch includes an anti-tampering device that

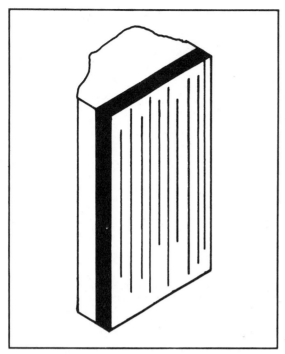

Fig. 2-80. Ultrasonic motion detectors monitor open spaces within the home.

Fig. 2-82. Portable radio transmitters allow you to activate the alarm from anywhere within range of the system (courtesy NuTone).

Fig. 2-81. An emergency panic button can be hooked into the system and placed anywhere in the home (courtesy NuTone).

Fig. 2-83. Exterior key-operated remote switch (courtesy NuTone).

Fig. 2-84. Indoor key-operated remote switch (courtesy NuTone).

Fig. 2-86. Entry /exit bypass switches for individual doors are used when access is required for only a moment (courtesy NuTone).

Fig. 2-85. Indoor remote controls can be with a digital controller (courtesy NuTone).

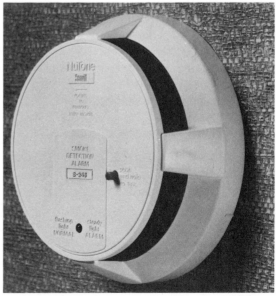

Fig. 2-87. Smoke detector alarm unit (courtesy NuTone).

Fig. 2-88. A rate-of-rise detector (courtesy NuTone).

Fig. 2-89. Fixed temperature detectors sound the alarm when a predetermined temperature is reached (courtesy NuTone).

protects it against attempted bypassing of the circuitry.

In addition to the perimeter and interior security of the home, no system is complete without a provision for fire detection. Most fatal fires start after midnight when families are asleep. Smoke, not fire, is often the killer. When seconds count, an early warning system can make the difference between life and death for all inhabitants.

A well-planned detection system should include *both* smoke and heat detectors in all critical areas and in sufficient number to assure full coverage of the home.

The primary location for the installation of smoke detectors (Fig. 2-87) is outside each bedroom area. Since fire travels upward, another important location is at the top of stairwells. The

National Fire Protection Association recommends the installation of smoke detectors on each level of a multistory home.

Rate-of-rise heat detectors (Fig. 2-88) and fixed temperature heat detectors (Fig. 2-89) should be installed in each enclosed living area, including bathrooms, closets, attics, and basements. In this particular system, up to 10 NuTone photoelectric smoke detectors and any number of heat detectors can be connected to the security system by using a fire protection module. Table 2-1 is a heat-smoke detector selection guide for use with this particular security alarm system.

No system is complete without a main control unit (Fig. 2-90). The control unit may be placed anywhere within the home, but it should

**Table 2-1. Heat-Smoke Detector Selection Guide for Use with NuTone SA-2300 Security Alarm System (courtesy NuTone)**

| Heat-Smoke Detector Selection Guide – Use With NuTone SA-2300 Security Alarm System | | | |
|---|---|---|---|
| Model No. | Description | Suggested Use | Dimensions |
| S-122 | Rate-of-Rise/135°F Fixed Temperature Heat Detector | Surface-mount on ceiling in ordinary living areas with normal room temperatures. | 4½" diameter, 1⅜" deep. Distance range: 25 ft. in all directions. Detector covers area up to 50' x 50'. |
| S-123 | Rate-of-Rise/200°F Fixed Temperature Heat Detector | Surface-mount on ceiling in areas where temperatures are higher than normal: furnace or boiler rooms. Note: Use S-123 or SA-125 in areas where temperatures consistently exceed 150°F. | |
| SA-124 | 135°F Fixed Temperature Heat Detector | Surface-mount on ceiling in ordinary living areas with normal room temperatures. | 1¾" diameter, ¾" deep. Distance range: 15 ft. in all directions. Detector covers area up to 30' x 30'. |
| SA-125 | 200°F Fixed Temperature Heat Detector | Surface-mount on ceiling in areas where temperatures are higher than normal: furnace or boiler rooms; attics. | |
| S-246 | Smoke Detector | Surface-mount on 4" sq. or oct. wiring box, primarily outside bedrooms. | 5¾" diameter x 2⅝" deep |
| S-246H | Smoke Detector with 135°F Heat Sensor | | |

Fig. 2-90. The main control unit can be located anywhere within the home (courtesy NuTone).

be concealed such as in a closet in the master bedroom or another out-of-the-way location.

Figure 2-91 illustrates the NuTone SA-2252 security system through a representative wiring diagram. All the items previously described are included here, giving you a view of a comprehensive security system. Note that this is not intended for an actual installation, nor does it include all the devices that might be used. It is provided to assist you in initial planning.

Space detection systems for a smaller home or apartment are usually easier to install mainly because you are limited by the places where such systems will be used (Fig. 2-92). Observe that only two areas are considered for a space protection system: the living room and its main door and the bedroom where the sliding patio door is located.

Assume that the patio door will require protection because the residence is too high from ground level. There are no other areas that can be used to reach this patio. The valuable material in the apartment is all in the living room. Figure

2-93 illustrates two positions where a space detection system could be positioned.

A microwave system may create problems because the detection field will go beyond the doors and walls. Toward the door, the system would be detecting other residents walking up and down the hallway; in the second position, the system can detect movement in the residence next door. A microwave system should not be used. The possibilities left would include an ultrasonic system, in which the waves will stay within the protected area (Fig. 2-94), a hardwired perimeter system (Fig. 2-95), or a sound discrimination system (Fig. 2-96).

## DO-IT-YOURSELF ALTERNATIVES

Perhaps you don't want to invest several hundred dollars or more in a professional alarm system. Low-cost alternatives are available, but they can't do all that a professional system can do.

To make your home or apartment more secure, some basic items from a hardware store can be used. Windows and doors can be used as a point to provide basic perimeter protection and alert you to potential problems that may occur. Through the use of a pull trap alarm, which you build and install yourself in less than 1 hour, you can have added security.

Figure 2-97 illustrates the pull trap device that is powered by batteries or standard ac power and sounds an alarm bell when activated.

The trip cord is firmly attached at the potential point of entry by a small screw eye. The other end is connected to the pull trap unit. When pressure is applied to the cord, in this case by the opening movement of a window or door, it pulls the cord out of the trap. This allows the two electrical contact points to close, activating the alarm bell.

## SENSORS FOR YOUR ALARM SYSTEM

Various intrusion sensors are used within intrusion detection systems. They include:

☐ Dry contact mechanical switches.
☐ Magnetic switches.

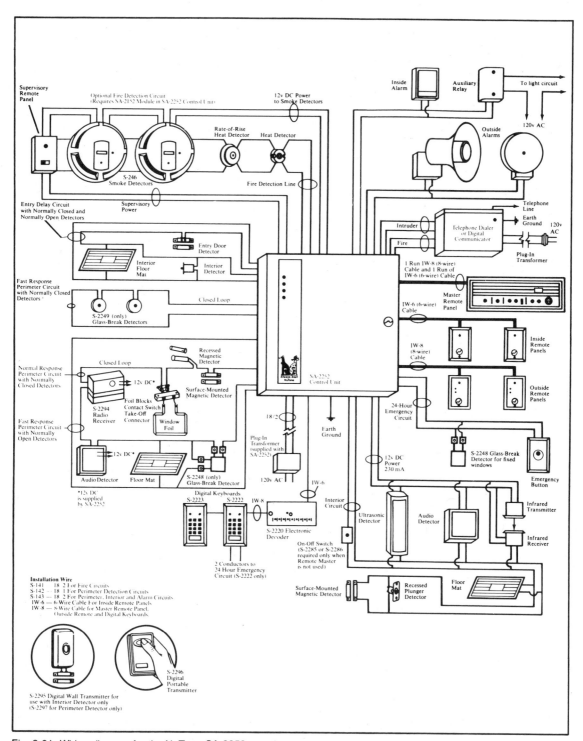

Fig. 2-91. Wiring diagram for the NuTone SA-2252 security system (courtesy NuTone).

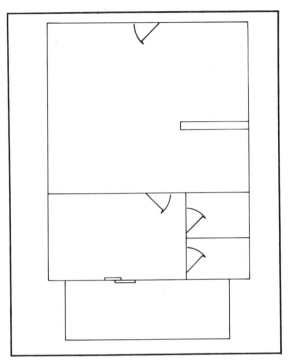

Fig. 2-92. Apartments (and small homes) are ideal for space detection systems.

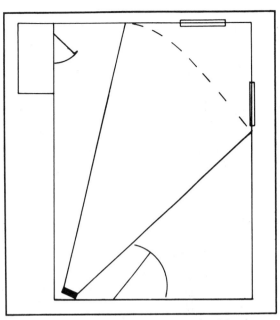

Fig. 2-94. An ultrasonic system is easy to locate and use.

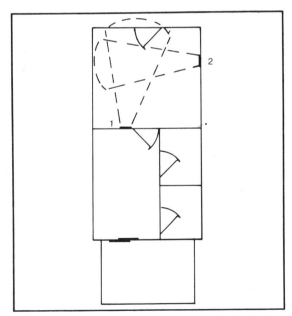

Fig. 2-93. Locating a space detection system is simple; here are two possible positionings for the unit.

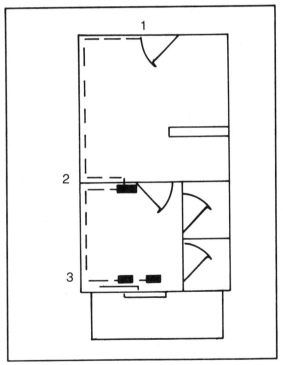

Fig. 2-95. Hard-wired systems take longer to install and are more expensive, but they can still protect the home: (1 and 3) magnetic switches, (2) control panel and alarm.

**Table 2-2. Comparison of Intrusion Sensors (source Law Enforcement Standards Laboratory of the National Bureau of Standards from Research Sponsored by the National Institute of Law Enforcement and Criminal Justice).**

| SENSOR | DRY CONTACT MECHANICAL SWITCHES | MAGNETIC SWITCHES | MERCURY SWITCHES | METALLIC FOIL | WIRE SCREENS | TRIP WIRES | PRESSURE MATS PRESSURE RIBBONS PRESSURE WAFERS |
|---|---|---|---|---|---|---|---|
| APPLICATIONS | DOORS, WINDOWS, GATES, TRANSOMS, HATCHES, ETC., USUALLY FOR PERIMETER PROTECTION. | DOORS, WINDOWS, GATES, TRANSOMS, HATCHES, ETC., USUALLY FOR PERIMETER PROTECTION. | | SHOW WINDOWS, OFFICE WINDOWS, GLASS DOORS, DRY WALL BOARD, ETC., USUALLY FOR PERIMETER PRO-TECTION. | ACCESS POINTS NOT SUBJECT TO EVERY-DAY USE, USUALLY FOR PERIMETER PROTECTION. | ENTRY WAYS SUCH AS TO CORRIDORS OR IN DOORWAYS FOR PERIMETER PROTECTION. | SMALL AREAS, DOORWAYS, OR UNDER SPECIFIC OBJECTS FOR POINT PROTECTION |
| ADVANTAGES | LOW COST. | RELATIVELY RESISTANT TO ENVIRONMENTAL EF-FECTS. RELATIVELY IMMUNE TO EFFECTS OF WEAR. LOW COST. | (SAME COMMENTS AS FOR MAGNETIC SWITCHES APPLY; APPLICATION IS USUALLY FOR ACCESS POINTS THAT HAVE COVERS THAT OPEN WITH CHANGING VERTICAL ANGLE. THUS THESE SWITCHES OPERATE WHEN TILTED BEYOND A CERTAIN POINT.) | EASILY REPAIRED. VISIBILITY SERVES AS DETERRENT. | LOW DEGREE OF MAINTENANCE. LOW VISIBILITY FOR ATTRACTIVE APPEARANCE. | LOW COST. | LOW COST. LOW DEGREE OF MAINTENANCE. ADAPTABLE TO WIDE VARIETY OF SHAPES AND SIZES. |
| DISADVANTAGES | LOW RELIABILITY. LOW SENSITIVITY. SUBJECT TO ENVIRON-MENTAL EFFECTS. HIGH INSTALLATION COST. | BECAUSE OF MOUNTING POSITION, MAY BE SUBJECT TO DAMAGE IN SOME APPLICATIONS. HIGH INSTALLATION COST. | | VULNERABLE TO DAMAGE BOTH IN-TENTIONAL AND THROUGH DAY-TO-DAY USE. | MUST BE REPLACED AFTER PENETRATION TO RESTORE PROTECTION. | MUST BE REMOVED TO ALLOW NORMAL ACCESS. THEN REPLACE TO RESTORE PROTECTION. | SUBJECT TO WEAR IF IN PATH OF HEAVY TRAFFIC. SUBJECT TO EFFECTS OF HUMIDITY AND STANDING WATER. |
| RESISTANCE TO DEFEAT | LOW. | BALANCED TYPE MORE RESISTANT TO COMPROMISE TYPES. | | LOW. | MODERATE FOR CON-CEALED TYPES. | LOW IF DETECTED BY INTRUDER. | RELATIVELY HIGH ONLY IF CONCEALED, OR PRESENCE UN-KNOWN TO INTRUDER. |
| FALSE ALARM SUSCEPTIBILITY | HIGH IF DOOR OR WINDOW HAS LARGE AMOUNT OF PLAY. LOW IF TIGHT. | HIGH IF DOOR OR WINDOW HAS LARGE AMOUNT OF PLAY. LOW IF TIGHT. | | HIGH DUE TO EFFECTS OF ENVIRONMENT. | LOW TO MODERATE. | LOW IF BUILDING IS SOLID. | SUBJECT TO ENVIRON-MENTAL CONDITIONS. |

SOURCE: LAW ENFORCEMENT STANDARDS LABORATORY OF THE
NATIONAL BUREAU OF STANDARDS; FROM RESEARCH
SPONSORED BY THE NATIONAL INSTITUTE OF LAW ENFORCEMENT
AND CRIMINAL JUSTICE

| ACOUSTIC SENSORS | ULTRASONIC MOTION SENSORS | MICROWAVE MOTION SENSORS | INFRARED MOTION SENSORS | PHOTOELECTRIC (ACTIVE) SENSORS | PHOTOELECTRIC (PASSIVE) SENSORS | CAPACITANCE SENSORS | VIBRATION SENSORS |
|---|---|---|---|---|---|---|---|
| AREA PROTECTION OF ENCLOSED SPACES (ROOMS, VAULTS, ETC.). | AREA PROTECTION OF SMALL EN-CLOSED SPACES (ROOMS, COR-RIDORS, ETC.) | AREA PROTECTION OF ENCLOSED SPACES (ROOMS, CORRIDORS, ETC.) CAN COVER LARGE AREAS. | AREA PROTECTION OF ENCLOSED SPACES (ROOMS, CORRIDORS, ETC.) CAN COVER LARGE AREAS. | ACROSS DOORWAYS, CORRIDORS, ETC., FOR PERIMETER PROTECTION: MULTIPLE BEAM SYSTEMS FOR LIMITED AREA PROTECTION. | POINT PROTECTION USING SENSORS WITH HIGH DIRECTION SEN-SITIVITY; LIMITED AREA PRO-TECTION OF SMALL ROOMS OR PORTIONS OF LARGER ONES. | PRIMARILY POINT PROTECTION FOR SAFES, FILING CABINETS, VALUABLE OBJECTS; LIMITED AREA AND PERIMETER PROTECTION. | PRIMARILY POINT PROTECTION FOR VAULTS, SHOW-CASES, ETC.; LIMITED SPACE PROTECTION WHEN INSTALLED TO PROTECT WALLS OR CEILINGS, ETC. |
| SENSITIVE. CAN USE EXIST-ING INTERCOM SYSTEMS. NOT AFFECTED BY AIR MOVEMENT. EFFECTIVE AGAINST "STAY-BEHINDS." | USUALLY NOT DETECTABLE BY INTRUDER. EFFECTIVE AGAINST "STAY-BEHINDS." NOT AFFECTED BY AIR MOTION, NOISE, LIGHT OR SOUND. EASY PHYSICAL INSTALLATION. | NOT DETECTABLE BY INTRUDER. EFFECTIVE AGAINST "STAY-BEHINDS." NOT AFFECTED BY AIR MOTION, NOISE, LIGHT OR SOUND. | RELATIVELY IMMUNE TO NOISE AND VIBRATION. | HIGH DEGREE OF FLEXIBILITY IN APPLICATION. INFRARED BEAM DIFFICULT TO DETECT. CAN COVER ACCESS POINTS WHERE PHYSICAL OB-STRUCTION NOT DESIRED OR CAN-NOT BE TOLERATED. | RELATIVELY UN-AFFECTED BY ENVIRONMENTAL FACTORS (EXCEPT ABRUPT CHANGE IN LIGHT LEVEL). HIGH DEGREE OF FLEXIBILITY IN APPLICATION. | HIGH DEGREE OF FLEXIBILITY IN APPLICATION. PROTECTIVE FIELD NOT DETECTABLE BY INTRUDER. | REQUIRE LOW MAIN-TENANCE. HIGH DEGREE OF RELIABILITY WHEN PROPERLY APPLIED. |
| MUST BE USED IN STABLE NOISE ENVIRONMENT WHERE BACKGROUND LEVEL IS LOW. | SEVERELY AFFECTED BY ENVIRONMENTAL FACTORS; AIR TURBULENCE AND MOTION, RATTLING DOORS, JANGLING KEYS, BLOWING DRAPERIES, VIBRATIONS, LOUD NOISES, ETC. ESSENTIALLY LINE-OF-SIGHT OPERATION; LARGE OBJECTS COULD SHIELD INTRUDER. MAY NOT DETECT EX-TREME RATES OF MOVEMENT (VERY SLOW OR VERY FAST). | COVERAGE DIFFICULT TO CONFINE TO DE-SIRED AREA. CAN BE SET OFF BY NEARBY FLUORES-CENT LIGHTS, LARGE OBJECTS OUTSIDE PROTECTED AREA, RADIO TRANSMITTER OPERATING NEAR SENSOR FREQUENCY | SOME SYSTEMS SENSITIVE TO CHANGES IN THERMAL ENVIRON-MENT (e.g., CHANGES IN SUNLIGHT AND TEMPERATURE). | NARROW BEAM OF PROTECTION. LINE-OF-SIGHT OPERATION; SMOKE OR DUST CAN HAMPER OPERATION. SUBJECT TO MIS-ALIGNMENT PROBLEMS. | NARROW BEAM OF PROTECTION. LINE-OF-SIGHT OPERA-TION; SMOKE OR DUST CAN HAMPER OPERA-TION. | CAN BE APPLIED ONLY TO OBJECTS NOT ELECTRICALLY GROUNDED; MAY REQUIRE SPECIAL CONSTRUCTION. | DETECTS ONLY FORCE-FUL ATTEMPTS AT ENTRY. CANNOT BE USED IN AREAS OF HIGH VIBRATION (TRAFFIC, CONSTRUCTION, ETC.) |
| HIGH IF PROPERLY INSTALLED. | HIGH IF PROPERLY INSTALLED. | HIGH IF PROPERLY INSTALLED. | HIGH. | LOW TO MODERATE, WITH SYSTEMS USING MODULATED BEAMS HAVING HIGHEST RESISTANCE. | HIGH. | VERY HIGH. | VERY HIGH. |
| CAN BE HIGH BUT REDUCED USING ADDITIONAL CAN-CELLATION MICRO-PHONE. | CAN BE HIGH UNLESS ENVIRONMENTAL FACTORES ARE CON-SIDERED BEFORE APPLICATION. | CAN BE HIGH UNLESS PROPERLY PLACED AND CAREFULLY ADJUSTED. | HIGH FOR RECEIVE-ONLY SENSORS. LOW FOR TRANSMIT-RECEIVE SENSORS. | CAN BE HIGH IF CERTAIN ENVIRON-MENT FACTORS ARE PRESENT (SMOKE, DUST) OR POOR PLANNING RESULTS IN MISAPPLICATION. | CAN BE HIGH IF IMPROPERLY INSTALLED SO THAT HEAT OR LIGHT LEVELS ARE NOT CONSTANT; IF COVERS FLOOR RODENTS MAY SET OFF ALARM. | LOW IF PROPERLY INSTALLED. | CAN BE HIGH IF ENVIRONMENTAL FACTORS ARE NOT TAKEN INTO AC-COUNT; MAY BE TRIGGERED BY MINOR EARTH TREMORS, SONIC BOOMS OR TRAINS. |

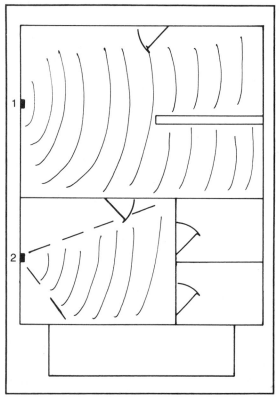

Fig. 2-96. A sound discrimination system is easy to install and provides excellent protection for the home: (1) main panel and alarm and built-in sensor, (2) remote sensor.

☐ Mercury switches.
☐ Metallic foil.
☐ Wire screens.
☐ Trip wires.
☐ Pressure mats, ribbons, or wafers.
☐ Acoustic sensors.
☐ Ultrasonic, microwave, and capacitance sensors.
☐ Active and passive photoelectric sensors.
☐ Vibration sensors.

Against these sensors, your system must be measured in terms of what it can do for you. You must be aware of the types of sensors, their specific applications, advantages, disadvantages, resistance to defeat, and false alarm susceptibility. See Table 2-2.

The controls, alarm, and sensor are all inside in a single unit piece. In multiunit pieces of a system, the sensors are located in different areas of the home. Each sensor protects a specific item—door, window, skylight, gun cabinet, etc. Numerous types of sensors are available on the market. Companies either develop their own or go to another company for them, but they have their own name imprinted. There may be no difference except for the name imprint and the exterior casing. Regarding magnetic contacts for use in security systems, though, only a few companies contract out to another manufacturer. In many pinpoint alarms, and even in hard-wind systems, the magnetic contacts used are probably manufactured by Sentrol Inc.

Sentrol specializes in surface-mouthed, recessed, high-security and wide-gap balanced contacts. They are designed to fit every interior and exterior need. Not content just to manufacture the contacts, Sentrol has spent many years

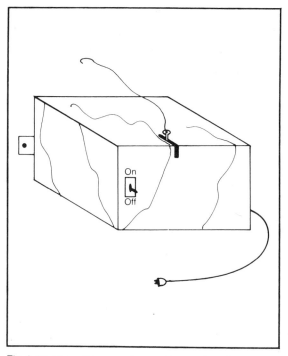

Fig. 2-97. The pull trap can be used in a variety of protection modes.

Fig. 2-98. Concealed switches for on-off control (courtesy Sentrol Inc.).

researching all alarm systems on the market. Numerous specific applications to meet about every security need have been developed.

When designing and/or installing a portion or all of a home security system, or just adding to an existing system, review the various applications. You can eliminate worry and time and get the job accomplished much sooner by using or adapting a proven security technique to meet your needs.

### Concealed Switches for Off-On Control

Closed loop magnetic contacts are used to arm and disarm certain alarm systems with a magnet. They replace the key switch. Some control panels are armed or disarmed using a momentary closure of a single switch (spring-loaded key switch), and others use two separate switches requiring a momentary closure of one switch to turn on and another switch to turn off (Fig. 7-98). It is possible to use hidden magnetic contacts in place of a key switch. Hiding the contact near entry door eliminates the need for a key. A small steel plate holding a magnet or a hole drilled to hold the magnet will allow entry. This eliminates the need for keys for employees or family to disarm the system.

Other applications include: controlling pumps, motors, and lights using a holding relay activated by magnet contacts (i.e., gasoline pump can be turned on only when switch has activated relay; and using sealed contacts to operate and control marine alarm systems).

### Protecting Double-Hung Windows

There are three methods of alarming double-hung windows with recessed or surface-mounted magnetic contacts. Method one is the recessed installation in the top of an upper window and the bottom of a lower window.

1. Use a magnetic contact. Select the position of the magnet in the window frame and the position of the switch in the head or sill. Slightly overdrill holes for the switch and magnet. Coat the switch and magnet with RTV mounting compound (this will permit easier insertion and help

67

hold them in place). Insert the switch and magnet in their respective holes.

2. Attach an ohmmeter to leads and check for proper operation.

3. Connect the switch to the loop.

4. If desired, cover the switch and magnet with wood filler to camouflage and to improve appearance.

Wide-gap Sentrol switches (those with W suffix) are polarity-sensitive. If the switch uses a bare magnet, observe correct polarity by mounting the magnet with the red end away from the switch.

Method two is the recessed installation in sides of windows. This type of installation is recommended only when the wall is open and readily accessible for running wires (e.g., during construction or remodeling). A finished wall will make this a very difficult job, requiring extremely awkward "fishing." This application requires perpendicular mounting of the switch and magnet, and it may require a wide-gap distance between the switch and magnet. A switch from the Sentrol concealed contact series should be used.

1. Drill a vertical hole in the window frame for the magnet. Coat the magnet with RTV mounting compound and insert it in the hole.

2. Pick a position for the switch. This will be determined by two requirements (Fig. 2-99). The magnet must not be centered under the switch; the end of the switch must be the opposite end of the magnet. If it's a wide-gap switch (switch with W suffix), observe correct polarity by mounting the magnet with the red end away from the switch end with wires.

3. Drill a hole for the switch. Insert the switch in the hole.

4. Attach an ohmmeter to leads, close the window, and test for correct operation.

5. Connect the switch to the loop.

Method three is surface installation on upper and lower windows.

1. Select an appropriate surface-mount switch. Mount the switches on the head, sill, or jamb in the desired position.

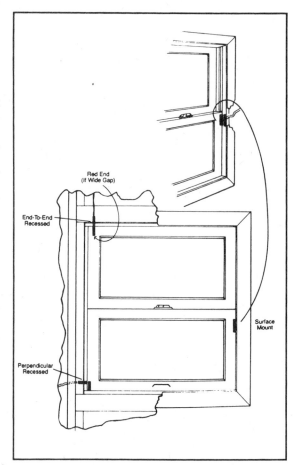

Fig. 2-99. Protecting double-hung windows (courtesy Sentrol Inc.).

2. Mount the magnet on the window. It should be directly opposite the switch when the window is closed. If you're using a switch with self adhesive, clean the surface with alcohol before mounting to assure a good bond. If it's a wide-gap or high-security switch, align labels on the switch and magnet so they read in the same direction (switch is polarity-sensitive).

3. Attach on ohmmeter and test for proper operation of the switch.

4. Connect the switch to the alarm loop.

### Protecting Thin Steel Frame Windows

A magnetic contact can be installed on windows with thin steel frames. Many casement, awning,

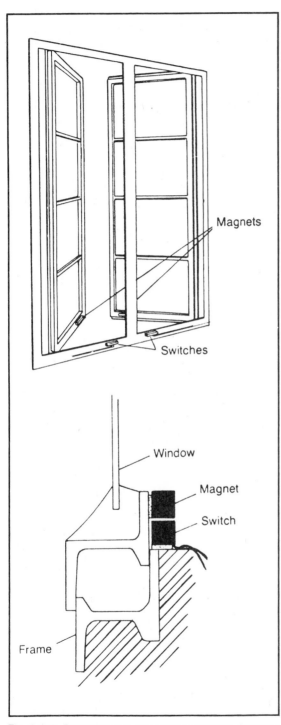

and classroom windows using a thin steel frame have been installed over the last 20 to 30 years. Due to the thin section of the metal and that it is steel, problems with drilling and tapping to install normal surface-mount contacts are common. This method uses two Sentrol self-adhesive clips and a Sentrol wide-gap magnetic contact, which will give about ⅝″ of gap when placed parallel to the magnet and ⅜″ of gap end to end with the magnet, when both the switch and magnet are in a clip on a steel surface.

Installation is as follows (Fig. 2-100):

1. Select a position for switches.

2. Drill a hole for wires if they are to be hidden.

3. Clean the frame with alcohol or soap and water.

4. Insert the switch and magnet in the clips.

5. Mount the switch and magnet on the frame and sash. The red end of the magnet must be away from the end of the switch—toward the wire end.

6. Test the switch with an ohmmeter.

7. Wire the switch into the loop.

8. Retest.

### Protecting Steel Frame Windows

This method permits recessed mounting of switches in casement or awning thin steel frame windows, which have a cross section as shown (Fig. 2-101). Because the steel environment will cause a decrease in gap distance, it is recommended that a wide-gap switch be used. To minimize the likelihood of water leakage, the switch and magnet should be mounted on the top or side of the window. Wire holes should be caulked with RTV mounting compound. Do not mount the switch and magnet on the hinge side of the window, or it will be possible to open the window too far before the switch will trip.

Installation instructions are as follows:

1. Select the position of the switch. Drill a hole in the frame for wires and insert wires in the hole.

2. Mount the switch on a header or side rail. Depending on the type of switch used, wipe the

Fig. 2-100. Protecting thin steel frame windows (courtesy Sentrol Inc.).

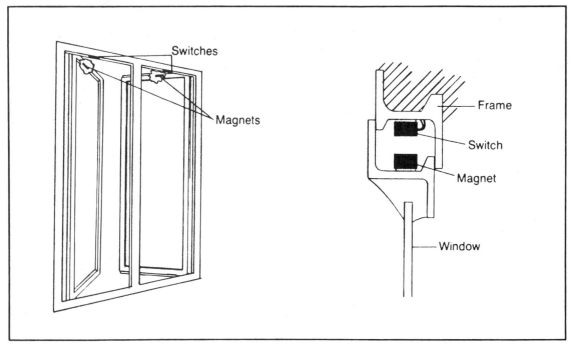

Fig. 2-101. Protecting steel frame windows (courtesy Sentrol Inc.).

surface with rubbing alcohol and attach with self-adhesive tape or RTV mounting compound.

3. Seal the wire hole with RTV mounting compound.

4. Mount a magnet on the sash opposite the switch. Wide-gap switches are polarity-sensitive. If Sentrol #1035 series, wipe the surface with alcohol and mount the magnet with self-adhesive tape. Align such that labels on the magnet and switch read in the same direction. If Sentrol #1055 or #1059 series, attach the magnet with RTV mounting compound, aligned parallel to the switch, with the red end of the magnet toward the wire end of the switch.

5. Attach an ohmmeter to the switch leads. Open and close the window to test for proper operation of the switch and to assure adequate clearance between the magnet and switch.

6. Connect the switch to the alarm loop. Retest for correct operation.

### Protecting Andersen Casement Windows

Protect Andersen casement windows with a re-cessed magnetic contact. A in Fig. 2-102 shows the standard method. B in Fig. 2-102 shows the method used if ventilation is required. Both methods require that the magnet be placed in the sash on the step closest to the inside of the window.

Installation is as follows:

1. Install the magnet in the sash on the step closest to the inside. Drill ¼″ hole × 1¼″ deep. This step has a cross section of about ½″ × ½″ and will hold the ¼″ diameter magnet by center-ing the hole in the section.

2. Drill a hole for the switch opposite the magnet. Angle this hole back toward the inside of the wall about 15°.

3. Install the switch and test.

4. Cover the ends of the switch and magnet with silicone rubber to protect from weather.

### Protecting Pella Brand Casement and Awning Windows

Protecting of Pella brand casement and awning windows with recessed magnetic contacts re-

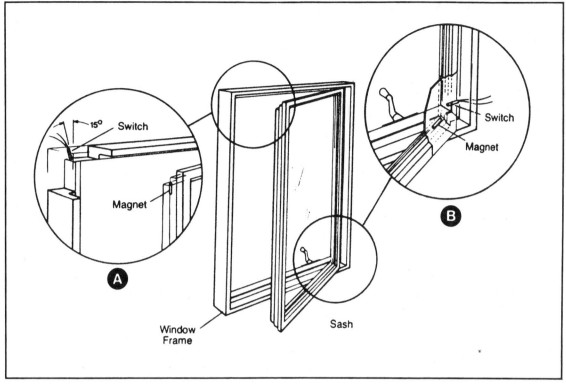

Fig. 2-102. Protecting Andersen casement windows (courtesy Sentrol Inc.).

quires extra care in installation because of the extra pane of glass. The windows may have two separate pieces of glass or one Thermopane. When drilling for the magnet, take care to miss the glass.

Installation is as follows (Fig. 2-103).

1. Select a position for the switch—in the top of the window frame if wires are going in the attic or in the bottom of the window if wires are going to run to the basement.

2. Drill a ¼″ diameter hole × 1¼″ deep in the window sash.

3. Insert a magnet.

4. Drill a ¼″ diameter hole in the frame. Drill at approximately 15° toward the inside of the wall. Align the switch hole center to within ¼″ of the center of the magnet.

5. Insert the contact into the hole.

6. Test the circuit and glue the switch and magnet in place.

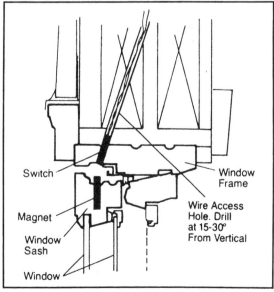

Fig. 2-103. Protecting Pella brand casement and awning windows (courtesy Sentrol Inc.).

71

### Arming Attic Entry Drop-Down Stairs

Secure drop-down stairways in garages against unauthorized entry. Frequently in residences, the entry door from the garage to the house will be alarmed, and the garage door will be left unsecured. An intruder can then gain access to the garage through the garage door, enter the attic via the drop-down stairway, cut a hole through a ceiling between the joists, and drop into the house without triggering the alarm.

Installation is as follows (Fig. 2-104):

Fig. 2-104. Arming attic entry drop-down stairs (courtesy Sentrol Inc.).

1. Position the switch on the stairway frame and the magnet on the drop-down portion of the stairway. Be certain there is no interference to the stairway mechanism from the switch or magnet.

2. Permanently attach the switch to the frame and temporarily attach the magnet to the stairway with masking tape. Connect an ohmmeter to the switch lead, close the stairway, and test for continuity.

3. Permanently attach the magnet to the stairway. Connect switch leads to the alarm loop.

### Protecting Roof Hatches

Unauthorized entry via a roof hatch can be thwarted by using surface-mount switches. The difference is in the method of mounting in the space available and the connection into the alarm circuit.

Installation is as follows (Fig. 2-105):

1. The most important thing to remember in hatch protection is to mount both the switch and the actuating magnet so they will not intrude into the open hatch space and cause hangup of clothing when climbing to the roof. Avoid any obstruc-

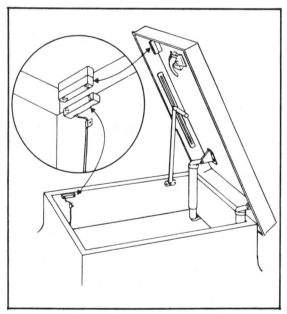

Fig. 2-105. Protecting roof hatches (courtesy Sentrol Inc.).

tion of entry and egress in normal hatch use. The use of spacer accessories will make installation within these criteria both quicker and easier.

2. Attach the selected switch on the hatch frame and on the side opposite the hatch hinges. Do this with the mounting of the magnet in mind and keep gap distance between the switch and magnet within specification tolerance. The switch and magnet elements need to be parallel for best operation.

3. If the roof hatch and/or frame is of steel, gap distance is usually halved and allowance needs to be made, or wide-gap switches should be used. Be sure to mount both the switch and magnet with the Sentrol name reading in the same direction. The switch is polarity-sensitive.

4. After completing the installation, check for proper operation and circuit continuity by opening and closing the hatch.

## Protecting Roof Skylights

Unwanted intrusion can occur by means of an unprotected skylight. Protection is easily achieved by using Sentrol contacts, with the difference being primarily in the method of fastening and connecting to the circuit.

Installation is as follows (Fig. 2-106):

1. If the skylight is hinged for an opening, locate the security switch on the side opposite the hinges. Follow standard mounting procedures with the switch unit being installed on the frame and the magnet on the skylight itself. Observe gap distance tolerances. In some installations it may be necessary to use spacers to achieve proper alignment.

2. If the skylight has a steel frame, gap distance is generally reduced by half. In this case, use Sentrol wide-gap switches. Be sure to mount with the Sentrol name reading in the same direc-

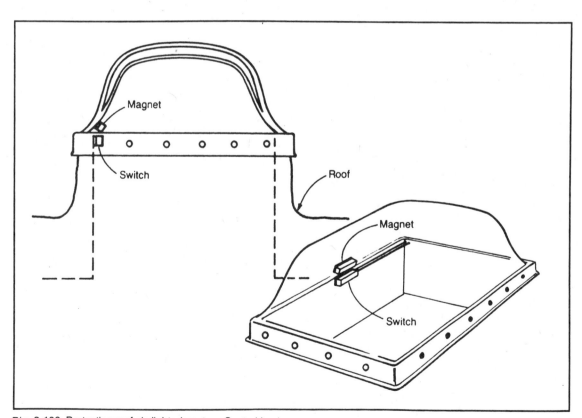

Fig. 2-106. Protecting roof skylights (courtesy Sentrol Inc.).

tion on both the switch and the magnet as the switch is polarity-sensitive.

3. In cases where the skylight is permanently installed, the operation of the switch should be checked for continuity and action by using a circuit checker before both parts are installed permanently. Do this by temporarily taping the magnet or switch in position and then move the companion piece toward and away. Mark the spot where you get positive action each time and install parts permanently in this position.

### Protecting Paintings

To protect hanging works of art (Fig. 2-107):

1. Inspect the frame for an area to place the magnet and switch.

2. Attach the magnet to the frame using a self-adhesive clip.

3. Attach the switch to the clip and install on the wall behind the magnet. The optional method is to install a switch in the wall at right angles to the magnet, forming an "L" with the switch and magnet.

4. Wire in to a 24-hour loop, if available, to protect even if the perimeter loop is off.

5. If a gap of more than ½″ is required, use a wide-gap switch, which allows more adjustment without false alarms.

### Protecting Art Objects

To provide security protection for statuary, vases, chests, or other works of art (not in cabinets or other coverings), use a roller/plunger magnetic switch.

Installation is as follows (Fig. 2-108):

1. Inspect the object to be protected for a flat resting surface where sufficient weight will be exerted to fully depress the roller/plunger of the switch when the art object is in place.

2. Drill a hole in the display stand ¾″ in diameter and at least 1½″ deep. Do this at the location selected in the first step.

3. Install the roller/plunger switch. Connect the wires in the 24-hour loop if available and to get protection even if a perimeter loop is inoperative.

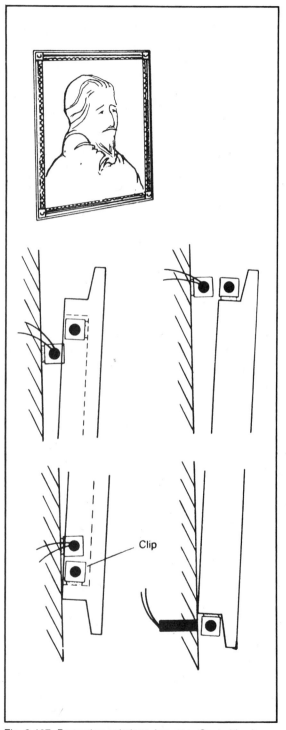

Fig. 2-107. Protecting paintings (courtesy Sentrol Inc.).

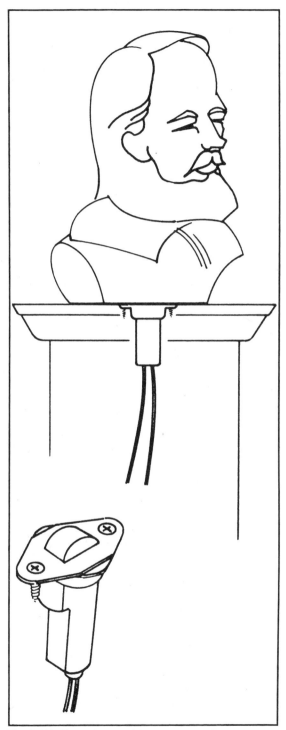

Fig. 2-108. Protecting art objects (courtesy Sentrol Inc.).

4. If the flange height of the switch causes the object being protected to "rock," the spacer supplied with the roller/plunger switch or an equal thickness of cardboard can be used as a wedge to assure mounting stability.

5. If the object to be protected is too light or too irregular in shape to provide a flat surface, it can be floated on a piece of hardboard or aluminum of sufficient size and weight that moving the art object still actuates the plunger and sets off the alarm. Some experimentation is usually required to get the proper balance.

### Protecting a China Cabinet

Secure a china cabinet to provide protection for silverware and works of art. Be sure to alarm both doors if protecting a two-door cabinet. Wire switches in series. Contacts should not be placed in a hinged portion of the door, because the door could be opened wide before the switch would trip. For aesthetic reasons, recessed installation is more desirable than the surface. See the next procedure to secure a drawer in a china cabinet.

Recessed installation is as follows (Fig. 2-109):

1. Choose an appropriate concealed contact.

2. Select positions for magnets in doors and switches in the cabinet.

3. Drill a vertical hole in the top of the door. Coat the magnet with RTV mounting compound and insert it in a hole. If it's a wide-gap switch, observe correct polarity by mounting a bare magnet with the red end away from the switch end without the wires.

4. Drill a vertical hole in the cabinet for the switch. Also, drill a hole at an angle from the inside of the cabinet to meet the switch hole, so wires can be run to the inside of the cabinet (be extremely careful to avoid drilling through the front of the cabinet).

5. Coat the switch with RTV mounting compound. Insert the switch in the hose and fish wires through to the inside of the cabinet. Route wires in the joints of the cabinet and around the

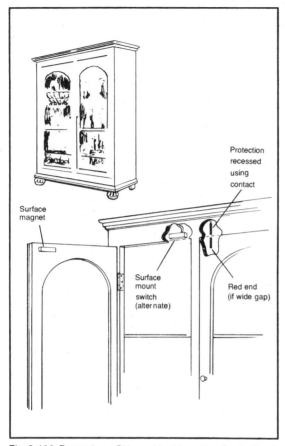

Fig. 2-109. Protecting a China cabinet (courtesy Sentrol Inc.).

top of the cabinet to the back. Drill a hole in back of the cabinet and run wires through.

6. Test for continuity with an ohmmeter; connect to alarm loop (on a 24-hour circuit if more security is desired, provide a shunt switch in the circuit to permit cabinet access as needed).

Surface installation is as follows:

1. Choose an appropriate surface mount.

2. Select position for magnets on doors and switches on the cabinet.

3. Mount switches and magnets. If wide-gap or high-security switches, align labels on the magnet and switch so they read in the same direction (switches are polarity-sensitive). If H-series, observe minimum gap distances.

4. Route wires in the joints of the cabinet and around the top of the cabinet to the back. Drill a hole in back of the cabinet and run wires through.

5. Test for continuity with an ohmmeter; connect to an alarm loop (on a 24-hour circuit if higher security is desired, provide a shunt switch in the circuit to permit access as needed).

### Protecting Gun Cabinets

This application is for an interior trap in a gun cabinet. Put a switch under the butt of a gun rather than on the door, because a burglar could break the glass in the door and remove the guns without opening the door (Fig. 2-110).

1. Select the gun that is going to be "bugged."

2. Drill a ¾" hole in the cabinet butt cutout.

3. Mount the switch in the hole.

4. Wire into a 24-hour (if desired) circuit to provide protection even when the person is home. All guns should be protected this way.

5. Instruct the user to disarm the system before removing the gun.

### Security a Valuables Drawer with an Interior Alarm Trap

To protect valuable coin collections, silverware, and jewelry, this application provides various means of alarming a storage drawer. Because of the difficulty of working with a screwdriver inside a drawer, a switch from the self-adhesive series should be used. Be certain to clean (with alcohol) the surfaces to which the switch and magnet are to be attached to assure good adhesion.

Surface installation instructions are as follows (Fig. 2-111).

1. Choose an area in which the switch and magnet will not interfere with drawer operation.

2. Install the switch in the cabinet, with the magnet on the drawer. If it's a wide-gap switch, align labels on the switch and magnet so the Sentrol name reads in the same direction (switch is polarity-sensitive).

3. Test for continuity with an ohmmeter; install in an alarm loop (on a 24-hour circuit if higher security is desired, provide a shunt switch

in the circuit to permit access as needed).

Recessed mounting is not recommended (and usually not possible on metal drawers, because the metal is usually too thin. On metal drawers, use self-adhesive contacts per surface installation instructions (allow for a 50 percent reduction in gap distance if in a steel environment).

Recessed installation instructions are as follows (Fig. 2-111).

1. Select the appropriate switch.

2. Drill a vertical hole in the side of the drawer. Coat the magnet with RTV mounting compound and insert it in the hole.

3. Coat the switch with RTV mounting compound and attach it to the cabinet perpendicular to the magnet (alternatively, 1055 or 1059 series switches can be mounted in plastic clips or self-adhesive clips). Be certain the magnet is not centered below the switch, but is near the end of the switch. If it's a wide-gap switch the red tip of the magnet must be away from the switch.

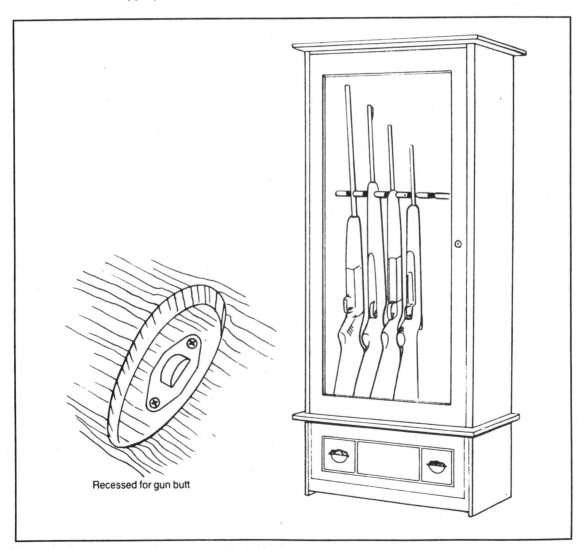

Recessed for gun butt

Fig. 2-110. Protecting gun cabinets (courtesy Sentrol Inc.).

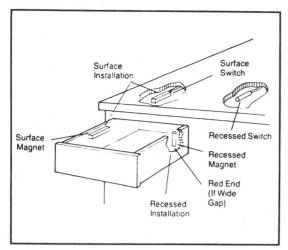

Fig. 2-111. Securing a valuables drawer with an Interior Alarm Trap (courtesy Sentrol Inc.).

4. Test for continuity with an ohmmeter; install in alarm loop (on a 24-hour circuit if higher security is desired, provide a shunt switch in the circuit to permit access as needed).

### Protecting Desk Drawers

The contact, when combined with a self-

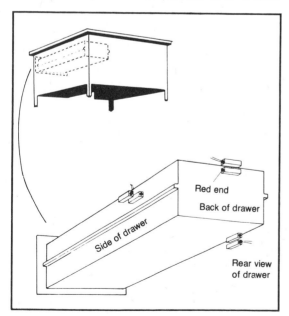

Fig. 2-112. Protecting desk drawers (courtesy Sentrol Inc.).

adhesive mounting clip, works very well on steel desk and cabinet drawers. The wide gap of the switch provides a good working distance on the steel, and the clip adheres very well for a long-term installation.

Installation is as follows (Fig. 2-112).

1. Choose an area with ¾" to 1¼" clearance between the moving and nonmoving portions.

2. Clean both surfaces with cleaning solvent to ensure good adhesion.

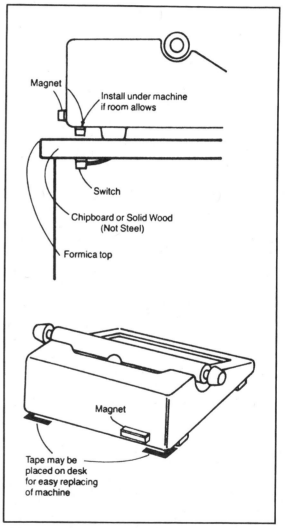

Fig. 2-113. Protecting office machines (courtesy Sentrol Inc.).

3. Install the switch and magnet. Install the magnet with the red-painted end away from the end of the switch (toward the end with wires).

4. Test with an ohmmeter and install in a loop.

### Protecting Office Machines

To protect office machines such as typewriters, word processors, adding machines, and home computer terminals from burglary, use the magnetic switch. Do not use magnetically actuated switches (such as the #1082W or #1082TW) in the vicinity of equipment sensitive to magnetic action such as magnetic tape.

This protection system will work on desks or tables with Formica-covered chipboard, plywood, or other tops. It will not work on desks or tables with steel tops.

Installation is as follows (Fig. 2-113):

1. Mount the magnet under or on the back side of the machine being protected. The under the machine position is preferred if room allows.

2. Mount the switch under the table or desk top so it is oriented with the magnet and parallel to it. A VOM (voltohmmeter) attached to the switch terminals will assist in achieving the best location. Be sure to observe polarity by having the Sentrol nameplate on both the switch and magnet read in the same direction (switch is polarity-sensitive). Fasten the switch in place with furnished screws (or use RTV mounting compound) and make the connection to the security circuit.

3. For office equipment likely to be moved during daily use, the use of "positioning" tapes to show the after-hours location will speed up the correct positioning at the close of the business day. Keep these markers as unobtrusive as possible.

### Interior Trap in a Closet for a 24-Hour Circuit

Using a small tool or tackle box with a brick inside and a switch, an interior trap can be devised.

1. Mark a small tool box "petty cash." Put a brick or other heavy object in the box (Fig. 2-114).

Fig. 2-114. Interior trap in a closet for a 24-hour circuit (courtesy Sentrol Inc.).

2. Drill a ¾" diameter hole through the floor in the corner of a closet. Locate the hole so that box can be set in a corner and won't be accidently moved.

3. Install Sentrol #3005 switch and wire into a 24-hour loop.

4. Set a box on the switch and test.

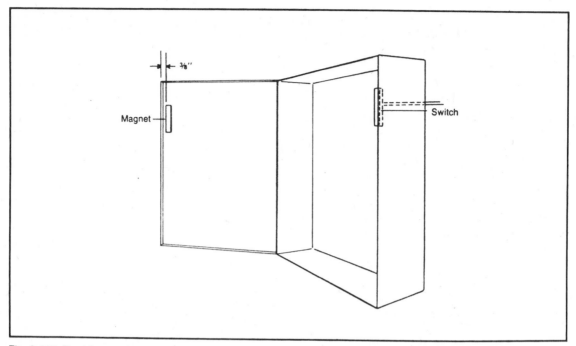

Fig. 2-115. Providing a tamper switch for a security alarm control cabinet (courtesy Sentrol Inc.).

### Providing a Tamper Switch
### for a Security Alarm Control Cabinet

Protect an alarm control cabinet from unauthorized entry by alarming the cabinet cover. Sentrol self-adhesive switches are recommended for this application, because they do not require screws (which would probably protrude through the front of the cabinet).

Clean the surface with rubbing alcohol before attaching the switch and magnet. This cleans off grease and dirt, assuring better adhesion.

Installation instructions are as follows (Fig. 2-115):

1. Attach a switch to the side, top, or bottom of the cabinet (as appropriate) near the front edge.

2. Attach a magnet to the inside of the cover, parallel to the switch, and in from the edge about ⅜″.

3. Connect an ohmmeter to switch leads. Close the door and test for proper operation.

4. Connect a switch to the 24-hour alarm loop for maximum protection. Retest for correct operation.

### Pressure Mats

Within the home and attached to your alarm system can be pinpoint security items. The *Secur-Step mat* (Fig. 2-116) gives positive operation and pinpoint security at a given point when tied into your system. The wafer-thin matting is unobtrusive when placed under carpets, rugs, or even on stairs—areas where unsuspecting intruders are likely to step. The footstep of a person closes the normally open switch, but the unit is unaffected by small household pets. The Secur-Step is versatile enough to actuate any standard alarm system signaling device, such as lights, bells, a siren, and even telephone dialers. Because the unit is adaptable, it can be used in combination with ultrasonic, microwave, or infrared sensors to extend protection to every corner of the home.

Let's discuss point protection at key locations within the home. Given the security system

Fig. 2-116. Concealed switch mat gives positive operation and pinpoint security (courtesy Recora Co., Inc.).

you require, it means protection at the right time immediately upon entry. At doors, it can provide protection from either side of the door. Porch, storm, and basement doors are commonly entered by burglars. Figure 2-117 illustrates a typical door positioning.

Near windows (Fig. 2-118) on the first and second floors of a home or condominium can be locations for the pressure mat. Even in the attic where there is an opening available, in addition to basement and garage openings, such devices should be seriously considered for point protection.

High-traffic areas leading from one portion of the home to another, such as stairs, must also be considered. Intruder movement is instantly

Fig. 2-117. Single and double doors can be protected with pressure mats tied into your security system (courtesy Recora Co., Inc.).

signaled when a mat is stepped on.

The matting is heat-sealed in durable polyethylene or dielectrically sealed in heavy gauge vinyl. The switch contact elements are of stainless steel. They are flexible and fully insulated, which means there are no "dead spots" in the mat. The mats will not rust or corrode, and they can be used on the exterior side of a door to detect a potential burglar.

Another pressure-type switch is shown in Fig. 2-119. This under-rug switching runner can be cut to fit desired rug lengths and then wired

Fig. 2-118. As the burglar enters through the window, his foot steps on the rug that conceals the Secur-Step mat, and he sets off the security alarm (courtesy Recora Co., Inc.).

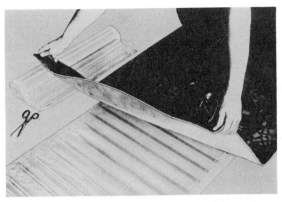

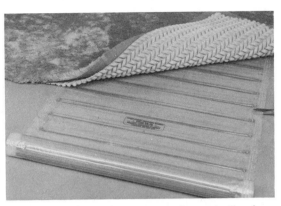

Fig. 2-119. This controlflex switching runner can be cut to any given length (courtesy Tapeswitch Corporation of America).

Fig. 2-120. The switching runner can be used with a foam insulator under the rug (courtesy Tapeswitch Corporation of America).

into any alarm circuit. It is extremely thin and requires no foam insulator, whereas other types may need one. Please note, though, that it is acceptable to use a foam insulator under the rug (Fig. 2-120).

A windowsill alarm switch has been developed by Tapeswitch (Fig. 2-121). This inconspicuous flat, white ribbon switch responds to the slightest pressure any place along its entire length. An intruder attempting to enter through a window will activate the alarm whether the window is partially or fully open or closed. While the windowsill alarm trip is available in various lengths (18″, 24″, 30″, 36″, and higher), the

length does not need to be exact because the central portion of the windowsill is the most important. The 24″ length is the most standard size used and should meet just about residential window need.

The switch, when laid and attached with an adhesive to the windowsill, only requires a 3/16″ hole drilled at each end for the wire leads (note arrows in Fig. 2-121). The circuit can be connected using one or both wire leads. The lead wires at each end connect to the switch conductors in identical fashion and may be used to conveniently interconnect to other switches or to provide a supervised circuit. The switch can also

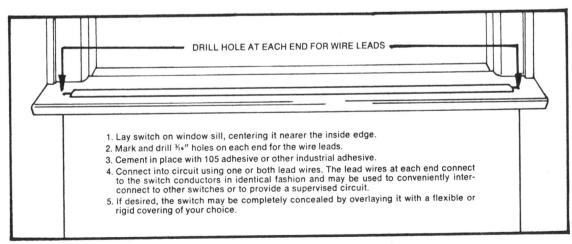

Fig. 2-121. An inconspicuous ribbon switch protects an open window (courtesy Tapeswitch Corporation of America).

be completely concealed by overlaying it with a flexible or rigid covering.

Using a switch under a hallway runner is inconceivable to some people because, in their minds, every time the dog or cat runs over it, the alarm will be activated if the alarm is in the active mode. "Bridges" are available that modify the under-rug detector so false alarms by pets are eliminated. These bridges are placed over the individually thin switches in the detector and taped into place (Fig. 2-122).

The sensitivity can be adjusted in other

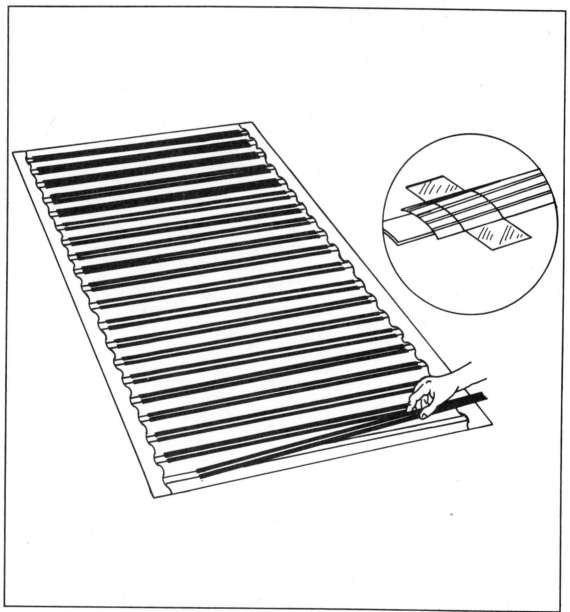

Fig. 2-122. Bridges placed over switches may be taped in place (courtesy Tapeswitch Corporation of America).

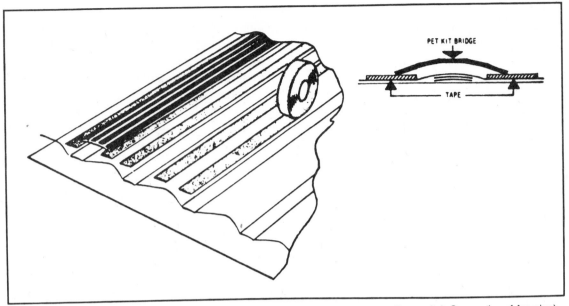

Fig. 2-123. Adhesive tape may be placed alongside each switching element (courtesy Tapeswitch Corporation of America).

ways. If the switching action is too sensitive, the pet strip can be raised by placing an adhesive tape or similar material alongside each switching element for the entire length of each (Fig. 2-123). This procedure raises the pet strip and increases the distance between the bridge and the switching element, thus reducing the switch sensitivity.

To increase the sensitivity of the switching action, a ½″ or ¾″ wide tape may be placed over the length of the switching elements. This will

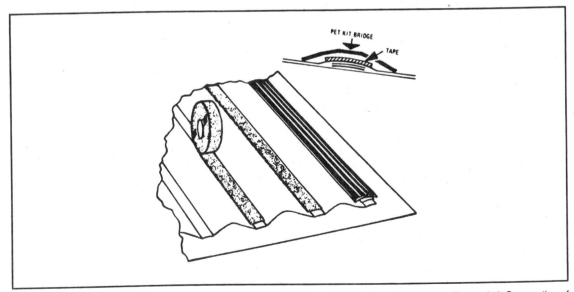

Fig. 2-124. A ½″ or ¾″ wide tape may be placed over the length of the switching elements (courtesy Tapeswitch Corporation of America).

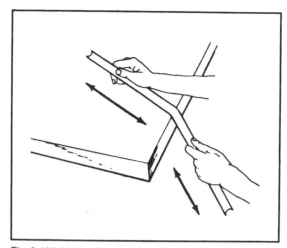

Fig. 2-125. Method for obtaining the greatest sensitivity of the under-rug detector (courtesy Tapeswitch Corporation of America).

decrease the distance between the pet strip bridge and the switching element (Fig. 2-124).

Figure 1-125 illustrates the method for obtaining the greatest sensitivity of the under-rug detector. Each pet strip may be preflattened by running the full length of the strip over the edge of a table or similar surface prior to placing it on the detector switches within the pressure mat.

## SELECTING A SECURITY SYSTEM

No particular alarm product may perform the same when compared to the same product of a different manufacturer. State-of-the-art technology, the specific use to which it is intended, and local environmental factors may produce a slight response difference. We maintain that the products in this book can provide the desired level of security necessary to protect your home. We do not recommend any one product over another; they are all currently available and meet the high standards within the security industry for home security systems.

There is no best system on the market as each intrusion detection is based on your specific needs and requirements. A well-designed system will include the basics of perimeter security, interior protection, and fire protection.

You get only what you pay for—that's a fact.

There is no way to have a cheaply made system, obtained at a very low price, and ensure that your overall protection is the same as a neighbor with a well-designed system created especially for his home. A quality product will sell itself based on the proper degree of protection it can provide to you and your family. You cannot select a system on the basis of price alone and know that the system is what you really need.

In looking for an intrusion detection system for your home, remember that the alarm system is only as good as its power supply. The dependable system will use household power and also have a backup battery in case of power failure.

Each system considered must have a visual and/or audible signal to alert you to a possible intrusion or malfunction of the unit. This is within the home. An audible signal is desirable, and the signal—when in an alarm mode—should be located on the exterior of the home or inside but adjacent to an exterior vent opening (such as the attic vent).

Any portion of the system, whether a major part or a subcomponent, should have tamper-proof protection designed into it.

A warranty from the manufacturer should cover both parts and labor. It should be further backed up by the alarm installer.

Finally, all component parts of the system should carry Underwriters Laboratories (UL), Factory Mutual (FM), or other standard. They should also meet and conform to local codes and requirements.

## SELECTING A BURGLAR/FIRE ALARM SERVICING COMPANY

You may have your own purchased burglar and/or fire alarm system, or perhaps you are renting such a system. Either way, the selection of a company to install and service the system, much less to monitor the system if it is a monitored one, is very important. Why? Security systems are constantly changing. Choosing a security servicing or monitoring company, rather than an actual security system, is extremely important. The difference comes from the people who design, install, maintain, and service the system.

There may be similar systems available on the market; you may select a standard system or have one designed specifically for your home. While the systems are similar in design and some specific functions, the overall quality and utility of the system can be dependent on the company selected.

Where you do start the search for the right company? The most logical place is your local telephone directory. Look under burglar alarms, fire alarms, or security services/systems. You might also contact your local police department. They may have a list of highly reputable companies. Your Better Business Bureau is another point of contact, and this can also be a valuable one in terms of company reliability. Check also with your own insurance agent. Many insurance companies give reduced premium charges for residences with a quality burglar/fire alarm system installed. Your insurance agent may also have a list of qualifying companies that can be used as a starting point in selecting a company and a system that is right for you.

When you have the list or have developed your own, check which companies are members of the National Burglar and Fire Alarm Association. This step may narrow your search to a management number. It may provide you with the specific company you are looking for.

Professional affiliations means reputability. Certain companies specialize only in business, some only in residences, and some in both. Determining the specialty area can also tell you something about the capabilities of the company. When you have tentatively selected several companies, consider the following:

—Can you work with the company? Does it provide generalized systems, or can it design one to meet your specific security needs?

—Is the alarm system monitored by the company, by another alarm monitoring company, or does the company just install it (and perhaps provide some type of service maintenance contract)?

—Does the company require a written contract? What is its length?

—If the system is monitored, what type of response time to an alarm can be expected? Is the response time reasonable for your neighborhood?

—Does the reponse time come from the company? Does the company contact the police and let them answer the alarm? Or do both the company and the police respond when notified of an alarm?

—If you purchase the system outright, can you still get a monitoring service contract?

—What specific services in terms of alarm checks and maintenance are provided, if any?

—Are there any hidden expenses not shown in the contract? What "no charge" services are provided for the system, if any?

—Can the system be expanded to meet future needs without an entirely new alarm system being installed?

Security business are rapidly changing to keep up with technological advances in alarm sophistication. These advancements are happening all the time. Alarm companies must keep abreast of the changes, and it is the companies' specialty to see if such changes and advances can further enhance your system. You should rely on their professional judgment in these areas; they are the experts.

When you have selected a company, it should perform a home security survey of your residence. Detailed feedback from the company representative to you should be more than just a short talk of your security shortcomings. It should be detailed enough to show what you currently have (if anything) regarding proper security and what areas should be considered for improvement. Make sure that the company representative realizes what specific measures you want included within your system, that they are included in the overall design, and that unnecessary articles are not included without your approval.

Before you sign the contract to have the system installed, check and make sure the company is properly licensed. Licenses are one more safety precaution to look for in a security company. Unfortunately, not all states require alarm companies to be licensed and bonded. In states where there are no licensing requirements, check with other people who have had alarm systems installed, with the Better Business Bureau, and also with the local police department about the company.

Consider what makes this company just a little better than its competitors. What is it that sets the company apart from others?

Finally, don't choose a company based on price alone. A smaller company in the suburbs may have a lower overhead so it can afford to price lower, but it may not have all the capabilities to back up the system with what you want, such as 24-hour reponse to alarm problems. On the other hand, such a company may have the personal approach and pride in business that makes it stand out from others. A large company may pride itself on personalized customer service.

# Chapter 3

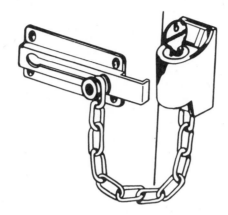

# Door and Window Protection

The first line of defense in any residence is the doors and the windows. Included are the basic outer structure and component parts such as the structural framing, locks, latches, and chains, along with sliding doors, grilles, security screens, and other accessory devices that can be attached.

The annual FBI reports and other studies indicate that the two main points of entry are the doors and the windows. The door is the easiest point of access for the burglar.

### BURGLARY FACTS

Depending on which study or report you read and believe, entrance by burglars into a home is anywhere from 50 percent to 70 percent. Entrance through windows is 25 percent to 35 percent.

A Department of Justice study, sponsored by the National Institute of Law Enforcement and Criminal Justice and the Law Enforcement Assistance Administration (LEAA), was conducted in three jurisdictions. The study found that entrance through the door was the most common, with windows being second. Even though the study was performed more than a decade ago (Table 3-1), the statistics are still quite relevant today because most people still consider their home as safe as it was the day they moved in. They never upgraded the security. In some respects, the figures are probably low. In June 1983, 15 years after these figures were compiled, a radio report stated that burglaries through doors alone accounted for approximately 70 percent of all residential burglaries.

The front door was the most frequent point of entry (Table 3-2). As for windows, the rear window was the most frequent point of entry (Table 3-3). Table 3-4 indicates the means of entry into the home by burglars. The study showed that more burglaries were done during the day when the residences were empty (Table 3-5).

Burglaries don't have to take place over a long period. Some people were gone from their

**Table 3-1. Percentage Distribution of Place of Breaking and Entering for Three Jurisdictions (Two-Year Average) (courtesy "Patterns of Burglary," Department of Justice, LEAA).**

| Place of Entry | Fairfax County VA | Washington DC | Prince George's County, MD |
|---|---|---|---|
| Door | 45.9 | 60.2 | 60.6 |
| Window | 23.3 | 25.5 | 28.4 |
| Roof | 0.8 | 1.2 | 0.8 |
| Other | 0.7 | 3.8 | 2.0 |
| Unknown | 29.3 | 9.3 | 8.2 |
| Total | 100.0 | 100.0 | 100.0 |

**Table 3-2. Percentage Distribution of Location of Door Entered Where Door Was the Point of Entry (Two-Year Average) (courtesy "Patterns of Burglary," Department of Justice, LEAA).**

| Location | Washington DC | Prince George's County, MD |
|---|---|---|
| Front | 73.3 | 49.1 |
| Rear | 23.1 | 42.9 |
| Side | 3.6 | 8.0 |
| Total | 100.0 | 100.0 |

**Table 3-3. Percentage Distribution of Location of Window Entered Where Window Was the Point of Entry (Two-Year Average) (courtesy "Patterns of Burglary," Department of Justice, LEAA).**

| Location | Washington DC | Prince George's County, MD |
|---|---|---|
| Front | 32.4 | 20.9 |
| Rear | 47.0 | 55.5 |
| Side | 20.6 | 23.6 |
| Total | 100.0 | 100.0 |

**Table 3-4. Percentage Distribution of Means of Entry in Washington, DC, and Prince George's County, Maryland (Two-Year Average) (courtesy "Patterns of Burglary," Department of Justice, LEAA).**

| Means of Entry | Washington DC | Prince George's County, MD |
|---|---|---|
| Break glass | 21.4 | 26.9 |
| Force lock | 51.1 | 29.0 |
| Open unlocked door/window | 7.4 | 10.1 |
| Use key to unlock door | 2.4 | 3.3 |
| Other | 4.6 | 15.3 |
| Unknown | 13.1 | 15.4 |
| Total | 100.0 | 100.0 |

**Table 3-5. Percentage Distribution of Residential Burglaries by Day and Night in Prince George's County, Maryland (Three-Year Average) (courtesy "Patterns of Burglary," Department of Justice, LEAA).**

| Time of Day | Percent of Burglaries |
|---|---|
| Day | 46.7 |
| Night | 28.9 |
| Unknown | 24.4 |
| Total | 100.0 |

home for as little as 20 minutes. Table 3-6 indicates length of absence from a residence in terms of burglaries.

Most burglaries are committed between 10 A.M. and 4 P.M. The time of burglary can also be considered in terms of frequency during the entire year. Table 3-7 illustrates the amount of burglaries throughout the year. Notice the peak burglary periods. These are when people are

**Table 3-6. Percentage Distribution of Length of Time Home Was Unoccupied at Time of Burglary (courtesy "Patterns of Burglary," Department of Justice, LEAA).**

| Home unoccupied | Resident Victim |
|---|---|
| Don't know | 5.6 |
| Less than 20 minutes | -- |
| 20 minutes to 1 hour | 27.8 |
| 2-4 hours | 24.4 |
| 5-8 hours | 5.6 |
| 9-12 hours | -- |
| 13-24 hours | 3.3 |
| 25-48 hours | 13.3 |
| Over 48 hours | 1.1 |
| No response | 18.9 |
| Total | 100.0 |

## Elements of a Door System

The entire door system of any residence consists of such parts as the door itself, the frame, the threshold, and the lock. An optional element, found mostly on apartment doors, is an automatic closure (Fig. 3-1). The burglar considers the door itself, determining what type of door it is (many types available and in use), the type of lock (poor, good, high, or very high security), whether the door opens inward or outward (hinges can be a very vulnerable point when the door opens outward), and the framing for the door.

Basically, there are four types of doors: the

**Table 3-7. Percentage Distribution of Burglaries by Month of Occurrence in the Three Jurisdictions (Two-Year Average) (courtesy "Patterns of Burglary," Department of Justice, LEAA).**

| Month | Fairfax County VA | Washington DC | Prince George's County, MD |
|---|---|---|---|
| January | 8.1 | 7.9 | 8.7 |
| February | 7.8 | 6.5 | 7.9 |
| March | 7.8 | 7.1 | 7.9 |
| April | 7.3 | 8.3 | 7.6 |
| May | 7.8 | 8.5 | 6.9 |
| June | 8.6 | 7.9 | 7.6 |
| July | 9.5 | 8.2 | 8.4 |
| August | 9.4 | 9.4 | 9.2 |
| September | 7.7 | 8.6 | 8.4 |
| October | 8.2 | 9.3 | 8.1 |
| November | 8.2 | 8.6 | 9.0 |
| December | 9.6 | 9.7 | 10.3 |
| Total | 100.0 | 100.0 | 100.0 |

going on vacation, out shopping because of special seasons of the year, or more likely to be absent from the home.

## DOORS

An intruder's attack on the residential door will usually center around only one point. This point can vary depending on the type of door and its surrounding element. Successful penetration of the door is usually due to the failure of the type of door or one of the various door components that make up the door security system.

Fig. 3-1. Check closures at least once a year to ensure they are adjusted so the door will fully close (courtesy Ideal Security Hardware).

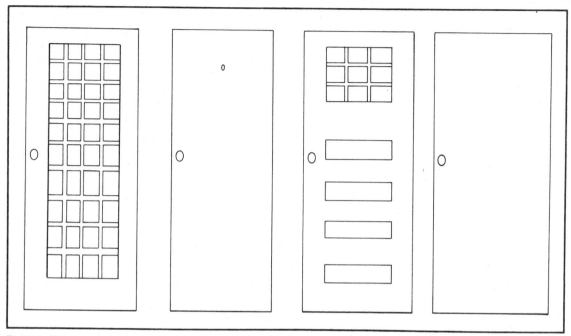

Fig. 3-2. Full-glass panel door, hollow core door with peephole, glass and panel door, and a solid core door.

solid core, the hollow core, the glass and panel door, and the steel door. Within these types, you can have one panel, two panels, full-view glass, flush, and ledged or braced doors (Fig. 3-2).

These doors can be graded in descending order of security levels. This order will represent the ability of the door to resist attack for a predetermined period of time and is based on the strength of the door, the types of materials of which the door is made for its construction elements, and also the framing around the door: steel, hardwood, hardwood with solid panels, softwoods with panels, glazed or glass panels, framed and braced doors, and frames with glass. There are solid or semisolid doors with trim glass panels surrounding the door itself (Fig. 3-3).

The most common doors found today are flush doors. These doors have no face panels, louvers, or recesses. Types of flush doors include solid core and hollow core, particle board, and glued block with a facing over them. Doors of steel construction and solid core doors with a steel facing are becoming more popular.

Fig. 3-3. If a door has glass slide panels, a thief can break in very easily.

Doors are of wood or metal and so are the frames. Metal jambs are normally of one-piece construction, whereas the wood jambs are of several pieces.

Doors are fastened to the frame by three hinges. Older homes may have only two hinges, though, and these are on lightweight, paneled/ glass doors. The locking device is opposite the hinge side and at the center edge. It can consist of a single unit or a double lock and can be built into the knob or be separate.

The framing for the door often can be a highly vulnerable point. If the home is old or a prefab construction unit, the framing and supporting wood can be made to give way under pressure. An intruder can push the door open without attacking the locking device.

The door must provide for maximum flexibility in design, but it also must have the security commensurate with the valuables kept within the home. Within the average home, the doors are most commonly constructed of wood, but not always of preferred solid core hardwood. Often the construction can be a combination of aluminum, some steel, and glass. It also can include hardboard, fiberboard, and even plastic.

Improvements that can be made include strengthening the entire area around the frame of the door with additional structural protection— essentially the inclusion of a perimeter barrier that cannot be easily punched through or spread apart. The solidification or hardening of the wall ensures that it will not become a focal point for a burglar when the door is too difficult to break through or the lock is too sophisticated to be picked or forced.

Standard door frame construction is shown in Fig. 3-4. When the door frame is removed, you see only the covering wood or other material over the wall framing. If this could be removed, it would probably look like Fig. 3-5. The possibility for entrance through spreading the frame is very good, these wood members must be strengthened.

The best method is to remove the entire wood frame and install a steel door and frame.

If the cost is high or you don't want a steel door, then consider the following methods:

☐ Add additional wood supporting members so the door cannot be spread.
☐ Fill in the gap with metal bars to create extra strength.
☐ If the frame is of cheap metal, it could still be spread. Consider filling in the air gap behind the framing by using steel bars and/or mortar.

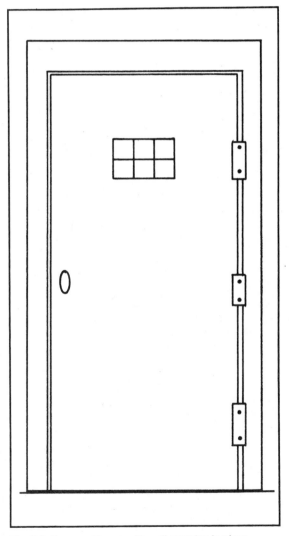

Fig. 3-4. Door and frame with wall covering in place.

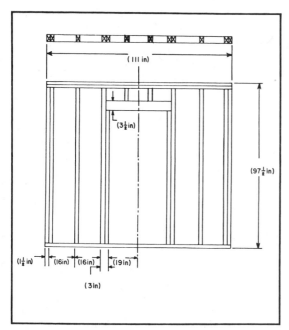

Fig. 3-5. Removal of the wall covering and frame, door, and door frame will reveal any deficiencies in structural security.

### Hinges

A door hinge has two parts called *leaves,* one of which is attached to the door and the other fastened to the door frame. When properly hung, the door swings on the hinges.

There are hinges with a removable pin and those with a nonremovable pin. The latter is also called a fixed pin hinge. The fixed pin, once installed, cannot be removed when the door is in the closed position.

The door must swing inward for proper security. By swinging outward, the hinge pins are exposed to a burglar and his tools, and his job is made much easier. Remove the hinges, relocate the door, and reattach the hinges so that the door opens inward.

As a temporary stopgap measure, especially when the hinge has a removable pin, weld or braze the pin to one of the hinge halves. This prevents someone from lifting the pin out of the hinge to remove the door. Another temporary measure is to attach a metal steel plate. The metal steel plate is bolted over the latching area

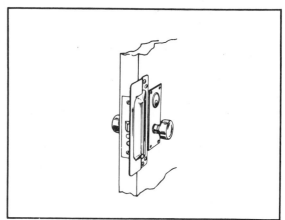

Fig. 3-6. Protect the locking bolt from attack with a temporary steel plate until one like this can be installed (courtesy Lori Corporation).

between the door handle and the door frame (Fig. 3-6). This prevents a person from easily forcing back the locking bolt.

### Weaknesses

There are seven weak areas that can make a door vulnerable to the potential burglar. They are:

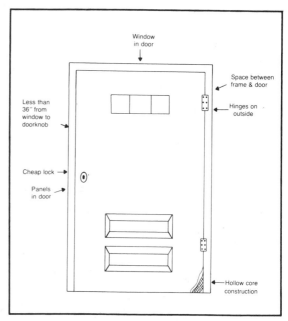

Fig. 3-7. This door has many weaknesses.

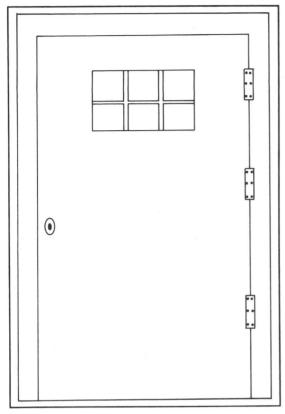

Fig. 3-8. Breaking a small glass panel makes little noise, and any glass within 36″ of the doorknob allows someone to reach inside and turn the doorknob.

- ☐ Poor or rotting frame or door edge.
- ☐ A cheap lock on the door.
- ☐ A window in the door within 25″-35″ of the inside door handle and the window or portions of it being less than 5′ from the bottom of the door.
- ☐ Thin wood panels in the door that can be easily kicked out.
- ☐ A hollow core construction door.
- ☐ Hinge pins located on the exterior side of the door.
- ☐ A space between the door and the frame.

Figure 3-7 illustrates these faults in the average door.

Figure 3-8 shows a door with unacceptable windows in terms of security. If a windowed door is necessary to see who is on the outside, it should be replaced with a solid door and a peephole viewer installed (Fig. 3-9). Various types of peepholes are available, with anywhere from a 150° to 180° viewing range. You should install a viewer with the maximum 180° viewing range (Fig. 3-10).

Let's consider each potential door fault and determine what can be done to remedy the situation.

**Poor or Rotting Frame or Door Edge.** Replace the door and/or frame with preferably a steel frame and door.

**Windows in the Door.** The glass can be replaced with wire glass, or an acrylic plastic can be installed over the glass and firmly attached. These plastics sometimes should be installed on both sides of the door (Fig. 3-11). The replacement may not be broken, but literally forced in-

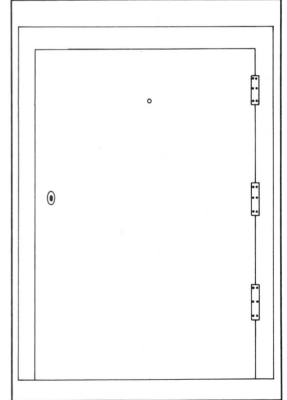

Fig. 3-9. A good door is a solid door.

95

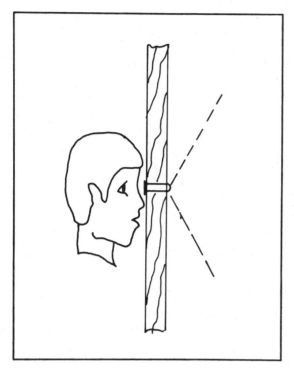

Fig. 3-10. A maximum viewing peephole ensures that you see everything and everyone outside your door.

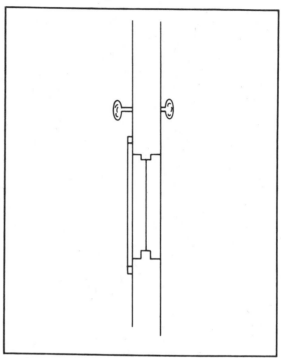

Fig. 3-11. Acrylic plastic should be at least on the inside and should extend 3″ minimum beyond the edge of door glass. Use 1″ screws minimum.

ward and out of the door by heavy blows with a blunt instrument. You should use two sheets of the acrylic plastic.

The best method is to replace the entire door, but this is expensive. The next best step is to remove the window and reseal the area with solid wood. Repaint the door so that the additional wood is not noticeable, then install a peephole.

**Cheap Locks on the Door.** Remove the lock and replace it with a heavy-duty one that has a minimum deadbolt throw of 1″ (Fig. 3-12). Install an auxiliary lock on the inside of the door (Fig. 3-13).

**Wood Panels in the Door.** Remove the panels and replace with solid wood. Repaint the entire door to conceal the change. Use other pieces of wood (hardwood) and cover over the panels (on both sides of the door), smoothing the edges down and repainting to conceal the renovation.

Finally, remove the door and install a solid wood or steel door in its place.

**Space Between the Door and the Frame.** A home tends to settle somewhat over a long period. This settling causes the door and frame to partially separate. Sometimes the lock will not work properly, and the latchplate must be re-

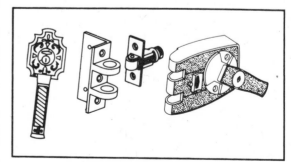

Fig. 3-12. Components of a very good replacement door lock that *will* provide above-average security (courtesy Ideal Security Hardware).

Fig. 3-13. An auxiliary lock (courtesy Abloy Security Locks).

Fig. 3-14. The basic lock cylinder (courtesy Abloy Security Locks).

moved or recut so that the lock bolt will continue to operate. You must shim up the frame, realign the door, and reset or replace the lock. Ensure alignment by replacing the lock last and making sure the latchplate is properly located.

**Hinge Pins on the Exterior of the Door.** This was discussed earlier in this chapter.

**Hollow Core Doors.** Replace the door with a solid core or steel door. A hollow core door is easily detected by rapping on the door in a couple of places. When a burglar determines that the door is hollow, he knows that it only takes a couple of really good kicks with his foot, or several hammer blows, to cause the wood to give way and allow the door to be opened.

### LOCKS

When looking at locking devices, consider not only the front (or main) door, but also side, back, basement, and second-story locks. Since the basic pin tumbler lock was designed and put into use by Linius Yale in the mid-1800s, continued improved technology has increased the security integrity of locking devices available for general use. Your lock must be the most technically developed and secure one possible for the level of protection and safety of your home and its contents.

The basic lock cylinder (Fig. 3-14) is de-

signed to provide a measure of security for your home. The average cylinder available, whether it is an individual cylinder or a key-in-the-knob type cylinder lock, is constructed of brass with at least five pin sets and springs (Fig. 3-15). These pins and the springs hold the lock cylinder in either the locked or unlocked position. As the proper key for the lock is inserted into the cylinder keyway, the pins will line up at the top of the cylinder plug, allowing the cylinder to revolve. As it revolves, the lock is either locked or unlocked.

Regretfully, though, many locks have been

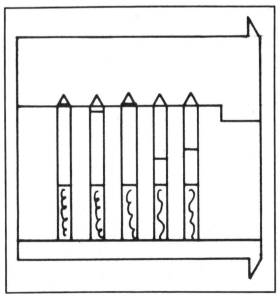

Fig. 3-15. The basic cylinder in any lock should have five pins and have no problems in operation.

installed in homes that really don't provide even a minimal amount of protection. These cheap locks are easily bypassed or defeated even by the amateur burglar. If you have such a lock, replace it immediately.

### Sargent Keso Security System

The *Sargent Keso* high-security locking system has several features:

- ☐ Highly pick-resistant cylinders. A fan-shaped arrangement of 12 key pins bars the way to picking.
- ☐ Key control. The owner retains control over duplication of keys by unauthorized individuals. Keys must be ordered from the factory.
- ☐ There are expanded levels of masterkeying with no loss of security. This allows for individual doors to have their own keys, and you can also have a master key that will operate all of them. If you have a different entrance to the home, such as through the garage, you can control access to the area without providing access to all areas.
- ☐ Each key system is proprietary. No Sargent Keso security system installation will ever be duplicated.

Figure 3-16 shows the unique Sargent Keso key. Notice that instead of the standard key cuts found on most keys, this one has dimples into the key. These dimples are precision drilled to varying depths that correspond with the various pins within the lock cylinder.

Figure 3-17 is a cutaway view of the cylinder and illustrates one of the 24,500 different patterns of key pins available within any one Sargent Keso security system installation. Exceptionally precise manufacturing tolerances and the absence of splits, even in masterkeying, make the cylinder highly pick-resistant.

The 7700 model line Sargent lock (Fig. 3-18) uses the standard knob trim for exterior appearance. This model has been consistently chosen

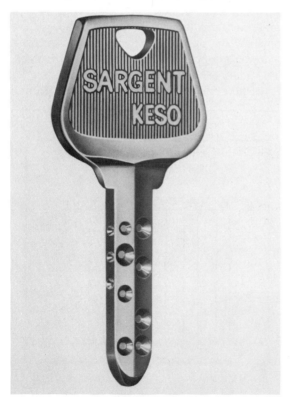

Fig. 3-16. The unique dimpled Sargent Keso high-security lock key (courtesy Sargent Division, Kidde, Inc.).

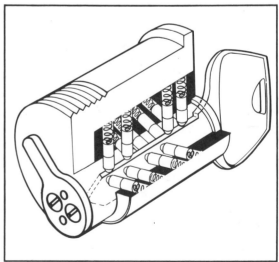

Fig. 3-17. Cutaway of the Sargent Keso high-security cylinder (courtesy Sargent Division, Kidde, Inc.).

Fig. 3-18. The 7700 series mortise lockset (courtesy Sargent Division, Kidde, Inc.).

Fig. 3-19. Model 8100 with modern handle trim (courtesy Sargent Division, Kidde, Inc.).

for security and dependability for more than 50 years. This model is available in all conventional locking functions with a choice of distinctive self-aligning screwless trim. It has a standard lock case for mortising and interchangeability and includes an anti-friction latch.

The 7700 series model can fit all doors 1¾" and over in thickness. It comes with a brass ¾" deadbolt throw, but a 1" throw with a hardened steel roller is also available.

For its strength and durability, the case is of wrought steel with a zinc dichromate finish applied. The front of the lock can be brass or bronze. Adjustable armored fronts can be adjusted at any angle from flat to beveled.

The 8100 line model lock (Fig. 3-19) has a level handle trim to fit in with the more modern designed doors. This is engineered specifically to bear the extra weight of level handles and increases torque generated by them.

The 8100 model will fit doors of 1¾" thickness and over. Also, a 1" deadbolt throw with hardened steel rollers is available if the standard ¾" throw is not what you want.

### Kwikset Locksets

The Kwikset locksets have been used for many years by builders in the construction of new homes. They have developed a proven reliability and dependability for long use and minimal lock part failure. If you are purchasing a home with builder-installed Kwikset locks, there's one thing with which you need not concern yourself. The builder will put the locks on and use them when the internal portions of the home are being finished. The builder is protecting the investment in merchandise and equipment put into the home. When the builder leaves and you take possession of the home, you may be concerned about extra keys floating around that may allow an unauthorized person direct access to your home. With Kwikset, this concern is unfounded.

Kwikset has a lockset with a "brain" as it were. This is part of the *Protectokey* lockset system and is available for all Kwikset keyed entry locksets. This is the first new lockset security

feature to be developed since the key-in-the-knob convenience.

When you use your personal key in this Protectokey lockset, all other keys formerly used during the construction phase of the home will now be automatically and permanently locked out. This is accomplished by four hidden, tiny steel balls that drop into a blind "pocket" in the cylinder when it is turned. This first turning of the cylinder changes the pin tumbler combination. If the builder's key is reinserted into the lock, the change in the pin tumbler combination will prevent the cylinder from turning and the lock from opening. The homeowner's key will continue to work perfectly in the lock. Figure 3-20 shows how the Kwikset Protectokey system works.

The Kwikset keyed lockset features an advanced five pin tumbler mechanism (Fig. 3-21). The advantages in security over inexpensive disk or wafer mechanisms allow for far more keying and masterkeying combinations with less chance of duplication. Pin tumbler locking is more precise, easier to operate, and will last longer than wafer or disk designs.

### Double Security Locksets

The double security lockset offers protection

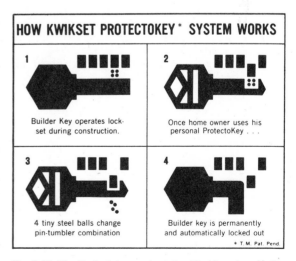

Fig. 3-20. The Protectokey system simplified (courtesy Kwikset Division, Emhart Industries).

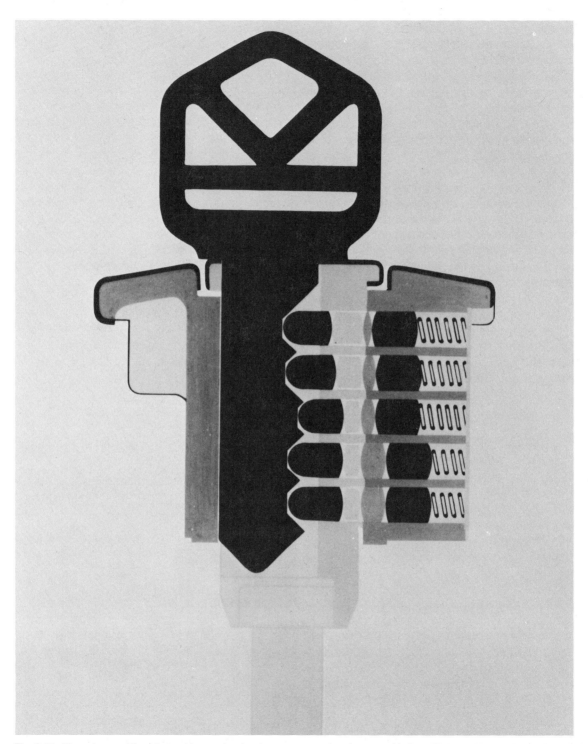

Fig. 3-21. The advanced five-pin tumbler mechanism in a cutaway view (courtesy Kwikset Division, Emhart Industries).

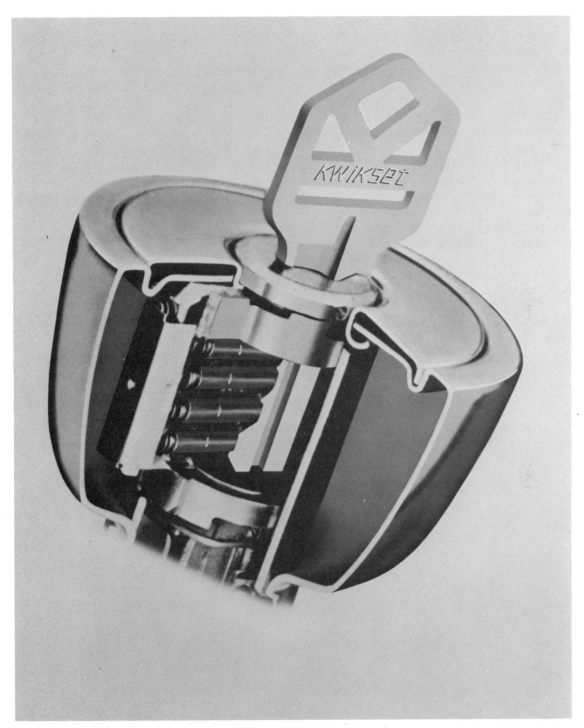

Fig. 3-22. Cutaway shows the extra security cylinder deadlock in a key-in-the-knob lockset (courtesy Kwikset Division, Emhart Industries).

against panic and burglary. The *Protecto-Lok* by Kwikset (Fig. 3-22) combines an extra security cylinder deadlock together with a key-in-the-knob lockset. Unlike ordinary deadlock and lockset combinations, the Protecto-Lok can be opened from the inside by simply turning the knob (Fig. 3-23). There is no need to turn both the thumbkey and knob before opening. This is the anti-panic portion of the lockset that allows for increased security against an external threat while also providing quick exiting in case of an emergency. This one action retracts the deadbolt and the deadlocking latch. Both the deadlock and lockset are keyed alike for easy locking and unlocking. The Protecto-Lok comes as a standard package or with optional exterior trim (Fig. 3-24) to allow the lock to better blend in with the door and surroundings.

Additional protection is provided by a 1″ steel deadbolt with a hacksaw-resistant steel rod and a solid steel cylinder assembly protected by a heavy-duty steel cylinder guard and solid steel reinforcing rings and plates. The cylinder guard itself is tapered and is free-turning. This disallows any attempt to remove it from the exterior. The companion lockset is equipped with an extra security latchbolt that deadlocks automatically when the door is closed.

You may want to keep your current lockset in place. A secondary lock can be installed—not just as a secondary lock for additional protection at night, but also to complement the initial door lock. Consider the following points when selecting such a lock:

Fig. 3-24. Exterior trim adds attractiveness to a home (courtesy Kwikset Division, Emhart Industries).

Fig. 3-23. Turn the knob to open the Protecto-Lok from the inside (courtesy Kwikset Division, Emhart Industries).

□ The lock must be rugged and heavy-duty in its use.

□ The internal turnpiece should be easy to operate for faster and easier locking and unlocking.

□ Within the lock, heavy-gauge steel interior reinforcing plates are a must to resist forceful attempts to remove the lock from the door.

□ Whenever possible, the lock should have a solid steel security shield that will protect the deadlocking mechanism against any pry-backs and hammer attacks on the lock.

□ The cylinder guard and the trim rings should be combined into one single piece—normally of solid brass construction. This allows for faster and easier installation.

□ The lock cylinder itself should have a hardened steel barrier in the keyway that provides a greater resistance to drilling or any other attempted violation of the interior locking mechanism.

Figure 3-25 shows an exploded view of a popular secondary lock.

Several cylinder deadlocks are available in

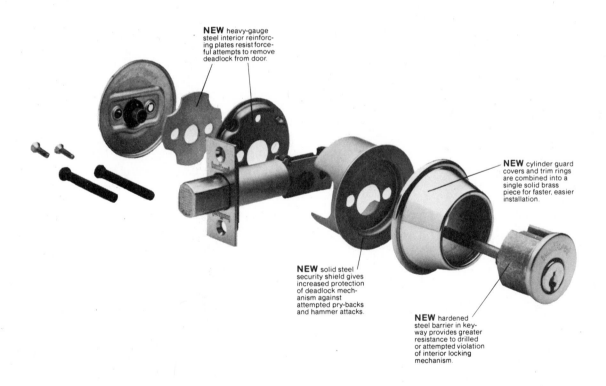

NEW heavy-gauge steel interior reinforcing plates resist forceful attempts to remove deadlock from door.

NEW cylinder guard covers and trim rings are combined into a single solid brass piece for faster, easier installation.

NEW solid steel security shield gives increased protection of deadlock mechanism against attempted pry-backs and hammer attacks.

NEW hardened steel barrier in keyway provides greater resistance to drilled or attempted violation of interior locking mechanism.

Fig. 3-25. Exploded view of a secondary lock (courtesy Kwikset Division, Emhart Industries).

Fig. 3-26. The Kwikset 885 double-cylinder deadlock (courtesy Kwikset Division, Emhart Industries).

Fig. 3-28. The Kwikset 880 cylinder deadlock (courtesy Kwikset Division, Emhart Industries).

different working models, depending on your specific desires and uses. Figure 3-26 shows the double-cylinder deadlock, which is key operated from both the interior and exterior. This deadlock has a 1″ bolt for increased security. Figure 3-27 shows a one-sided keyed deadlock. The key retracts a 1″ deadbolt from the exterior; there is no exterior access to this lock. Figure 3-28 shows a single-cylinder deadlock with the key retracting the deadbolt from the exterior side. A thumb key on the interior side operates the bolt mechanism. The one-way deadlock (Fig. 3-29) is operated only from the exterior. There is no thumb key on the interior side. This lock provides additional protection for the entranceway to the home while you are away.

### Lori Kaba Locks

Many people are replacing individual cylinders in their locksets to provide increased security. The Lori Kaba cylinders often are installed because they increase security. The Kaba cylinders are operated by a unique, dimpled key made of nickel silver that has a smooth, flat profile. Figure 3-30 shows an exploded view of a Kaba 14 series cylinder. It has 14 pins set at various positions

Fig. 3-27. The Kwikset 884 one-sided keyed cylinder deadlock (courtesy Kwikset Division, Emhart Industries).

Fig. 3-29. The Kwikset 881 one-way deadlock (courtesy Kwikset Division, Emhart Industries).

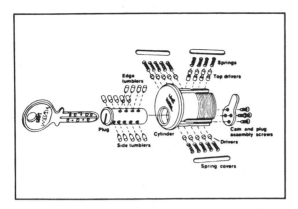

Fig. 3-30. Exploded view of a Lori Kaba 14 series cylinder. Multiple pins provide a higher than normal level of lock security (courtesy Lori Corporation).

Fig. 3-32. Kaba mortise cylinder with high security (courtesy Lori Corporation).

around the cylinder for security. These cylinders are extremely high in their resistance to picking because of the pins' convergence on the key from several directions to overlap the center of the keyway when locked. Figure 3-31 shows a Kaba 14 rim cylinder that can be installed in the home.

Mortise cylinders are also available for replacement. These cylinders (Fig. 3-32) also use the dimpled key for high security. Literally millions of key combinations are possible on any given key, so the chance that another key could be made with your particular key dimples is very remote.

Mortise cylinder deadbolts from Lori feature

Fig. 3-33. Mortise cylinder deadbolt with heavy-duty cylinder housing (courtesy Lori Corporation).

Fig. 3-31. A Kaba 14 rim cylinder (courtesy Lori Corporation).

Fig. 3-34. Double-cylinder deadbolt (courtesy Lori Corporation).

107

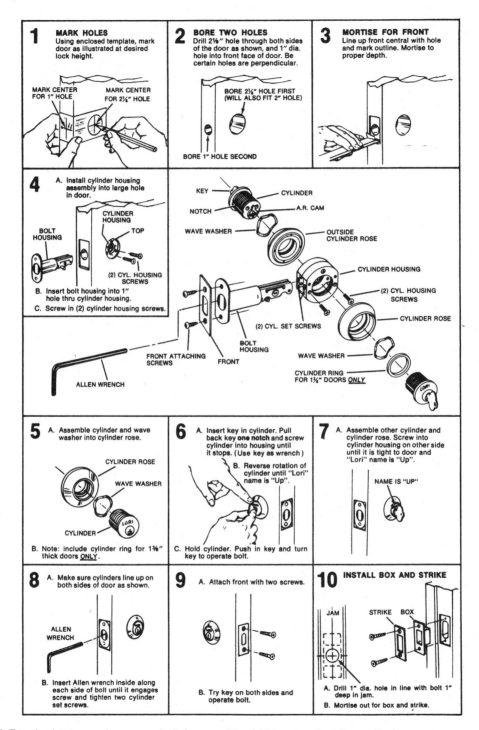

**1 MARK HOLES**
Using enclosed template, mark door as illustrated at desired lock height.

MARK CENTER FOR 1" HOLE    MARK CENTER FOR 2⅛" HOLE

**2 BORE TWO HOLES**
Drill 2⅛" hole through both sides of the door as shown, and 1" dia. hole into front face of door. Be certain holes are perpendicular.

BORE 2⅛" HOLE FIRST (WILL ALSO FIT 2" HOLE)

BORE 1" HOLE SECOND

**3 MORTISE FOR FRONT**
Line up front central with hole and mark outline. Mortise to proper depth.

**4**
A. Install cylinder housing assembly into large hole in door.

BOLT HOUSING

CYLINDER HOUSING

TOP

(2) CYL. HOUSING SCREWS

B. Insert bolt housing into 1" hole thru cylinder housing.
C. Screw in (2) cylinder housing screws.

KEY    CYLINDER

NOTCH    A.R. CAM

WAVE WASHER    OUTSIDE CYLINDER ROSE

CYLINDER HOUSING

(2) CYL. HOUSING SCREWS

CYLINDER ROSE

(2) CYL. SET SCREWS

FRONT ATTACHING SCREWS    FRONT

BOLT HOUSING

WAVE WASHER

CYLINDER RING FOR 1¾" DOORS _ONLY_

ALLEN WRENCH

**5**
A. Assemble cylinder and wave washer into cylinder rose.

CYLINDER ROSE

WAVE WASHER

CYLINDER

B. Note: include cylinder ring for 1⅜" thick doors _ONLY_.

**6**
A. Insert key in cylinder. Pull back key **one notch** and screw cylinder into housing until it stops. (Use key as wrench)
B. Reverse rotation of cylinder until "Lori" name is "Up".

C. Hold cylinder. Push in key and turn key to operate bolt.

**7**
A. Assemble other cylinder and cylinder rose. Screw into cylinder housing on other side until it is tight to door and "Lori" name is "Up".

NAME IS "UP"

**8**
A. Make sure cylinders line up on both sides of door as shown.

ALLEN WRENCH

B. Insert Allen wrench inside along each side of bolt until it engages screw and tighten two cylinder set screws.

**9**
A. Attach front with two screws.

B. Try key on both sides and operate bolt.

**10 INSTALL BOX AND STRIKE**

JAM    STRIKE    BOX

A. Drill 1" dia. hole in line with bolt 1" deep in jam.
B. Mortise out for box and strike.

Fig. 3-35. Ten simple steps and your security is increased ten-fold (courtesy Lori Corporation).

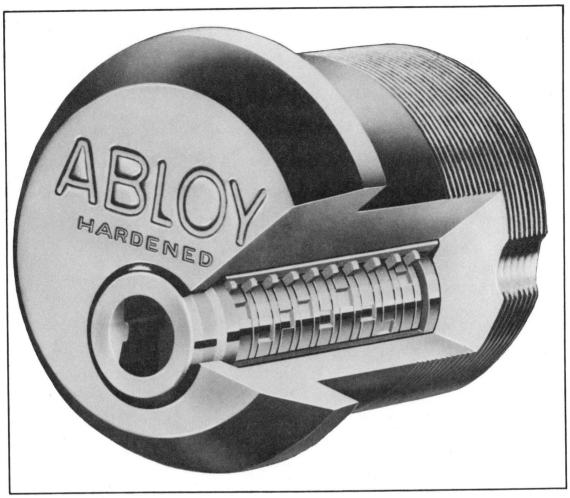

Fig. 3-36. Cutaway view of the unique Abloy security lock cylinder (courtesy Abloy Security Locks).

Fig. 3-37. Unique key for Abloy security locks (courtesy Abloy Security Locks).

a heavy-duty cylinder housing (Fig. 3-33) and a 1″ throw bolt utilizing two hardened steel pins to prevent hacksawing. These are ideal for both new doors and as replacements on current doors. The double-cylinder deadbolt (Fig. 3-34) has no exposed screws. The two mortise cylinders are held in place by cylinder setscrews under the armored front. Notice that in Figs. 3-32 and 3-33 the cylinders have the standard pin keyways. The locks can fit into other keying systems such as Yale, Schlage C and C-K, Lockwood, Segal, Ilco, Corbin, and Russwin. The keyways available also mean rekeying to other keys such as those of Arrow, Corbin, Dexter, E-Z Set, Harloc, Kwikset, National, Sargent, Segal, Russwin, Weslock, and Weiser. Instructions for installing a Lori double-cylinder deadbolt are in Fig. 3-35.

### Abloy Locks

*Abloy* is a manufacturer of high-security locks and is fairly new to the United States. In Europe, Abloy has many distinguished years of service in providing exceptionally high-security locking devices.

Virtually every other lock in the world uses pins and springs, but Abloy has unique rotating detainer disks that operate like tumblers in a safe. The installation of a *DiskLock* into a conventional door lock housing will give you the highest security door lock of its kind available.

The detainer disk system provides for two-way key operation with a unique key. A cutaway view of a DiskLock is shown in Fig. 3-36, while the unique key is shown in Fig. 3-37. The Abloy DiskLock keys cannot be duplicated on any conventional key machine.

The Abloy system offers certain advantages that ordinary springs and pins can't:

☐ Disks are virtually impossible to pick.
☐ The disks are physically scrambled by turning the key. There are no springs involved.
☐ The disks allow for millions of key combi-

Fig. 3-38. A 1″ mortise cylinder (courtesy Abloy Security Locks).

Fig. 3-39. A 1¼″ mortise/rim cylinder (courtesy Abloy Security Locks).

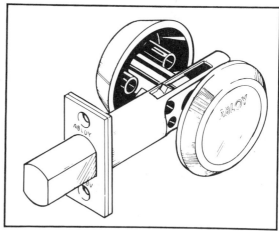

Fig. 3-40. Tubular deadbolts (courtesy Abloy Security Locks).

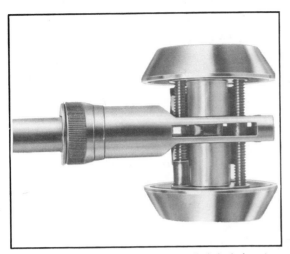

Fig. 3-41. Top view of the Abloy deadbolt lock (courtesy Abloy Security Locks).

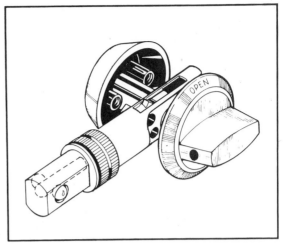

Fig. 3-42. Note the steel ball; it will interlock with the protrusions within the strike box (courtesy Abloy Security Locks).

nations. Ordinary pin locks can't even come close.

□ The large number of key combinations greatly increases masterkeying capabilities.

□ The disks are more durable and reliable because they resist fouling caused by dirt and corrosion.

□ Security cannot be compromised by the lock's extensive use because the disks don't wear out like springs and pins over a long period.

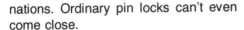

The Abloy locking concept is available in mortise cylinders (Fig. 3-38), mortise/rim cylinders (Fig. 3-39), and tubular deadbolts (Fig. 3-40).

The tubular deadbolt has several important features that may not be in other deadbolt locks:

□ Other lock cylinders, even high-security ones, are made of brass. The Abloy is the only cylinder made with a hardened steel housing and spinning keyway ring to defy drills, chisels, or saws.

□ The tubular deadbolt penetrates a full 1″ into the strike. The bolt is made of case-

hardened steel throughout for maximum resistance to sawing.

□ Unique patented steel balls interlock the door and the frame to prevent jimmying. No other deadbolt offers this optional maximum security feature. Figure 3-41 shows the lock in an overhead view. Figure 3-42 shows the same lock with the ball bearing. Figure 3-43 is a view of the strike box. Notice the protrusion on the interior of the strike box. When the bolt has entered to the strike box, the two steel balls will interlock at this point to secure the lock against jimmying.

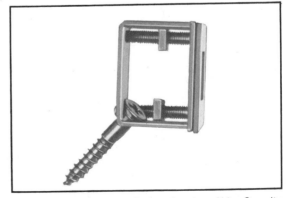

Fig. 3-43. The deadbolt strike box (courtesy Abloy Security Locks).

☐ The heavy-duty strike is mounted with four screws. Two of these are angled, 2″ reinforcing screws and come in addition to the standard screws. These reinforcing screws anchor directly into the wall studs instead of just the door frame.

Whether you use a conventional doorknob lockset or an individual cylinder aside from the knob area, you should also include a guardplate that complements the cylinder (Fig. 3-44). The guardplate is a one-piece steel plate and is case-hardened throughout, which totally shields the cylinder. It is virtually the toughest and largest plate made. No other guardplate on the market can match it for drill resistance.

The drill plate has four specially machined ¼″ mounting studs that are anchored behind the steel plate. This prevents them from being drilled, pried, chiseled, or punched out.

The Abloy tubular deadbolt requires only five installation steps:

1. Mark the door (Fig. 3-45). Use the template provided with the deadbolt, position it properly and mark the door at the desired height.

2. Bore the holes (Fig. 3-46). The holes (1⅝″) for the deadbolt cylinder should be drilled first, working from both sides of the door.

3. Prepare the strike plate mortise (Fig. 3-47). Mark the center of the strike cutout *exactly opposite* the center of the latch hole.

4. Install the strike (Fig. 3-48). Mortise the jamb to accept the strike plate face and then install the strike plate. Attach the strike with the two smaller screws, then use the subframe anchoring screws last.

5. Install the deadbolt (Fig. 3-49). Insert the bolt assembly into the door as shown and fasten with the screws provided with the lockset. Install with the slot up. If resistance is met while insert-

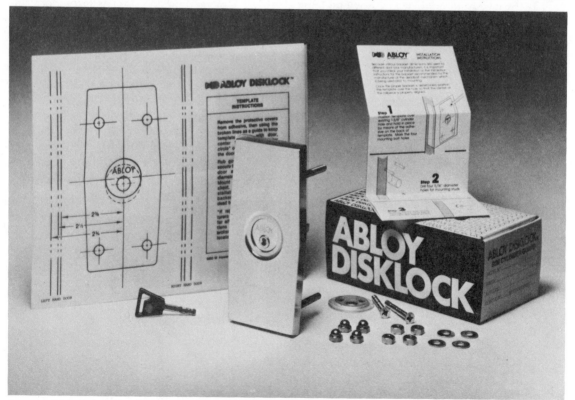

Fig. 3-44. The Abloy DiskLock guardplate (courtesy Abloy Security Locks).

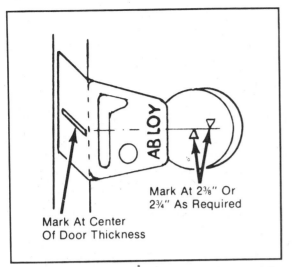

Fig. 3-45. Use a template at the desired height to mark the door (courtesy Abloy Security Locks).

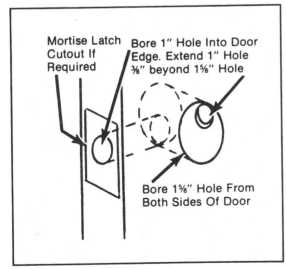

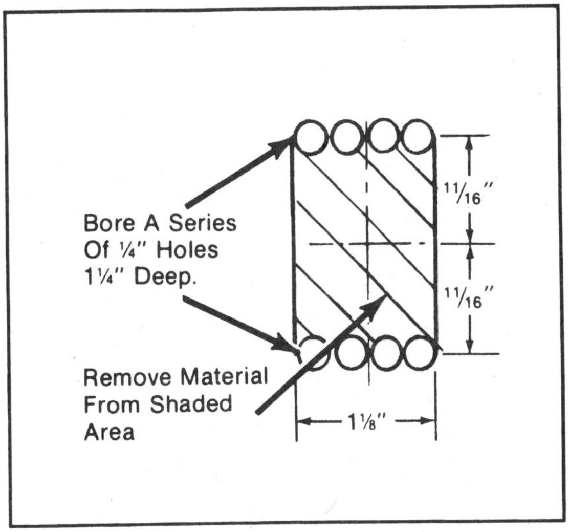

Fig. 3-47. Mark the center of the strike cutout exactly opposite the center of the latch hole (courtesy Abloy Security Locks).

ing the bolt, move it in the retracted position and press firmly on the latchplate. Place the appropriate accessories required to properly install the unit according to the thickness of the door.

Secure the cylinders and check the operation of the bolt. If it functions smoothly, seal the installation with balls provided.

Break the cylinder ring retaining screws to the proper length. With the steel ball inserted in the outer cylinder ring, install the retaining rings.

### SuperguardLock II

The *SuperguardLock II* (Fig. 3-50) comes in two models—either a double-cylinder key locked from either side, or a single-cylinder key locked

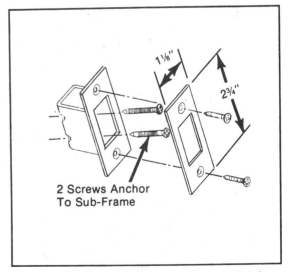

Fig. 3-46. A tubular deadbolt can be installed in a 2⅛" cross bore (courtesy Abloy Security Locks).

Fig. 3-48. Mortise the jamb to accept the strike plate face. Install the strike plate (courtesy Abloy Security Locks).

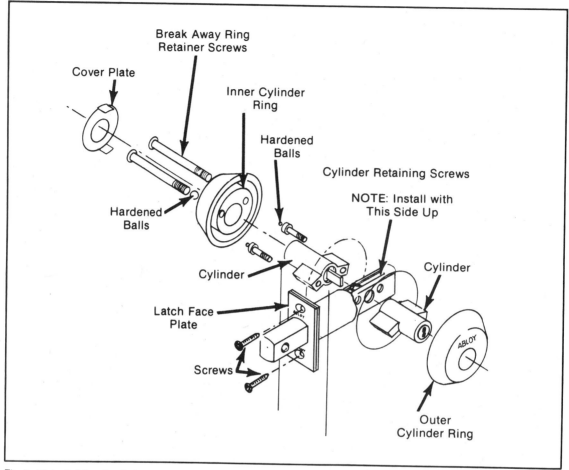

**Break Away Ring Retainer Screws**

**Cover Plate**

**Inner Cylinder Ring**

**Hardened Balls**

**Cylinder Retaining Screws**

**NOTE: Install with This Side Up**

**Cylinder**

**Hardened Balls**

**Cylinder**

**Latch Face Plate**

**Screws**

**Outer Cylinder Ring**

Fig. 3-49. Install the deadbolt (courtesy Abloy Security Locks).

from the outside and having a lockout button and turn handle on the interior side. Features include the following:

☐ Automatic locking. Just close the door and it's locked.

☐ Lockout button. By sliding the lockout button to the locked position, entry with a key from the outside is prevented.

☐ Protective locking sliding bolt. The door cannot shut on you accidentally and lock you out.

☐ An adjustable roller catch that allows the door to remain in the closed position when the door is not engaged.

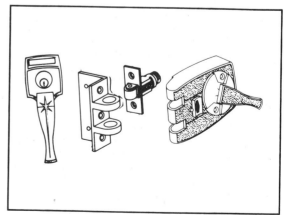

Fig. 3-50. The SuperguardLock II with modern design (courtesy Ideal Security Hardware).

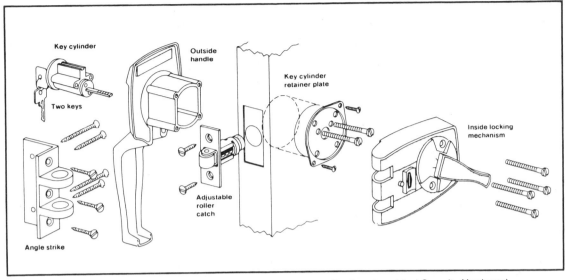

Fig. 3-51. Exploded view shows ease of assembly for the do-it-yourselfer (courtesy Ideal Security Hardware).

☐ The brass cylinder contains five solid pins. Both the interior and exterior locks are keyed alike, so two separate keys are not necessary.

☐ An interchangeable lock on the inside function can be reserved to accommodate a key for left- and right-hand doors.

☐ The lock installation screws are concealed by a patented inside pull handle; this prevents the removal of the screws without the insertion of a key into the inside assembly.

☐ The angle strike uses seven screws, entered into the door frame from two directions, to provide a high level holding posture against attempts to force the strike away from the framework.

☐ The lock is of jimmyproof construction.

☐ This lock is up to eight times stronger than the lock on your door.

☐ The lock can be installed in less than 30 minutes. A screwdriver is the only tool required.

☐ The SuperguardLock II can eliminate the need for a second lock on the door.

An exploded view of the SuperguardLock II is shown in Fig. 3-51. You can install it on either wood or metal doors.

### Keyless Door Locks

Keyless door combination locks have been successfully used in many homes, offices, storage buildings, etc. The mechanical push-button combination lock (Fig. 3-52) can eliminate keys and key control problems.

The *Preso-Matic* keyless combination lock means no more lost or misplaced keys. By pressing a four-number combination in just the right sequence, the lock bolt automatically releases. You have one of 10,000 possible combinations available when you obtain a lock with a four-digit combination. A lock with a seven-digit combination has 10,000,000 possible combinations. Because of the push-button feature, there is no keyhole and no way to pick open the lock. A four-digit lock could be mastered so if more than one were installed, you could have the same opening combination for each lock.

A keyless combination door lock means:

☐ Elimination of all key and key control problems.

☐ No keys to carry around or lose.

Fig. 3-52. The Preso-Matic keyless security lock for the home (courtesy Preso-Matic Lock Co., Inc.).

☐ Absolute security.
☐ One finger operation—the locking bolt retracts automatically when the correct combination is pressed.
☐ The combination can be changed in seconds to maintain security.
☐ There is no keyhole to pick.
☐ Jimmyproof hardened steel deadbolt or deadlatch is available (Fig. 3-53).

The deadlatch spring bolt model (Fig. 3-53, right) can be reversed to fit either swing of your door. The lock will lock automatically when the door is closed, but it can be unlocked instantly from the inside by pushing a single button, allowing for quick emergency exiting. A night latch mode allows the setting at night to render the combination inoperable from the outside.

The Hercules model has a revolving hardened steel deadbolt (1" throw) to defy forcible entry. It has automatic unlocking by pressing the combination correctly, but also has manual locking, ensuring the bolt will stay retracted until the exterior reset bar or the interior lock button is pressed.

Many questions have arisen concerning keyless push-button combination door locks. Below are the most commonly asked questions and the answers:

☐ Exactly how do these keyless combination locks operate? The lock is mechanically operated. There are no electrical components. Press your combination from the outside. The deadbolt or deadlatch bolt retracts automatically, which unlocks the door. The deadbolt model locks from the inside by pressing the lock button and from the outside by pressing the reset bar. The deadlatch models lock automatically each time the door is closed. All models feature an instant exit by pressing the unlock button on the inside of the door. The night latch mode is set by exerting a slight extra pressure on the button and turning it right or left until it stops. It remains depressed along with the "reset" bar on the outside, indicating that the lock cannot be opened even with the combination.
☐ What if I forget my combination? You probably won't forget the combination any more than your telephone number, street address, or social security number.
☐ How can I change the numbers that open my lock if necessary? Simply remove the inside cover plate, then turn two spring clips clear of the slot in the lock body. Lift off the small cover, remove the two brass combination slides, and insert new ones. These slides determine the correct numbers and sequence for operating the lock. The slides can be changed from the old to the new combination in less than 5 minutes.

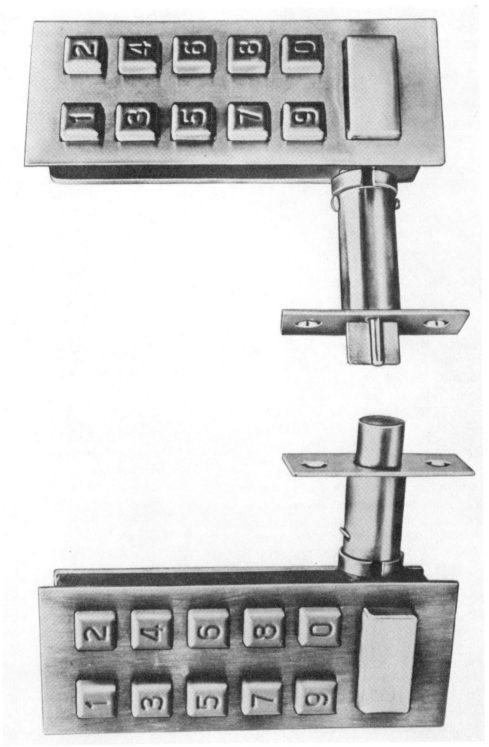

Fig. 3-53. Hardened steel deadbolt or deadlatch versions are available (courtesy Preso-Matic Lock Co., Inc.).

☐ Could anyone open this lock by pushing the buttons at random? An unauthorized person is confronted with 10,000 possible combinations. Computers tell us that it would take about 35 hours to try them all. That's only for the model that requires four digits to open. For the model that uses seven digits, the odds are about 10 million to 1. This is equal to 41,660 consecutive hours of button pushing, which represents 5,208 normal working days or 20 years. No burglar is going to stay around that long in an attempt to figure out the combination.

☐ Can the combinations be mastered, such as masterkeying standard cylinder locks? The answer is yes. As many locks as desired can be mastered to be unlocked by the master combination, and yet each lock will also have its own individual combination number. Master combinations can replace master key systems currently used in small or large apartments. You could install locks in your home and outbuildings and have them operated by a master combination and also an individual combination. If you have a room rented out with a separate entrance, this would be excellent.

☐ Why are keyless combination locks more secure than an ordinary key lock? They are absolutely pickproof. There is no keyhole to pick, no tumblers to feel or hear, and no telltale sound or feel to the push buttons. Because there is no key to become lost, stolen, or copied, you can realize and appreciate that the key is the weakest link in any security setup. Also, if you give out the combination, you know you have done so. Your keys though, can be copied without your knowledge. Because these locks are deadbolt or deadlatch bolt locks, they cannot be jimmied or slid free of the doorjamb with a piece of celluloid.

☐ Are the locks weatherproof? Yes. They have been tested on Air Force and commercial installations from South America to the Arctic. Under the most extreme conditions, these locks have set new standards for dependence and reliability.

☐ If I purchased the lock, how difficult is installation? You can install it yourself quite easily. The only differences between installing this lock and an ordinary lock is a different shaped cutout in the door and that the Preso-Matic has an extremely simple one-screw assembly.

☐ Are the Preso-Matic locks more expensive than ordinary locks? Compared with equally durable deadbolt or deadlatch bolt key locks, the Preso-Matic lock is moderately priced. Because you can eliminate the cost of duplicating or replacing keys, as well as the high expense of changing cylinders if your keys are lost or stolen, you can save the cost of the lock many times over during its lifetime.

☐ What level of security does the lock provide? What level of security do you envision would be the proper response? The lock is used by the U.S. Army; numerous commercial, industrial and government organizations; by the FAA (Federal Aviation Administration) and major airlines. It protects computer and data processing rooms, banks, hospitals, schools, fire and police stations, and many other public buildings in addition to homes and apartment dwellings.

Figure 3-54 illustrates a combination slide unit (they come in pairs) for a keyless combination lock. These units are all that is required to change the combination in the lock. There are no complicated procedures to follow.

If you install a deadlatch model, the lever on the interior plate would be left in the unlocked position to keep the device unactivated (Fig. 3-55). The Preso-Matic lock can be installed and used in all types of doors.

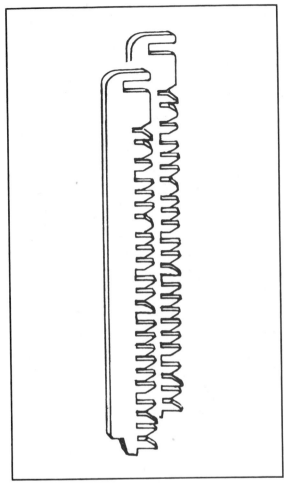

Fig. 3-54. A pair of master combination slides for the Preso-Matic keyless lock (courtesy Preso-Matic Lock Co., Inc.).

## Installing the Preso-Matic Lock

The Presto-Matic lock can be installed by anyone who can handle a hammer, screwdriver, saber or coping saw, and an electric or hand drill. For the person who can afford a cylinder lock but can't install it because he or she lacks mechanical aptitude, the keyless lock is very easy.

Step one: cut the opening in the door. Take the template provided with the lock unit (Fig. 3-56) and fold it along the line indicated. Attach it to the door with masking tape. If a saber or coping saw is used, punch mark the corners, drill 3/16" holes in each corner, and cut out the

rectangle. If a power drill is used, punch the center marks of the circles and drill 1" holes through the door in each circle using a ½" electric drill (Fig. 3-57). Form a rectangle by chiseling from both sides of the door. Try inserting the lock from both sides of the door; it should fit loosely. Mark the correct door edge center on the template line that is folded over the door edge. Use this center mark to drill a 1" hole into the door edge for the bolt housing.

Step two: install the bolt housing. Gouge out a clearance for the lugs (inside of the 1" hole drilled in the edge of the door) (Fig. 3-58). Use a ½" drill or chisel. Drill or chisel at an angle inside

Fig. 3-55. A simple movement of the interior level keeps the lock in either the locked or unlocked modes (courtesy Preso-Matic Lock Co., Inc.).

119

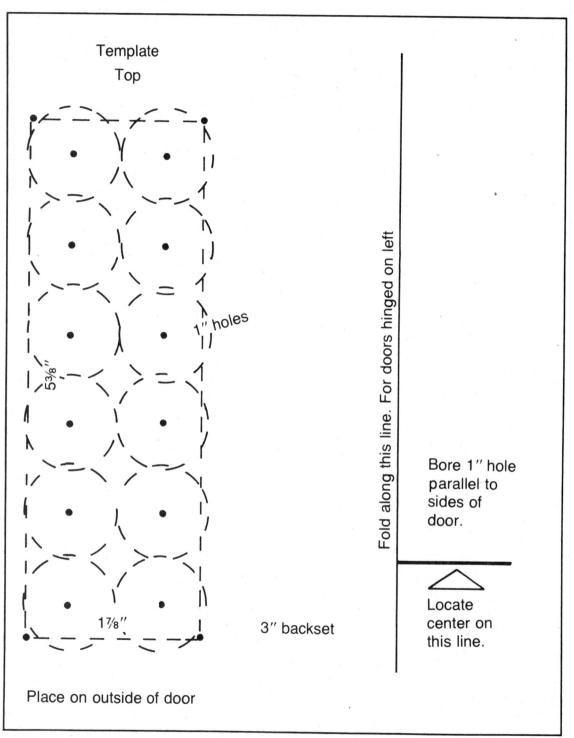

Template
Top

1″ holes

5³⁄₈″

Fold along this line. For doors hinged on left

Bore 1″ hole parallel to sides of door.

1⁷⁄₈″

3″ backset

Locate center on this line.

Place on outside of door

Fig. 3-56. Fold the template along the line indicated (courtesy Preso-Matic Lock Co., Inc.).

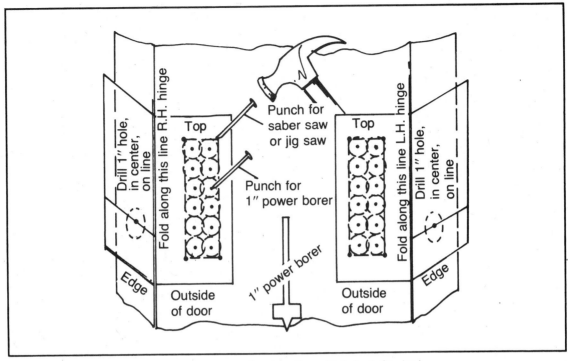

Fig. 3-57. Details for drilling holes through the door (courtesy Preso-Matic Lock Co., Inc.).

of the 1″ hole as shown, so wood is left for the screws to attach the bolt housing. The lugs must have positive clearance with no rubbing. Set the bolt housing in the opening with the bolt extended all the way. The brass pin is toward the inside of the door (Fig. 3-59). Mark the outline and recess slightly with a chisel. Clean out the sawdust and set the bolt housing in place with two wood screws.

Step three: if an escutcheon or space is used, it must be slid onto the lock before installing the lock in the door.

Step four: install the lock body in the door. Make sure the bolt actuator and brass pin are in place (Fig. 3-60). Remove the large-headed screw and also the long thin spring in the hole under the screw. Insert the lock body into the door opening, ensuring that the buttons are on the door outside. Make sure the dovetails in the lock body mate with the dovetails in the bolt housing. Push in as far as possible, then insert the long thin spring into the hole and turn the

large-headed screw until the bolt housing casting touches the body casting. Do not overtighten the screw. Slightly back off the screw after tightening. Tap the head of the brass pin with a screwdriver lightly to set the actuator. Note that it must

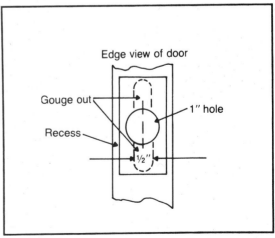

Fig. 3-58. Gouge out a clearance for the lugs (courtesy Preso-Matic Lock Co., Inc.).

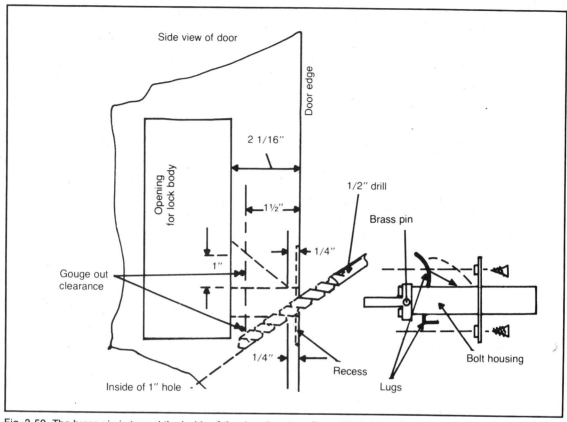

Fig. 3-59. The brass pin is toward the inside of the door (courtesy Preso-Matic Lock Co., Inc.).

be in a straight line with the bolt. Pull the brass pin out and save it. Keep the door ajar and work the combination several times.

Step five: mount the inside cover plate (Fig. 3-61). Insert the appropriate screws into the holes on the corners of the inside cover plate. Before tightening them, align the inside cover plate correctly by observing the straightness of the unlock button. When this button is straight and center, tighten the screws, but do not over-tighten. Keep the door open and test the lock to see that it operates properly from the inside and the outside.

Step six: install the strike plate. Place a drop of paint or fingernail polish on the center of the bolt in the retracted position. Shut the door and press the rest button to extend the bolt. This will transfer the paint dot to the jamb indicating the

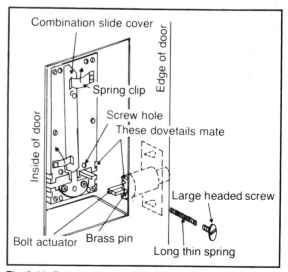

Fig. 3-60. Position the bolt actuator and brass pin (courtesy Preso-Matic Lock Co., Inc.).

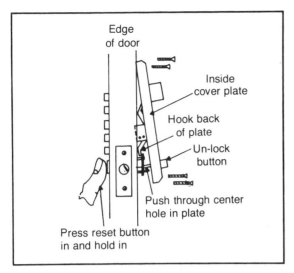

Fig. 3-61. Mount the inside cover plate (courtesy Preso-Matic Lock Co., Inc.).

center for the strike plate opening. Drill a 1″ hole 1¼″ deep. Recess the strike plate in the doorjamb and attach.

### Simplex Keyless Access Control Locks

*Simplex Security Products* is another manufacturer of keyless access control locks. Originally developed for government and industry, these locks are also widely found in small stores, computer rooms, and in the home. They are ideal door locks for apartment complexes, individual apartments, and individual residential applications.

**Unican 1000.** The Unican 1000 (Fig. 3-62) is a five-button push control for access to a home. It is easy to operate. Thousands of combinations are possible, and you can change the combination in seconds.

Fig. 3-62. Unican 1000 keyless access control system (courtesy Simplex Security Systems, Inc.).

The Unican 1000 can save you the cost of new keys and key cylinders. There is no electrical wiring or electronics to go awry and no keyways that can be picked.

The Unican 1000 is durable, performs well, and is attractive. It is rugged, weatherproof, and wear-tested for 30 years of intensive use. Easily installed, the Unican 1000 will fit on wood or metal doors from 1⅜" to 2¼" thickness.

The lock uses a standard strike and has a 2¾" backset (the distance from the center of the lock to the door edge), so it easily replaces cylindrical and tubular locksets. If you incorporated one on each of your residential doors, you could also have the lock keyed for a bypass function (Fig. 3-63).

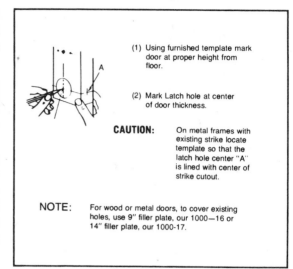

(1) Using furnished template mark door at proper height from floor.

(2) Mark Latch hole at center of door thickness.

**CAUTION:** On metal frames with existing strike locate template so that the latch hole center "A" is lined with center of strike cutout.

NOTE: For wood or metal doors, to cover existing holes, use 9" filler plate, our 1000—16 or 14" filler plate, our 1000-17.

Fig. 3-64. Mark the door (courtesy Simplex Security Systems, Inc.).

From the interior, you have the option of a thumb turn or key cylinder, allowing the outside knob to be set to open the lock without the need for using the push-button combination (i.e., the unlocked position of the lock). This would be excellent for families with small children who are in and out of the house constantly during the day,

Fig. 3-63. Unican 1000 with key bypass (courtesy Simplex Security Systems, Inc.).

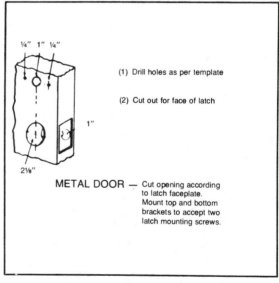

(1) Drill holes as per template

(2) Cut out for face of latch

METAL DOOR — Cut opening according to latch faceplate. Mount top and bottom brackets to accept two latch mounting screws.

Fig. 3-65. Bore holes and prepare the latch cutout (courtesy Simplex Security Systems, Inc.).

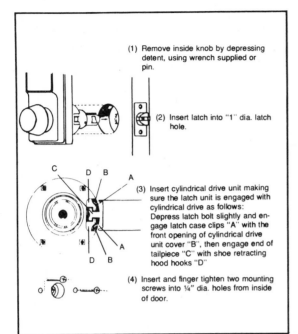

(1) Remove inside knob by depressing detent, using wrench supplied or pin.

(2) Insert latch into "1" dia. latch hole.

(3) Insert cylindrical drive unit making sure the latch unit is engaged with cylindrical drive as follows: Depress latch bolt slightly and engage latch case clips "A" with the front opening of cylindrical drive unit cover "B", then engage end of tailpiece "C" with shoe retracting hood hooks "D"

(4) Insert and finger tighten two mounting screws into ¼" dia. holes from inside of door.

Fig. 3-66. Install the latch and lock (courtesy Simplex Security Systems, Inc.).

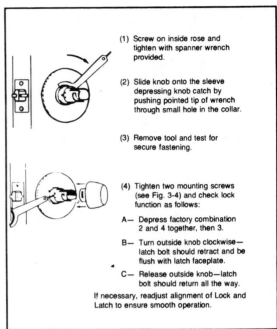

(1) Screw on inside rose and tighten with spanner wrench provided.

(2) Slide knob onto the sleeve depressing knob catch by pushing pointed tip of wrench through small hole in the collar.

(3) Remove tool and test for secure fastening.

(4) Tighten two mounting screws (see Fig. 3-4) and check lock function as follows:

A— Depress factory combination 2 and 4 together, then 3.

B— Turn outside knob clockwise— latch bolt should retract and be flush with latch faceplate.

C— Release outside knob—latch bolt should return all the way.

If necessary, readjust alignment of Lock and Latch to ensure smooth operation.

Fig. 3-68. Install the inside knob (courtesy Simplex Security Systems, Inc.).

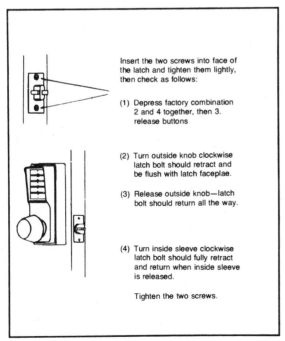

Insert the two screws into face of the latch and tighten them lightly, then check as follows:

(1) Depress factory combination 2 and 4 together, then 3. release buttons

(2) Turn outside knob clockwise latch bolt should retract and be flush with latch faceplae.

(3) Release outside knob—latch bolt should return all the way.

(4) Turn inside sleeve clockwise latch bolt should fully retract and return when inside sleeve is released.

Tighten the two screws.

Fig. 3-67. Secure the latch (courtesy Simplex Security Systems, Inc.).

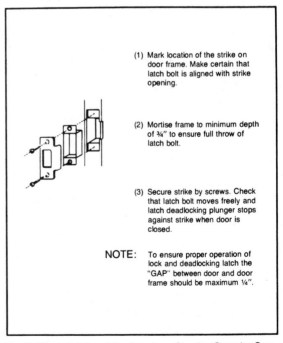

(1) Mark location of the strike on door frame. Make certain that latch bolt is aligned with strike opening.

(2) Mortise frame to minimum depth of ¾" to ensure full throw of latch bolt.

(3) Secure strike by screws. Check that latch bolt moves freely and latch deadlocking plunger stops against strike when door is closed.

NOTE: To ensure proper operation of lock and deadlocking latch the "GAP" between door and door frame should be maximum ¼".

Fig. 3-69. Install the strike (courtesy Simplex Security Systems, Inc.).

Fig. 3-70. A Simplex "tuch-but'n" push-button combination door lock (courtesy Simplex Security Systems, Inc.).

while the parent may be inside working. The Unican 1000 requires only six installation steps (five if the lock is replacing a cylindrical or tubular lockset). See Figs. 3-64 through 3-69.

**The Tuch-but'n Door Lock.** This is another excellent Simplex lock that has residential applications. Like the Unican 1000, the tuch-but'n combination lock comes in two versions: the deadlock (with a full 1″ deadbolt—Fig. 3-70), and the automatic spring latch model (Fig. 3-71). From the inside, the lock can be opened with a finger lever or a 2½″ lever handle (Fig. 3-72). Numerous homes have these locks in addition to the standard keyed door for increased security protection. In some cases, these locks have even replaced the standard door lock.

With the deadlock model, the lock will remain open (with the bolt retracted) until either the

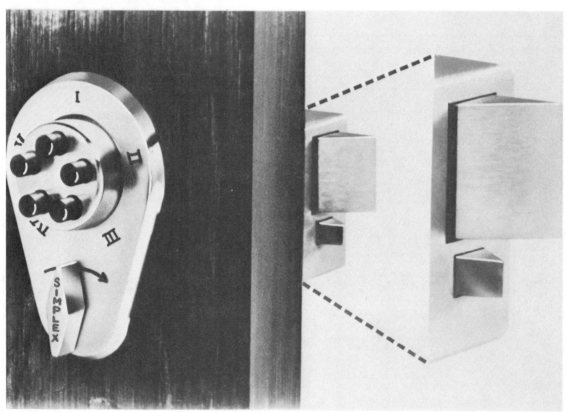

Fig. 3-71. Automatic spring latch model combination door lock (courtesy Simplex Security Systems, Inc.).

Fig. 3-72. One finger lever or a 2½" lever handle can open the lock for emergency exiting (courtesy Simplex Security Systems, Inc.).

the combination setting being used. Several locks can be installed in various parts of the home and outbuildings. Each has a separate combination, but all can be opened by one key.

Installation of the Simplex tuch-but'n combination lock is much easier than that for a regular lockset. Using the template provided with the lockset when purchased (Fig. 3-74), attach it to the door and drill the appropriate holes into the door.

Slide the lock housing into the holes in the door (Fig. 3-75). If the holes were drilled at an angle and the undersurface of the lock housing is not in full contact with the door, file out the hole to correct the error. Screw the lock housing to the door.

Place the holding bracket on the front of the door surface with the slotted legs engaging the aligning pin on the barrel (enlarged view in Fig. 3-76). The large radius of the holding bracket mates with the radius of the barrel.

Remove the lock housing from the door. Slide the holding edges of the faceplate *behind* the formed-up edges of the holding bracket. Make sure that the faceplate is securely held on both sides.

Replace the lock housing while holding the control knob marked "Simplex" in the vertical

inside lever or the outside knob is turned to throw the bolt into the locked position. On the spring latch model, the door will lock automatically when in the closed position. There is a thumb slide on the inside to hold the bolt in the retracted position if necessary. If desired, the latch hold-back can be eliminated by having a different model of the spring latch lock. The deadlatch feature available with the spring latch will prevent prying the latch back on the closed door, thus ensuring that the lock bolt is not forced back to allow an unauthorized entry.

A key bypass may be desirable (Fig. 3-73). The optional key cylinder provides the flexibility of a key system and the advantages of a combination lock. The key assures entry regardless of

Fig. 3-73. Push-button door lock with key bypass (courtesy Simplex Security Systems, Inc.).

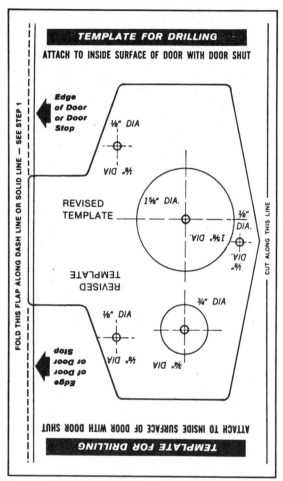

Fig. 3-74. Ensure alignment of the template for proper lock positioning (courtesy Simplex Security Systems, Inc.).

position. Turn the knob to ensure proper engagement and fasten the lock housing to the door.

### Single- and Double-Cylinder Deadlocks

Local ordinances in many areas have required that apartment houses or other multiple dwelling units including condominiums, have another lock in addition to the basic lockset. These ordinances and laws were enacted to counter the crime being committed in multiple dwelling units. What was not legislated was the real need for these units to be considered for individual residences.

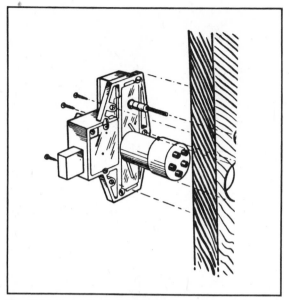

Fig. 3-75. Insert the housing from the interior of the door (courtesy Simplex Security Systems, Inc.).

Figure 3-77 illustrates two single-cylinder deadlocks. The interior uses a thumb turn to lock and unlock the unit. Two different strikes are included depending on the type of mounting. The angled strike would be used in wood frames or

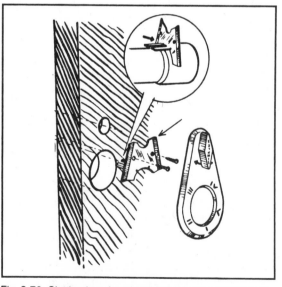

Fig. 3-76. Slotting legs face inward toward the locking body (courtesy Simplex Security Systems, Inc.).

128

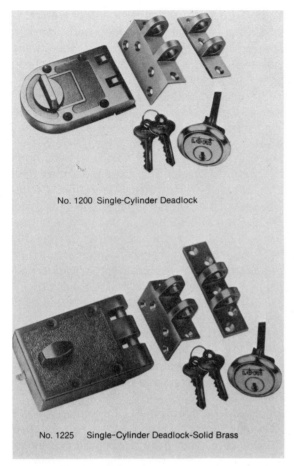

No. 1200 Single-Cylinder Deadlock

No. 1225    Single-Cylinder Deadlock-Solid Brass

Fig. 3-77. Single-cylinder deadlocks with vertical deadbolt and interior thumb turn (courtesy Lori Corporation).

those metal frames that have a wide gap between the door and the frame.

Figure 3-78 illustrates two double-cylinder deadlocks. Each has two strikes depending upon the installation required.

Notice that each of these deadlocks has a vertical deadbolt. The vertical deadbolt lock is jimmyproof.

### Night Latch Locking Units

As a replacement for existing night latch units or as a new installation, rim cylinders or 1″ square bolt deadlocks are exceptional for added security protection (Figs. 3-79 and 3-80). These units are rugged, dependable, and offer a greater degree

of security against vandalism. Each also comes with a standard cylinder to allow external locking of the unit when you leave home.

### The Fox Police Double Bolt Lock

The *Fox double bolt lock* is designed to provide maximum security for single doors (Fig. 3-81). Although designed primarily for use on doors that open out, the lock can also be installed on other types of doors by using special hardware.

Properly installed, the lock will work smoothly from outside the door, as the key is inserted and the cylinder turned. Turning the cylinder will rotate a spindle and bolt activating

No. 1250 Double-Cylinder Deadlock

No. 1275 Double-Cylinder Deadlock-Solid Brass

Fig. 3-78. Double-cylinder deadlocks (courtesy Lori Corporation).

Fig. 3-79. Rim cylinder night latch (courtesy Lori Corporation).

gear. As this gear turns, the bolts are retracted to unlock the door or extended to lock the door.

When operating the lock from inside the door, the knob is pulled out slightly while turning. This procedure is necessary to disengage the spindle from the portion of the lock cylinder tailpiece. If this was not done, the spindle and tailpiece would be locked in position, and the spindle could not be turned to activate the bolt gear. Figure 3-82 illustrates the unit in the locked position; the dotted lines show the extension of the bolt into the surrounding wood or metal of the frame. Figures 3-83 illustrates a variation of the basic unit, the E lock model, that allows for three bolts inserted into the frame on the most susceptible side of the door—the side that would be used for an attempted forced entry into the home. The C lock model (Fig. 3-84) has two bolts extending into the frame.

## AUXILIARY DOOR HARDWARE

Some people need auxiliary devices and accessories for their doors. Some are required, some are nice, and others are just an extra measure of security.

The *barrel bolt* (Fig. 3-85) can be used on side or rear doors that are seldom used. The steel barrel bolt uses at least ¾″ screws for installation. These units come in lengths from 3″ to 6″.

Every solid wood or steel front door that has no windows, or a window up high where children cannot see who is at the door, should have a *door viewer* installed (Fig. 3-86). The door viewer should have a wide angle, at least 160° viewing, but a 180° viewer is better. You can combine the door viewer with a *door knocker* (Fig. 3-87)

for better decor aesthetics. The door viewer allows you to identify the invited and uninvited guests, without having to open the door. Make sure the viewer is one way and has a precision optical lens for clarity.

Some individuals do not care to open the door all the way to strangers, even when accepting a small package or registered letter. You may want a chain door locking device. The *Superguard Chain-Dor-Loc* (Fig. 3-88) lets you open the door only slightly. This is the finest chain door lock ever designed. The Superguard Chain-Dor-Loc has a five pin tumbler specifically designed so that it can be interchanged with most rim cylinders to enable the lock to be keyed to other existing entry locksets. A secret catch on the slide stops the chain from being pried off, slipped off, or pushed off from the outside.

The chain is made of ¼″ case-hardened steel. The unit comes with 2½″ screws to ensure that the lock housing is firmly attached to the doorjamb, and that all installation screws are concealed for additional security. A special shim is included to offset various curvatures on existing jambs.

Even when you leave the home, you can secure the unit to provide that extra edge of security protection. If the initial door lock is forced or opened, there is still another lock to contend with, and with the location of the cylinder keyway it is virtually impossible to pick.

If you have an outswinging door, you should install a *latch guard*. It provides added protection against forced entry attempts and mounts to the door with four heavy-duty bolts.

Fig. 3-80. A 1″ square bolt deadbolt (courtesy Lori Corporation).

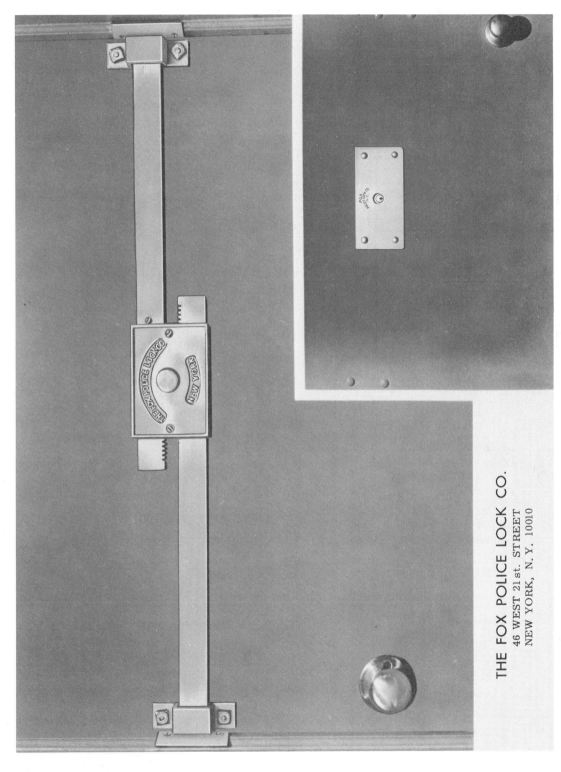

THE FOX POLICE LOCK CO.
46 WEST 21st. STREET
NEW YORK, N.Y. 10010

Fig. 3-81. Fox double bolt lock for maximum security for single doors (courtesy Fox Police Lock Co.).

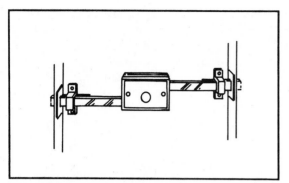

Fig. 3-82. Bolts extend a full 2″ into the frame (courtesy Fox Police Lock Co.).

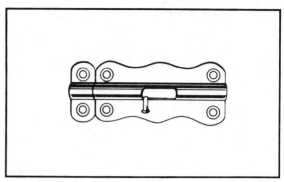

Fig. 3-85. The barrel bolt for side and rear doors (courtesy Ideal Security Hardware).

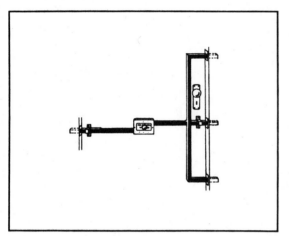

Fig. 3-83. The E lock model Fox bolt lock (courtesy Fox Police Lock Co.).

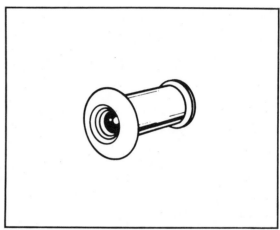

Fig. 3-86. Every solid door should have a door viewer installed and used by the homeowner (courtesy Ideal Security Products).

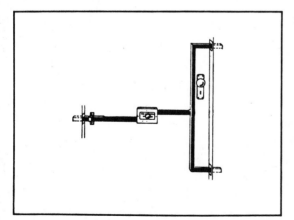

Fig. 3-84. The C lock model (courtesy Fox Police Lock Co.).

Fig. 3-87. Some door viewers are combined with the door knocker (courtesy Ideal Security Hardware).

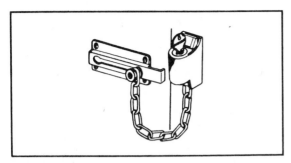

Fig. 3-88. Chain locking devices provide extra security when the door must be left open slightly (courtesy Ideal Security Hardware).

The Super Blocker is for outswinging doors (Fig. 3-89). The Super Blocker has a covering over the cylinder edging to prevent the cylinder from being wrenched out of the door.

When installing or replacing a flat strike with another, use a heavy-duty strike with more than two screws (Fig. 3-90). Screws used should be at least 2″ long; 2½″ is preferable.

Whether the door swings inward or outward, you can add a security stud to the door hinge (Fig. 3-91). On an outswinging door, removal of the hinge pin would still not allow the door to be removed because the lock stud screw, inserted in the place of one set of hinge screws, prevents the door's removal.

Hinge security studs are also available for wood and metal doors, but they are not used to replace a screw in the door hinge. While mainly applicable to doors that swing outward, they also provide an added measure of security for in-swinging doors. Figure 3-92 illustrates the hinge security stud for metal doors. Figure 3-93 shows the hinge security stud for wood doors. Note that the stud is completely hidden when the door is in the closed position.

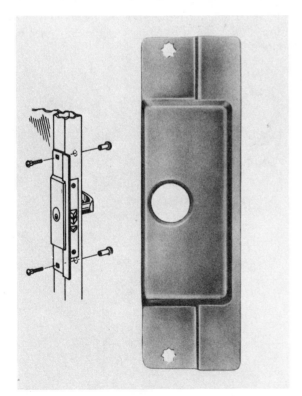

Fig. 3-89. The Super Blocker protects the door from tampering (courtesy Lori Corporation).

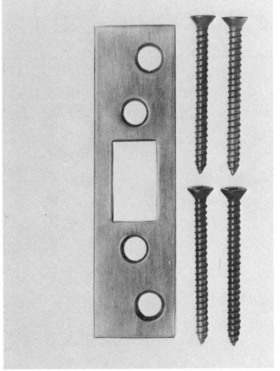

Fig. 3-90. Heavy-duty strike with longer and more (four) screws than an average door strike gives increased security (courtesy Lori Corporation).

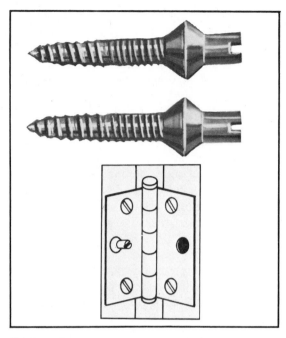

Fig. 3-91. Door hinge with security stud replacing a screw (courtesy Lori Corporation).

The *Fox Brace Lock* (Fig. 3-94) is a jimmy-proof lock that uses a positive steel bar to prevent forced entry. It has been recommended for use by police departments and burglary insurance underwriters.

## SECURING PATIO DOORS

Patio doors consist of three pieces: the frame that surrounds the entire door unit, the stationary door, and the movable door. Each of these pieces must work as part of a unit to keep the movable door open or closed, and each can be made more secure.

A highly secure method for the patio door is to have a unit that securely locks the door at the top and bottom by operating from a standard handle located at the door edge. One available unit is the *EntryGard* patio door lock and handle set (Fig. 3-95). The EntryGard unit seems to be a standard lock and handle set, but two concealed steel deadbolts are located within the narrow door stile (Fig. 3-96).

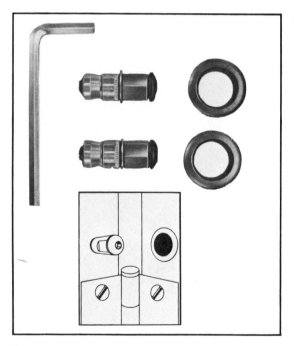

Fig. 3-92. Metal door security stud (courtesy Lori Corporation).

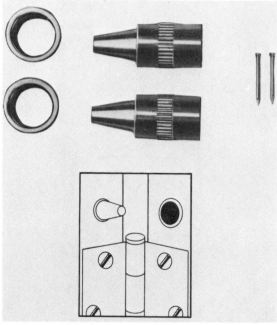

Fig. 3-93. Wood door security stud (courtesy Lori Corporation).

THE FOX POLICE LOCK CO.
46 WEST 21st. STREET
NEW YORK. N. Y. 10010

Fig. 3-94. The Fox Police Brace Lock is jimmyproof and prevents forced entry (courtesy Fox Police Lock Co.).

Fig. 3-95. The EntryGard patio door lock and handle set is the best available on the market today (courtesy Truth, Inc.).

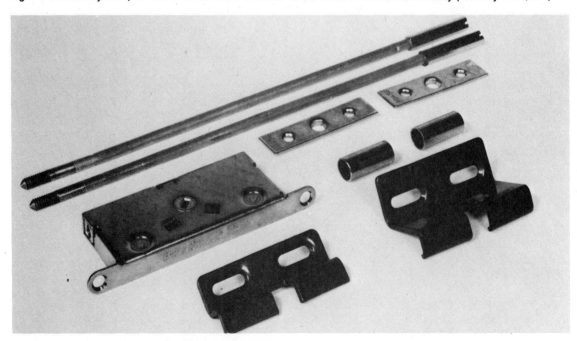

Fig. 3-96. The concealed deadbolts (left) are the heart of the patio door security system (courtesy Truth, Inc.).

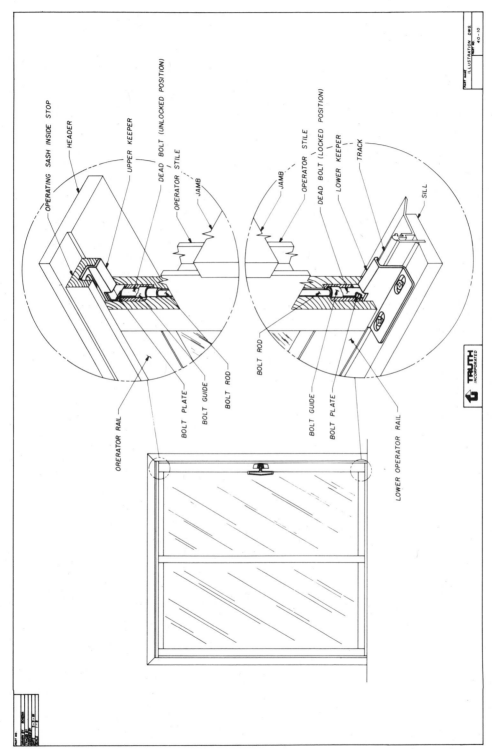

Fig. 3-97. Door frame edge hides deadbolts that completely secure the door in the locked position (courtesy Truth, Inc.).

137

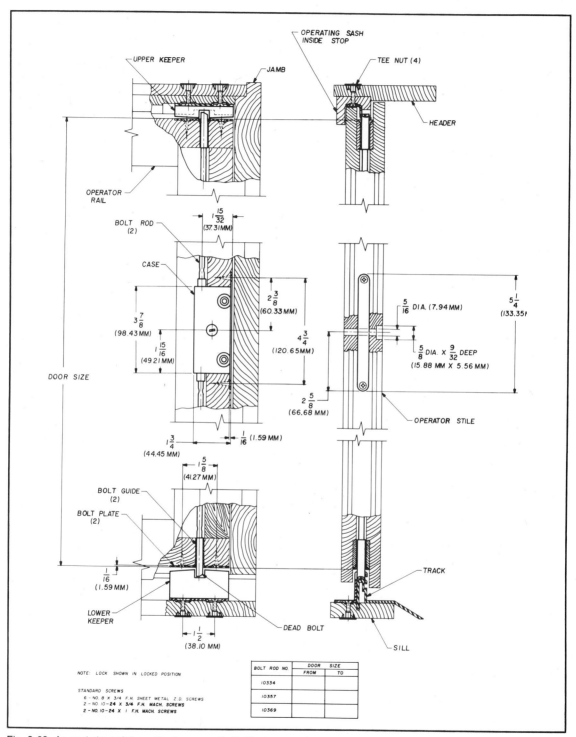

Fig. 3-98. An end view of the patio door security locking system (courtesy Truth, Inc.).

Note the main points of the deadbolt system at the top and bottom of the door (Fig. 3-97). An end view (Fig. 3-98) shows other specifications of the unit.

After the lock and handle set has been installed, the patio door looks just like any other (Fig. 3-99). Forced entry tests on the EntryGard have withstood loads in excess of 1,000 pounds applied parallel to the travel of the door. This is more than three times the forced entry resistance prescribed for the patio door standard.

The patio door security lock shown in Fig. 3-100 is a foot-operated device that is easily released from the inside for ready escape. The spring-loaded device easily locks or is released with either the hand or foot. This unit can be mounted to the bottom rail, locking into the sill, or into the face of the stationary door. The two mounting methods are shown in Figs. 3-101 and 3-102.

Another way to protect a sliding patio door is

Fig. 3-100. Foot-operated patio door lock will withstand more than 400 pounds of pressure (courtesy Truth, Inc.).

to install metal screws or bolts into the top of the frame and down the channelway where the door moves when the door is in the closed position. Installing a couple of screws or bolts (Fig. 3-103) properly set in, but allowing the door to move horizontally, we also prevent the door from being removed easily by an intruder.

The *patio door bar lock* is an adjustable unit (Fig. 3-104) that allows for the sliding door to be locked in a ventilating position, but automatically locks when the door is closed. It conveniently swings upward and out of the way when unlocked. A patio door pin lock is a hardened steel pin that securely holds the moving door to the stationary door when in the locked position. A hanging saddle is attached to the metal door frame to hold the pin when it is not in use.

The thumbscrew patio lock (Fig. 3-105) allows the door to be locked into either the ventilating or closed position. Two thumbscrews provide more protection. The thumbscrew requires no installation and can be used immediately. The keyed sliding patio door lock is attached by a series of three screws to the edge of the moving door. A hole is drilled into the stationary door for the locking bolt to enter. A second hole can be drilled to allow the unit to be locked when in a ventilating position. The patio door can be opened (or closed) only after the keyed lock has been opened. A main keyed patio door is used

Fig. 3-99. Once installed, it looks like any other patio door (courtesy Truth, Inc.).

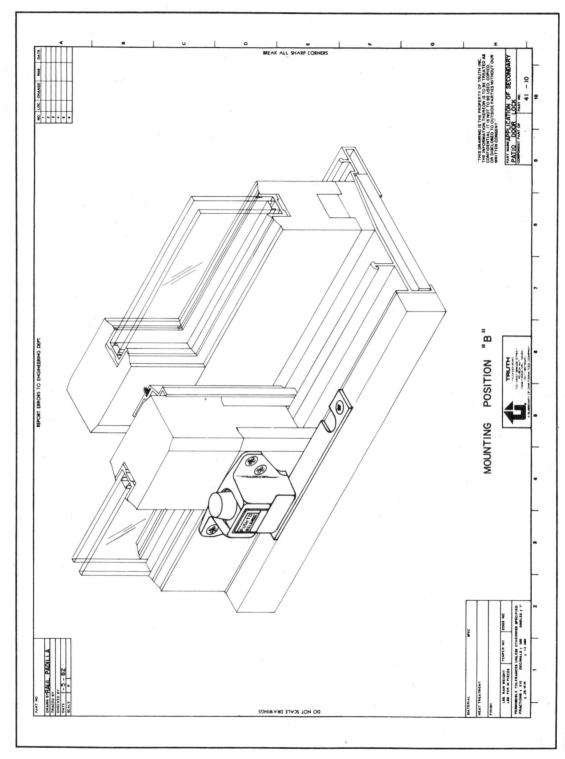

Fig. 3-101. The most common method of mounting the foot-operated patio door lock (courtesy Truth, Inc.).

140

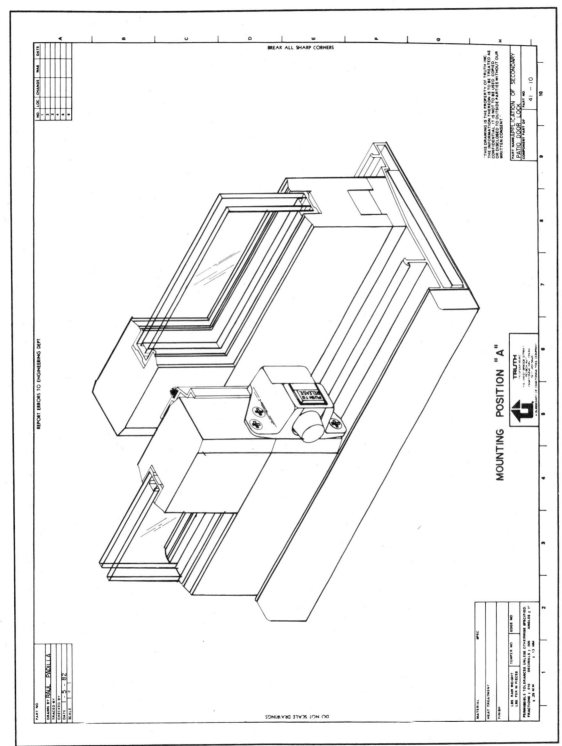

MOUNTING POSITION "A"

TRUTH

"THIS DRAWING IS THE PROPERTY OF TRUTH INC. THE INFORMATION THEREON IS TO BE TREATED AS CONFIDENTIAL. IT IS NOT TO BE USED, COPIED OR DISCLOSED TO OUTSIDE PARTIES WITHOUT OUR WRITTEN CONSENT."

PART NAME APPLICATION OF SECONDARY
PATIO DOOR LOCK

COMPONENT PART OF                PART NO
                                 41 — 10

DRAWN BY  PAUL PADILLA

Fig. 3-102. An optional but excellent method of mounting the patio door lock (courtesy Truth, Inc.).

141

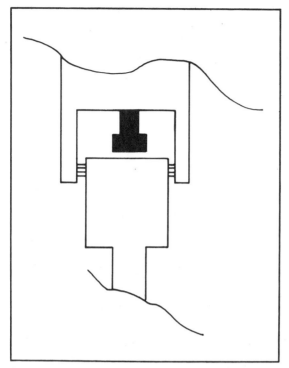

Fig. 3-103. Use a metal screw or bolt in the top of the track frame. This prevents the door from being lifted out.

for locking the door against the frame (Fig. 3-106). It can only be locked and unlocked with a key. An indicator button shows you at a glance if the door is locked or unlocked. Another patio door lock is shown in Fig. 3-107.

## WINDOWS

Windows are the most critical area for security in

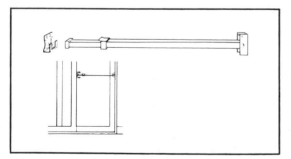

Fig. 3-104. The patio door bar lock will allow the door to be locked either fully closed or in a ventilating position (courtesy Ideal Security Hardware).

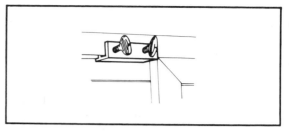

Fig. 3-105. Thumbscrew lock allows the patio door to be in the ventilating or closed position (courtesy Ideal Security Hardware).

the home. A burglar will usually attempt to gain access through the doors to a home; failing this, he will resort to the windows. They do not have the strength or durability of a door, and windows are very easy to penetrate.

Whenever possible, a burglar will avoid breaking window glass because noise attracts attention—the last thing a burglar wants. A burglar will attempt to force or pry open the window to gain entry.

If a burglar does break the glass to gain entry, there is nothing you can do. If you or a neighbor hears the sound of breaking glass, contact the local police. You can take steps to prevent your windows from being forced or pried open by a burglar.

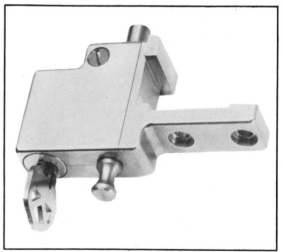

Fig. 3-106. A keyed patio door lock (courtesy Kwikset Division, Emhart, Industries).

Fig. 3-107. A nonkeyed patio door lock (courtesy Kwikset Division, Emhart Industries).

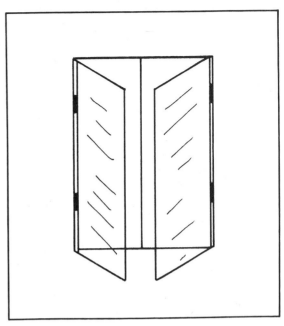

Fig. 3-109. Casement window.

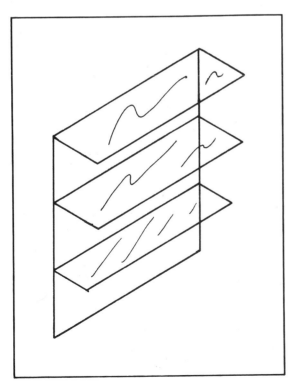

Fig. 3-108. Awning window.

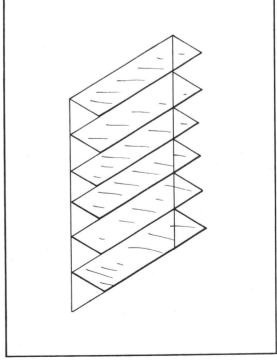

Fig. 3-110. Louver window.

143

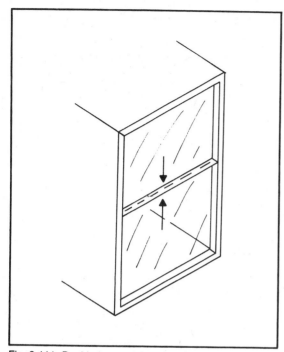

Fig. 3-111. Double-hung window.

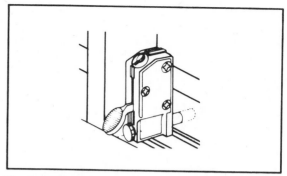

Fig. 3-113. A sliding door lock also works well on sliding windows (courtesy Ideal Security Hardware).

Basically, there are five types of windows: the *awning*, which projects inward or outward (Fig. 3-108); *casement* (Fig. 3-109); louver (Fig. 3-110); double-hung (Fig. 3-111); and the sliding (Fig. 3-112).

Protective measures taken depend on the type and style of the window, its location within the home, and your assessment of the window's vulnerability to attack. As an example, a double-hung window on the first floor side, which is partially hidden from casual observation by a large bush, is more of a prime target than a double-hung window on the other side of the house that is clearly visible from the street and by your neighbors.

A sliding glass door lock (Fig. 3-113) can be used on a sliding glass window. A keyed window sash lock, turned vertically, can be used to secure a sliding window.

### Double-Hung Windows

Most double-hung windows have a crescent

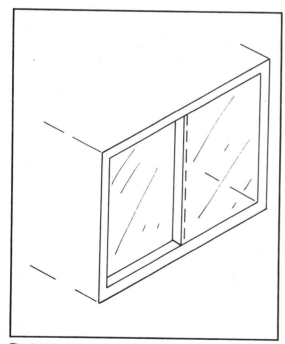

Fig. 3-112. Sliding window.

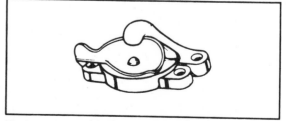

Fig. 3-114. The crescent lock is really only a closure device—not a lock (courtesy Ideal Security Hardware).

Fig. 3-115. Keyed window locks should be on all ground level windows at a minimum (courtesy Ideal Security Hardware).

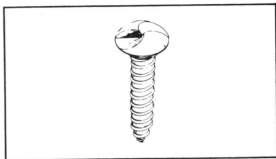

Fig. 3-117. Tamperproof screws can't be removed with an ordinary screwdriver (courtesy Ideal Security Hardware).

sash lock to hold them closed. Unfortunately, this isn't really a lock but a closure device (Fig. 3-114). When its located in a window that is easily accessible from the ground or by ladder, a burglar only needs moments to open this insecure unit. A better level of protection would be obtained by removing the closure unit and installing a keyed window lock (Fig. 3-115). This locking unit mounts directly to the window sash and comes with two lock plates and grommets, allowing for the locking of the window in both the closed and ventilating positions. A key is needed to unlock the unit, but it can be conveniently locked without a key.

There are also standard key-operated window sash locks that replace the standard crescent sash closure device. In addition to holding the windows secure and preventing them from rattling during storms and heavy winds, the sash lock must be locked and unlocked with a key. For newer homes that have windows with a narrow

stile bar, a key-operated narrow sash lock is available (Fig. 3-116).

When installing keyed sash locks, use tamperproof screws (Fig. 3-117). The screws prevent the lock from being removed even after the glass has been broken by a burglar.

Other methods of securing a double-hung window include drilling a hole or several holes in the window sash (Fig. 3-118) and inserting nails

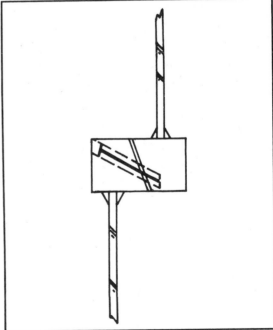

Fig. 3-118. A quick method for keeping windows closed is to use nails droped into drilled holes. A magnet is needed to pull out the nails.

Fig. 3-116. Keyed window sash locks are available even for narrow windows (courtesy Ideal Security Hardware).

into the holes. By making the holes slightly longer than the nails, you can insert the nail fully. Use a magnet to remove the nails.

If the window is never opened, nail it shut. Paint over the area so that the nails will not be evident.

### Awning Windows

An awning window opens inward or outward and may or may not have an operating handle and gear mechanism. Keyed locks can be mounted at the edge of the window to prevent them from being opened by burglars.

### Casement Windows

Found in homes as a single window and in many apartments as double-casement windows, these units operate by a handle and gear mechanism. They also have a locking handle.

Remove the standard casement locking handle (Fig. 3-119). Like the crescent window device, it is really a closure to hold the window shut and not a lock. Replace the handle with a locking handle. The locking handle (Fig. 3-120) has a built-in lock to secure the window when it is in the closed position. These locking handles are available in both left- and right-hand models to fit both types of casement windows.

If you have a set of adjoining casement win-

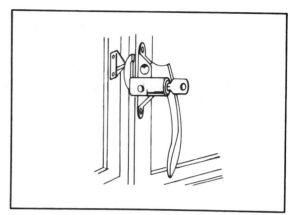

Fig. 3-120. A keyed locking handle is best for casement windows (courtesy Ideal Security Hardware).

dows, or even a single window that you do not open much, you can permanently close them. Drill several holes along the edge of the frame and use metal screws to hold the window closed. On the exterior side, file down the screw points and then paint over.

### Louver Windows

The Louver window is a bad security risk. To improve security, the window crank (Fig. 3-121) should be removed when not in use. Another technique is to obtain a quality glue (not plastic or regular glue) and glue the various windows into the window slat frames.

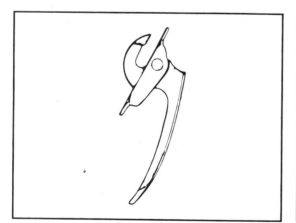

Fig. 3-119. Remove this casement locking handle and replace (courtesy Ideal Security Hardware).

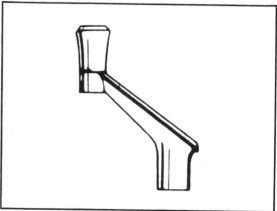

Fig. 3-121. Remove the crank so the window can't be opened by a burglar to gain entrance (courtesy Ideal Security Hardware).

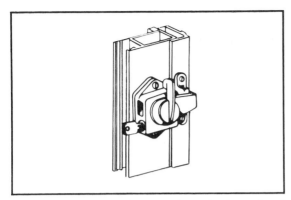

Fig. 3-122. A keyed lock secures the patio doors closed (courtesy Ideal Security Hardware).

Remove the window and replace it with a double-hung, sliding, or casement window. If this is not feasible, you should consider installing a heavy-duty protective grille over the window.

### Sliding Windows

The sliding window is essentially the same as a sliding door, and some protective measures used on the door can also be used on the sliding window. Preventing the window from being removed from its track is a prime concern, and you can use several screws or a tamper plate. A keyed lock (Fig. 3-122) or the keyed sliding patio door lock can be used (Fig. 3-123). The advantage of the keyed patio door lock is that it also allows you to have the window locked in a ventilating position.

For windows on the second floor or in a position where burglars can't gain entry through them, you can use a thumb sliding window lock (Fig. 3-124) to secure a window in either the closed or ventilating positions.

For apartment or home dwellers that have inward projecting or casement windows on a second or third floor or higher, overall security is less than on a lower floor. A spring-loaded security lock can be installed to provide secure locking of such windows (Fig. 3-125). This lock can be used in venetian blind applications where a key might interfere and key security is unnecessary. Front- and rear-mounted versions of this lock are shown in Fig. 3-126.

Double-hung and sliding windows on higher floors, while still requiring protection, do not always need a keyed security lock. A cam lock often will suffice. Figure 3-127 illustrates a lock that is ideal for windows with a narrow stile and check rail. Note the specifications in Fig. 3-128. A more standard cam lock action for a standard check rail is shown in Fig. 3-129. Both will ensure proper sash alignment and a weathertight seal. The spring action keeps the cam handle in the unlocked position to prevent damage to your windows.

For vertical pivoting (Fig. 3-130) and casement windows opening inward, a spring-loaded, key-operated security lock is available (Fig. 3-131). The security lock has a special tamper-proof key slot in its housing. The key is remov-

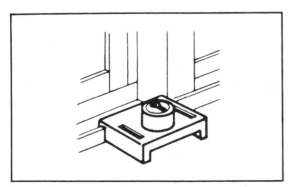

Fig. 3-123. A keyed sliding patio door lock allows the door to be locked in a ventilating position or fully closed (courtesy Ideal Security Hardware).

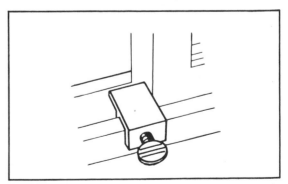

Fig. 3-124. Use only in areas where the window is extremely difficult to reach from the outside (courtesy Ideal Security Hardware).

147

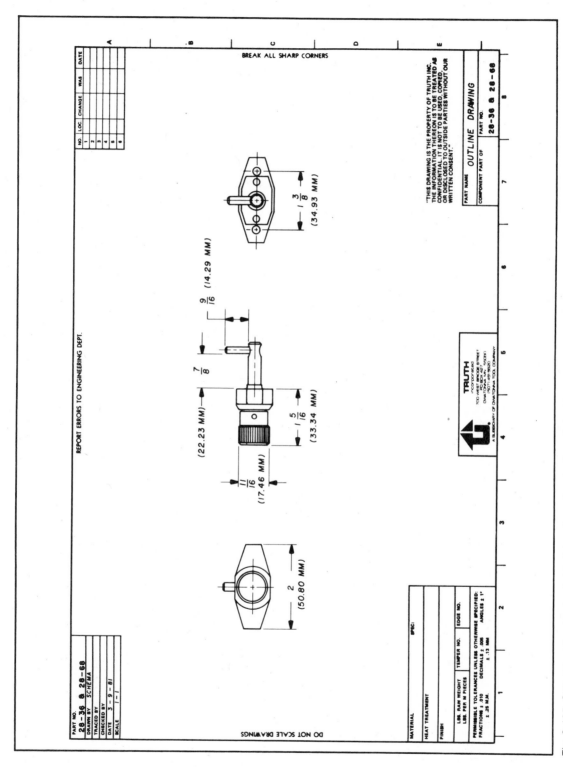

Fig. 3-125. Side view of spring-loaded lock in a inward projecting window frame (courtesy Truth, Inc.).

Fig. 3-126. Front- and rear-mounted versions of a spring-loaded lock (courtesy Truth, Inc.).

able only in the locked position. The lock can be either front-mounted or rear-mounted. The rear-mounted model has concealed screws. In window frames of extruded aluminum, the lock is actually fairly easy to mount.

### Glass Block Windows

An attractive way to protect your basement windows is to use glass blocks. Glass blocks restrict viewing from the outside, but they still let the sunlight into your basement. Blocks come in sizes ranging from 3″ × 6″ to 12″ × 12″.

The *Pittsburgh Corning Corporation* has many patterns and sizes available through local dealers. Installing windows made of glass blocks is as easy as laying cement blocks. You need only a few basic tools, a little planning, and your favorite patterned glass blocks. Several blocks are shown in Figs. 3-132 through 3-134. Glass blocks can be installed in either wood or masonry openings.

Measure each window opening. While the old windows are still in, measure the height and width of each opening. Measure the openings as

though the old windows, frames, and other obstructions had already been removed.

Make a list of all window sizes. Figure 3-135 shows a window sizing list. Number each window on the sill or surrounding wall area, then record the height, width, and appropriate block size and quantity for each window in the proper columns. Take the list to your nearest glass block dealer and have him show you the size and patterns available to do a complete job.

Select the glass block size and pattern that best accommodates your window openings. The following glass block sizes can be used in multiples to fill a window opening sizes: 3 × 6, 4 × 8, 4 × 12, 6 × 6, 6 × 8, 8 × 8, and 12 × 12. These sizes allow for a ¼″ mortar joint when used in multiples.

A hammer, chisel, crowbar, trowel, pre-mixed mortar, striking tool, and level are needed for installing glass block windows. If you install the glass block windows in a wood frame opening, you will also need a caulking gun, wood molding, and wood preservative.

Old windows are constructed with wood, steel, or aluminum frames. Wood and aluminum frames are easily removed using a claw hammer or a crowbar (Fig. 3-136). Steel frames may require cutting with a hacksaw.

Level the windowsill. Old windowsills may not be level because of high spots or slumps or

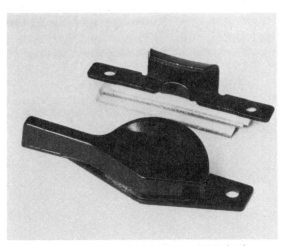

Fig. 3-127. A cam closure lock (courtesy Truth, Inc.).

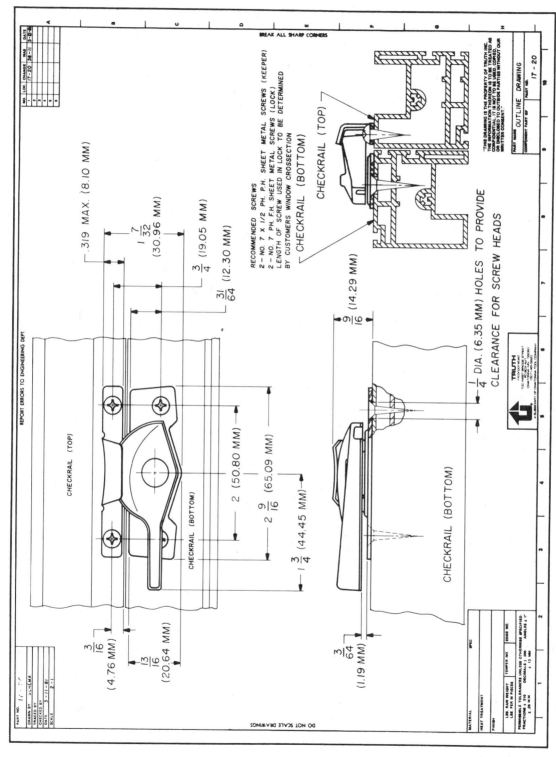

Fig. 3-128. Technical specifications for the low profile cam (courtesy Truth, Inc.).

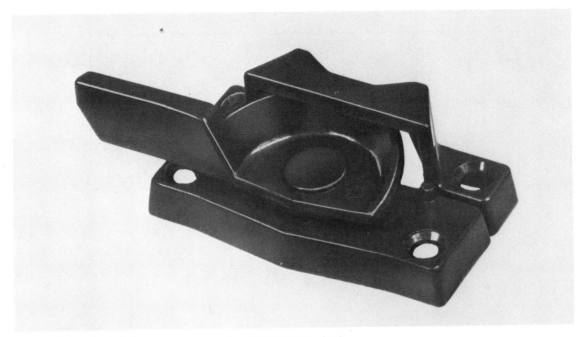

Fig. 3-129. Standard window cam closure device (courtesy Truth, Inc.).

settling of the home after it was originally built. Level up the sills so that the glass blocks fit properly in the window openings.

With high spots, use a hammer and chisel to chip away the old mortar. If the sills slope to either side or the middle, the first bed of fresh mortar will level them out. The first bed of mortar is part of the overall window opening measurement.

Before actually mortaring the glass blocks into place, make a test run. Place the loose blocks in each window opening to create one complete horizontal and one vertical row. Place folded cardboard or wood spacers between the glass blocks to simulate even mortar joints. When you have a complete horizontal and vertical row in place, make check marks on the wall surrounding the window opening to line up with the top and bottom of each spacer (Fig. 3-137). By setting the blocks loosely, you can make whatever changes are necessary for easy installation.

Mortar consistency must be workable but dry enough so that the glass blocks won't "float"

Fig. 3-130. Outward swinging vertical pivot window (courtesy Truth, Inc.).

151

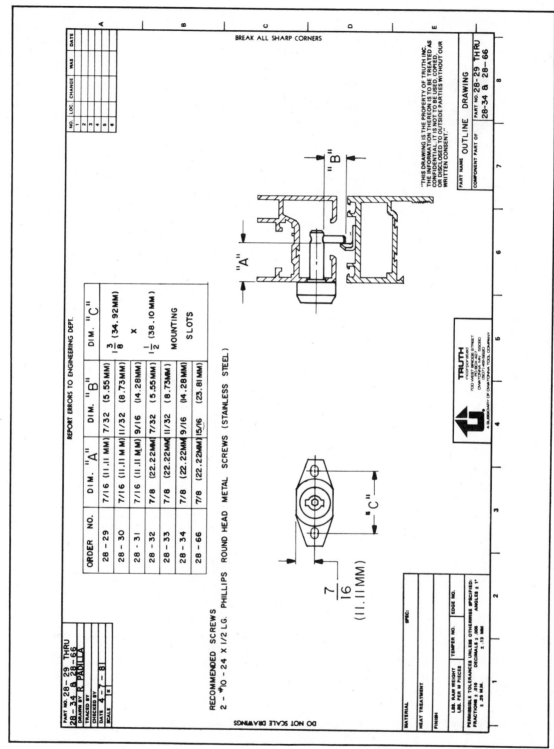

Fig. 3-131. Schematic (side view) of window framework with a spring-loaded lock in place (courtesy Truth, Inc.).

152

Fig. 3-132. A Vue glass block (courtesy Pittsburgh Corning Corporation).

Fig. 3-134. A Delphi glass block (courtesy Pittsburgh Corning Corporation).

Fig. 3-133. A Decora glass block (courtesy Pittsburgh Corning Corporation).

|  | Height | Width | Block Size | Block Quantity |
|---|---|---|---|---|
| Window #1 |  |  |  |  |
| Window #2 |  |  |  |  |
| Window #3 |  |  |  |  |
| Window #4 |  |  |  |  |
| Window #5 |  |  |  |  |
| Window #6 |  |  |  |  |

Fig. 3-135. Use a chart similar to this one to ensure that your glass blocks are the correct size when installed. Your local Pittsburgh Corning dealer will assist you in the proper selection of the glass blocks (courtesy Pittsburgh Corning Corporation).

153

Fig. 3-136. Use a crowbar to remove a window frame (courtesy Pittsburgh Corning Corporation).

154

Fig. 3-137. Make check marks on the wall (courtesy Pittsburgh Corning Corporation).

Fig. 3-138. Position the glass blocks carefully (courtesy Pittsburgh Corning Corporation).

Fig. 3-139. Smooth all joints to remove excess mortar (courtesy Pittsburgh Corning Corporation).

out of place, causing uneven joints. Mortar with the consistency of bread dough will produce the best result. Any commercial premixed dry mortar is adequate. Follow the direction on the sack and prepare approximately one bucket of mortar for each window. If you prefer, make your own mortar by using a mixture of 1 part masonry cement to 3 parts sand.

To install a glass block window in a masonry opening, put a layer of mortar on the windowsill and smooth it out with a trowel to create an even bed. Put a layer of mortar on the side of the opening where the first block will butt against the wall. Put mortar on one vertical edge of each block at a time and place the blocks to create the first row.

Make sure that the first row is even to the eye. You can check it with a level. Remember to position each glass block row so that all mortar joints line up with the check marks on the wall. Put a bed of mortar across the top of the first row. Make sure that all spaces between the glass blocks are filled. Repeat the process for each new row until all blocks are mortared in place and the window is complete (Fig. 3-138).

If the blocks "sink" or "float," mix some drier mortar to create more substantial joints. You can firmly press the tops of the blocks with your hand or the trowel handle to line them up.

If you're installing a ventilator in the window, simply mortar it in place of one or more glass blocks depending on the size unit that you install. Ventilators generally are positioned in the center of the window for aesthetic purposes.

Smooth all mortar joints. Let the glass blocks settle for approximately 2 hours or until the mortar is almost dry. Smooth all joints to remove excess mortar (Fig. 3-139). This will give you a clean and very professional-looking job and will compact the mortar to create a moistureproof seal.

Allow the blocks to set long enough for all mortar joints to firm up. Wipe off the excess mortar using a cloth and some water. Don't let excess mortar totally dry before you attempt to clean the window surface. Do not use steel wool or other abrasive materials to remove partially dried mortar. When this procedure is finished, your completed window should look like Fig. 3-140.

Fig. 3-140. A completed glass block window (courtesy Pittsburgh Corning Corporation).

If you are installing a glass block window in a wood frame opening, apply a coating of preservative to all the exposed wood frame areas around the window openings. When you start to put in the block, use mortar between the glass units only. Do not use mortar between the glass blocks and the wood frame. Glass blocks should be shimmed in tight to the frame.

To complete the job, fasten wood molding to the house frames so that it overlaps the glass blocks approximately ½″ and holds them in place. Caulk wherever glass blocks butt against the trim on both the interior and exterior surfaces.

### Windows as a Means of Escape

Windows must provide a means of escape for occupants. You should not forsake security to ensure an emergency exit, but you must take care in your security precautions so that if escape is necessary, it can be done swiftly.

The National Fire Prevention Association (NFPA), in the Life Safety Code of 1981, addressed the issue of means of escape in the following code sections:

22-2.1.1—"In any dwelling of more than two rooms, every bedroom and living area shall have at least two means of escape, at least one of which shall be a door or stairway providing a means of unobstructed travel to the outside of the building at the street or ground level."

22-2.2.1—"The second means of escape shall be either: a door or stairway providing a means of unobstructed travel to the outside of the building at street or ground level, or an outside window operable from the inside without the use of tools and providing a clear opening of not less than 20″ (50.8 cm) in width, 24″ (60.96 cm) in height, and 5.7 square feet (.53 sq m) in area. The bottom of the opening shall not be more than 44″ (111.76 cm) above the floor."

Bedroom windows should never be permanently closed by nails, screws, or other fasteners. If you have keyed locks for windows, the keys must be placed so that they are accessible to the occupants of the room. A key can be placed at a point near the window where it can be easily reached by the occupant of the room. It shouldn't be put on a nail at an extreme height or hidden in a drawer. The key should not be hung on a nail right beside the window. This would assist a person who had to exit the room rapidly because of an emergency, but it would also facilitate a burglar entering the room. Keep the key in an easy-to-reach place for all, but it should be at least 50″ away from the window.

## SECURITY DOORS AND WINDOW GRILLES

Security doors do not have to be of solid steel. Beautiful security doors are becoming popular. Security doors are available for single door entranceways (Fig. 3-141) and patio doors (Fig. 3-142).

What should you look for when considering a security door for your home? The door should be made of quality steel for rigidity, strength, and durability. The frame and bars should be of fully

Fig. 3-141. Security gate for a single door (courtesy Allen Manufacturing Co.).

Fig. 3-142. Security door for a patio door (courtesy Allen Manufacturing Co.).

welded steel. The steel tubing frame should be of 16-gauge steel, and the bars must be fully welded all the way around for strength. A double deadbolt lock provides great security because when the key is turned, the door is locked into the jamb at the lock point. A bolt simultaneously pops out into the opposite jamb, securing the door into the frame of the house itself (Fig. 3-143).

The security door should be 100 percent prehung. For easy installation, the hinges and the weather-stripped metal frame should already be attached at the factory and ready to set into the door opening.

Security doors use tempered glass that is usually in two panels. This glass has been tempered for strength and safety, then framed in a vinyl weather seal and fitted to the door. Your security door should also have a screen panel. One of the panels of tempered glass should be exchangeable with a glass panel to be used during periods of high temperatures.

Finally, your security door should have an

# SECURITY

is really an outstanding feature with Allan doors because people today, even those living in suburban areas, are very concerned about break-ins. They are afraid their loved ones may be hurt or killed and their possessions stolen or damaged by vandals.

The cost of Allan doors and window guards are insignificant compared to the comfortable feeling their security provides.

# ← BOTH WAYS →
## Dead Bolt Locking System

**Super Security** is provided because when the key is turned, the door is locked into the jamb at the lock point, and a bolt simultaneously pops out into the opposite jamb securing the door into the frame of the house itself!

Fig. 3-143. Double locking on both sides of the security gate will provide excellent security (courtesy Allen Manufacturing Co.).

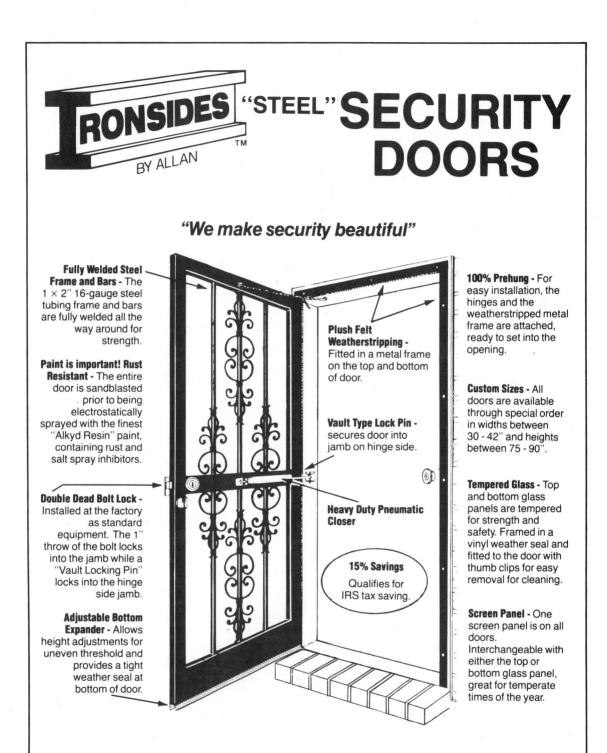

# IRONSIDES "STEEL" SECURITY DOORS

BY ALLAN ™

## "We make security beautiful"

**Fully Welded Steel Frame and Bars -** The 1 × 2" 16-gauge steel tubing frame and bars are fully welded all the way around for strength.

**Paint is important! Rust Resistant -** The entire door is sandblasted prior to being electrostatically sprayed with the finest "Alkyd Resin" paint, containing rust and salt spray inhibitors.

**Double Dead Bolt Lock -** Installed at the factory as standard equipment. The 1" throw of the bolt locks into the jamb while a "Vault Locking Pin" locks into the hinge side jamb.

**Adjustable Bottom Expander -** Allows height adjustments for uneven threshold and provides a tight weather seal at bottom of door.

**Plush Felt Weatherstripping -** Fitted in a metal frame on the top and bottom of door.

**Vault Type Lock Pin -** secures door into jamb on hinge side.

**Heavy Duty Pneumatic Closer**

**15% Savings**
Qualifies for IRS tax saving.

**100% Prehung -** For easy installation, the hinges and the weatherstripped metal frame are attached, ready to set into the opening.

**Custom Sizes -** All doors are available through special order in widths between 30 - 42" and heights between 75 - 90".

**Tempered Glass -** Top and bottom glass panels are tempered for strength and safety. Framed in a vinyl weather seal and fitted to the door with thumb clips for easy removal for cleaning.

**Screen Panel -** One screen panel is on all doors. Interchangeable with either the top or bottom glass panel, great for temperate times of the year.

Fig. 3-144. The many features of a well-constructed steel security door (courtesy Allen Manufacturing Co.).

Fig. 3-145. Four of the popular designs available in security doors (A) Century '81.

Fig. 3-145. (B) Bird of Paradise.

Fig. 3-145. (C) Villa.

Fig. 3-145. (D) Bastille (I) (courtesy Allen Manufacturing Co.).

adjustable bottom expander to allow for height adjustments for uneven threshold. This also provides a tight weather seal at the bottom of the door.

Figure 3-144 illustrates a security door and pertinent features. When selecting a security door, consider your decor and choose a design that will complement your home. Figures 3-145A through 3-145D show some security door decor designs.

## SECURITY GATE

A patio security gate should be made of quality steel. A security guard plate (Fig. 3-146), a double cylinder, tapered collar, and a deadbolt lock should be on each gate.

## BURGLAR BARS

Some burglars bars consist of thin hollow sliding bars that do not provide true security. Consider custom-built burglar bars specifically designed for your home windows. The price of such bars may be prohibitive, but there is an alternative.

Standard burglar bars are made of steel and adjustable for width (Fig. 3-147). Stationary bur-

glar bars should only be installed over windows that are not used for emergency exiting. Stationary burglar bars have adjustable side mounting brackets to allow a 3″ offset from the window casement. This allows the burglar bar to be installed over most window styles.

Adjustable burglar bars are constructed of ½″ tubular steel vertical pickets. The pickets are welded onto the steel bars at the top and bottom. There is stability is quality burglar bar units when the pickets overlap the top and bottom cross bars by at least 3″ and are tiered by 1″ increments.

Burglar bar units located over bedroom windows should be equipped with an emergency escape kit. These kits may be obtained from distributors of security equipment that deal in burglar bars. Such kits are designed to adjust in height to fit up to 64″ high burglar bars, but they can be reduced to fit a minimum height of 24″. Essentially, one side of the burglar bar unit is hinged, while the other side has an interior key-operated lock that can be opened in an emergency.

### Window Security Screen

Window locks are fine, but in some cases you may want a window security device that ties into your general alarm system. Also, you may want the window to be in a partially or fully open position and still have an alarm mechanism. The alarm screen in Fig. 3-148 is appropriate. The screen looks like any other quality fiberglass screen you can purchase for your window.

Plug in your security system, and the screen activates an alarm if it is tampered with. Even from the inside with the system on, you can open and close a screened window as you please. The Imperial alarm screens are very effective in scaring off burglars before they can even break a window or enter through an open one.

No complicated electronic equipment or devices need to be hooked up. Small wires are woven vertically through the screen at 4″ intervals. Once connected, these wires form a protective barrier. If the screen is cut or removed, the

Fig. 3-146. Any patio security gate *must* have the security guard plate, a double-locking cylinder, taper collar, and a deadbolt (courtesy Allen Manufacturing Co.).

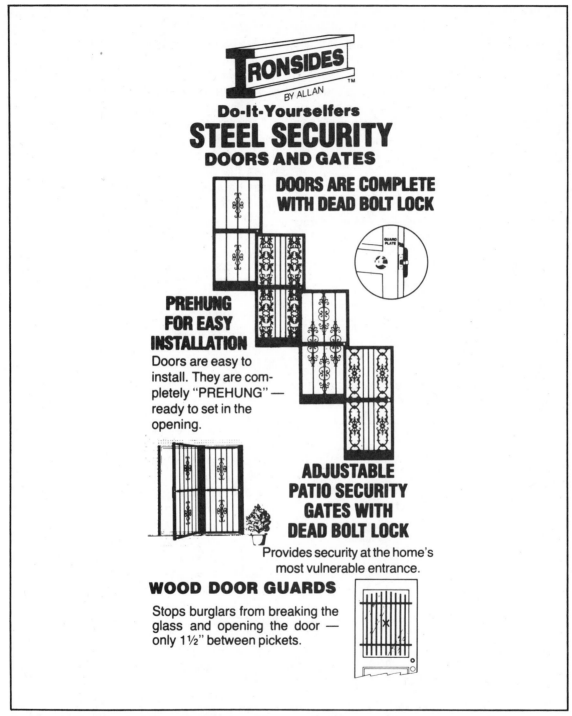

**IRONSIDES**™
BY ALLAN

**Do-It-Yourselfers**
# STEEL SECURITY
## DOORS AND GATES

### DOORS ARE COMPLETE WITH DEAD BOLT LOCK

### PREHUNG FOR EASY INSTALLATION

Doors are easy to install. They are completely "PREHUNG" — ready to set in the opening.

### ADJUSTABLE PATIO SECURITY GATES WITH DEAD BOLT LOCK

Provides security at the home's most vulnerable entrance.

### WOOD DOOR GUARDS

Stops burglars from breaking the glass and opening the door — only 1½" between pickets.

Fig. 3-147. Window with the Trombone Burglar Bars installed. The adjustable width allows the bars to cover the full width of the glass area (courtesy Allen Manufacturing Co.).

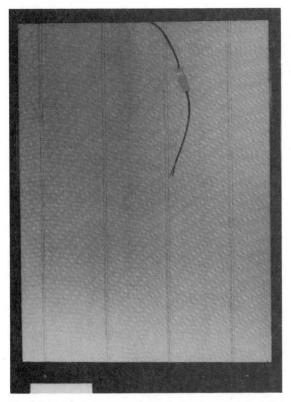

Fig. 3-148. An alarm screen for a window (courtesy Imperial Screen).

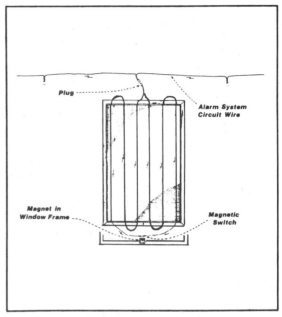

Fig. 3-149. It's easy to hook up the alarm screen to your alarm system (courtesy Imperial Screen).

alarm goes off. The burglar can be stopped before the home is entered. The Imperial alarm screen can be added to any alarm system already used in your home.

Figure 3-149 illustrates the alarm screen and the simplicity of hooking it up to your current home alarm system. At the top, wires are soldered to a plug. At the bottom, outside wires connect to a switch. All the wiring is sealed under the spline. A magnet in the window frame aligns with a magnetic switch in the screen, and the plug at the top of the screen hooks into your alarm system circuit wiring.

# Chapter 4

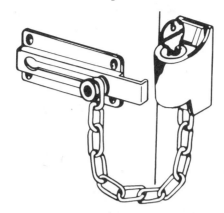

# Apartment, Condominium, and High-Rise Security

The chances for burglary and theft in small apartment buildings, condominiums, and high rises are just as great as for houses. It is easier for a burglar to operate in these places because there are more residences closer together. This makes for a shorter time element and more places to hide or escape to for a burglar in case he is spotted.

Most dwellers are working people. Hardly anybody is home except for maintenance and apartment staff personnel during daylight hours. A burglar can work in greater freedom and with a lesser fear of being caught. Most people have a passing acquaintance with their neighbors, but are not really "friends" with them. More than likely, a resident probably won't know more than 5-10 percent of the other residents. A resident may have more than a passing conversation with only one or two people. If the complex or building is relatively small, 50 percent or more of the residents may know and talk to the other residents.

When the complex is large, sometimes encompassing 5, 10, or even 20 buildings, there may be 200 to 1000 people or more. Eighty percent or more of these people may be strangers.

The daytime burglar may wear a business suit or look like a construction worker or a maintenance person from your complex. The burglar looks like everyone else and is going about his daily routine—crime.

## POTENTIAL FOR CRIME

Each building and individual living area has potential for a burglar or thief. Older buildings may have doors that sag or are made of poor quality wood. A hollow core door, even recent, is just as bad as a door that has been hanging on the same frame for the last 30 years. Some older buildings have doors that swing *out* into the hallway or stairwell area. The hinges are old, and they also have removable hinge pins.

Have the locks been changed since the last tenant moved out? Were all the keys turned in? If you have lived there for several years, have you considered having a new lock installed?

Do you have a night latch or lock (a secondary one) on the door? What about a peephole to view visitors to your residence?

Your windows are a prime target for entry, especially if they are on the ground or second floor. Numerous bushes and trees abound on the grounds of many complexes. A burglar may hide behind bushes while waiting to break in through a first floor window. Branches on tall trees may protrude over close enough to a second floor window to allow someone to climb up and enter an unlocked window.

Separate storage areas within an apartment complex are usually located in the basement. A storage area usually has a separate entrance—sometimes two.

A small storage compartment is probably made of wood and chicken wire. You probably purchased a simple, relatively cheap hasp device to lock it. Most storage areas contain plenty of valuable merchandise in them such as winter tires, collections of old records or books, furniture, television, trunks and suitcases, and gifts you have been hiding for other family members. Bicycles are probably stored in the halls outside the locker, if they aren't kept within the apartment/condo or are chained to the stairwell outside the main door. A simple storage area may contain several hundred dollars of merchandise that is worth something to somebody else.

## DOORS AND WINDOWS

To a great extent, the protection required here is the same as that discussed in Chapter 2. There are a few new items, though, that are valuable and of interest.

Let's look at three examples of possible living arrangements. These are shown in Figs. 4-1 through 4-3.

Each has sliding doors going to the outside. One has a garage. The sliding doors and the garage door will be the weakest points. These areas will have the lightest security present. In

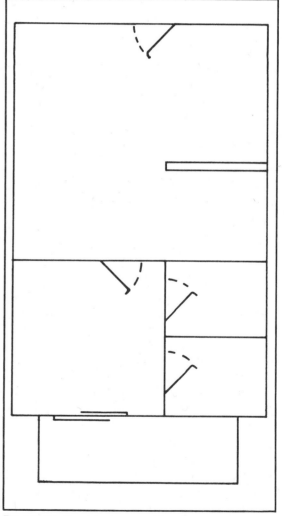

Fig. 4-2. Small one-bedroom apartment.

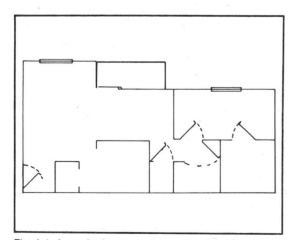

Fig. 4-1. A one-bedroom apartment turned condo.

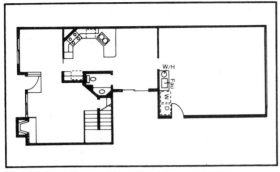

Fig. 4-3. First floor condo with a two-car garage.

addition, the sliding door provides for a greater view of the residence's interior.

The second most critical points will be the entrance doors to the residence. What types of locks are present? How secure are they and how old are the locks?

If the locks are key-in-the-knob type, hope-fully they are of high quality and have a deadlock feature on the door. If the building is a decade or older, the lock has limited qualities. The lock should be changed. You may have to check with the management when selecting a new lock, and may require that one of their locks be put on the door. Management may also say that because your residence hasn't been broken into, there is no reason to change the lock. Don't take no for an answer. Management has an obligation to pro-tect the residents, and one major step in this process is to ensure that the doors and the locks are of high quality and in good working condition. The door itself must not be cheaply made. It should be solid. A hollow core door is not worth much more than cardboard in terms of security. A 12-year-old can kick in a hollow core door in just a few minutes.

Figure 4-4 shows various doors that are ac-

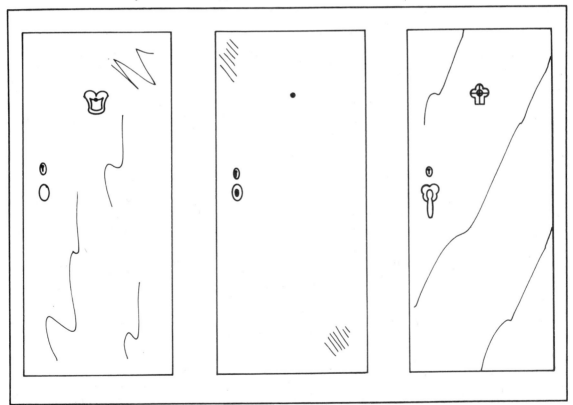

Fig. 4-4. Solid wood, stud-plated hollow core, or a steel door are recommended. Notice that all doors have some type of viewer installed.

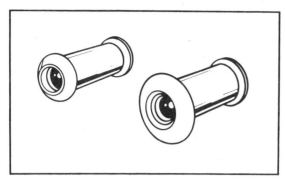

Fig. 4-5. All multifamily complexes, like individual houses, should have a door viewer. A 180° viewing range is optimum, but the 160° viewer is the standard (courtesy Ideal Security Hardware).

ceptable for apartments, condominiums, and other high rises. Besides an excellent lock, you should have a door viewer (Fig. 4-5) installed and a chain door lock (Fig. 4-6). A secondary lock should be a deadbolt with at least a 1″ throw or else a vertical deadbolt (Fig. 4-7).

Unless you live in an extremely old apartment or a renovated older building, you probably will have fairly good walls surrounding the door frame. The old wooden frames are out in many buildings and metal frames are the standard.

Figure 4-8 shows windows found in apartments and condominiums. You may need different types of locking devices—not fastening devices.

The only value of fasteners is ensuring that a window does not rattle and keeps out drafts. Fasteners do not provide security. Figure 4-9

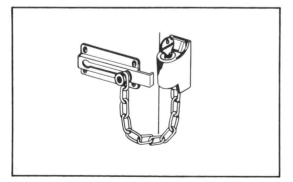

Fig. 4-6. Don't get just a door chain. Proper door security is a door chain with a lock (courtesy Ideal Security Hardware).

shows a simple fastener and a window lock. The lock should be on the window. Figure 4-10 illustrates several window locks that you may consider installing.

Some people consider sliding doors as extremely large picture windows. They are a prime point of entry into the home. The sliding door in Fig. 4-1 is slightly protected from winds by two walls on opposite sides of the door. The door in Fig. 4-2 has no protecting barriers. The wall can provide a hiding place for a burglar.

The sliding door is extremely easy to get through. The door often can be lifted out of its frame by the burglar so he can enter. The burglar

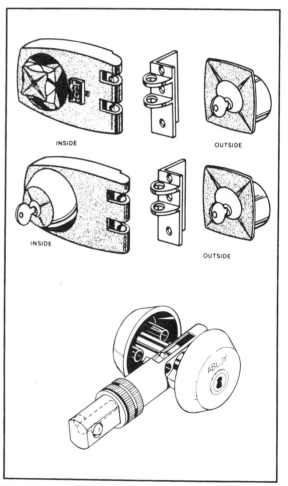

Fig. 4-7. Secondary locks (courtesy Abloy Security Locks and Ideal Security Hardware).

174

Fig. 4-8. Four window types found in apartments and condominiums. (A) A casement window. (B) Note the locking devices. (C) A double-hung window. (D) This window has two latches (courtesy Truth, Inc.).

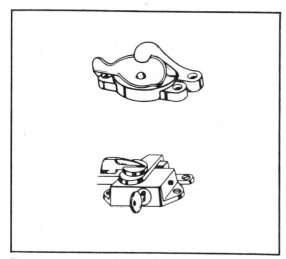

Fig. 4-9. A simple window closure (top) should be replaced with a window lock (bottom) (courtesy Ideal Security Hardware).

replaces the sliding door and leaves by the front door.

Ensure that the sliding glass door cannot be lifted out of its tracks. Insert screws into the upper track frame. The screws shouldn't be more than ¼ " from the top of the door (Fig. 4-11). The sliding door must be lifted at least ½ " so it can be removed from the door track. Add another lock to the door (Fig. 3-42).

The garage door (Fig. 4-12) is a prime point of entry. Some condominium dwellers may not have an attached garage. Most garage doors have a simple keyed locking lever in the center of the door.

When you are home or away, keep the door locked. Add a second lock. Figure 4-13 shows how to use a standard padlock to provide increased security.

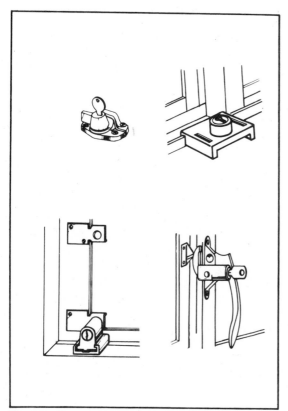

Fig. 4-10. The type of window, its location, and how it might be used may dictate what type of locking device you should use (courtesy Ideal Security Hardware).

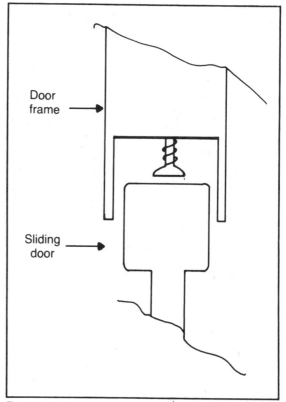

Door frame

Sliding door

Fig. 4-11. A screw into the top of the track can eliminate the possibility of a sliding glass door being lifted out of the frame.

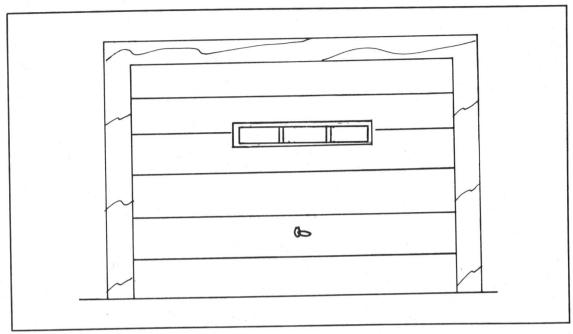

Fig. 4-12. A garage door.

If your garage has a base line point of metal where the door meets when closed, put a hasp at this point. Secure it from the interior with a padlock.

## TIPS FOR APARTMENT AND CONDOMINIUM RESIDENTS

Unless you have a controlled access system at the main door of your apartment and the other doors can only be opened from the inside, but require a key from the outside, you already have fundamental perimeter protection. The outer perimeter in this case is the building itself. If you can delay or, preferably, deter a person from unauthorized entry, you have stopped crime in your building.

Many apartments and condos do not have a doorman; nor do they have a lock on the main door. If there are any locks, they will be found on side doors and doors to storage and work areas. These are more than convenience locks for the management. They are there to protect and secure the building operator's working materials and equipment. These locks may be superior to the one on your front door. In some cases, management may have two locks or even three on their rooms. You may have one or two on your door. Management is concerned about the protection of their property; the protection of your property is secondary.

In some cities, codes and regulations state that you must have a competent deadbolt or a vertical deadbolt lock on your door. Management is obligated to install them.

Locks and alarms are only part of your personal and security protection. Here are some other guidelines:

☐ Never leave notes on your door; they advertise that you are not at home.
☐ Urge your friends and neighbors never to leave any notes on their doors or yours.
☐ Keep all ground floor windows locked when not at home.
☐ Secure first and second floor patio doors and balcony doors with a commercial bar (Charlie Bar) or metal pass-through track and frame.

177

☐ Use a secondary lock on patio and balcony doors.

☐ Do not hide door keys under a doormat, in your mailbox, on the patio, or in patio flower/plant tubs.

☐ If you go out at night, leave one or more interior lights on. Have a radio playing and the blinds/drapes closed. Use a timer device for lights and the radio.

☐ If you have an air conditioner installed, and you expect to be gone quite a while, don't turn it off in hot weather.

☐ Don't leave your television on. It may burn out and start a fire.

☐ If you will be away overnight, have a neighbor pick up your mail and paper.

☐ Report suspicious strangers to the police and/or the building management, particularly those who loiter in laundry rooms, near basement storage areas, and near children's play areas and garages.

☐ Use only your initials on your mailbox and apartment door.

☐ When parking, keep your car keys handy, but your apartment keys should be tucked away in your pocket—not your purse or handbag.

☐ Don't wait until you get to your door to remove the key from your pocket, purse, or handbag.

Apartment dwellers are transient people, especially in larger cities. They must stay at an apartment for only one or two years before moving to another apartment or to a home. Especially with younger people moving into apartments, you should contact your local police department and join Operation Identification. Many people have not been able to identify their property as

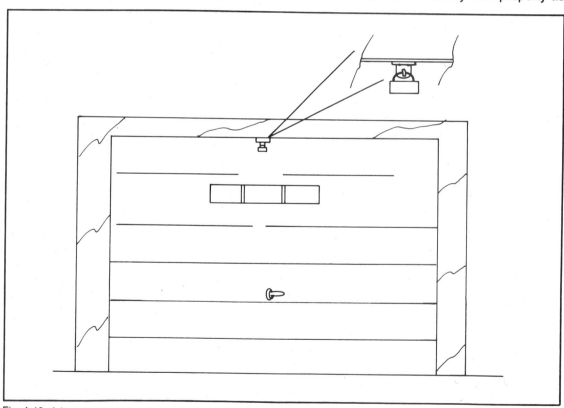

Fig. 4-13. A lock and hasp located at the top of the garage door secures it and are difficult for burglars to reach.

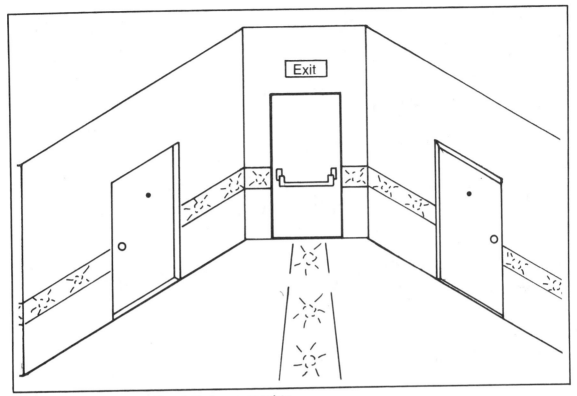

Fig. 4-14. In the dark, Escape Tape lights the way to safety.

stolen because they did not have identifying marks on it, and they didn't know the serial numbers of the property.

### ESCAPE TAPE

Suppose you are on the fifth or sixth floor of an apartment building, and there are 30-50 residents to a floor. In an emergency, can you find your way easily to an inner stairwell or even to the elevator and then determine your access route to the first floor and possible safety. How will children find a safe exit route?

*Escape Tape* is a reliable and inexpensive nontoxic, self-adhesive tape that can be applied to the hallway walls and/or floor (Fig. 4-14). The tape is about 1″ wide, and the light-emitting arrows take over when other emergency lighting systems cannot do the job. Escape Tape needs no other power source. The use of phosphor enhancement technology ensures the highest intensity of light emission. It is easily installed

and has a slightly raised surface to aid the sight-impaired. The tape can be seen and felt from a crawling or walking position. Escape Tape will reduce injury, aid in rescue, ease panic and confusion, and save lives. The glow-in-the-dark feature will last for more than 4 hours, which is adequate time for people to safely and calmly exit from the building.

Escape Tape could be used within the apartment. If you have to move to another room at night, you can do so without turning on the lights.

### APARTMENT ALARM CONTROL

Many apartments have a single room or two rooms. Even with apartments that have more rooms, there is still usually only one entranceway available—not counting the windows. A one-zone protection alarm control unit (Fig. 4-15) can provide 24-hour panic protection. This unit is

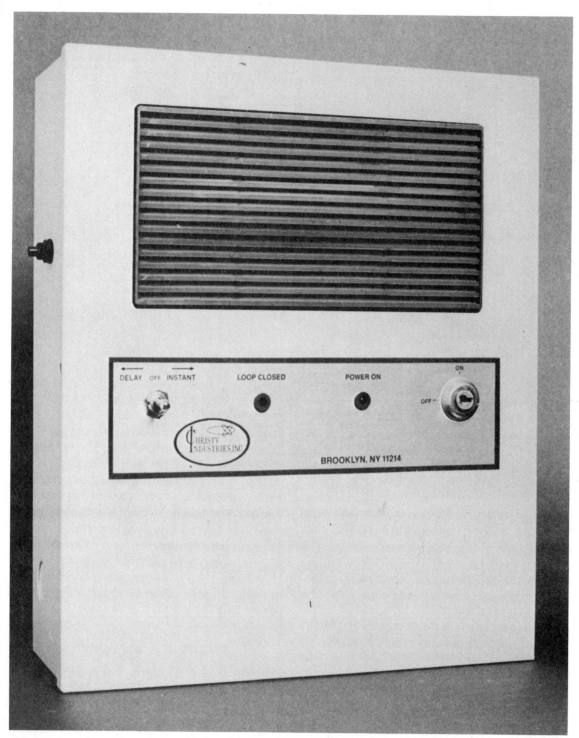

Fig. 4-15. A one-zone alarm system is ideal for many apartments (courtesy Christie Industries, Inc.).

Fig. 4-16. A digital coded control system uses radio transmitter sensors to provide reliable and efficient alarm security protection (courtesy Interstate Engineering Co.).

key-controlled and provides entrance door security.

A built-in open circuit gives entrance door delay prior to the alarm sounding, so you have time to switch off the unit before the electronic siren is activated. Note that the electronic siren has an adjustable pitch. This adjustable pitch will be more easily heard should the siren activate.

The LED indication of zone status lets you know that the ac power is properly on and the unit is operating. The unit also has a built-in 12-volt power supply, with the transformer included. This gives a constant 12-volt dc output and dry contacts. The built-in charging circuit will keep your battery ready so that should the ac power be off for any reason, the alarm control unit will remain operational.

### Crime Watch Units

*Interstate Engineering Company (IEC)* has developed several excellent home security and fire systems.

The IEC *Crime Watch* control consoles (Fig. 4-16) are digital coded control units that work with radio transmitters. They are hooked to various intrusion and space protection sensors.

Crime Watch is the leader in rf security

equipment. Crime Watch controls come in wooden desk top models or attractive metal cabinets for closet- or wall-mount installations. Space is provided inside the control for a separate battery and digital communicator. Both have the same security and *high quality*.

All Crime Watch controls have a filtered and regulated power supply that will recharge a sealed lead acid battery. A built-in siren driver will drive up to 40-watt speakers. Standard features are:

☐ Adjustable automatic cutoff and reset.
☐ Adjustable entry/exit delay.
☐ Plug-in connectors for digital communicator and receiver.

Each control has a 24-hour monitoring device that will sound when a protected door or window is opened.

The *Eight Channel Control* can be armed with a remote digital wireless key pad. The hand-held/portable two-button transmitter provides remote operation of floodlight and personal protection. The Eight Channel Control features are:

☐ Channel 1—instant.

- [ ] Channel 2—delay.
- [ ] Channel 3—24-hour panic.
- [ ] Channel 4—24-hour fire.
- [ ] Channel 5—remote arm/disarm.
- [ ] Channel 6—remote lights on and off.
- [ ] Channel 7—automatic interior trap arm/disarm.
- [ ] Channel 8—optional panic or zone.

The control has four LEDs. The power light will illuminate when ac power is connected to control. If the control is activated, the system will alarm for approximately 10 minutes, then cut off and reset. The violation light will remain on as a visual indicator until the control is reset manually.

When the system is in the home position, all protected windows and doors, if violated, will instantly activate the alarm. Channel seven will automatically disarm when the system is in the home position.

When the system is in the away position, the door selected for delay will allow you time to exit or enter when the system is armed. The channel will automatically arm in the away position.

Figure 4-17 shows the Crime Watch Princess model. It is not expensive. Features include:

- [ ] Instant or delayed alarm response.
- [ ] Panic button.
- [ ] LEDs for power-violation-away-home settings.
- [ ] Touch only one button to alarm in the home or away settings.
- [ ] Four-number customer code to disarm—360 possible codes.
- [ ] Tamper Pruf button for additional security.
- [ ] Piezo tone on each button assures contact.
- [ ] Drives up to four 40-watt speakers.

Fig. 4-17. The Princess system is another excellent selection when considering residential security (courtesy Interstate Engineering Co.).

Fig. 4-18. Various sensors can be used to enhance security. (A) Photoelectric smoke detector. (B) Ionization smoke detector. (C) Passive infrared detector. (D) Two-button transmitter. (E) Open circuit door/window transmitter (courtesy Interstate Engineering Co.).

☐ Twenty-four hour monitoring of all protected openings.
☐ Lights will illuminate during activation and delay cycle for entry and exit.
☐ Terminals for communicators or dialers.
☐ Simple installation and operating instructions for the do-it-yourselfer.

The Princess is designed specifically for residences.

Figure 4-18 shows the various transmitters available for Crime Watch units. All rf transmitters have simple digital coding schemes using digital switches. Each transmitter can be easily coded to a channel of your choice by changing the switch setting.

Figure 4-18A is a photoelectric smoke detector with built-in transmitter. This unit features delay. The detector will not falsely transmit in a low-battery warning condition.

Figure 4-18B is an ionization smoke detector with a built-in transmitter. This unit features a built-in delay. The detector will not falsely transmit in a low-battery warning condition.

The low-battery warning condition is important. When the battery becomes low, an audible signal tells you to change the battery. The design ensures that you will not get false alarms by having the low-battery warning condition accidentally transmit an alarm signal to the Crime Watch console.

Figure 4-18C is a passive infrared detector. The detector features a transmitter in the same housing. It protects an area 35′ by 25′ and will transmit a signal to the master control when violated.

Figure 4-18D is a hand-held/portable two-button transmitter. This transmitter can be programmed for many uses. The left button can be used for remote arm or floodlights on/off. The right button can be used for panic or silent alarm.

Figure 4-18E is the open circuit door/window transmitter. Digital settings and terminals are housed inside the case to neatly conceal and connect wires directly from contacts. The LEDs let you know the transmitter is transmitting a signal.

The closed circuit door/window transmitter and delay transmitter also are available. The delay transmitter has a 10-second exit/entry time.

### Entraguard

The *Entraguard* (Fig. 4-19) has been designed to protect people and property in condominiums, apartment houses, closed community complexes, and residential trailer parks where visitor control is a must. Because Entraguard's advanced system employs exclusive microprocessor circuitry and is designed to be tamperproof, repairs and maintenance are virtually eliminated. The Entraguard is the recommended entry control system in many HUD (Department of Housing and Urban Development) projects. If your apartment building or complex does not have an Entraguard or similar unit for entry control, contact your building management.

The Entraguard concept has two parts: *intercommunication* and *keyboard entry*. These work to provide you with excellent protection against unwanted visitors. The unit is designed to be the most practical solution of intercommunication in existing buildings. It uses the regular telephone lines in an apartment house, con-

dominium, or other building or closed community. It provides the occupants with intercommunication and convenience to operate the security entryways. Costly wiring from the lobby or entryway to each occupant is completely unnecessary. With the elimination of wire, conduit, and in-wall intercom panels, plus the labor required to install this material, the unit is a most economical choice.

Instead of costly magnetic cards or keys, a heavy-duty keyboard allows entry to restricted areas through a door, gate, or elevator. On-site programming allows owners to invalidate a code instantly on a tenant's moving from the premises or a change of employee status.

For small or medium-sized buildings, the series 54 Entraguard is recommended (Fig. 4-20). This is the lowest-priced entry security system and is cost-competitive with most others.

Fig. 4-19. Exterior systems, such as the Entraguard, allow you to check out a visitor before entrance is allowed into the building. The Department of Housing and Urban Development (HUD) has recommended this system for many multifamily complexes (courtesy Marlee Electronics Corp.).

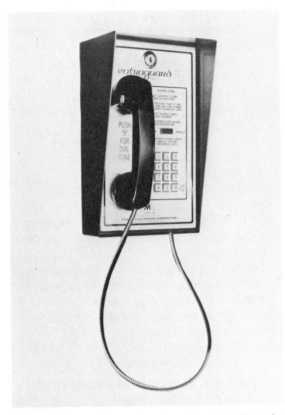

Fig. 4-20. For smaller apartments and condominiums, the series 54 Entraguard will meet all your needs (courtesy Marlee Electronics Corp.).

Designed into a most compact cabinet, the model has 100 memories for tenant telephone numbers. There are 10 Entrakey codes for maintenance personnel, the newsboy, or management to use.

For buildings with 10 occupants or less, the model 4C is perfect. Each person has a confidential Entrakey number for family members or close friends to use.

Features of the Entraguard models are:

☐ Durable stainless steel front panels.
☐ Armored handset cables held in place with a steel restraint.
☐ Unit operates on 12 volts for safe, economical operation.
☐ Registered with the FCC (Federal Com-

munications Commission) for direct connection to the telephone network.
☐ Door or gate release relay is actuated by the tenant's rotary or Touch-Tone telephone.
☐ Front panel push-button programming.
☐ Limited speaking time.
☐ Audible background "beeps" to advise tenant that the call is from the lobby.
☐ Audible tone warning of the call termination.
☐ Standby battery for operation during a power outage.
☐ Volume controls.
☐ Protective fuses.
☐ A visual "enter" indicator.
☐ Provisions for a postal lock connection.
☐ Off-premises calling capability.

The FCC Entraguard system consists of a telephone handset, keyboard, and programming computer in one sturdy case (in most Entraguard models).

A visitor to the building selects from a directory the code assigned to the occupant. He then removes the handset and dials this code. The Entraguard will transmit these digits into the oc-

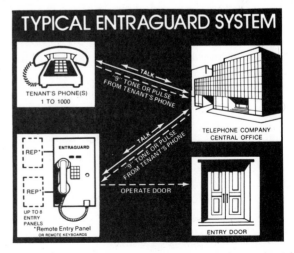

Fig. 4-21. The Entraguard system can meet the needs of residents in complexes of all sizes (courtesy Marlee Electronics Corp.).

cupant's telephone number and dial it automatically. The normal two-way telephone conversation can now occur between the visitor and the occupant. The visitor is identified. If the occupant wishes to allow entry, he dials or touches "9." This signal is transmitted through the Entraguard to the entry lock, allowing entrance to the visitor. Figure 4-21 visually illustrates the typical Entraguard system.

The Entraguard series 5610 is a deluxe single-entry system. It can come with a handset or as a hands-free unit (Fig. 4-22). A hands-free unit prevents potential handset vandalism. The hands-free models have concealed and protected built-in speakers and microphones in place of the handset.

Other advantages of the 5610 include the following (* indicates vandal-resistant features):

☐ Exclusive metal keyboard buttons for added durability.*

☐ Rugged stainless steel front panel.*

☐ A provision for a mail carrier's postal lock.

☐ Heavy-duty armored cable on the handset with a stainless steel restraint lock for handset models.

☐ Background "beeps" tell the occupant that the call has originated from the Entraguard. A steady tone warns that the system will hang up after 75 seconds.

☐ Immediate relocking of the door on entry of an authorized visitor.

☐ Entrakey allows occupants to enter the building by unlocking the door electronically through the use of a private, individual number combination using only four digits plus a symbol.*

☐ A "three strikes, you're out" local or remote alarm prevents abuse of the Entrakey feature.

☐ Specialized Entrakeys for workmen, which are valid only during certain times of the day. A time clock such as the Intermatic T101B or equal is needed.)

☐ Various models are capable of handling

up to 1000 occupants.

☐ A choice of three or four-digit occupant codes allows for high-rise suite/apartment numbers on a directory.

☐ Off-premises calling to the police, fire department, property manager, etc., allows for owner's convenience and emergency service.

☐ Works with any kind of telephone line. It accepts both rotary and Touch-Tone occupant telephones.

☐ Recessed Lexan illuminated signs.*

If the building has more than one entrance, a series 5610 unit can be used that allows for multiple entry points.

Apartment complexes, individual apartment buildings, and condominiums require modular flexibility in a system that meets the needs of effective door communication and lock control to keep out unwanted visitors.

## NuTone's System 4

The *System 4* from NuTone installs easily for even the most sophisticated requirements. This comprehensive system meets all the requirements for tenant safety.

Depending on the size of the building, the entrance directory should be tailored to meet the needs of the tenants. Figure 4-23 shows a directory that includes a telephone handset for contacting tenants of the building. A variation would be to have speaker panels and a postal lock door release tied in with the panel (Fig. 4-24). There is no telephone handset for vandals to destroy.

A compact directory (Fig. 4-24) is ideal for low-rise or garden apartments having from four to 20 units. This unit has a name directory for the tenants' names, which would have signal push buttons adjacent. A speaker is built in, so there is no telephone handset.

There should be a speaker within each apartment (Fig. 4-25). The tenant pushes a "talk" button to speak with a visitor at the door.

A separate single switch can control the door locks. An entry door release switch is acti-

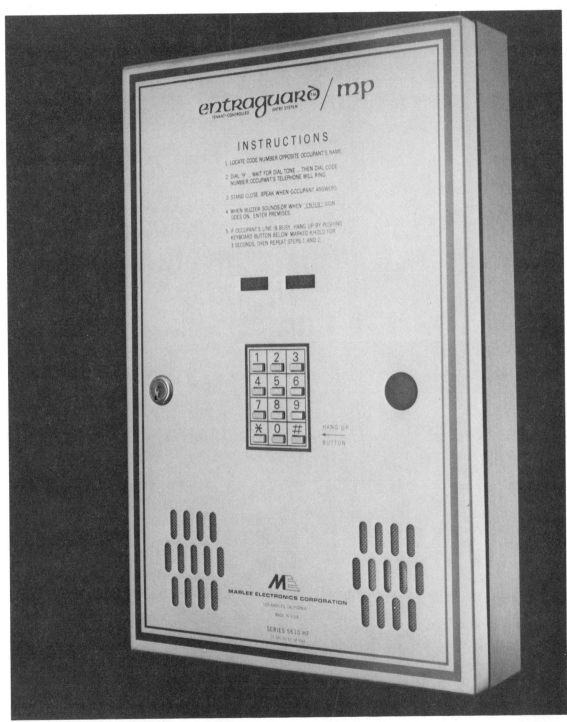

Fig. 4-22. To prevent vandalism, units are available that use built-in speakers instead of telephone handsets (courtesy Marlee Electronics Corp.).

Fig. 4-23. Wall-mounted unit for small or medium-sized buildings (courtesy NuTone).

Fig. 4-24. To the lower left of the speaker panel is the postal lock door release box. This size directory is very appropriate (courtesy NuTone).

Fig. 4-25. Each apartment has a speaker so the tenant can talk with visitors at the main door (courtesy NuTone).

vated, allowing the tenant to let the visitor enter the building.

Because postal boxes are located within the building, a postal lock door release (Fig. 4-26) should be mounted outside the building entranceway. It contains a door release button behind the lock (which is a U.S. Postal Service master lock supplied by that agency). The postman opens the door with his master lock key and depresses the button to activate the door release. If there is no door release in the building, the unit can be used to store a door key for the postman's use.

Figure 4-42 shows a representative wiring diagram for a one- or two-entry system with momentary or timed door release provisions for apartment tenants. For low-rise garden apartments and townhouses, a low-cost main entry system with door answering and lock control

Fig. 4-26. The postman has his own entry control access when entrance is required (courtesy NuTone).

190

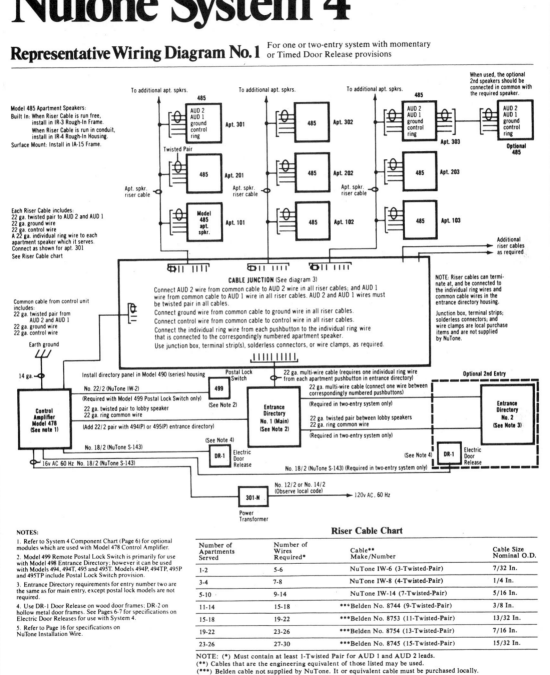

# NuTone System 4

## Representative Wiring Diagram No. 1
For one or two-entry system with momentary or Timed Door Release provisions

When used, the optional 2nd speakers should be connected in common with the required speaker.

**Model 485 Apartment Speakers:**
Built In: When Riser Cable is run free, install in IR-3 Rough-In Frame.
When Riser Cable is run in conduit, install in IR-4 Rough-In Housing.
Surface Mount: Install in IA-15 Frame.

To additional apt. spkrs.

**485**
AUD 2
AUD 1
ground
control
ring
Apt. 301

Twisted Pair

**485** Apt. 201

Apt. spkr. riser cable

**Each Riser Cable includes:**
22 ga. twisted pair to AUD 2 and AUD 1
22 ga. ground wire
22 ga. control wire
A 22 ga. individual ring wire to each apartment speaker which it serves.
Connect as shown for apt. 301
See Riser Cable chart

**Model 485 apt. spkr.** Apt. 101

To additional apt. spkrs.

**485** Apt. 302

**485** Apt. 202

Apt. spkr. riser cable

**485** Apt. 102

To additional apt. spkrs.

**485**
AUD 2
AUD 1
ground
control
ring
Apt. 303

**485** Apt. 203

Apt. spkr. riser cable

**485** Apt. 103

AUD 2
AUD 1
ground
control
ring
**Optional 485**

Additional riser cables as required

**CABLE JUNCTION** (See diagram 3)
Connect AUD 2 wire from common cable to AUD 2 wire in all riser cables; and AUD 1 wire from common cable to AUD 1 wire in all riser cables. AUD 2 and AUD 1 wires must be twisted pair in all cables.
Connect ground wire from common cable to ground wire in all riser cables.
Connect control wire from common cable to control wire in all riser cables.
Connect the individual ring wire from each pushbutton to the individual ring wire that is connected to the correspondingly numbered apartment speaker.
Use junction box, terminal strip(s), solderless connectors, or wire clamps, as required.

NOTE: Riser cables can terminate at, and be connected to the individual ring wires and common cable wires in the entrance directory housing.

Junction box, terminal strips; solderless connectors; and wire clamps are local purchase items and are not supplied by NuTone.

**Common cable from control unit includes:**
22 ga. twisted pair from AUD 2 and AUD 1
22 ga. ground wire
22 ga. control wire

Earth ground

14 ga.

**Control Amplifier Model 478 (See note 1)**

Install directory panel in Model 490 (series) housing

Postal Lock Switch

**499**
(See Note 2)

No. 22/2 (NuTone IW-2)
(Required with Model 499 Postal Lock Switch only)

22 ga. twisted pair to lobby speaker
22 ga. ring common wire
(Add 22/2 pair with 494(P) or 495(P) entrance directory)

No. 18/2 (NuTone S-143)
(See Note 4)

**Entrance Directory No. 1 (Main) (See Note 2)**

22 ga. multi-wire cable (requires one individual ring wire from each apartment pushbutton in entrance directory)

22 ga. multi-wire cable (connect one wire between correspondingly numbered pushbuttons)
(Required in two-entry system only)

22 ga. twisted pair between lobby speakers
22 ga. ring common wire
(Required in two-entry system only)

**Optional 2nd Entry**

**Entrance Directory No. 2 (See Note 3)**

**DR-1** Electric Door Release

(See Note 4) **DR-1** Electric Door Release

16v AC 60 Hz No. 18/2 (NuTone S-143)

No. 18/2 (NuTone S-143) (Required in two-entry system only)

**301-N**
Power Transformer

No. 12/2 or No. 14/2 (Observe local code)
→ 120v AC, 60 Hz

**NOTES:**
1. Refer to System 4 Component Chart (Page 6) for optional modules which are used with Model 478 Control Amplifier.
2. Model 499 Remote Postal Lock Switch is primarily for use with Model 498 Entrance Directory; however it can be used with Models 494, 494T, 495 and 495T. Models 494P, 494TP, 495P and 495TP include Postal Lock Switch provision.
3. Entrance Directory requirements for entry number two are the same as for main entry, except postal lock models are not required.
4. Use DR-1 Door Release on wood door frames; DR-2 on hollow metal door frames. See Pages 6-7 for specifications on Electric Door Releases for use with System 4.
5. Refer to Page 16 for specifications on NuTone Installation Wire.

### Riser Cable Chart

| Number of Apartments Served | Number of Wires Required* | Cable** Make/Number | Cable Size Nominal O.D. |
|---|---|---|---|
| 1-2 | 5-6 | NuTone IW-6 (3-Twisted-Pair) | 7/32 In. |
| 3-4 | 7-8 | NuTone IW-8 (4-Twisted-Pair) | 1/4 In. |
| 5-10 | 9-14 | NuTone IW-14 (7-Twisted-Pair) | 5/16 In. |
| 11-14 | 15-18 | ***Belden No. 8744 (9-Twisted-Pair) | 3/8 In. |
| 15-18 | 19-22 | ***Belden No. 8753 (11-Twisted-Pair) | 13/32 In. |
| 19-22 | 23-26 | ***Belden No. 8754 (13-Twisted-Pair) | 7/16 In. |
| 23-26 | 27-30 | ***Belden No. 8745 (15-Twisted-Pair) | 15/32 In. |

NOTE: (*) Must contain at least 1-Twisted Pair for AUD 1 and AUD 2 leads.
(**) Cables that are the engineering equivalent of those listed may be used.
(***) Belden cable not supplied by NuTone. It or equivalent cable must be purchased locally.
USE COLOR CODED CABLE.

Fig. 4-27. A representative system for an apartment or condominium complex (courtesy NuTone).

capabilities that can be used with or without an entrance directory is ideal.

Main door speakers used to provide communication between the door and individual tenants are shown in Fig. 4-28. At the apartments, a wall speaker (Fig. 4-29) allows a tenant to speak with a person at the door and, if desired, to remotely unlock the door and let the visitor into the building.

### Talk-A-Vision

*Talk-A-Vision* (Fig. 4-30) is a CCTV (closed-circuit television) unit that provides visual and verbal communication safely from within the home to a visitor at the door. The system consists of a small television screen monitor with a built-in handset in one unit, a lightweight camera that is easily installed outside and covers your door and doorstep, and the system power box.

Fig. 4-28. Two wall-mounted main door speaker types are available (courtesy NuTone).

Fig. 4-29. This speaker has listen-talk capability plus the ability to remotely open the door (courtesy NuTone).

Fig. 4-30. When observation of visitors is required, this system more than meets your needs (courtesy Koyo International, Inc. of America).

The system also includes a buzzer and door opener switch. You may not have to install the switch or use it.

The system power box operates off the standard household current. It should be centrally located for ease of access.

Different from other CCTV systems for home, the *Koyo* system has a quick-start function switch built in. When this function is turned on, the television screen monitor will operate while the video is being provided. When off, the monitor will operate only when a video signal and buzzer signal are provided simultaneously. The monitor should continue its operation while a video signal is being provided.

In addition to the apartment security systems in this chapter, consider the various units discussed in Chapter 2. Many systems are applicable to more than just a single family dwelling. Delete the various accessories that do not meet your needs and requirements so that the system fits your apartment or condo.

### PORTABLE DOOR LOCK

The *Lifelock*, a portable door lock, can be used in the apartment or condo. Figure 4-31A shows the unit being put into place. Figure 4-31B shows how easy it is to remove the lock.

One of the aluminum bars has a lip that hooks under the closed door. Prongs at the other end dig into carpeting on the floor, and along with the middle bar, from a strong angular brace. On tile or hardwood floors, a rubber cup footing re-

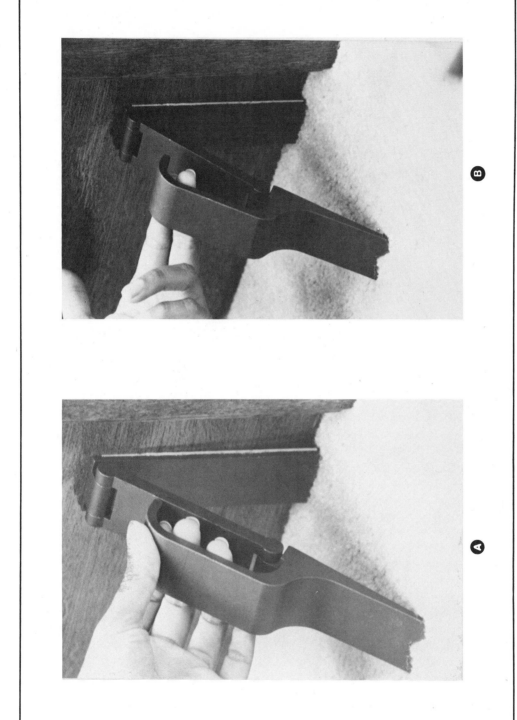

Fig. 4-31. (A) The Lifelock can be positioned in less than 15 seconds. (B) A simple pull removes the Lifelock (courtesy October Group Systems, Ltd.).

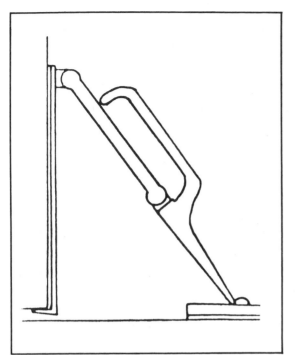

Fig. 4-32. The hardwood and tile floor adapter plate is placed under the lock prongs while the lock is adjusted to its optimum closing position. Hold the adapter plate securely and close the lock. Be sure the floor is smooth, clean, and dry (courtesy October Group Systems, Ltd.).

places the carpet-gripping prongs. To remove the Lifelock, a simple tug on the curved handle folds the hinges and releases the brace instantly. The lock is made of aluminum and weighs only 7 ounces.

The L-shaped end catch is inserted flush under the door's bottom edge. It is firmly placed against the door. There should be no gaps between the L-shaped catch and the bottom of the door.

With the handle approximately 2″ from closure, press the pronged end into the rug. Push the handle down until it snaps shut. If the lock feels loose, the pronged tip should be closer to the door. If the handle is difficult to close, the pronged tip should be further from the door. Test the lock's placement by pulling inward on the door handle; the door should be snugly secured. If not, repeat these steps.

Proper placement of the unit allows removal

with just a slight pull backward on the handle. When the lock springs back, remove it completely from under the door and its path.

Under no circumstances should this lock be used on a "throw rug" or other loosely secured rug. The lock should be used only on any standard inward swinging door. It will not work on two-way swinging doors or sliding doors, nor on doors with a space greater than ¾″ between door bottom and floor or doors with a decorative protruding metal lip along the bottom.

This lock can be used for hotel room doors and adjoining room doors. While at home, you can use it for the front door or on a back door that is not utilized often. Before you leave your home, it can be used for back or side doors where a thief may be more likely to attempt a break-in.

For hardwood and tile floors, an adapter plate comes with the unit. The adapter plate is placed under the lock prongs while the lock is adjusted to its optimum closing position. Hold the adapter plate securely and close the lock. Figure 4-32 illustrates the Lifelock with an adapter plate.

### PROTECTING VALUABLES

The *Safe-N-Sekure wall safe* (Fig. 4-33) safeguards your valuables against theft and provides fire protection. It has a deadbolt combination lock and a steel door to prevent tampering. A 6″ × 12″ opening permits easy loading and removal of valuables, such as cash, gold, silverware, small firearms, jewelry, credit cards, important papers, medication, and keys. This unit can be installed in various locations (Fig. 4-34).

Locate the wall studs in the area where you wish to mount the unit. Drill a hole to locate the exact stud positions, draw an outline of the box exterior and, cut the drywall panel out using a small handsaw. Fit the Safe-N-Sekure unit into position between the wall studs. Insert screws through the holes inside the unit into the wall studs.

You could mount the unit flush to the wall, such as inside a closet or cupboard. Drill holes through the back panel and then secure the unit with the screws provided.

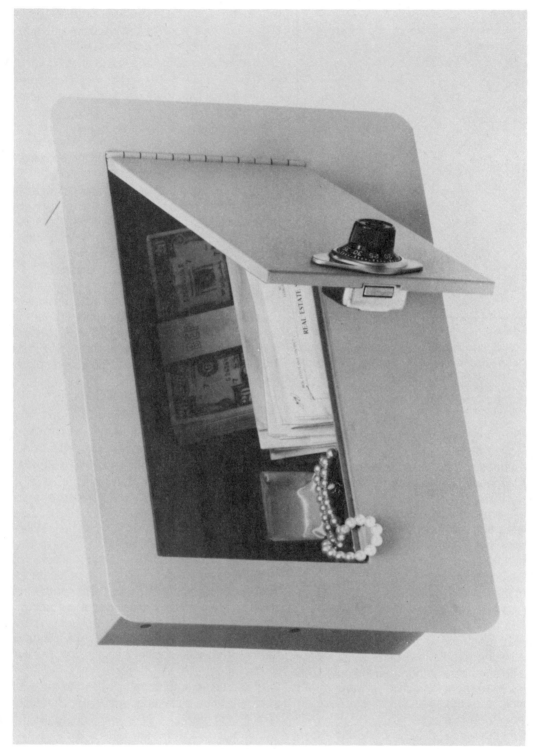

Fig. 4-33. Wall-mounted units protect valuables and are fire-resistant (courtesy Se-Kure Controls, Inc.).

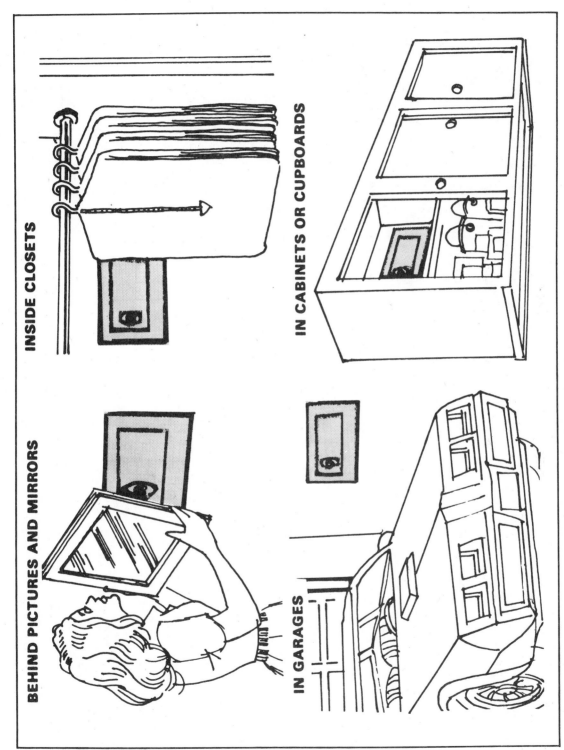

**INSIDE CLOSETS**

**IN CABINETS OR CUPBOARDS**

**BEHIND PICTURES AND MIRRORS**

**IN GARAGES**

Fig. 4-34. Numerous locations can be found in the home to place the wall safe (courtesy Se-Kure Controls, Inc.).

Fig. 4-35. Stop Loss wall unit uses a sliding door and the highly popular Ace circular key to protect valuables (courtesy Stop Loss Security Systems).

model 200 would be applicable. It can be mounted into the wall between the studs.

Always check with the management concerning installation of these units. Without permission, you could be evicted and even charged with damaging or destroying property. With permission, you would, have to replace/repair the wall when you move from the apartment.

This locking ski rack (Fig. 4-39) is a welded steel unit with nonremovable screws for mounting to studs. A solid steel bar can be slid into place and padlocked to keep your skis to yourself.

## GAS DETECTORS

By the time you can see, smell, or taste them,

Another security vault is from *Stop Loss Security Systems*. This cabinet (Fig. 4-35) mounts between wall studs. It has two shelves and a sliding door that is locked and unlocked by a circular key. The door slides down but not out of the unit. The sliding door cannot be pried away or bent out of shape. Figure 4-36 shows the unit with the door in the locked position.

The small gun cabinet (Fig. 4-37) can be mounted in an out-of-the-way place or even locked and put into your automobile for transport. It is rugged and uses the tubular key for added protection.

Gun cabinets come in several sizes and depths. The model 420 is heavy-duty and can hold six or more rifles in addition to other smaller items (Fig. 4-38).

For the home or apartment dweller, the

Fig. 4-36. Unit in the closed /locked position. Notice the door edge is not easily accessible to pry bars and other devices used to force entry (courtesy Stop Loss Security Systems).

Fig. 4-37. The gun cabinet can be mounted in the home or transported in your automobile (courtesy Stop Loss Security Systems).

most hazardous gases have already reached or exceeded those levels determined to be harmful to humans. Early detection and control of these gases is essential.

Certain detectors are combination models that also can detect smoke. Gas detectors can be used in the home, office, garage, and in areas where there may be a concentration of gases, such as carbon monoxide, natural gas (methane), propane, butane, and LP (liquid petroleum) gas.

The *Macurco* gas detectors (Fig. 4-40), can complement smoke detectors, which do not detect any gases and can't sound an alarm until a fire occurs. These detectors can provide protection from deadly carbon monoxide, which is pro-

duced by faulty furnaces or exhaust fumes from engines.

Any gas detector selected and used in the home must have a fail-safe design. The sensors and other critical functions must be supervised. Also, a detector must be immune to explosion. Any detector selected should require no maintenance or recalibration and should last for at least 10 years. The 481 models and the MRI remote

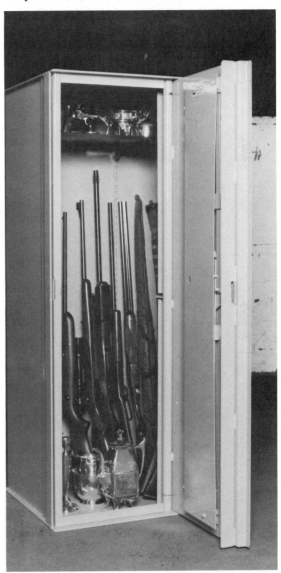

Fig. 4-38. The larger model can store weapons and other valuables (courtesy Stop Loss Security Systems).

alarm unit meet these safety requirements.

Operating off standard ac power at less than 10 watts, the detectors use electronic sensors and circuitry and can be plugged into any ac outlet. The detector's alarms can be triggered up to 500' away by a remote sensor. Unless you have a large estate, the units will more than meet your needs.

The detectors operate on an FM signal that is transmitted over the standard ac power line with the residence. The MRI detector, on sensing smoke or gas, sends an FM signal to the main unit, which activates an alarm sound level of 88 decibels. The detector has a buzzer silencing switch with an automatic restoration after a 2-minute delay. The main unit will also detect and activate the alarm.

If you have a detached garage perhaps 25' from the home; a detector here can sense danger and still alert the main unit. This is as long as the carrier signal is on the same power system from the main power transformer. You can be alerted to danger in a neighbor's home if both of you have the system, and you are on the same power system from the main power transformer.

Figure 4-41 lists gases that one or more Macurco units can detect. Specific calibrations

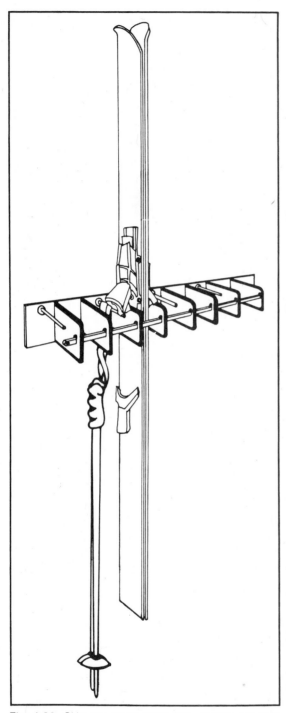

Fig. 4-39. Skis are costly items. The locking ski rack adequately protects your skis (courtesy Stop Loss Security Systems).

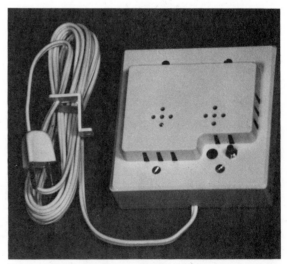

Fig. 4-40. Gas detectors should be in any residence where gas is used. A gas detector can save your life by warning you early about a leak (courtesy Macurco, Inc.).

| | |
|---|---|
| Butane | Alcohol |
| Propane | Ethanol |
| LP Gas | Carbon Monoxide |
| Methylene Chloride | Acrylonitrile |
| Lacquer Thinners | Benzene |
| Acetone | Methyl Acetate |
| Hexane | Ethane |
| Ethylene Oxide | Hydrogen |
| Methyl Chloride | Vinyl Chloride |
| Methanol | Ammonia |
| Dimethyl Amine | Gasoline Fumes |
| Methane | Pentane |
| Ethylene | Acetylene |
| Natural Gas | Methyl Ether |
| Sulfur Dioxide | Hydrogen Sulfide |
| Freon | Methyl Ethyl Keton |
| | Trichloroethylene |

Fig. 4-41. Gases that the Macurco detectors can detect (courtesy Macurco, Inc.).

for these gases would be determined by which model of the 481 series was used. If such a system is purchased, you should check with the factory representative in your area for specifics.

The OSHA (Occupational Safety and Health Administration) standards and most building codes require that carbon monoxide concentrations not exceed 50 parts per million (ppm) averaged over an 8-hour period. Peak levels are allowed up to 400 ppm during that 8-hour period.

The Uniform Building Code requires either an automatic controller or a continuous operation of exhaust fans in enclosed parking garages. For those who live in townhouses, apartments, and condominiums where there is a central garage area, this becomes a must. If you do not have a detection system capable of monitoring carbon monoxide detection, you may be in serious danger.

When automobiles or other machines containing internal combustion engines are operated in garages or enclosed structures, they rapidly fill the building with carbon monoxide (CO). An elextronic detection and fan control system that turns on an exhaust fan when the level of CO reaches 100 ppm and operates until at least the building is exhausted to a level of 50 ppm is a must. Figure 4-42 illustrates a typical location in an in-building or underground parking garage. Figure 4-43 shows a master control unit and remote sensor, each of which would contain a carbon monoxide sensor.

The master control unit works off standard ac electrical power. The remote sensor is connected to the master control unit via a low-voltage, three-conductor cable.

In a building with seven apartments and a small basement containing workshop and perhaps a gas heater, a gas detection system would be excellent. One detector would be installed in each apartment. An eighth detector would be in the basement area. A receiver and

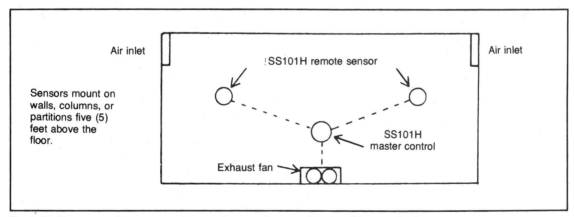

Fig. 4-42. Placement of gas sensors in an underground garage (courtesy Macurco, Inc.).

Fig. 4-43. Master control and remote sensor units (courtesy Macurco, Inc.).

alarm control panel could be set in the hallway or inside the door.

Figure 4-44 illustrates the eight units, the receiver, and alarm control panel. There are no problems as long as the power for all apartments is on the same power system from the main power transformer. Plug in a detector in each apartment, then plug in the main alarm control panel, and the system is in use.

This particular system, while excellent for apartments, can also be used with reliability in a home. The system provides protection from fire, explosion, smoke, and toxic gases. This *Quadra-Safe* gas detection system can be calibrated to detect the gases listed in Fig. 4-41.

## PORTABLE DOOR ALARM

A simple portable alarm can be used on a main door, a side door, or even inside your bedroom to alert you to danger (Fig. 4-45). The Majima Company of Japan claims this alarm is the world's smallest and lightest door alarm. The alarm is in a safe mode when the pin is left inserted into the alarm unit. When the alarm is positioned and the pin is removed (Fig. 4-45), the unit is ready to be activated. When activated, the alarm sounds at over 90 decibels until the pin is reinserted.

The *Super Ace* wireless door or window alarm (Fig. 4-46) is based on alarm systems that

utilize a reed switch alarm circuit. This unit can be used in semipermanent alarm locations. The unit and reed switch are held to the door by a self-sticking adhesive prepositioned on the back of the unit component.

The Majima Company recently redesigned this alarm to include an automatic heat/fire sensor. Besides making a shrill sound when used as an alert to unauthorized entry, the alarm will also sound automatically when the temperature reaches 104° F (40° C).

## BUILDING AN ALARM

A basic alarm can work on a single door, several doors, on one or more windows, or on a combination of doors and windows. A sensor, battery, and an alarm are needed (Fig. 4-47). A simple switch

Fig. 4-44. Sensors on an alarm panel (courtesy Macurco, Inc.).

Fig. 4-45. Set against the door with the pin removed, the alarm unit is ready to activate when the door is opened by an intruder (courtesy Majima Co., Ltd.).

is needed to allow you to activate the system, say, from your bed in case of an emergency (Fig. 4-48). You can build and install the alarm in an evening. Figure 4-49 illustrates the positioning of an installed system in a small apartment.

## FIRE EXTINGUISHERS

There are four main extinguishing agents: *water,*

Fig. 4-46. The Super Ace wireless door or window alarm (courtesy Majima Co., Ltd.).

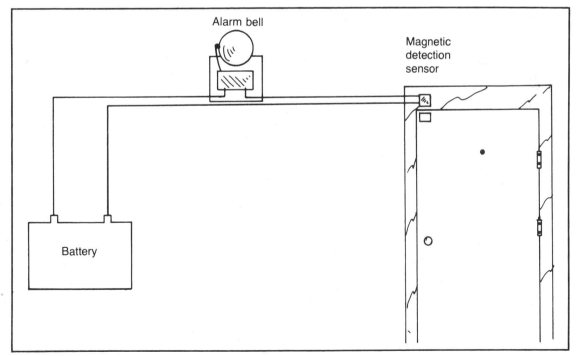

Fig. 4-47. A simple alarm system you can make yourself.

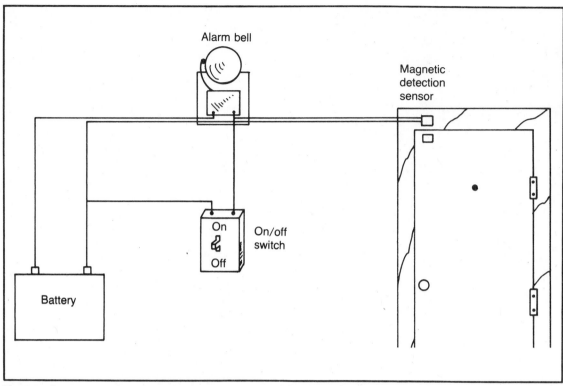

Fig. 4-48. By attaching a local control switch, you can sound the alarm when necessary.

*carbon dioxide, dry chemicals,* and *Halon*. Living in an apartment does not mean your responsibility toward fire protection has been transferred to management. Even the small efficiency or one-bedroom living quarters should be equipped with a fire extinguisher. A 2¾-pound dry chemical extinguisher should be centrally located for use.

Your extinguisher should be capable of suppressing A, B, and C classes of fire. Figure 4-50 shows the classes of fire and what types of materials are in each class. Notice the triangle, square, and circle. These are easy symbols to recognize and remember. Your fire extinguisher should have these symbols on it.

Look at the gauge on an extinguisher. The pointer should be in the vertical position. The extinguisher is fully charged and ready for use. If the needle should drop into the recharge position, do not assume a malfunction. You're being alerted that the optimum pressure is not avail-

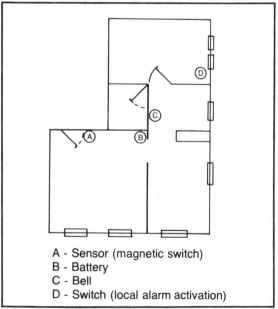

A - Sensor (magnetic switch)
B - Battery
C - Bell
D - Switch (local alarm activation)

Fig. 4-49. Placement of the alarm system in a small apartment. The on-off switch is placed beside the resident's bed.

Fig. 4-50. Even your children should be able to recognize these basic symbols (courtesy Pem All Fire Extinguisher Corp.).

able. Get the extinguisher recharged at the earliest possible moment.

In an apartment or condominium, the corridors should contain at least two fire extinguishers. The 2¾-pound model is nice, but it should be supplemented with a 5-pound model (Fig. 4-51).

Of the main types of extinguishing agents, only two types are effective on A, B, and C classes of fire: dry chemical and Halon. Water is excellent on class A fires, but it is generally unsuitable for chemicals and grease fires and is never used on electrical fires.

Carbon monoxide is poor on class B fires. It is not effective at all on class A fires, but it is effective on class C fires.

The dry chemical extinguisher is the most popular type used today, but Halon is gaining ground fast. There is no equipment damage with Halon (dry chemicals spew powder all about). Cleanup is easy with Halon and extensive with dry chemicals. Visibility is poor with dry chemicals and good with Halon.

Halon is a natural fire extinguishing agent. It interferes with the actual process of combustion and works extremely fast. This gives Halon a definite edge over other systems, especially in fire fighting.

Figure 4-52 is a Halon hand-held extinguisher that can be used effectively against all three classes of fires. Several sizes are available, and all except the smallest come with a pin, tie, and wall bracket.

Halon units are fairly new, having been introduced by ASP International only in the last few

Fig. 4-51. A 5-pound dry chemical fire extinguisher (courtesy Pem All Fire Extinguisher Corp.).

years. While widely available, the Halon units are more expensive than carbon monoxide or dry chemical ones but they are of higher quality.

Hand-held Halon fire extinguishers offer the following advantages over the competition:

☐ A high emission discharge valve.
☐ Lower toxicity.
☐ Disposable—maintenance-free.
☐ Offers better visibility to the fire.
☐ More effective on obstructed fires.
☐ Unequaled factory warranty.
☐ No dangerous obscuring of vision as with carbon monoxide and dry chemical extinguishers.
☐ Can be discharged in the presence of people before evacuating the area.
☐ No damage to delicate equipment, such as a word processor or computer system. (Shock caused by extreme cold (−90°F) with carbon monoxide and power residue from dry chemicals can be very damaging).
☐ The patented formula is expelled as a vapor rather than a liquid, thereby eliminating possible damage to sensitive equipment, furniture, or the surrounding area.

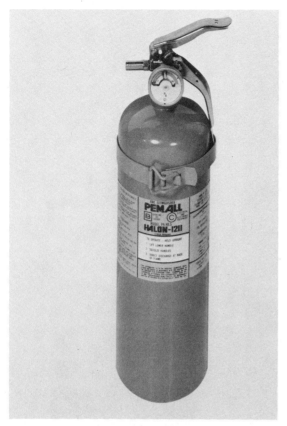

Fig. 4-52. A Halon hand-held fire extinguisher (courtesy Pem All Fire Extinguisher Corp.).

# Chapter 5

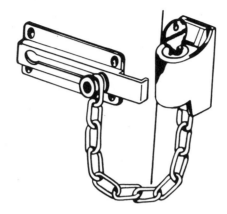

# Eliminating Home Hazards

Hazards include liquids that burn, clothing fires, gas dangers, rubbish and trash, home construction and decoration materials, cooking and heating appliances, electrical fires, and lightning.

### FIRE PROTECTION AND PREVENTION

Fire is a very common household problem. It can be caused by faulty electrical wiring and appliances, oily rags, grease, and smoldering cigarettes. There are more than 3.5 million fires a year. More than 10,000 people die and some 300,000 people are injured in fires. Hundreds of millions of dollars are lost in terms of destroyed property.

Every person in your home should know what to do and how to safely escape from the home in case of fire. Your preplanning for an emergency can make the difference between life and death.

### Nighttime Fires

Most fires start between the hours of midnight and 6 A.M. At this time you are asleep and are least prepared for an emergency situation. Fires may likely block your usual hall and/or stairwell escape route. Table 5-1 indicates the percentage of fires occurring in the various household rooms.

### Fire Detection Devices

Your home fire alarm system can be a single smoke detector outside the bedrooms or a complete system covering all rooms. The smoke detector forms the main ingredient of your home fire alarm system. It senses an abnormal amount of smoke or the invisible combustible gases in the air. The smoke detector gives you an early warning of a smoldering or flaming fire.

You may also have a heat detector (either a rate-of-rise or fixed temperature type) that operates and alerts you when it is heated to a preset temperature. The temperature for most heat detectors is 135°F.

Smoke detectors should be located:

**Table 5-1. Percent of Fires
Occurring in Various Household Rooms.**

| Room | Percent |
|------|---------|
| Living room | 37 |
| Kitchen | 22 |
| Basement | 14 |
| Bedrooms | 13 |

☐ Adjacent to sleeping areas in the home (Fig. 5-1).

☐ At the top of stairways in the home (Fig. 5-2).

A smoke detector should be in the living room, or study or any other room when the entrance to these rooms is more than 15"-20" away from the bedroom smoke detector(s) (Fig. 5-3).

### Fire Escape Planning

Planning for a potential fire is important. Prepare a floor plan of your home (Fig. 5-4). Divide a piece of paper into ¼" squares and indicate the rooms, windows, doorways, and stairs.

There should be at least *two* escape routes (Fig. 5-5). For upper rooms, indicate on the floor plan any rooftop that could be used as a fire escape (Fig. 5-6).

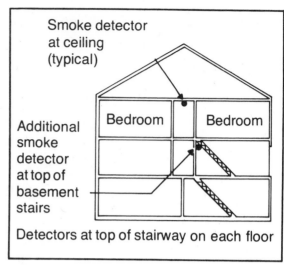

Fig. 5-2. Smoke detectors are placed up high to receive rising smoke that will activate the alarm.

Go to each bedroom and select the best window for an emergency escape. Test the window to see that it works easily. Have the occupant of the room also test the window. Is the window large enough, and is it also low enough for the person to open and get through quickly?

Indicate on your floor plan each normal exit through the hall or stairwell (Fig. 5-7). Use a different color code to indicate an emergency exit (the second exit route) in case a fire blocks the hall or stairwell exit.

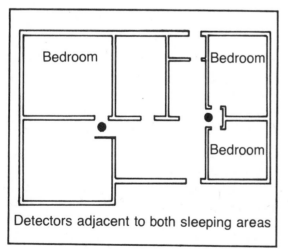

Fig. 5-1. A fire detector should be placed outside *every* sleeping area in the home.

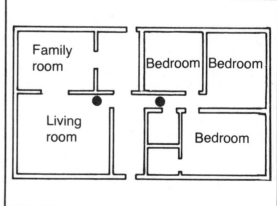

Fig. 5-3. Locate detectors in areas of congregation.

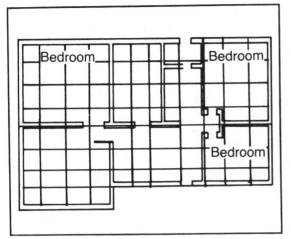

Fig. 5-4. Divide the room into subareas by using squares.

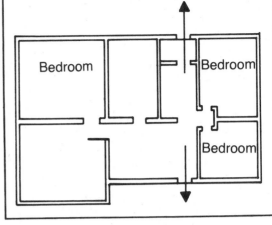

Fig. 5-5. Have at least two escape routes.

Be sure that everyone has an emergency escape route and that each bedroom has a second emergency exit. You may have to install an escape ladder or rearrange the bedroom occupants so that children have an easy rooftop escape.

Have practice fire drills regularly. Hold a family meeting and discuss fire prevention in your home. Afterward, show everyone the escape plan and walk through it with them. Does each person understand his role during a fire? Does each person understand what he should

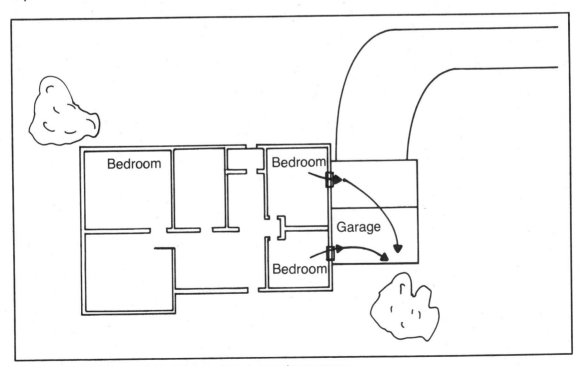

Fig. 5-6. Use everything available in terms of terrain to make an escape.

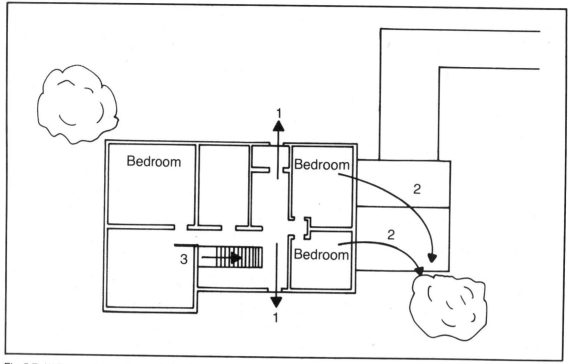

Fig. 5-7. (1) Escape ladder down; window has escape ladder stored by it—primary route. (2) Escape out over garage and down tree—emergency route. (3) Downstairs to basement and out the back door if you can't get to another route—emergency route.

and should not do during a fire? Does each person know the outside meeting place? Do you have the fire department's telephone number on your telephone and on the neighbor's telephone?

Conduct at least one drill every six months. Points to remember during a fire drill include:

☐ Don't make it scary for the children—make it a game for them.
☐ In an emergency, children must understand that the "game" is now real. They must follow directions instead of hiding under beds or in a closet.
☐ Don't announce the drill to anyone. It is best to hold a drill in the early evening just after darkness falls.
☐ Sound the alarm (possibly giving a child the practice of doing it).
☐ At this point everyone should move out of bed and check the door. Carefully test the door before opening it.

☐ Escape by the normal exit (the hall or stairwell) during the first fire drill. For the second fire drill, assume the doors are hot because the fire is in the hall or stairwell. Use the emergency escape exit.
☐ All family members must test their emergency escape exits.
☐ Ensure that everyone can open windows, remove screens, place the emergency ladder properly, etc.
☐ Have everyone gather at the outside meeting spot. What was the amount of time required to exit safely and gather at the meeting spot?

Everyone should know how to notify the fire department. Also, they should know how to help infants, elderly, or those who are physically impaired. If you have a third floor, is there a ladder nearby that can be raised?

To reduce the risk of fire, you must learn and

follow the basic safety rules. Also, ensure that your children follow them:

- ☐ Don't smoke in bed.
- ☐ Repair faulty electrical cords, switches, and plugs on lamps, appliances, and other electrical equipment. If you can't repair them, replace them.
- ☐ Don't play with matches or lighters.
- ☐ Don't use multiple extension cords from one outlet or overload your electrical circuits.
- ☐ If your kitchen stove has a ventilation hood, use it to keep the stove free from grease buildup. If you don't have a ventilation hood, clean the stove regularly inside and out and under the top (if removable) to remove grease.
- ☐ Get a professional electrician to replace electrical house wiring.
- ☐ Keep space heaters and stoves away from furniture and draperies. Ensure that only the manufacturer's recommended fuels are used in these heaters.
- ☐ Keep gasoline out of the house.
- ☐ Have your chimney checked for cracks, crumbling bricks or cement, obstructions, and residue buildup. Clean the chimney at least once a year.
- ☐ Always use a fire screen with the fireplace. Never remove a screen just because the fire has been extinguished.

Every homeowner should have a fire safety check performed. Check with your local fire department for help. Many have routine programs and employ individuals who are trained in home fire safety checks.

The following items are looked for during a fire safety check:

- ☐ Piles of old papers, magazines, and oily rags.
- ☐ Clutter that builds up in out-of-the-way rooms, such as the basement and attic.
- ☐ Paint cans should be properly resealed.

- ☐ Only approved storage containers should be used for flammable liquids. Store flammable liquids outside the house.
- ☐ Hidden electrical cords, frayed cords, improperly repaired cords, etc. Limit the number of extension cords in your home. Electrical outlets should be inspected.
- ☐ Combustibles in your utility room or in the basement. Areas around your hot water heater and furnace should be kept clean.
- ☐ Fireplaces should have metal fire screens or tempered glass doors. Chimneys should be checked and cleaned annually. The chimney top should have a mesh screen to prevent sparks from flying out onto the roof and to keep birds and other small animals from entering.
- ☐ Television sets and stereos should not be up against the wall. They need room to let out the hot air.
- ☐ Stairwells are kept clean and in good repair.
- ☐ Fire/smoke detectors properly placed throughout the home where required.

### Home Construction and Remodeling

Survival during a fire is greatly influenced by the type of materials used in the construction and/or remodeling of your home. Materials such as gypsum board (drywall) and plaster are considered safe building materials. Thin plywood, uncoated wood fiber ceiling tiles, and many plastics are not.

If your home has plastic laminates on the walls, acoustic ceiling tiles, wood paneling, and exposed insulating materials, a fire can develop and spread very rapidly. Your chances of escaping safely have been greatly reduced. Most ceiling tiles and panels on the market today have reduced flamespread capability, so your safety is greater than if the tiles and wall panels were several years old.

Prefinished plywood paneling, plastic laminates on plywood or hardboard, corkboard, and particle board are other materials capable of

Ceiling tiles or prefinished wood paneling that is
  UL labeled with a flamespread of 200 or less
Plaster
Gypsum wallboard
Wallpaper, canvas, or thin plastic (under 1/16″) over
  plaster or gypsum wallboard
Fiberglass
Ceramic tile
Metal tile
Mineral fiber ceiling types

Other types of wall finish materials should only be
  used in small quantities such as partial wallcovering
  in a small room like a bathroom

Fig. 5-8. This list covers primary fire-safe building materials that can be used in the home (courtesy Department of Housing and Urban Development).

rapidly spreading a fire once it starts. Some of these materials can have special treatments applied that can reduce their flammability.

Cover these materials with gypsum wallboard and install smoke detectors. If you have low-density fiberboard that is unfinished, apply a generous coat of ordinary latex paint to make the fiberboard safer. Figure 5-18 lists materials considered sufficiently fire-safe for use in the home.

### Faulty Lighting and Electrical Wiring

Light bulbs that are left exposed can cause problems when they are located in closets or other areas where, if too close to paper or clothing, they can scorch and burn it. Encase such lights with a protective cover or shell to ensure that they will not come in contact with anything. If your light bulbs are too close to the shelves, consider moving the shelves away or moving the light source and electrical wiring.

During the Christmas holiday season, many fires are reported. Use only UL labeled Christmas tree lights. Check the electrical wiring *before* you put the lights on the tree. A bare wire or bad connection may blow a fuse, but more than likely it will start a fire without blowing the fuse. When you go out or go to bed, turn off the lights for at least 30 minutes to give them time to cool.

Decorations for Christmas or other occasions should be flame-retardant. Don't put decorations close to electrical fixtures and outlets.

### Clothing Fires

Not all clothing is flame-retardant. If your own clothing catches fire, don't run. Running will fan the flames. Lie down and then roll over and over. Do it fast; seconds do count. As soon as possible, remove the clothing if you can do so without pulling it over your head.

If another person's clothing catches fire, don't let the person run. Get the person onto the ground and roll him or her over and over. Whenever possible, take handy articles such as a throw rug, heavy coat, or blanket to smother the flames. When outside, use dirt, sand, or anything else that is available.

Don't get too close to any open flames or hot surfaces. Instruct children on the dangers of playing with matches, lighters, and candles. For parties or special occasions, use costumes that are made of flame-retardant materials.

Flame-retardant sleepwear for children is a necessity. Manufacturers are required by law to make flame-retardant sleepwear up through size 14.

### Combustible Liquids

Many household products, such as cleaning fluids, are extremely combustible. Aerosol can products are dangerous when punctured or left close to heat or fire or to a warm window. Other combustible products include paint thinner, kerosene, lighter fluid, and turpentine. Cooking oil and melted grease, which burns rapidly, can be dangerous.

Keep combustible products in a cool storage area. For cooking oil and grease, clean up the stove and any spills as soon as possible. Keep excess grease in a container away from the stove and place in your garbage can as soon as possible; don't keep it in the kitchen.

Contact cements, such as common airplane glue, are extremely flammable. Don't use them near open flames.

Hair sprays can be ignited before and after using, especially if you are near open flames. Don't use matches or lighters or smoke while you are using hair spray. Don't use hair spray in a kitchen, and keep away from a stove until the hair spray has dried.

### Gas Appliances

Butane, LP, and portable gas stoves may be found around the home. Such gas cylinders contain enough gas to cause an explosion in confined areas. Read and follow the safety precautions on the labels of these products.

### Kitchen Safety

Many kitchen items can burn: paper towels, napkins, garbage, clothing, cooking oil and grease, cleaning fluids under the sink, etc. The electric grill, deep fryer, toaster, the stove burners, and even the pilot light can start a fire.

Keep all items that burn far away from a flame or removed to another room. Grease and cooking oil will not burn at room temperature. When heated on the stove, though, they can easily ignite if spilled or dripped too close to the open flame.

### Electrical Fire Safety

Electrical fires can occur due to overcurrent, high-resistance faults, hot surfaces, and arcing. *Overcurrent* is when too much electricity is passed through the wiring to the extent that it burns through the insulation and starts a fire. High-resistance faults occur when there is frayed wiring. Outside surfaces of appliances, such as toasters, are not hot enough to ignite paper, wood, and clothing.

*Arcing* occurs when a spark of electricity jumps across an open gap. This can be caused by a short-circuit in an electrical cord or a switch. A spark in an area where open paint thinner or gasoline is stored can cause the vapors to explode.

Here are a few simple rules:

☐ Never replace a fuse with another fuse having a higher ampere rating.

☐ Don't overload electrical circuits.

☐ Keep all appliance cords and extension cords in good condition; replace rather than repair.

☐ Keep paper and cloth away from open light bulbs.

☐ Don't use a regular extension cord for appliances that require a lot of electricity, such as a heater, air conditioner, iron, etc.

☐ Provide a ground connection for an outside television antenna.

☐ Keep all appliances with hot surfaces away from any item that could be ignited.

☐ Don't use an appliance that is not working properly.

### Emergency Fire Ladder

Second-floor bedrooms should be equipped with a fire ladder if there is no adjoining roof outside the window. One 15' ladder weighs only 9 pounds, and a child can use it. The ladder has a continuous loop cable that is nonkicking and non-tangling. It has braced 1" rails that lock securely over the windowsill. Heavy-duty 4" standoffs keep the ladder away from the wall, allowing for an easy and smooth descent to safety. The ladder may be stored under a bed, in a closet, or by the window in its own storage case. If you live in a three-story home, 25' long emergency ladders are available.

### Security Lite

Waking up in a home without electricity or one with dense smoke requires you to see where you are going. The Security Lite in Fig. 5-9 can work in both situations. The unit will light automatically when the power goes off. It doubles as a night-light in children's rooms. The unit can be removed and act as a flashlight. This light is continuously rechargeable when left in the wall outlet, so you can have a readily usable light at all times. The special beaming lens illuminates directly in front of you and also off to the sides with its wide beam.

Fig. 5-9. Each bedroom should have a Security Lite (courtesy Rival Manufacturing Co.).

## WATER DETECTORS

Water damage from a flash flood due to an excessive heavy rain, which can easily put 10″ or more of water flowing down your street, cannot be stopped in time. Minor water line breaks, sump pump failure, and surface water coming through cracks in your basement wall can easily be detected early and eliminated.

The *Informer water detector* (Fig. 5-10) electronically senses water. Models provide either a dry contact or audible alarm.

Imagine a fairly heavy rain that overflows the sewer system. Surface water runoff enters your basement through a crack in the basement wall or floor. The Informer water detector will alert you early so that you can move items in the basement or possibly stem the water flow.

A probe can be placed near a gas furnace, bathroom, or laundry area in the basement. Water may snuff out a gas flame, resulting in an excessive buildup of gas.

The water alarm consists of the basic electronics and a small probe. The amount of water required for the probe to activate the detector is determined by you. When the water level reaches a certain level, the device sounds the alarm. When the water level returns to a point below the probe, the unit will reset automatically and is instantly ready to continue monitoring the water level. The Informer can be used with an alarm panel, dialer, or an external alarm that is compatible with it.

Figure 5-11 shows one unit that can work in virtually any situation. The smallest amount of water coming into contact with its two water sensors causes the *Flood Alert* to send an easily heard high-pitched warning beep. A battery-powered unit can fit in locations where electricity may not be available or warranted, such as in a boat or a remote area of a home basement. Figure 5-12 illustrates six possible areas where a water alarm should be used. Other areas include a water meter, water beds, chimney stack, roof, the base of an aquarium, and in basements. For hard-to-reach places, such as the bilge of a boat, a remote sensor that can be attached to the Flood Alert (Fig. 5-13).

## INTERIOR/EXTERIOR EMERGENCY LIGHTING

Every home should have some type of emergency lighting. Items such as a simple flashlight, candles, and matches are not found in every home. We recommend permanently installed solid-state lighting units. These units should be:

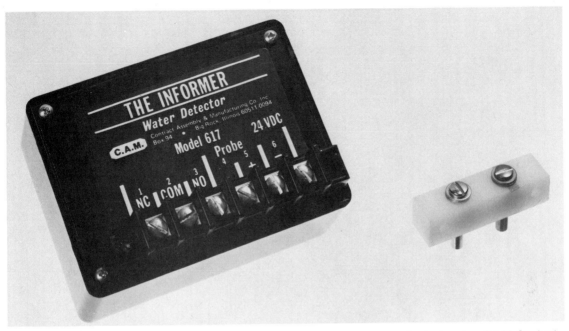

Fig. 5-10. Water detectors should be in a laundry room, by open drains, and near a water heater (courtesy C.A.M. Co., Inc.).

- ☐ Maintenance-free.
- ☐ Self-contained.
- ☐ Automatic.
- ☐ Low voltage to permit battery discharge.
- ☐ Equipped with an LED to indiate battery charging and "readiness" conditions.
- ☐ A minimum of 2 hours illumination.
- ☐ Equipped with long-life batteries (five to 10 years).

Units can have one or two lamps (Figs. 5-14 and 5-15). Emergency lights can be located at the top of stairwells (single lamp unit pointed downstairs; a double lamp unit with one lamp pointing down the hallway and the other on the stairs) and also near exits.

For an apartment dweller, such units could be mounted to illuminate the pathway to the apartment door. Multilevel homes should have at least one emergency lighting unit on each floor. Emergency lighting unit deter burglars.

Mount a unit on the side corners and back of the home. When power goes out, the sides and back of the home are well-lighted.

Fig. 5-11. The Flood Alert can be used in the home, in outbuildings, or on your boat (courtesy Datasonic, Inc.).

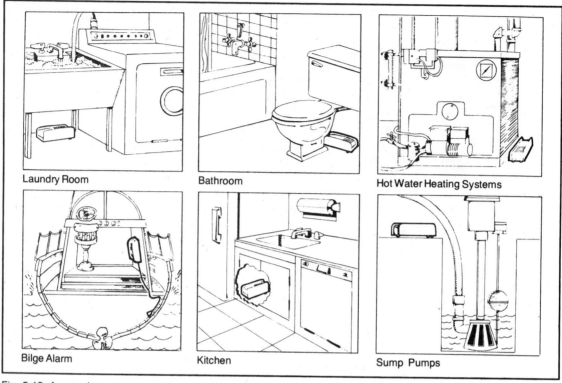

| | | |
|---|---|---|
| Laundry Room | Bathroom | Hot Water Heating Systems |
| Bilge Alarm | Kitchen | Sump Pumps |

Fig. 5-12. Areas where a water alarm should be used (courtesy Datasonic, Inc.).

A flush-mounted overhead fixture (Fig. 5-16) is acceptable in foyers, hallways, side rooms, at the top and bottom of stairwells, work areas, in the basement, and even in some main rooms. The fixture will fit in with most decors.

For very large homes and small apartments, a mini-central system is appropriate (Fig. 5-17). The cabinet can power up to four remote lamps or a combination of lamps and exit lights. The cabinet may have two lamps attached.

Exit sign lights can be used in a basement or hallway near a young child's bedroom. In buildings with six to 12 apartments, a unit should be installed at every apartment door. If your apartment house does not have such a unit, or an equivalent unit, contact your apartment management.

### LIGHTNING PROTECTION

Lightning will strike from 90 to 135 times each year within a half-mile radius of your residence. More people will be injured by lightning than by floods, hurricanes, or tornadoes. every year at least 37 percent of all fires in rural and suburban areas are caused by lightning. The Lightning Protection Institute (LPI) has noted that proper lightning protection systems must meet the requirements of the Underwriters Laboratories and the National Fire Protection Association's lightning code.

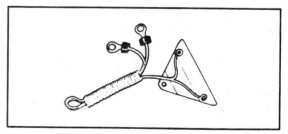

Fig. 5-13. For hard-to-reach places, a remote sensor should be used (courtesy Datasonic, Inc.).

Fig. 5-14. An emergency lighting unit with one lamp (courtesy Carpenter Emergency Lighting).

Fig. 5-15. An emergency lighting unit with two lamps (courtesy Carpenter Emergency Lighting).

Fig. 5-16. Flush-mounted emergency lights do not stand out, which makes them acceptable to almost every room (courtesy Carpenter Emergency Lighting).

Fig. 5-17. Wall-mounted lamps and exit sign lights (courtesy Carpenter Emergency Lighting).

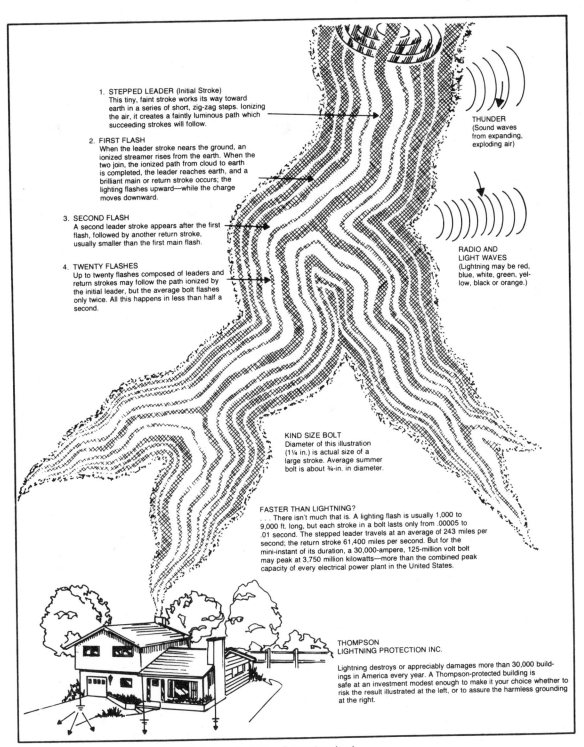

1. **STEPPED LEADER** (Initial Stroke)
This tiny, faint stroke works its way toward earth in a series of short, zig-zag steps. Ionizing the air, it creates a faintly luminous path which succeeding strokes will follow.

2. **FIRST FLASH**
When the leader stroke nears the ground, an ionized streamer rises from the earth. When the two join, the ionized path from cloud to earth is completed, the leader reaches earth, and a brilliant main or return stroke occurs; the lighting flashes upward—while the charge moves downward.

3. **SECOND FLASH**
A second leader stroke appears after the first flash, followed by another return stroke, usually smaller than the first main flash.

4. **TWENTY FLASHES**
Up to twenty flashes composed of leaders and return strokes may follow the path ionized by the initial leader, but the average bolt flashes only twice. All this happens in less than half a second.

**THUNDER**
(Sound waves from expanding, exploding air)

**RADIO AND LIGHT WAVES**
(Lightning may be red, blue, white, green, yellow, black or orange.)

**KIND SIZE BOLT**
Diameter of this illustration (1¼ in.) is actual size of a large stroke. Average summer bolt is about ¾-in. in diameter.

**FASTER THAN LIGHTNING?**
. . . There isn't much that is. A lighting flash is usually 1,000 to 9,000 ft. long, but each stroke in a bolt lasts only from .00005 to .01 second. The stepped leader travels at an average of 243 miles per second; the return stroke 61,400 miles per second. But for the mini-instant of its duration, a 30,000-ampere, 125-million volt bolt may peak at 3,750 million kilowatts—more than the combined peak capacity of every electrical power plant in the United States.

**THOMPSON LIGHTNING PROTECTION INC.**

Lightning destroys or appreciably damages more than 30,000 buildings in America every year. A Thompson-protected building is safe at an investment modest enough to make it your choice whether to risk the result illustrated at the left, or to assure the harmless grounding at the right.

Fig. 5-18. A lightning bolt (courtesy Thompson Lightning Protection, Inc.).

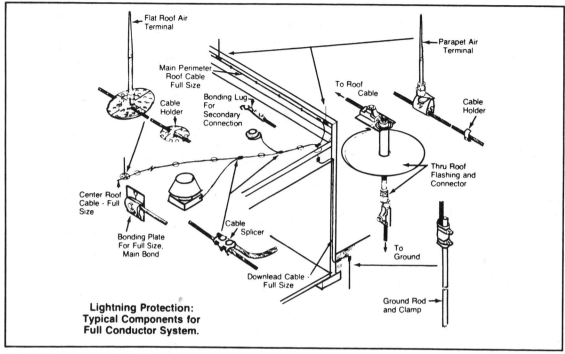

Flat Roof Air Terminal

Main Perimeter Roof Cable Full Size

Parapet Air Terminal

Cable Holder

Bonding Lug For Secondary Connection

To Roof Cable

Cable Holder

Thru Roof Flashing and Connector

Center Roof Cable - Full Size

Bonding Plate For Full Size, Main Bond

Cable Splicer

To Ground

Downlead Cable - Full Size

Ground Rod and Clamp

**Lightning Protection: Typical Components for Full Conductor System.**

Fig. 5-19. Components for a full conductor system (courtesy Thompson Lightning Protection, Inc.).

A lightning bolt is composed of millions of ions of negative electrons and positive protons. These ions of opposite polarity attract and make a sparking point when they meet. They neutralize each other. Figure 5-18 illustrates a lightning bolt.

Residential homes, farm buildings, and apartment houses all require lightning protec-tion. This is not a do-it-yourself project. Let an experienced, LPI-certified installer do the work. Figure 5-19 illustrates the components for a full conductor lightning protection system. For further information about lightning protection, contact the Lightning Protection Institute and/or check your local telephone directory for a light-ning protection specialist in your area.

# Chapter 6

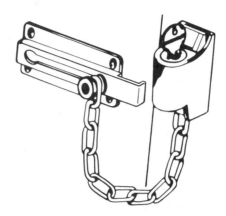

# Automotive Security

The FBI reports that two cars are stolen every minute. Of the millions stolen during the year, the replacement cost will exceed $1.5 billion. Less than 20% of all auto theft cases will be solved by law enforcement personnel.

It may make no difference to a thief whether or not your car is new or five years old. If he's out for a joyride, it doesn't matter what type of car he steals. He may be stealing the car to obtain a few parts for his car or a friend's car. He may belong to a ring dealing in stolen car parts.

Numerous vehicle theft detection/deterrent systems are on the market, ranging from a few dollars to several hundred in cost. Some provide a very low level of protection, while others will sound an alarm if somebody attempts to move or lift the car, pry open a door, or whatever.

Some automobile security systems have given the public a false sense of security. While there are many excellent systems and devices on the market, others may deter an amateur auto thief, but a full-time thief will not be deterred.

Because of the rising auto theft rate, alarms have become more sophisticated and have more component parts and special equipment than they did a decade ago. The basic auto alarm system consists of a horn or siren, control unit, some type of access control, door sensors (or microsensors), sound discrimination devices, vibration (motion) detectors, key sensors, etc. The minimal auto security system usually has an alarm for the doors, an outside key to arm and disarm the system, possibly a motion detector, a siren or horn, and the system control unit.

## AUTO THEFT INFORMATION

Over a seven-year period, FBI crime reports showed the number of automobile thefts in the United States increased by 23 percent. It was only because of the increase in other crimes that the proportionate share of auto theft appeared to be less. As an example, during one period surveyed, the percentile was 11.7 percent. Seven years later it was 9.5 percent. Other crimes in-

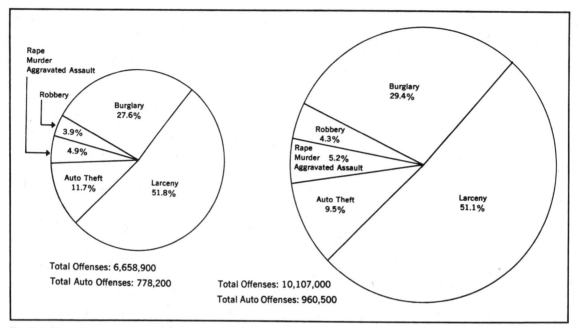

Fig. 6-1. Serious crimes in the United States (seven-year difference between left and right figures). Crime increased almost 50 percent in total offenses, while increase in auto was less than 37 percent) (courtesy FBI Uniform Crime Reports).

creased, which gave auto theft a lower statistical averaging. The number of cars increased, so the percentile could be lower due to the number of cars versus the number stolen.

During any one year of the seven-year survey period, losses due to theft easily exceeded $1 billion, based on an average value of $2,000. Figure 6-1 shows serious crimes in the United States based on total offenses and total auto offenses.

### Reasons for Auto Theft

Automobiles are stolen for many reasons:

joyriding, for use in committing another crime, stripping, use for scrap, material or reselling. The frequency with which cars are stolen and never recovered represents an index of theft for personal gain by either scrapping or reselling. Those cars recovered that are stripped are a conservative indication of stripping as the purpose for the theft. Stolen cars that are recovered undamaged have generally been stolen for joyriding. Table 6-1 shows statistics for the recovery of stolen cars. The left-hand column represents a study done only in California. The right-hand column represents data from FBI surveys. Based on the

Table 6-1. Percentage of Automobiles Recovered (source FBI).

| Car Status | Percentage Recovered |
|---|---|
| Intact | 29% |
| Damaged | 12% |
| Stripped | 28% |
| Not Recovered | 31% |

Table 6-2. Age Distribution of Apprehended Auto Thieves (source FBI).

| Age | FBI General Survey Percent | FBI UCR Percent |
|---|---|---|
| Under 18 | 54% | 57% |
| 18 to 24 | 31% | 29% |
| 25 and Over | 15% | 14% |
| Unknown | - | - |

sampling represented by these surveys, at least one-fifth of all stolen cars were never recovered, and almost one-third of the thieves probably were joyriding. Table 6-2 indicates the age distribution of apprehended car thieves.

### Methods of Vehicular Theft

Vehicular theft includes the categories of joyriding, (a need for) transportation, getaway vehicles, and commercial thefts.

**Joyriding.** Most reported thefts fall under the category of joyriding because it is an offense of opportunity. The offender, who is usually a juvenile, finds an unoccupied vehicle with the keys in the ignition or such a situation that allows easy theft of the vehicle. The thief does not want to permanently deprive the owner of his vehicle.

Joyriding is usually a single-step operation wherein the thief steals, uses, and then abandons the vehicle. By plan or afterthought, the thief may strip the vehicle of easily removable parts for personal use or resale.

**Transportation.** A vehicle stolen for transportation purposes is usually abandoned after it has served its purpose. The car may be abandoned after being driven from one city or state to another. This type of thief may attempt to sell spare tires, radios, or other parts from the vehicle.

**Getaway Vehicles.** A car may be stolen just prior to or several days before a robbery and then abandoned later.

**Commercial Thefts.** These thefts are for monetary gain and usually involve high-performance or luxury vehicles. These cars constitute the largest portion of unrecovered vehicles.

Investigations of organized theft rings are complicated and extremely difficult. Professional auto thieves know that law enforcement is generally confined to the area in which it normally serves, so most stolen vehicles involved in organized theft ring operations are removed from the area where they were stolen.

### AUTO THEFT PREVENTION TIPS

Here are some precautions:

—Always lock your car when leaving it. Leaving your car unlocked or, even worse, leaving the keys in the car while you make a quick stop somewhere is an open invitation to theft.

—Never leave valuables in view in your car. Valuables are tempting targets for thieves. Keep such items in the trunk. Whenever possible, never keep any valuables in the car. Take them with you on errands or leave them at home.

—Avoid leaving the car in a deserted area, especially for a long period. If you must abandon it for one reason or another, take simple precautions, such as removing the distributor cap or center wire from the distributor. If the car is broken into, the car cannot be started and driven away.

Park in well-lighted areas. Whenever possible, make sure an attendant is on duty in parking lots.

—Use a hood lock that must be controlled by a lever from inside the car.

—Use a steering column lock.

—Reduce the chance of break-ins and theft by removing accessories, such as CB radios and antennas. Keep them at home or locked in the trunk of the car if not actually being used. Tape decks fall into this category.

### ANTI-THEFT DEVICES FOR CARS

Jay Kolinsky, a recognized expert in automobile theft devices and technology, has lectured for years on automobile theft and anti-theft devices. The following information is based on his years of experience and expertise in the field.

With car thefts at record levels—more than 1 million each year—and continuing to rise at an alarming rate, sales of anti-theft devices are also increasing. You should carefully investigate the advantages and disadvantages of the many anti-theft products before making any purchase for your own automobile.

Some highly sophisticated security systems can cause more problems than they solve, and they can provide you with a false sense of security. Some can even jeopardize your life. Note, though, that certain anti-theft devices can more than pay for themselves with reduced insurance premiums.

Automobile thefts are becoming more prevalent and more damaging to car owners because the recovery rate has decreased sharply in recent years. Car owners must take important steps to safeguard their vehicles from experienced car thieves who can steal a locked car in less than 30 seconds. These thieves can strip the car of major body parts and mechanical components at so-called "chop shops" in less than 40 minutes. You will never see or recognize your car again. With insurance depreciation rates as they are, you will not be able to receive adequate compensation from your insurance company. Most companies today don't even pay you for stolen stereo or CB equipment.

Security devices may prompt the thief to look for an easier target. Kolinsky states that several states are requiring insurance companies to give owners who buy certain devices premium discounts that can range from five to 20 percent.

Surprisingly, insurance companies are increasing the incidence of car thefts by insisting on used parts to repair damage on an insured car because they are less expensive than new parts. "Steal-to-order" theft rings have prospered due to this increased demand for used parts.

There are three basic types of anti-theft devices available: alarms, locks, and ignition or fuel system immobilizers. Each has its advantages and limitations. The best system may be a combination of these items.

An alarm may be effective in scaring off a thief or for telling you when a theft is occurring, but it will not cut off the ignition system or keep the hood locked. Many alarms have severe disadvantages.

Kolinsky believes automatic (passive) electronic alarms that work on a time delay principle may offer the most protection with the fewest problems. The alarm should have a hidden defeat switch so you can disengage the system when leaving your car at a public garage manned by attendants or when mechanical work is being done on the car.

There is no lock to open or switch to push with a time delay alarm. You merely leave your car and an alarm sets itself after a minute or two. On entering the car, simply turn on the ignition. Depending on the alarm, you may have from 10 seconds to 2 minutes to turn the ignition on before the alarm sounds. You don't have to carry any special key, there is no need to mar the car's fender with a key switch hole, and you never have to remember to set your alarm each time you leave the car. With automatic alarms it is important to get a prealarm warning, such as an audible sound or buzzer. This will remind you to disable the alarm before it sounds.

Alarms are available in several degrees of sophistication, but some of the most modern and complex alarms can cause the most problems. Certain so-called modern alarm systems use either a numbered keyboard or thumb-wheel switches that require you to dial or punch in the proper code to shut the alarm off each time you enter the car. These systems look impressive, but they are not all that simple to use, most car owners will not bother using them every time they get in or out of their cars. Also, you have to tell people your code if you let them drive your car. Try punching the proper code when it's dark.

Kolinsky notes that silent alarms and radio pagers also have severe limitations because the car owner must be within a few miles of the car to hear the alarm. Range also is sharply curtailed by hills, large buildings, etc., and silent alarms do not scare a thief away. Sirens and flashing lights do. Many people installing silent alarms do so because they want to catch the thief before he leaves. Newspapers often carry stories about professional thieves killing carowners trying to apprehend them.

Many alarms with shock sensors, sonic, vibration, audio, glass-break, microphones, or motion detectors have built-in false alarm problems. Although they are equipped with sensitivity adjustments, be prepared to have false alarms at all hours of the day an night. Most false alarms are triggered by thunderstorms, lightning, strong rainstorms or hailstorms, normal vibrations, cars parking and touching your car, loud noises, etc. Many alarms will use only a sensor that triggers the alarm when any light bulb goes on, such as courtesy lights and hood and trunk lights. If these alarms are equipped with automatic shutoff timers, they will shut off even if the doors, hood, or trunk is left open. This leaves your car totally unprotected. The alarm won't function if the bulb is burned out or missing. Use caution when considering these alarms.

If you still want to use a motion detector or some other sensor, make sure there is a switch that can isolate and control that particular part of the system. Multiple devices that operate independently are more difficult to defeat than a single system that does everything.

Kolinsky says you should purchase an electronic siren instead of a mechanical one and make sure it has an automatic shutoff after 5 or 10 minutes so your car battery won't go dead, and so you won't receive a summons for disturbing the peace. The older mechanical sirens draw tremendous amounts of power from the battery and need very heavy wiring. They also are more susceptible to damage from salt, road grime, water, and sand. A mechanical siren only emits a monotonous single tone, which has been used for years and has become so common that people often ignore the sound.

Kolinsky warns against purchasing an alarm that requires the electronic circuitry to be mounted in the engine compartment where heat buildup can be as high as 225°F. Constant exposure to extreme temperatures eventually damages the components used in these alarms.

When installing an alarm, he also suggests including a device that sets off flashing parking lights, side markers, and taillights. They are particularly effective at night.

In the last 10 years auto manufacturers have been required by federal mandates to design anti-theft features into every vehicle. On pre-1970 cars it isn't difficult to open the hood and hot-wire the ignition or to push in the vent window and open the door. Theft by hot wiring today is much more difficult and usually is limited to the professional car thief who has tools to deal with the toughest locks.

Specialized steering wheel locks and locks for the ignition switch probably will deter the novice or amateur car thief. These locks must be switched on and off or be installed and removed at all times when leaving and entering the car. They also add an unsightly element to the appearance of the car. Too many car owners today who purchase specialized locks costing from $50 to $250 continually forget to use them, and they have no added protection against car thieves.

Ignition or fuel cutoffs are perhaps a more effective way to prevent your car from being stolen. A so-called passive disabling system prevents someone from starting the engine (or will stall the engine) unless a hidden button is activated. There is nothing for the car owner to switch on or off when leaving the car. There are no keys to carry and no unsightly locks.

Passive ignition cutoff devices can cost as little as $20 (for a unit with separate disabling switch for use when lending the car or parking in a manned parking garage) to $220. Because these devices require the car owner only to press a secret button when starting the ignition, they generally qualify for the maximum insurance discounts.

Kolinsky prefers an ignition cutoff device that prevents the vehicle from starting to one that causes the vehicle to stall after several seconds. "I wouldn't want the thief to abandon my stalled car in the middle of a busy highway where it could get clobbered by oncoming traffic," he notes. "And there also is a liability problem if someone smashes into your car when it is blocking traffic," he warns.

Fuel cutoffs also stall the engine, and they can cause restarting difficulties because fuel lines are empty. This can be dangerous if the owner forgets to deactivate the device and stalls on a busy street.

Kolinsky also adds that a passive ignition cutoff device, when used with an independently operating alarm system, probably affords the best protection for the investment. "One prevents the thief from starting and driving the car; the other sounds an alarm and scares him away or attracts the police," he says.

Passive anti-theft devices are "invisible" after being installed. Professional thieves automatically look for external key switches, coded keyboard, and hood lock/ignition kill controls on a dashboard. They will immediately take steps to neutralize them. If they can't see it, they won't defeat it.

Before selecting a device for your car, make sure the product is of the highest quality and comes from a reputable firm. Consider your driving and parking habits.

Kolinsky's firm, Kolin Industries, offers a 24-page guide describing how to select the best theft prevention system for your car. For a copy, reference this book in your request letter and send 50¢ for handling to *Kolin Industries, Box 357, Bronxville, NY 10708.*

### Automatic Ignition Killer

The *Big Stop automatic ignition killer* (Fig. 6-2) is a palm-sized unit that sells for about $20. This electronic unit stops a thief from stealing your car even if he has the ignition key. You can install the device in less than an hour and without any special tools.

The unit automatically immobilizes the engine in any vehicle with no dangerous grounding of electrical circuits and no fuel lines to cut. It automatically opens a circuit in the vehicle's ignition or starting system and will disable the engine each time the motor is turned off. The engine will crank, but it won't start with a key, if the ignition lock is pulled out, or if an attempt is made to hot-wire the car to start. Unlike other ignition cutoff devices that ground the automobile's spark coil and can damage certain electronic ignition systems, the Big Stop can use any ignition wire or the relay control wire for the starter motor. If you choose the ignition wire, the starter motor will turn, but the engine won't start. If you decide to control the starter motor relay, nothing will happen when you try to start the engine,

unless a hidden deactivation button is pressed.

The Big Stop's black box contains electronic circuitry and a toggle switch that can be used to disconnect the system when the car is being serviced or driven by a parking attendant. A single wire connected to a switched 12-volt wire, a double wire connected in series with the negative lead of the ignition coil, a single wire to a ground metal part of the car, and a push button are needed. The black box and push button are installed beneath the dashboard and hidden from view, but accessible to the driver.

Once the unit is installed, the engine won't turn over unless you turn the ignition switch to the on position and press the hidden button for ½ second or until a distinct click is heard. If the

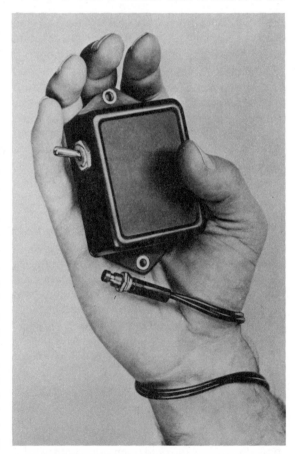

Fig. 6-2. The Big Stop automatic ignition killer (courtesy Kolin Industries, Inc.).

**INSURANCE DISCOUNT CERTIFICATE**
*Complete this certificate and MAIL to your Insurance Agent along with copy of Sales Receipt.*

Insurance Company_____

My Policy Number_____

Insured Name_____

Street_____

City _____ State_____Zip_____

Insured
Vehicle: Make_____Year_____ID#_____

*Gentlemen:*
*I have installed in the above named vehicle a ''Big/Stop'' Passive engine disabling device. (Copy of receipt enclosed.) This unit automatically disconnects my ignition when the engine is turned off. It requires NO manual steps to perform this function. The engine cannot be started unless a hidden secret button is first pressed before starting is attempted.* **Please apply the appropriate discount to my comprehensive insurance and notify me of same including actual cost savings I receive.**

Date_____Signature _____

**''Big/Stop'' manufactured by Kolin Industries, Inc. Box 357, Bronxville, N.Y. 10708**

DISCOUNTS *not* available in some states - ASK YOUR AGENT ◆ **914-961-5065**

**Some companies require a Hood Lock. Indicate if equipped with Hood Lock** ☐Yes ☐No

Fig. 6-3. An insurance discount certificate is included with the Big Stop (courtesy Kolin Industries, Inc.).

engine stalls, there is no need to press the push button again before attempting to restart, unless you turn the ignition to off.

The Big Stop is operated as follows:

☐ Get into the driver's seat.
☐ Set the toggle switch to the on position.
☐ Turn on the ignition switch.
☐ Press the secret push button ½ second. You hear a click.
☐ Start the engine.

When the engine is shut off, it can't be started unless the secret button is pressed after the key has been turned on.

Normally you leave the toggle switch in the on position. To bypass the unit when the car is being serviced or driven by a parking lot attendant, flip the switch to the off position.

Some people go that extra distance for automotive protection. Use one Big Stop to disable the ignition circuit, another to disable the starter relay, and a third one to disable the electronic ignition module. A thief would have to be a very good mechanic and familiar with electrical systems to steal a car equipped with three Big Stops. If you use a relay to control high-current draw, you can even use a Big Stop to disable automobile headlights.

A special insurance discount certificate is included with the Big Stop. With the Big Stop installed, you do nothing to activate the electronic system; it is classified as a passive engine disabling device. Insurance companies are required by many states to pass on a five percent to 15 percent discount on comprehensive insurance rates. Figure 6-3 illustrates such an insurance discount certificate. The five percent-15 percent discount can more than pay for the cost of one or several Big Stop units used for vehicle protection.

### Earsplitter Vehicle Alarm

The second Kolin Industries automotive protective unit is the *Earsplitter.* This alarm has 10 features. Some of these features are found on other alarm units, but not all are on any single unit:

- ☐ The Earsplitter doesn't use keys.
- ☐ The Earsplitter turns itself on every time. Simply leave your car. The unit automatically arms itself in about 2 minutes. This is accomplished with a sophisticated integrated circuit exit time delay. The computer does the thinking for you.
- ☐ The Earsplitter is simple to operate. Enter your car and turn on your ignition. You've got 15 seconds from the time you open your door.
- ☐ The Earsplitter has a hidden off switch. You can use it to completely disable the alarm when you're leaving the car at a public garage manned by attendants or when mechanical service is being performed on the car.
- ☐ The Earsplitter has a sensing or voltage drop. The computer monitors the vehicle's electrical condition. It knows when any light is turned on, even if it stays lit for just ½ second. The alarm will sound between 10 and 15 seconds after any light comes on. Perhaps you don't have a hood or trunk light. Then a "tilt"-operated hood and trunk light can be used in either place. It will trigger your alarm, and you'll also see in the dark. You will have instant triggering (no delay) for hoods and trunks with this system.

- ☐ Another feature is a high-low siren. If the alarm is activated, a siren sound like a European police car or emergency vehicles goes off. It uses only one-twentieth of the energy required by the mechanical sirens on the market. Plus, it won't kill your battery. This powerful siren sound is amplified by a special speaker mounted into the engine compartment. It has no electronics and is not affected by heat, dirt, water, or ice. There are no moving parts and nothing to break, wear out, or get clogged.
- ☐ If an intruder breaks in, the Earsplitter blasts for 3 to 5 minutes, then automatically shuts off and instantly resets. The automatic shutoff timer is controlled by sophisticated integrated circuitry, and it is very reliable.
- ☐ Some car alarms require the electronic circuitry to be mounted in the engine compartment. These alarms are subjected to tremendous heat, sometimes as high as 300°F. Constant exposure to such extreme temperatures eventually damages the components of the alarm system. The electronic circuitry of the Earsplitter remains protected in the driver's compartment of your vehicle. It is not subject to such tremendous heat as other alarms.
- ☐ Many insurance companies consider the Earsplitter a passive alarm. Arming is completely automatic. Many insurance companies are now giving special discounts off their policy rates if you have a system like this installed. In many cases, the money saved will pay for the entire system. Check with your insurance company for details.
- ☐ The Earsplitter is easy to service. Many alarm systems are connected with many wires into the car's electrical system. If something goes wrong, you have to remove all the wires that you originally put in. Your initial installation time is wasted.

All components of the Earsplitter are of very high quality. They're specially selected to give trouble-free performance. The Earsplitter has a new computer plug-in harness that allows you to simply unplug the alarm for a quick test of the unit. The alarm's wiring harness remains in your vehicle, and not one single wire has to be removed to disconnect the alarm unit.

☐ When you open the door of your car, you can hear a short "beep" sound. This sound lasts about ½ second and is loud enough to alert you, but it won't disturb others. The computer is telling you, "Hey, you've got just 15 seconds to turn the ignition on so I won't make any more noise."

☐ At the same time the siren is sounding, the unit will automatically flash your taillights, front yellow (parking lights), and side marker lights. The flashing will occur about 60 times a minute. Even if your vehicle is in a parking lot with more than 1,000 cars, everyone will know your car has just been illegally entered.

☐ If someone opens your door and leaves it open, the siren and flashing lights won't shut off. If someone opens the door and immediately closes it, the siren and light would operate from 3 to 5 minutes before automatically shutting off and resetting.

### In-Line Gas Lock

The *in-line gas lock* (Fig. 6-4) allows you to shut off the gas running from the tank to the engine. By doing this, you can stop a person from driving your car away.

The gas lock stops the car from being started, stolen, and then stripped at another location. By taking a few minutes to drill a hole, cut the gas line, and install the gas lock, you ensure that even if the car is hot-wired, it cannot run without gas. The thief would have to locate the problem, jack up the car, and then figure a way to get gasoline to the engine. The gas line often is not outside the car, but it is concealed. Without the gas line available, the thief isn't going anywhere with your car.

Figure 6-5 illustrates the fuel line and gas

Fig. 6-4. The in-line gas lock (courtesy Clark Manufacturing Co.).

Fig. 6-5. Locating the in-line gas lock (courtesy Clark Manufacturing Co.).

lock location. A convenient location for the gas lock is at a point where it is easily accessible to being unlocked from inside the car. The best and easiest point is by the driver's or passenger's seat (Fig. 6-6). A side view of the location is shown in Fig. 6-7.

(Don't smoke or have lighted objects near the car while installing the gas lock.) Here are installation procedures:

☐ Locate the gas line on your vehicle. The gas line normally runs along one side of the frame from the gas tank to the engine.

☐ Find an appropriate place where the valve can be mounted in the floor pan and is convenient to operation from the driver's seat. This requires a ¾" hole in the floor pan and room for the valve location under the car. A neoprene gas hole and hose clamps are supplied with the gas lock kit for valve installation.

☐ Cut the gas line in half where the lock valve will be placed.

☐ Install the neoprene hose and hose clamps on each end of the valve.

☐ After locating the car's gas line, pull it away from the frame or bottom of the vehicle to allow room for cutting.

☐ After the fuel line is cut, put your finger over the end of the line coming from the tank. Slip the neoprene hose from one end of the valve and put a clamp over the gas line. Approximately 1½" are overlapped, then the clamp is tightened. This will stop the flow of gas. A small amount will run out of the other end. You can drain this gas into a container or put the other end of the hose from the opposite side of the valve onto the gas line and clamp it. This completely stops the flow of gas onto the ground (and your hands).

☐ Double-check your location of the valve and cut a ¾" hole in your carpet or floor pad (do not drill through the carpet). Use a razor blade or sharp knife. After the hole is through the carpet or pad, use a center punch and punch the metal floor pan. This can be done with any ¼" hand drill. Be sure you know where you are drilling.

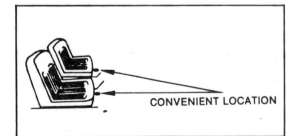

Fig. 6-6. Under the front seat is a convenient location for the in-line gas lock (courtesy Clark Manufacturing Co.).

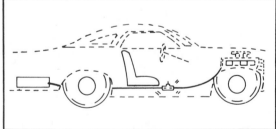

Fig. 6-7. Side view of gas lock placed convenient to driver's seat (courtesy Clark Manufacturing Co.).

☐ Remove one nut and insert the unit up through the floor pan. Tighten the nut. The unit is now secure and in operation.

☐ By using your gas lock key and turning it 90°, you can now turn the gas flow on or off. When you leave the car, turn the key 90° and remove it.

☐ The gas lock valve must be installed between the tank and the fuel pump to operate.

Do not turn or adjust the sealed nut. If it is tampered with, permanent damage will result.

### Steering Column Lock

This anti-theft steering column lock withstands pulling, drilling, and picking (Fig. 6-8). Installed in just minutes, the unit features a hardened face guard, special deadlocking retainer, and a unique stress displacement ring. It uses the well-known Medeco high-security cylinder and keys.

The recessed ignition cylinder is out of reach of a lock puller. it cannot be penetrated with the screw tip of a slide hammer, and the Medeco cylinder that replaces your standard ignition switch cannot be picked. With more than 250,000 key combinations, the steering column lock key can be duplicated only by an authorized Medeco locksmith or by the manufacturer.

This ignition lock conforms to NHTSA Standard 114-1 with a case-hardened steel protective cap that prevents removal of the lock with conventional tools. The lock is considered a passive anti-theft device as defined by the Insurance Service Bureau bulletin, because it disables the ignition when the key is removed. If your car is equipped with this security lock and a hook lock that can only be released from the car's interior, you may qualify for an insurance premium discount. Contact your automobile insurance agent for specifics.

### Master Disconnect Switch

Automobiles, trucks, vans, antique cars, RVs, boats and construction equipment can be protected with the *master disconnect switch* (Fig. 6-9). The switch protects the vehicle from theft, guards against the loss of life and damage to equipment resulting from electrical fires and vehicle accidents, ends the battery drain from faulty wiring and electrical accessories that are accidentally left on, and stops tampering and unau-

Fig. 6-8. The steering column lock withstands pulling, drilling, and picking (courtesy Lock Technology Corp.).

Fig. 6-9. The master disconnect switch is ruggedly built (courtesy Bathurst, Inc.).

233

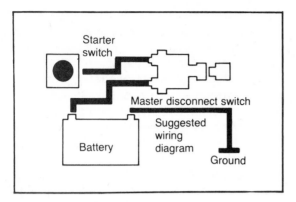

Fig. 6-10. Suggested wiring diagram for the master disconnect switch (courtesy Bathurst, Inc.).

thorized operation of the vehicle.

The switch is ruggedly built for reliable and lasting service. The lock is a tumbler type of cylindrical design with a shutter closure. It uses specially coded keys for operation. When in operation, the switch will disconnect and lock up all vehicle electrical systems. It is for all 6-, 12-, 24-, and 36-volt systems.

Easily installed on all vehicles inside or outside, the switch can be on or under the dash, on the firewall, floorboard, engine compartment, the body of the vehicle, or hidden away for maximum theft protection. A suggested wiring diagram for the master disconnect switch is shown in Fig. 6-10.

## Battery Lock

The *Battery Protect-A-Lock* eliminates the theft of your automobile, truck, boat or RV battery from a vehicle. This unit is easy to install and has a nine-pin tubular lock. While you may not consider your battery worth that much, remember that your car is not going anywhere without it.

## Driver Seat as Alarm Activator

The *FlexSwitch* can activate a signal when it is flexed approximately ⅛″ on a 6″ radius. A prominent actuating bead assures positive performance.

The FlexSwitch can be used as a sensor when tied into your auto security system. Figure 6-11 illustrates the FlexSwitch inserted within the foam of the driver's seat. When the alarm is activated, any individual that is able to gain entry into the car will activate the alarm when weight is put on the driver's seat (Fig. 6-12).

As a safety feature, a second FlexSwitch can be mounted beside the first and tied into the ignition and seat belt warning light (if your auto has one). In this case, with proper wiring, the ignition cannot be started until the seat belt has been properly secured.

## CompAlarm

*Adalarm Manufacturing Company* (Laguna

Fig. 6-11. Placing the sensor switch is relatively easy and, including attachment to the alarm, should take no longer than 30 minutes (courtesy Tapeswitch Corporation of America).

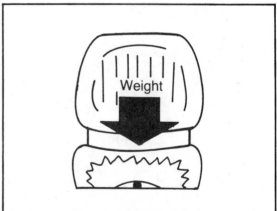

Fig. 6-12. When weight is applied to the driver's seat without the alarm being turned off, the alarm will sound (courtesy Tapeswitch Corporation of America).

Niguel, California) supplies the *CompAlarm*. This computerized anti-theft system is controlled by a 12-digit keyboard system that also incorporates an ignition kill system. It can have either passive or active arming. Optional equipment includes an electrically-operated hood lock, paging system, sound discriminator unit, and a motion detector.

### Alarm System from Autosafe Electronics

*Autosafe Electronics* (Los Gatos, California) has an alarm system featuring pre-entry perimeter protection. A front panel switch allows only the owner to disarm the system. It utilizes a sound discriminator that will listen for typical sounds made during an unauthorized entry, while ignoring all normal sounds. This sound detection is separate from the doors, which are on another adjustable entry delay portion of the security system. A special ignition cutoff can prevent the auto from being stolen, even if the thief has possession of the car keys.

### Hood Locks

*Maci-Guard TuBar automotive security lock* makes a vehicle virtually theftproof by deadbolt locking the hood and killing the ignition system. This automatic hood deadbolt lock also pick-proof, is hardened steel and has a 5.5 million possible key combinations.

The Monrolock from the *Monroe Timer Company* includes a hood locking device and automatic ignition cutoff. The ignition cutoff is secured and locked under the hood for maximum protection. A case-hardened tubular steel conduit is employed to prevent the cable from being severed. A dual switch deadbolt casing provides for optional diesel cutoff, dual ignition cutoff, and operation with any alarm system.

Another hood locking device from *Vehicle Security Electronics, Inc.* (Chatsworth, California) can be installed on any vehicle having an inside hood release lever. It is operated by an electronic solenoid and steel cable to lock the hood by allowing the vehicle's inside hood release lever to operate only when the solenoid is energized.

A hood lock is a vital element of any comprehensive vehicle security system, because other critical components of a system are normally located within the engine compartment, such as the vehicle battery, the siren or horn to the alarm system, and bypass circuits for the vehicle's ignition and/or starting systems. A thief must be denied access to the area under the hood.

### Ungo Box

For more expensive automobiles, such as Porsches, Rolls, Mercedes, etc., the *Ungo Box* from Techne Electronics is available. This very sophisticated system detects entry into the auto's interior, engine compartment, or trunk, even if the car is left unlocked or the keys are stolen. The Ungo Box can also detect attempted forced entry through an extremely advanced motion sensing system. It sounds an intermittent horn when the alarm is triggered, disabling the car's engine so that it cannot be driven even with the car's own keys.

### Door Lock Button

If you have an older automobile, the door lock button can be pulled up by using a coat hanger,

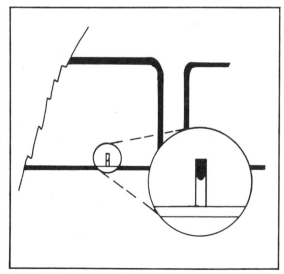

Fig. 6-13. Door lock buttons such as this one cannot be pulled upward by a thief.

thus unlocking the door. Replace those standard buttons with the new slim, tapered type that cannot be pulled out. Figure 6-13 illustrates the door with the tapered door lock button in place.

### SENSORS FOR INCREASED POINT PROTECTION

Point protection of the car doors, trunk, and even van doors can be added through individual sensors. The sensors are tied into your auto alarm system. With a little imagination and ingenuity, you can come up with other techniques besides the ones mentioned.

### Protecting Van Doors

This method is for protecting rear doors of vans, so a minimum opening will trigger an alarm system (Fig. 6-14). By using an adjustable gap contact, it may be possible to use only one switch to protect both doors, if an adjustment can be made to trigger the alarm before the second door can be opened.

This switch is rated at 110 mA. If it is to be used to operate a horn, siren, or lights, buffer with

a relay. Use a magnetic contact to drive the relay coil and the relay contacts to drive a high-current load.

Installation is as follows:

☐ Select a position for the switch and magnet on the hinge side of the door that opens first (door one).
☐ Drill 1″ diameter hole with a hole saw in the door and body. Line up centers within ⅛″.
☐ Insert a switch in the frame (1076B).
☐ Insert a magnet in the door.
☐ Attach a meter to the switch. Adjust a screw in the end of the switch. Set the gap for the minimum opening to trigger the alarm.
☐ Wire a switch to the alarm.
☐ Check to see if door one triggers the alarm before door two can be opened. If door two can be opened without setting off the alarm, add a switch to door two.

### Protecting Car Doors

This application provides a method of protecting car doors so a minimum opening will trigger the alarm system (Fig. 6-15). The Select-A-Gap steel door contact has an adjustable gap dis-

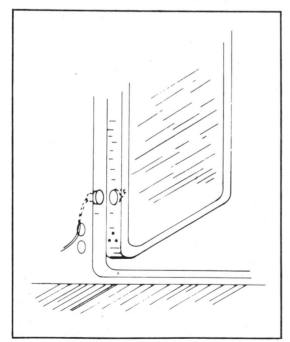

Fig. 6-14. Protecting van doors (courtesy Sentrol Inc.).

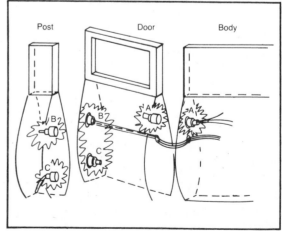

Fig. 6-15. Protecting car doors (courtesy Sentrol Inc.).

tance between 1/8" and 1" in steel doors, permitting adjustment to the desired sensitivity.

This switch is rated at 300 mA. If it is to be used to operate a horn, siren, or lights, it should be buffered with a relay. Use the Sentrol 1076B Contact to drive the relay coil and the relay contacts to drive a high-current load.

Installation instructions are as follows:

To install in the hinge end of the front door or the handle end of the rear door (switch in body), select positions for the magnet in the door and for the switch in the body. Be certain that neither will interfere with operation of the door. Drill 1" diameter holes in the door and body. Line up centers within 1/8". Insert the switch and magnet (a dab of RTV mounting compound around the rims of the switch and the magnet will help seal the holes and protect the metal from moisture).

Attach an ohmmeter to the switch leads. Adjust the screw in the end of the switch to set the gap for the minimum opening to trigger the alarm. Wire the switch to the alarm.

To install in the handle end of the front or rear door (switch in door), select positions for the switch in the door and for the magnet in the body. Drill 1" diameter holes in the door and body. Line up centers within 1/8". Insert the switch and magnet. Seal the rims of the magnet and switch with RTV mounting compound.

Attach an ohmmeter to the switch leads. Adjust the screw in the end of the switch to set the gap for the minimum opening to trigger the alarm. Run the wire from the switch through the door to the opposite end of the door.

Drill holes in the door and body of sufficient diameter to allow wire to pass through. Insert rubber grommets in holes to keep the wires from rubbing on bare metal. Seal grommets with RTV mounting compound. Allow enough slack to keep wire from breaking when the door is opened. Wire the switch to the alarm.

To install in the handle end of the front door or the hinge end of the rear door (switch in post), select positions for the magnet in the door and for the switch in the body. Drill 1" diameter holes in the door and post. Line up centers within 1/8".

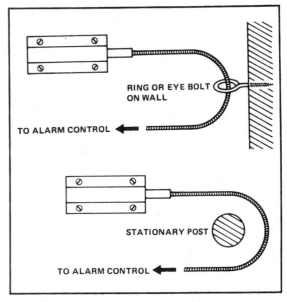

Fig. 6-16. Installing a Sentrol 2105 magnetic pull-apart cable (courtesy Sentrol Inc.).

Insert the magnet and switch. Seal the rims of the magnet and switch with RTV mounting compound.

Attach an ohmmeter to the switch leads. Adjust a screw in the end of the switch to set the gap for the minimum opening to trigger the alarm. Wire the switch to the alarm.

### Pull-Apart Alarm Activation Cable

A cable can be installed so that when a vehicle is moved, the cable detaches, activating the alarm.

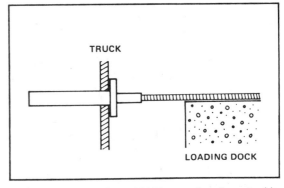

Fig. 6-17. Installing a Sentrol 2115 magnetic pull-apart cable (courtesy Sentrol Inc.).

237

Fig. 6-18. Audio-Safe is the only auto stereo protection device available (courtesy Burbank Enterprises).

To install a *Sentrol 2105 magnetic pull-apart cable* (Fig. 6-19), drill a ¾″ diameter by 3½″ deep hole in the unit being protected (boat, truck, trailer, etc.) that can be moved. Also, drill two 3/16″ diameter holes for mounting screws. Install the magnet portion of the takeoff in the ¾″ diameter hole and mount with two number 8-32 flathead screws. To prevent easy removal of the screws, damage the threads after the nuts are tight, use epoxy or glues, or use high-security screws and nuts.

Mount the cord section with clamps so the cord will pull straight out of the magnet when it reaches the end of the cord. Make sure the cord has the correct slack and loop, so it will not hang up on anything as the protected object is moved.

To install a Sentrol 2115 magnetic pull-apart cable (Fig. 6-1), mount the magnet block on the object to be protected that will be moved in case of theft. Install with tamper-resistant screws.

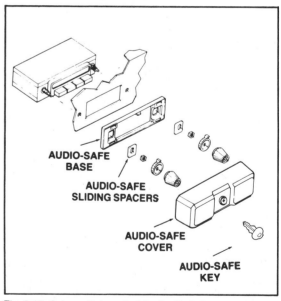

**AUDIO-SAFE BASE**

**AUDIO-SAFE SLIDING SPACERS**

**AUDIO-SAFE COVER**

**AUDIO-SAFE KEY**

Fig. 6-19. Schematic layout of the Audio-Safe (courtesy Burbank Enterprises).

Fig. 6-20. (A) A car stereo. (B) The Audio-Safe in place (courtesy Burbank Enterprises).

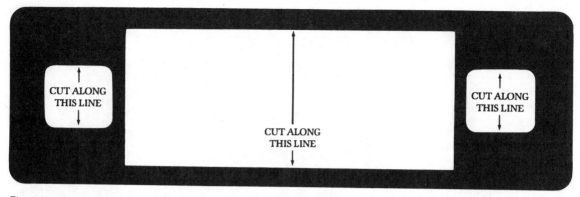

Fig. 6-21. Use this illustration to determine if the Audio-Safe will fit your car stereo (courtesy Burbank Enterprises).

Mount so the "make" portion of the cable can pull out straight to keep damage from occurring. If there is an alignment problem, mount the magnet block on a hinge and the hinge on the item being protected.

Mount the cord section with clamps so the cord will pull straight out of the magnet when it reaches the end of the cord. Make sure it has the correct slack and loop so it will not hang up on anything as the protected object is moved. For alternate mounting, loop the cord through the item being protected or through a stationary item.

### CAR STEREO LOCK

The *Audio-Safe* protects most in-dash stereos from theft. It fits most cars, vans, and RVs (Fig. 6-18). Because most in-dash sound systems are mounted by just one nut to each control shaft, all a thief needs to do to get at your system is to unfasten these two nuts.

Manufactured of heavy-duty aircraft quality cast aluminum, the Audio-Safe was developed specifically to prevent car stereo theft. The unit, consisting of a base and a cover, locks together to enclose the stereo and the mounting nuts. With these nuts shielded from access, your in-dash sound system is protected from theft. The Audio-Safe literally hides the in-dash system from view. When you want to use the system, the Audio-Safe cover can be removed quickly with a key. Figure 6-19 illustrates, schematically, the placement of the Audio-Safe to protect the car stereo.

Features of the Audio-Safe include:

☐ Easy installation in most cars, vans and RVs.

☐ Handles most currently popular car stereos.

☐ Locks with an 11-blade tumbler lock— the standard of the industry.

☐ Can be mounted either right side up or upside down to slide right or left, respectively, when unlocking.

☐ Added protection for tape drives from dust or moisture—great for off-the-road vehicles, convertibles, and motorcycles.

☐ Protects the stereo from unauthorized use or programs changes.

☐ Completely hides the stereo from sight (Figs. 6-20A and 6-20B).

Perhaps you feel the Audio-Safe may not fit your car stereo. If you're not sure, try the template shown in Fig. 6-21. Outline the template on another piece of paper and cut out the three openings as indicated. Next, remove the knobs from your car stereo. Place the template over the face of your stereo, then over your dashboard, and check for interference. If it fits, the Audio-Safe will work for you. Please note, though, that the dashboard must allow for at least 3/16″ clearance on one side for the cover to slide on and off.

# Chapter 7

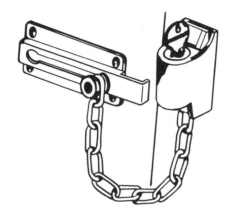

# Garage and Driveway Protection

The garage, attached to or detached from the home, must be protected. This may be no more than a lock and hasp on the door and an exterior night-light. Protection may be more—an extension of the home security system perhaps, or maybe a separate security system, if the value is high and the building is totally separate from the home. In another case, the security provided could be a combination of the above.

Garage security includes three main points for protection: the main garage door(s), the side door entrance, and any windows in the structure. When these have been protected properly, your concern is focused on individual point protection of specific items that may be stored within or near the garage, such as certain power tools, a moped, motorcycle, bicycles, and perhaps a boat and its trailer. The driveway must also be protected.

## GARAGE DOORS

Most garage doors can be pried or forced open with little difficulty. Garage doors can be of wood, wood with windows, or metal. They can open outward or upward.

For basic wood doors that open outward or upward (not controlled by an automatic door opening device), install cane bolts on the inside of the door. For double doors, one door would have a cane bolt that is secure in the vertical position, while two would be used—one on each side—on upward moving doors (Fig. 7-1).

In addition to cane bolts, a top center hasp mounted on the interior side of the door would provide further security. Such a hasp would be used only when there is a standard side door for entrance. If there is no other door, a padlock and hasp should be mounted on the outside—at the sides and at the top.

## HASPS

For garage main doors or the side door, several types of heavy-duty hasps may be considered for basic or supplementary security (Fig. 7-2). Do

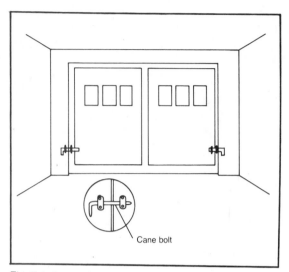

Fig. 7-1. A cane bolt on each side secures the door.

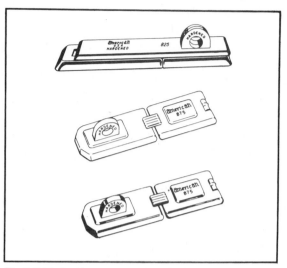

Fig. 7-2. Typical hasps to secure main and side doors of the garage (courtesy American Lock Co.).

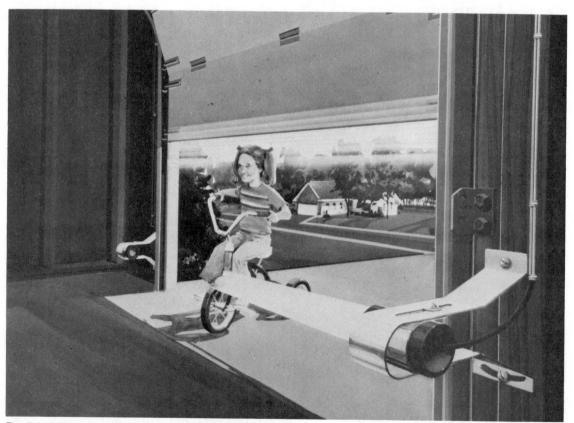

Fig. 7-3. Sensors automatically stop the door from lowering further and reverse its movement when an object or person interrupts the beam (courtesy Chamberlain Manufacturing Co.).

not buy hasps made of lightweight aluminum. Select a heavy-duty hasp that contains a steel staple. If the hasp will be used outside, it should also be rustproof-plated to protect against the weather.

## PROTECTOR SYSTEM
## AUTOMATIC GARAGE DOOR OPENER/CLOSER

The Protector System provides more than just automatic opening and closing of your garage door for the safety of your automobile. It includes an invisible light beam across the inside of the garage door opening (Fig. 7-3). If anything or anyone interrupts the light beam as the door is descending, the door instantly reverses without contact. This feature is important for children's safety.

The automatic door system is better than others on today's market. The powerful ½-horsepower motor will operate even the heaviest residential garage door with a push of a button. The system comes in a box, and the components look like any other garage door system (Fig. 7-4). Note the protector obstruction sensors (Fig. 7-5). Once installed, the sensors are located low down on the interior side of the garage door (Fig. 7-6). The transmitter and receiver must be installed so that the path of the light beam is not obstructed by the garage door, door tracks, springs, hinges, rollers, or any other part of the door mechanism. You may have to add a piece of wood to the wall at the mounting locations to ensure the proper clearance or do so for masonry wall installations (Fig. 7-7).

Features of this system include:

☐ A ½-horsepower, full chain-driven motor drive that will lift the heaviest residential garage door (Fig. 7-8).
☐ The Protector System safety feature that "sees" obstructions and reverses the door instantly without making contact with the subject.
☐ A code selection on the transmitter/

Fig. 7-4. The Protector System looks like any other system until you see it work (courtesy Chamberlain Manufacturing Co.).

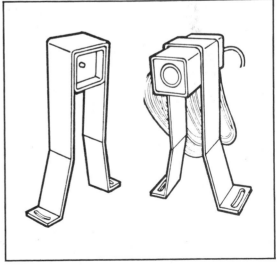

Fig. 7-5. Transmitter (left) and sensor (right) (courtesy Chamberlain Manufacturing Co.).

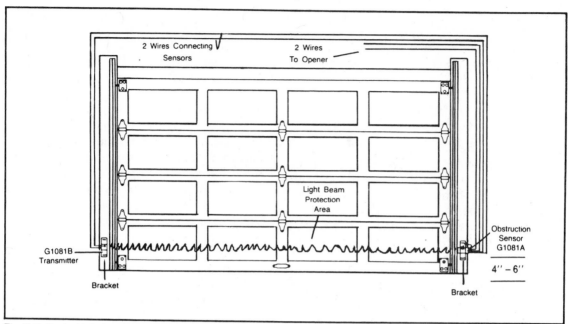

Fig. 7-6. Typical interior view—notice how low to the floor the sensor and transmitter are located (courtesy Chamberlain Manufacturing Co.).

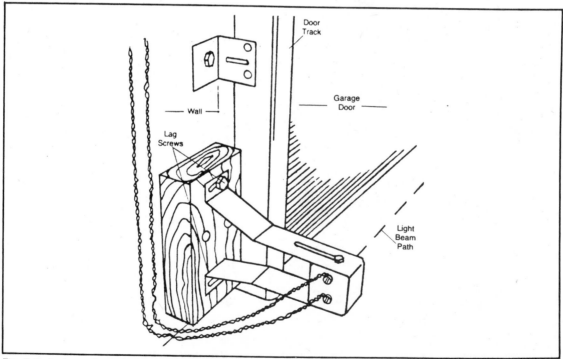

Fig. 7-7. A piece of wood can ensure that the Protector System's light beam is not obstructed (courtesy Chamberlain Manufacturing Co.).

244

Fig. 7-8. A heavy-duty motor will operate the heaviest garage door (courtesy Chamberlain Manufacturing Co.).

receiver, with a total of 3,375 codes to provide excellent security because the secret code is determined by you and can be changed at any time (Fig. 7-9).

☐ A lighted button in the wall-mounted receiver that stays lit so it is easy to see in the dark.

☐ A key switch that lets you open the garage door from the outside without the transmitter (Fig. 7-10).

☐ A convenient pull chain that allows you to turn on the opener lights when the unit is not in use.

☐ The garage is automatically lighted for safe entry. You see what is there before you enter instead of going into a darkened garage to find a light switch at night.

☐ The receiver is wall-mounted and has convenient push-button door operation from inside the garage, allowing for easy access to change the security code in use.

☐ A vacation/security switch (an on/off switch) that shuts out all radio signals for added security when you're away for extended periods.

☐ A light time delay that means the light will remain on for safe entry into the home, then shuts off automatically.

☐ An emergency release with auto reconnect allows manual door operation in case of a power failure. You only have to push a button to automatically reconnect the unit to the control unit when power is restored.

☐ Constant door control means the door can be stopped at any height for safety and ventilation with a push of the button.

## SECURITY ALARMS AND SENSORS

Following are the more apparent sensor applications that should be considered when garage security must complement that within the home. Each of these applications provides protection at a certain point within the garage. By using individual sensors, in this case magnetic contacts,

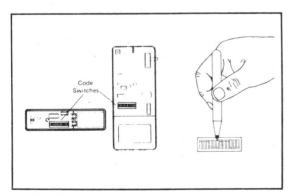

Fig. 7-9. It takes but a minute to change the operating code of the transmitter (courtesy Chamberlain Manufacturing Co.)

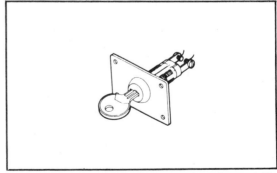

Fig. 7-10. The key switch can be mounted anywhere outside the garage to be used when you don't have the transmitter ready (courtesy Chamberlain Manufacturing Co.).

you increase your security protection beyond the minimal amount that may be present when only a lock and hasp are used.

### Protecting an Overhead Garage Door with a Floor Switch

It is sometimes necessary to bury a magnetic contact in the floor due to door construction (Fig. 7-11). The switch has been designed for this installation. It is stainless steel for corrosion protection and has the extra gap distance.

Installation instructions include the following:

☐ Select a position for the switch that will minimize the amount of concrete to be chipped out.

☐ Install the magnet on the door and place the switch on the floor. Test to make sure of at least a 1" gap. If not 1", adjust the magnet.

☐ Chip concrete out approximately ½" deep by ½" wide.

☐ Place the switch in the floor and test. Make sure of at least ½" extra gap.

☐ Fill in over the switch and cable with concrete patch.

### Protecting a Garage Curtain Door

Installation instructions are as follows (Fig. 7-12):

☐ Both the switch and the magnet should be located near the floor and away from

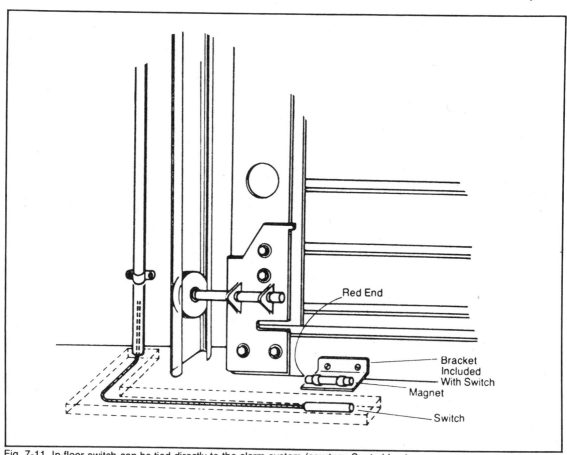

Fig. 7-11. In-floor switch can be tied directly to the alarm system (courtesy Sentrol Inc.).

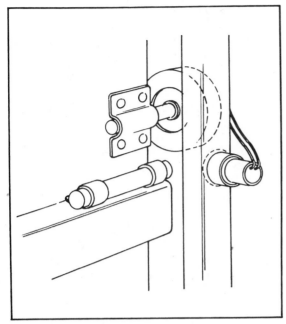

Fig. 7-12. Correct mounting to protect a steel curtain roll-up door (courtesy Sentrol Inc.).

checker to observe switch operation. Make the connection into the alarm loop. Recheck for operation and clearance.

### Contacts on Garage Door Track

Installation instructions are as follows (Fig. 7-13):

☐ Make sure the door does not have a guard that extends around the track on the bottom of the door.

☐ Choose the side opposite the rope pull or

traffic, so the switch and its connecting wires will not be accidentally disturbed.

☐ Saw a 1″ hole in the face surface of the door track. This hole should be in line with an inside door segment centering on the segment and being about ¾″ in from the edge of the track.

☐ Insert the switch from the back into the hole you have sawn in the track face. It should snap into place.

☐ Using the clamps provided, mount the magnet on the outside door segment that is in line with the switch. This alignment would be with the door closed. You can temporarily tape the magnet in place and open and close the door to be sure there is no binding or interference with operation. Fasten the magnet via the clamps using #6 and ¾″ sheet metal screws.

☐ In mounting the magnet, be sure the red end is *away* from the face of the switch. The switch is polarity-sensitive.

☐ Open and close the door to check the proper operation. Use a continuity

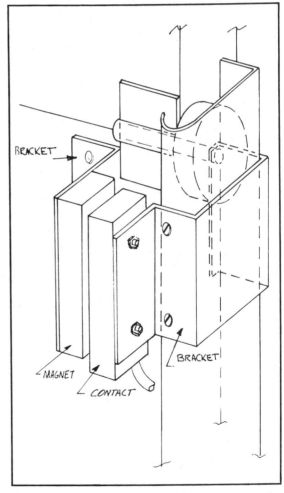

Fig. 7-13. Magnetic contacts can also be mounted on the garage door track (courtesy Sentrol Inc.).

move the rope pull to the side opposite the switch.

☐ Mount the bracket on the track with two self-tapping screws. Tighten evenly against the track.

☐ Mount the switch to the bracket.

☐ Mount the magnet to the bracket. Observe the polarity of the switch and magnet. Always line up the switch and magnet labels to read in the same direction.

☐ Mount the bracket and magnet to the garage door, allowing about ½″ gap between the switch and magnet.

☐ Test for clearance and operation.

☐ Loosen holding screws on the bracket and apply RTV mounting compound to the flat side of the track. Reinstall and tighten screws. Retest.

## High-Security Switch on an Overhead Garage Door

The triple-biased, high-security balanced mag-

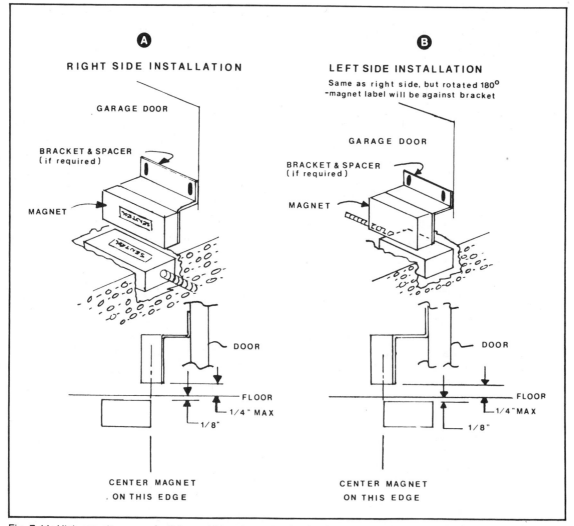

Fig. 7-14. High-security sensor/switch provides extra protection for the garage door and garage contents (A) Right-side installation. (B) Left-side installation (courtesy Sentrol Inc.).

netic contact in this application is virtually impossible to defeat with an external magnet. The switch used is polarity-sensitive and balanced. Be certain to align the magnet and switch so that labels read in the same direction. The switch has a nominal operating gap between the magnet and switch of 0.2" minimum and 0.6" maximum. Installation instructions take these operating parameters into account, but you should check for correct operation of the switch before encasing in concrete.

Installation instructions are as follows:

☐ Select a position for the switch that will minimize the amount of concrete to be chipped out.

☐ Install the magnet on the door, either directly or with bracket as necessary. For installation on the right side of the door (looking at door from inside—see Fig. 7-14A), attach the magnet with the label *upside down* and facing *away* from the door. For installation on the left side of the door (Fig. 7-14B), attach the magnet with the label *upside down* and facing *toward* the door.

☐ Close the door; be certain that the lower edge of the magnet is no further away from the floor than ¼".

☐ Position the switch such that the label on it reads in the same direction as the label on the magnet and that the bottom edge of the switch is centered on the bottom edge of the magnet. This will ensure proper operation of the switch.

☐ Chip away enough concrete (approximately 4½" × 1¾" × ⅞") to permit placement of the switch about ⅛" below the surface of the floor. Chip out a channel for the flex cable (approximately ⅜" × ⅜").

☐ Lay the switch in the chipped out area, with the cable in the channel. Attach an ohmmeter to the switch, close the door, and test for proper operation.

☐ Pour concrete to cover the switch and

cable. After the concrete is dry, test the switch again. Connect to the alarm loop. For maximum security, it is best to continue the cable run in the conduit after it exits from the floor.

### Additional Methods of Curtain Door Switch Mounting

A curtain door can be protected by mounting a switch to the side of the channel of the door, with a hole cut in the channel to provide a "window" for the switch to see the magnet (which is mounted on the door). In some instances this will not work, because the steel door and channel will weaken the magnetic field to the point where the switch will not operate. Here are mounting methods that will overcome this difficulty.

To install on the "stop" near the top of the door, close the door. Tape the magnet in place with masking tape. Position in the recessed portion of the slat, adjacent to the doorstop, with the red end mounted as shown.

Roll up the door, making sure the magnet clears and does not interfere with the operation of the door. Close the door. Attach a magnet to the door with clips or RTV mounting compound.

Attach wires to the terminals of the switch. Attach the switch to the inside of the long portion of the bracket, such that the label will be right side up and facing toward the door when the bracket is mounted on the stop (Fig. 7-15). Attach the bracket to the stop with self-tapping screws.

Close and open the door to test for proper operation of the switch. Dress wire leads with wire clips and hook them into the alarm loop. Retest for operation and clearance.

To install on the channel, close the door. Tape the magnet in place with masking tape. Position it in the recessed portion of the slat, as close to the edge of the door as possible, with the red end mounted as shown.

Roll up the door, making sure the magnet clears and does not interfere with operation of the door. Close the door. Attach the magnet to the door with screws.

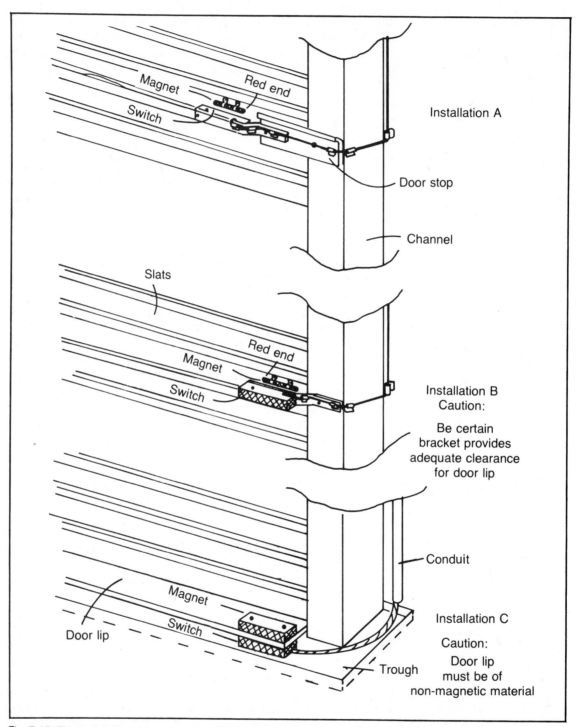

Fig. 7-15. This installation gives you options depending on the particular model and type of curtain door in your garage (courtesy Sentrol).

250

Attach wires to the terminals of the switch. Attach the switch to the outside of the long portion of the bracket, so that the label will be right side up and facing away from the door when the bracket is mounted on the channel. Attach the bracket to the channel with self-tapping screws. Position the bracket so that there will be adequate clearance for the corner of the door lip as the door is opened and closed.

Close and open the door to test for proper operation of the switch. Dress wire leads with wire clips and hook them into the alarm loop. Retest for operation and clearance.

To install the magnet on the door lip, with the switch on the floor (using an industrial wide-gap switch), the door lip must be nonmagnetic. The door must close into a trough to provide recessed mounting for the switch. Also, the door lip must not be flush with the bottom of the door, or there will be no clearance for the switch when the door is shut.

Attach the magnet to the corner of the door lip with screws. Attach the switch to the floor with appropriate fasteners. Position with the label facing up, reading in the same direction as the label on the magnet.

Open and close the door to test the switch for proper operation. Run stainless flex cable in the trough to the conduit. Connect to the alarm loop; retest for proper operation.

## WINDOWS

Garages usually have either double-hung or

Fig. 7-16. A secured garage window may prevent the theft of numerous tools stored in the garage (courtesy Ideal Security Hardware).

single-piece windows installed. If the window in question is double-hung, ensure that the closure device is one that locks (Fig. 7-16). Many garages have been entered through the windows because they could not be locked. For single-piece windows, usually those that are on a set of hinges located at the top and secured with a hook and eye, use magnetic contacts or make the windows permanently closed by nailing them to the frame.

Window protection can be spot protected with a local self-contained locking alarm. Figure 7-17 illustrates a multipurpose lock that can be used in the home and also in the garage. The battery-operated unit can be mounted to a vulnerable window to provide a quick alerting signal of attempted penetration through the window. With the chain, it also means the window can be open 1″ or 2″ for ventilation and still provide security.

## LOCKS

The rugged steel padlock shown in Fig. 7-18 provides very high security in home situations. The hardened steel shackle fights sawing and prying, while the solid steel body gives maximum protection against ordinary hand tools and general abuse. The double-ball feature (Fig. 7-19) means the shackle also will resist forcing. This type of heavy-duty security padlock can be used for securing expensive tools, high-cost bicycles, mopeds, motorcycles, and boats and trailers to a security post adjacent to your garage.

Brass or stainless steel padlocks may also be used to secure tool chests and other valuable equipment (Fig. 7-20). These locks, like standard bicycle locks, should at least be case-hardened at the shackle (you can tell this by the word "hardened" imprinted into the shackle).

Avoid cheaply made foreign import locks and locks that do not have a regular pin tumbler and standard cylinder key. The cheaper locks usually have a flat key. They provide a measure of security, but will not stand up to any excessive force applied.

This is not to imply that all foreign locks are

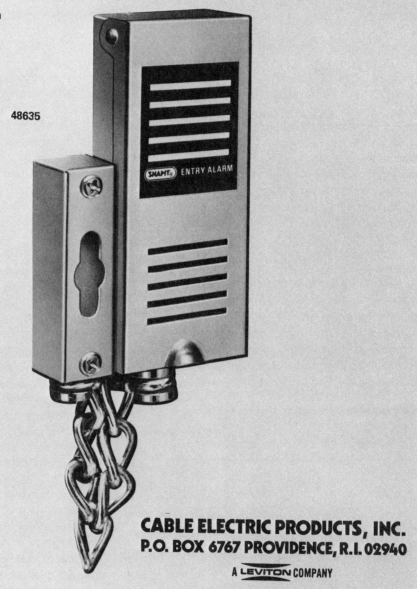

Fig. 7-17. Spot protection for a garage door can be obtained with a self-contained door alarm (courtesy Cable Electronics).

Fig. 7-18. Good security requires that a quality lock with a hardened steel shackle be used (courtesy American Lock Company).

Fig. 7-20. All-brass marine locks provide excellent security in all environments (courtesy Campbell Chain Co.).

cheap. Some are exceedingly superior to many American-made locks.

Medium security needs do not require the more expensive padlocks. A laminated steel padlock will suffice in many instances (Fig. 7-21).

This lock should have a five-pin tumbler mechanism and a hardened shackle to resist saws and files. To resist weather, select a padlock that is zinc-plated.

Outside doors, such as those leading to

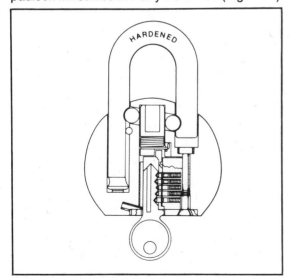

Fig. 7-19. The double-ball feature further protects the shackle from tools and abuse by vandals (courtesy American Lock Company).

Fig. 7-21. Any laminated lock used should have a pin tumbler cylinder for medium security (courtesy Campbell Chain Co.).

Fig. 7-22. Rustproof locks that also provide a medium or higher lever of exterior security may have a tubular key mechanism (courtesy Campbell Chain Co.).

small storage rooms, need the standard weather-resistant lock. Locks that must stand up to seashore weather need locking devices designed to ensure maximum weather resistance Fig. 7-22. These rustproof, stainless steel locks have the circular type eight-pin key tumbler mechanism and include a hardened steel shackle and double-ball shackle locking mechanism to provide maximum security. These locks can secure mopeds, bicycles, and other items.

Figure 7-23 shows a model *2000 Superlock*.

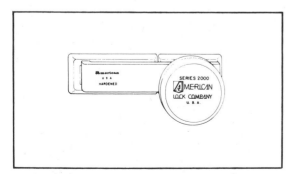

Fig. 7-23. The shrouded shackle leaves nothing exposed to attack (courtesy American Lock Co.).

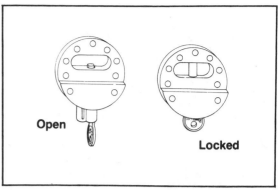

Fig. 7-24. The vertical locking pin is completely hidden from view when the Superlock is in use (courtesy American Lock Co.).

It has a shrouded shackle, meaning that nothing is exposed to make it vulnerable to attack. The lock fits over and completely covers the area when it is fitted onto the door hasp. This is a new patented hasp lock that has a solid reinforced one-piece body containing a high-security six-pin tumbler with mushroom pins, making it vitrually impossible to pick. Figure 7-24 shows a rear view of the Superlock in the opened and locked posi-

Fig. 7-25. A ⅜-inch thick anti-theft chain, provides a strong deterrent against theft (courtesy Campbell Chain Co.).

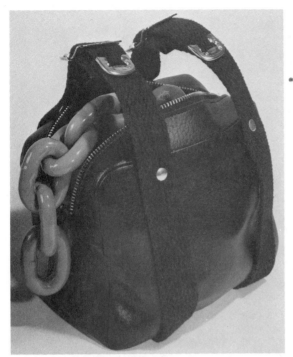

Fig. 7-26. Each link is vinyl-coated to protect your property from scratches while still giving optimum protection (courtesy Campbell Chain Co.).

tions. You can see how the lock fits flush up to the door hasp, protecting the lock from attempts to cut or saw at a shackle that cannot either be seen or reached by the perpetrator.

### SECURITY CHAINS

Various anti-theft chains are on the market for motorcycles, trailers, boats, and large equipment in the home that requires protection (Fig. 7-25). The chain for ultimate security (Fig. 7-26) is case-hardened and heat-treated to the core of the link. Putting it in a zipper tote bag allows for easy storage and transportation, especially when mounted to a motorcycle or in a boat.

Chains that are ¼″ or 9/32″ are designed for securing 10-speed bikes, go-karts, trail bikes,

Fig. 7-28. A case-hardened and vinyl covered chain protects mopeds against even bolt cutters (courtesy Campbell Chain Co.).

Fig. 7-27. The 6′ length allows numerous items to be secured to stationary objects (courtesy Campbell Chain Co.).

Fig. 7-29. A popular and highly successful lock for motorcycle and moped security (courtesy Campbell Chain Co.).

snowmobiles, mini-bikes, gates, and other items.

Flexible galvanized aircraft cables for bicycles have been popular among sporting and health enthusiasts. Because of the "snap-back" feature, the self-coiling feature makes it easy to store when not in use. The 6′ length is adequate to go through both bicycle wheels, around the frame, and to attach to a stationary object (Fig. 7-27).

Motorcycle and moped security can be pro-

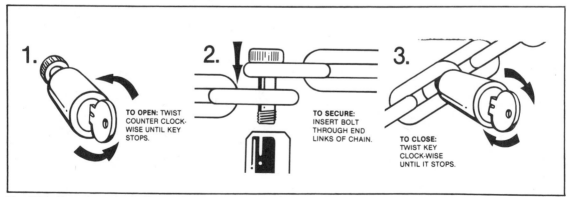

Fig. 7-30. Procedures for locking and unlocking the lock (courtesy Campbell Chain Co.).

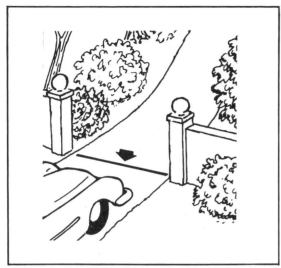

Fig. 7-31. The Road Switch provides an immedate alert to approaching vehicles (courtesy Tapeswitch Corporation of America).

vided with a case-hardened, boron bearing chain (5/16″ × 4′ long) specifically designed to resist saws and cutters (Fig. 7-28). To further protect the finish of the moped or motorcycle, the chain should be sleeved in vinyl. The lock is of an unusual design, but it allows more protection. There is no shackle. Figures 7-29 and 7-30 illustrates the lock and procedures for locking and unlocking it.

## DRIVEWAY ROAD SWITCH SENSORS

A weatherproof *Road Switch* installed across the entrance to a driveway provides a momentary warning of a vehicle entering your property (Fig. 7-31). This new heavy-duty road switch operates as a normally open, momentary switch. It has a closing contact when pressed by any vehicle wheel. The pressure sensitivity is 20 pounds. The Road Switch can be attached to the road surface mechanically or with an adhesive. Two versions are available: a standard one mounted in a steel mounting channel with flanges for fastening with studs, nails, or cement; or a ribbon

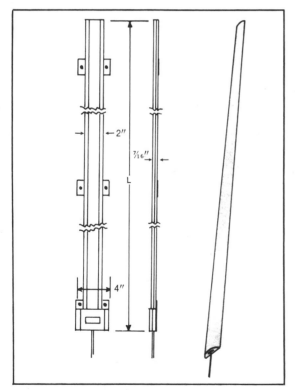

Fig. 7-32. A standard Road Switch or a ribbon switch (courtesy Tapeswitch Corporation of Amercia).

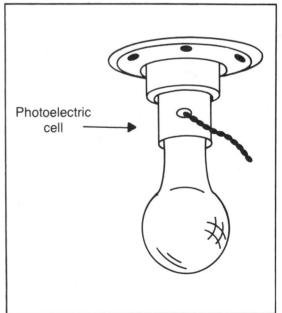

Fig. 7-33. While the photoelectric cell will turn on the light at dusk, a pull chain gives you the ability to check the lamp during the day.

257

switch that will slip into a protective rubber sheath (Fig. 7-32).

## LIGHTING

Install a light on the outside of your garage. The exterior lights may cover the garage. If not, you may consider installing one or two floodlights on the garage. Otherwise, have an exterior light, using a photoelectric cell (Fig. 7-33). Do not leave the lamp directly exposed. Cover it with a metal shield on top for weather protection and perhaps a wire mesh beneath the lamp.

# Chapter 8

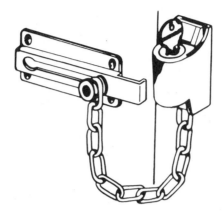

# Self-Protection

Self-protection is the ultimate. This chapter examines procedures and products that will help keep you safe.

### RAPE

Rape is a very ugly action. It is a crime against society and a viscious crime against the individual on whom it is perpetrated.

Rape is one of the most terrifying of crimes for women. Rape no longer must be locked away like a guilty secret. It can be dealt with in a way that can help the victim overcome the anguish and degradation that results from the act of an unjust aggressor.

Across the country police departments, hospitals, prosecuters, and other rape victims are prepared to give increased assistance and compassionate treatment to women who have been raped. Private nonprofit rape crisis centers in many localities can provide short- and long-term assistance to rape victims.

Your city police department has a sex crime division of men and women teams on a 24-hour/day basis. When a rape is reported, the team responds immediately. The woman officer usually questions the victim while the male officer conducts the investigation. The police evidence technician often obtains physical evidence from the scene of the crime.

These officers have received advanced training in sexual assault investigation. They are extremely aware of the problems, traumas, and fears of the rape victim. They will provide every possible assistance to the victim.

In some communities, the life crisis center or rape crisis center is prepared to counsel and make contacts for the victim. This is done on a 24-hour/day basis. The victim receives the best treatment and care possible from both the hospitals and police involved with the rape case and its investigation.

### What To Do If Rape Occurs

Rape can happen to any woman, no matter how

young or old, at any time and place. If it happens to you, call the police at once. A regular patrol officer will probably respond first, followed very quickly by a special investigator trained in rape matters.

Officers will take you to the hospital. An examination will be made. Don't change clothes, bathe, or douche before going to a hospital or seeing a doctor. You will destroy vital evidence.

You may wait to describe details of the incident until the woman officer arrives from the sex crime/sexual assault investigative unit. She and her partner have had special training on the treatment of rape victims, as well as investigating for a solution to the crime.

You may find it difficult to describe all that happened, but try hard. The person who attacked you must be caught for your protection and that of others.

Talk freely to someone close to you—your husband, parents, daughter, boyfriend, or girlfriend—or call a local rape crisis counseling center. If you bottle up the experience in an effort to forget it, you may have serious problems later. It is not a disgrace. It wasn't your fault. There are many professionals ready to help you.

### Note to the Family of a Rape Victim

Your understanding, compassion, and support are very important to the victim. Some women have suffered long-term injury because of mistaken attitudes shown by family members (or neighbors, friends, or relatives) after a rape. There is a rejection by a husband who feels that his "property" has been damaged, that his wife must have asked for it, and that no woman is raped unless she wants to be. This is a hangover from a time when even the word rape was taboo.

There are other examples when families were too embarrassed, felt guilty, or simply wanted to help a woman forget and thus refused to talk about it. Talking about the crime is a reasonable method of getting out the fears the woman feels. It may also help her to remember important details she may have forgotten, and it will help her face the situation more sensibly.

### Court

The police have a dual role in any violent crime. First, they must assist the victim in every way possible; second, they must catch the criminal before he can victimize someone else.

If you are a victim, it is your duty to help by giving every clue you can. You may know your attacker's name. If you don't the police have aids to help you reconstruct a picture of the man. They will show you photographs of known rapists. They can put together a composite picture at your direction. Try to remember things such as height, weight, clothing, type of hair, coloring, any identifying scars or blemishes, the make of automobile, and any special features.

You may appear before a grand jury to tell what happend, so that the grand jury can issue an indictment. An appearance before the grand jury is private—no reporters, no public, and no lawyers, except the prosecutor who is representing you and the citizens of your community.

It may be several months before the trial. Meanwhile, if you should receive any threats, the police will investigate and should give you protection. If you need help or just want an understanding person to talk to during this period, go to or call the rape crisis center in your area for assistance.

The trial will probably be the only time you have to see your attacker after the original identification. You will be far separated from him, with many officials between you. Your attorney from the prosecutor's staff will try to protect you from embarassment.

### Why Get Involved?

You may be thinking now, "Why should I, or anyone, have to go through all this? None of it was my fault." True, but apathy is one reason why there is so much crime today.

Your cooperation in getting the rapist convicted can prevent hundreds of additional crimes—not just from this one man, but from the many others who think women are too weak to fight back. You can't always fight back physically and win, but you can fight back in court. This is your most powerful weapon against your attacker.

## Keys to Rape Prevention

Do you:

- ☐ Lock your car doors and close windows?
- ☐ Keep your car in good condition, with plenty of gas and good tires?
- ☐ Keep alert for suspicious followers in cars or on the street?
- ☐ Train yourself to be alert as to identification of people, cars, or circumstances?
- ☐ Walk dark streets or alleys alone or unnecessarily?
- ☐ Talk to perfect strangers (men in particular) and let them buy you a drink, take you home, get in their car, invite them, or even worse, go into a stranger's house or apartment?
- ☐ Allow your date to park on lonely streets or out-of-the-way places where marauders may be lurking?

Some unthinking women believe that just because a man becomes friendly in a grocery store, cafeteria, tavern, cocktail lounge, or at a party or singles bar, it's all innocent fun and no harm can come to her if she lets her guard down. The woman, though, probably knows nothing about that stranger.

A woman who is hitchhiking may be putting herself in jeopardy. She may be raped, assaulted, physically maimed, or even killed. Some forms of behavior put you in a compromising position—actually inviting trouble. They are not worth it.

## What Can You Do?

If you are outdoors:

- ☐ Always have a whistle and keys in your hand for the car, home or office.
- ☐ When walking alone anywhere, be alert, aware, and perhaps even suspicious.
- ☐ When walking at night, stay in well-lighted areas whenever possible. Know where you are going and *take the most direct route*, preferably one that is well-lighted and well-traveled.
- ☐ Notice stores or other establishments that are open at night; these are places to go for help.
- ☐ If you have to be out alone at night, let other people know your plans so they know where you are and will be on the lookout for you.
- ☐ If you are suspicious about being followed, go to the nearest store or walk out into the street for help where you can be seen. If you carry a whistle, blow it for help.
- ☐ Always drive with your car doors locked.
- ☐ If you are being followed, drive to the nearest open gas station or police station and honk your horn for help.
- ☐ If you feel threatened by another car or by pedestrians while stopped or parked, use your horn.
- ☐ If your car is disabled, display a "send help" sign and don't get out of the car.
- ☐ If accosted, carefully consider the situation and use your best defense—scream and run. If caught, try and talk the attacker out of it. Distract him and use all the delaying tactics at your command.
- ☐ If your attacker has a weapon, put your life first. Struggling may result in your being seriously hurt or killed.

If you are indoors:

- ☐ Always keep the shades or curtains pulled at night.
- ☐ Never open the door to a stranger. Check credentials of repairmen.
- ☐ Keep doors and windows locked at all times.
- ☐ Never give the impression that you are home alone. Don't tell strangers on the telephone about your plans.
- ☐ If living alone, never use Miss or Mrs. on your mailbox or in a telephone listing.

261

Use your initials, like J. K. Smith, instead of Josephine K. Smith.

☐ Avoid empty basement laundry rooms or empty laundromats; also, don't use such areas late at night.

☐ Change the locks when you move into a new apartment or home.

☐ If you aren't home, use one or more timers for lights in the home.

☐ Dogs can be excellent protectors. Even friendly dogs can sound the alarm.

☐ Never allow young children to answer the door. Because they are friendly and unafraid, they usually will admit anyone.

The *Shriek Alert* (Fig. 8-1), a hand-held unit, produces a very loud and high-pitched sound that is continuous until you release the activation button. In addition to alerting other people to your distress, it can produce enough noise to scare off a potential attacker.

## SELF-DEFENSE

Self-defense, be it against a potential mugger, robber, or rapist, is good to know. Hopefully, people who have taken such training, and continue to keep themselves in physical condition, will never have to use it. If you are required to use it, do so properly.

Self-defense training is available in just about every city. There are usually several professional training organizations in addition to various clubs and locally sponsored activities that can assist you. Basic training in *jujitsu, judo, karate, aikido,* and other martial arts is excellent. Such training is not just a one-time event. It must be continuous. Even if not formal, the training and body conditioning must go on as long as you want to retain proficiency.

Do not assume that you can purchase a book, follow the words and pictures, and become an expert in self-defense. Books provide basic information and the pictures illustrate the various moves, but they are no substitute for proper training under a professional.

## BABY-SITTERS

For teenagers, baby-sitting is an excellent way to

Fig. 8-1. A push of the button alerts people to your need for help and also frightens away a potential mugger/rapist (courtesy The Peterzell Co.).

**Babysitter's Checklist**

The address here is: _____
Neighbor to contact, if necessary: (Name) _____
(Address) _____ (telephone) _____
Police/sheriff's department _____
Fire department _____
Doctor _____ (telephone) _____

We will be at _____ until _____
Telephone number(s) _____

Will return home at _____
Children's bedtime is _____
Any medication required is located at _____
Dosage of medication _____
Other instructions to follow _____

When answering the telephone, *never* announce to the caller that you are the baby-sitter. Merely inform the caller that we are not at home at the present. Take the caller's name and number and indicate they will be contacted as soon as possible.

Do not open the door to anyone you do not personally know and trust. If you see, hear, or become overly suspicious of anything that is happening outside, contact the police immediately. Keep the doors locked at all times. We will ring the doorbell when we return and then use our key to open the door. Do not open the door yourself if you are unable to positively identify us.

Fig. 8-2. The baby-sitter checklist should be filled out and placed by the telephone; always go over the list with the sitter before departing your home.

earn money and allows them to learn a lot about children. For a parent, it's a method of earning extra money, or by hiring a baby-sitter, getting away from the kids for an evening. Figure 8-2 is a baby-sitter checklist that should be completed and used by the sitter.

Note the first line—address. If there is a real emergency, the fire department and/or police must know the address to provide assistance. Go over the list with the baby-sitter prior to your departure from home. The sitter should:

☐ Always keep the doors and windows locked.
☐ Know the people to contact in case of an emergency.
☐ Not try to be a doctor or nurse except for any minor cuts, bruises, or abrasions.
☐ Know the dangerous items in the home: medicines, bleaches, household cleaners, and electrical and gas appliances. Keep children away from such items and keep the items out of the children's reach.
☐ Know what to do in emergencies.
☐ Know the emergency exits from all occupied rooms in the house.
☐ Know where a portable fire extinguisher is kept and how to use it properly.

## NEIGHBORLY ALERT SYSTEM

The *Neighborly Alert* system (Fig. 8-3) provides personal security protection and neighborhood protection. It also acts as an emergency alert.

Note the component parts in Fig. 8-3. This is one system that any do-it-yourselfer can handle. Plug in the basic receiver unit, ensure the various component parts have been attached, and the system is ready to use. The unit can have a buzzer, or a siren can be substituted. When activated, either will sound. If a lamp is plugged in, it turns on. Touching the portable clip-on panic button activates the unit. A simple touch of the panic button and the alarm is activated. People

can walk within or outside the home for short distances and still be in wireless contact with the unit. The system may be expanded so it can be used to work with floor pressure mat switches or to connect a transmitting device to a smoke detector.

The system is flexible enough to use in apartment buildings and private homes. One receiver per corridor and a transmitter in every apartment will suffice. The siren can be replaced by a bell. In homes where elderly parents have separate rooms, a buzzer can replace the bell.

Radio-intercom systems provide a communications link to every area of your home, both inside and outside, whenever you choose. A good intercom system allows you to speak to people all over the house. A good system will also have a listening capability. You can check night sounds outdoors without leaving the home and check sounds that occur in the middle of the night within the home. The system must provide you with security when determining who is at the door. Perhaps you are upstairs or in the basement when the doorbell rings. Instead of coming to the door and opening it, you have the convenience of answering the door from anywhere in the home. Speakers are located throughout the home to allow individual room monitoring and

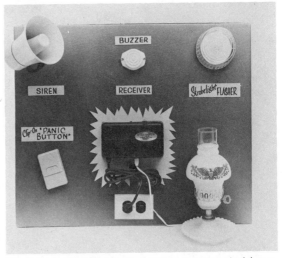

Fig. 8-3. The Neighborly Alert system is economical (courtesy Life Guard Products Co.).

Fig. 8-4. Master Control Center has various functions you can use (courtesy NuTone).

Fig. 8-5. Even when working, you can answer from anywhere in the home (courtesy NuTone).

Fig. 8-6. When the visitor is recognized, you can open the door and greet him (courtesy NuTone).

also the ability to answer the door via the intercom system.

Figure 8-4 illustrates the *CommuniCenter Master Station* radio-intercom system. In addition to security, the system also provides for weather radio/alert, a digital clock, AM/FM radio, and a tape deck.

The unit provides for "hand-free" door answering from anywhere in the home (Fig. 8-5). At the door, a simple push-button speaker unit (Fig. 8-6) is available for unknown visitors to your home.

A portable speaker that can be plugged into a wall receptacle is available for use from your bed. Besides the bedroom, it can be carried and used anywhere in the home where you don't wish to install a permanent speaker (Fig. 8-7).

To some people, radio intercoms and speakers are luxuries that aren't required. If they are needed in your home, look at the system carefully before purchasing it. It must meet your needs and home requirements.

## WATCHDOGS

The knowledge of a watchdog close by gives you a feeling of added protection.

Almost any dog will provide added home and personal protection. Before selecting the dog, though, you must consider exactly what functions the dog will perform. Will the dog be used solely as a watchdog, or will it also be a family pet? Must the dog be aggressive in its manner to all except the owner? Will the dog be used to warn (bark) you of potential intruders, scare away intruders by its barking, or will it be used as an attack dog? What level of training do you desire for the dog?

In a typical family (especially those with children), you probably won't require an attack dog but merely one that will bark to ward off strangers and potential intruders. Dogs don't have to cost a lot of money. You can lower your initial cost greatly by selecting a crossbreed or a mongrel. Many times the local dog pound, ASPCA (American Society for the Prevention of Cruelty to Animals) local animal protection society, or even the pet store will have such dogs available.

Dogs should have a good temperament, and be intelligent, courageous, and loyal. Agressiveness in a dog may also be desirable, but only if the dog will be performing guard duties. A dog must not be overly aggressive around children.

The German shepherd, Boxer, Great Dane, Doberman pinscher, and Airedale can easily be trained as watchdogs and home pets. Smaller dogs, such as Scottish and fox terriers, can also be used for protection. Even a beagle or a poodle can be used effectively. The bark from the dog alerts the homeowner to a prowler in the area, but it also alerts the prowler that his presense is known and that he should quickly move on.

Dogs can be too docile to act as watchdogs in the home. Although the *collie* has a good temperament and is excellent with small children, it may not bark when a stranger is around. It is too easily placated by such things as a bone or a piece of meat.

If the dog is to be a full-time guard dog, consult a professional dog trainer. If you are

Fig. 8-7. A portable, plug-in unit can be moved anywhere in the home for use (courtesy NuTone).

using the dog for its deterrance and noise value, you can train it yourself and save a lot of money. Any training will include initial obedience. Allowing the dog to be around children and in a family atmosphere will give it basic obedience and tol-erance to everyday family situations. The dog will learn from daily experiences what it should and shouldn't do.

A dog can be taught to respond to specific commands in a single or several languages. A

Fig. 8-8. The Super Hailer can signal for help or talk to people in distress from afar (courtesy Ovenaire-Audio-Carpenter).

specific word or combination of words with the specific function (action reponse by the dog) can be easily taught and remembered by the dog when it is taught in repetition several times. Check your local library to see what books it has available on training dogs.

A dog in the home cannot replace your other security features. It will not replace a quality lock; nor will the dog (especially if it is untrained) ever be as reliable as a burglar alarm. The dog can only be used as a supplement to your other security devices.

## HAND-HELD SIGNALING DEVICES

The *Super Hailer* is an extremely powerful 20-watt, hand-held megaphone that can also double as a portable public address system (Fig. 8-8). It is transistorized, is the commercial version of the military model, and operates solely on "D" batteries. A variation includes a penetrating electronic siren that will alert people at a greater distance to your need for assistance.

A second possibility that cannot be overlooked, especially for those with large boats, is that version shown in Fig. 8-9. This public ad-

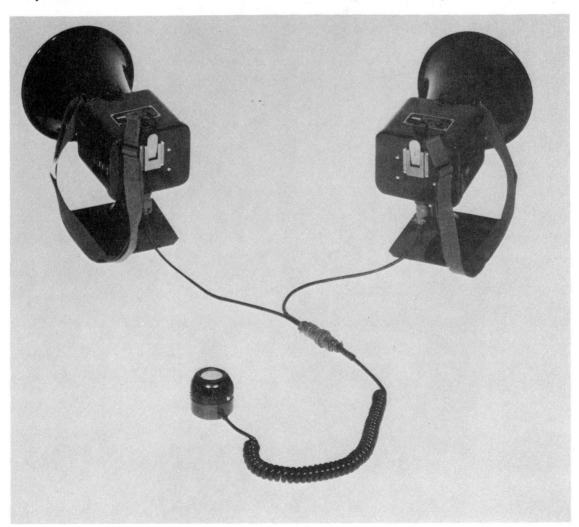

Fig. 8-9. Dual Super Hailer can perform many duties (courtesy Ovenaire-Audio-Carpenter).

Fig. 8-10. A personal public address system can be a real help to lost hikers, hunters, or those looking for them (courtesy Ovenaire-Audio-Carpenter).

dress system, which is a pair of 20-watt Super Hailers interconnected with a dual hookup cable to allow for voice projection in more than one direction at a time, is especially good under unfavorable conditions, such as fog. Like the previous unit, it is also portable and self-contained, requiring no external power.

Another unit can be clipped to a belt or hung from a neck strap (Fig. 8-10). Light and compact, it is a personal public address system using transistorized circuitry and 9-volt transistor batteries for operation. It has a long life and is very dependable.

Those units can be used to search for people, allowing your voice to carry further away to hear your normal shouting voice. The megaphones may be used when you are alone in secluded areas.

## SUSPICIOUS ACTIVITY

Police cannot be everywhere. For this reason, the effective functioning of a police department is dependent on citizens' cooperation and their resistance to crime. Many crimes would never be committed if more citizens would be alert to suspicious activity and notify the police.

The police should be contacted whenever you observe suspicious activity, even though you may not be the only observer to the activity. Never rely on the next guy to do what you should have done. The police would rather get many calls concerning the same incident than no calls at all.

Citizens often fail to act because they are not sure if what they are observing is suspicious activity. When in doubt, call the police immediately. Don't wait to discuss events with friends or neighbors first. Valuable police response time is lost this way. By not calling in immediately, a crime may take place—and you may have been able to prevent it by acting immediately. Suspicious activity is not necessarily a crime about to be committed or one in progress. It's better to have the police check it out than to assume that it isn't your responsibility.

Don't be concerned about bothering the police. Don't dwell on your possible embarrassment if your suspicions should prove unfounded. Think of what could happen if you don't act.

The following examples of what to watch for may be helpful in determining when to call for help:

☐ A stranger entering a neighbor's home while the neighbor is away, someone crossing your yard or a neighbor's yard, anyone trying a neighbor's door, and a moving truck or van pulling up to a neighbor's home while he is away should be investigated.

☐ Someone carrying certain items (such as a television, stereo, etc.) at an unusually late hour in or in an unusual place, especially if it does not appear that the property is wrapped as if just purchased.

☐ The sound of breaking glass could indicate possible burglary, vandalism, or larceny.

☐ Anyone observed peering into vehicles as they walk down the street, someone removing tags, gasoline, or accessories from a vehicle; or someone attempting to enter a vehicle using a coat hanger or other gadget are suspicious. Never assume that it is the owner who has mistakenly locked his keys in his vehicle. Be suspicious of anyone tampering with the hood or the trunk of a vehicle.

☐ An improperly parked car, an abandoned vehicle, and someone leaving one vehicle and driving away in another may be signs of vehicle theft.

☐ Anyone being forced into a vehicle could indicate a possible abduction.

☐ Persons loitering around schools, parks, secluded areas, or in neighborhood locales where they do not live or work. These could be possible burglars or sex offenders.

☐ Apparent business transactions conducted from a vehicle, especially around schools or parks and if juveniles are involved, or a constant flow of strangers to and from a particular house regularly, especially at late or unusual hours, could be indicative of drug sales or, in the latter case, of a possible fencing operation.

☐ Offers of merchandise or repair work at unusually low prices could indicate stolen property or some form of fradulent scheme.

☐ Persons involved in a fight or any loud explosions or screams are suspicious. Sex offenses, robbery, and assault are among the crimes that could be occurring.

☐ Door-to-door solicitors without a properly issued permit to conduct such business are suspicious.

Use the police's emergency number to report suspicious activity. You will be asked for your name, address, and telephone. This information is requested in case additional contact with you becomes necessary. Any information provided to the police department is kept in confidence. You should know the emergency number for your police department. Contact your police crime resistance unit for telephone stickers and other information that may aid you and your neighbors in stopping crime.

### ROBBERY AND PURSE SNATCHING

*Robbery* occurs when someone steals or takes anything of value from your person or in your presence against your will by force or violence or by putting you in fear of force or violence. Statutes commonly classify robberies by the means employed, such as armed robbery, or the place of the offense, such as bank robbery.

A robbery has elements of both crimes against persons and crimes against property. The motive is momentary gain, but property must be taken from or in the presense of another person.

*Burglary* is the breaking and entering of your home (or business) with the intention of stealing or committing some felony. It isn't necessary for the theft or felony to be consummated; the crime is committed at the moment of breaking and entering. Your home or business may be burglarized, but when you are personally involved, you have suffered a robbery.

Robbery and purse snatching are crimes against you. Is your money worth more than your life? Some people take foolish risks and lose. If a robber threatens you with a gun or indicates that he has a gun in his pocket, assume that he does. Your chance of safely disarming him is small. Your best protection lies in thinking out ahead of time what you will do under certain conditions. Hopefully, you will be realistic in your thinking; do nothing that might make the individual panic or become angry with you.

☐ Don't panic; stay calm.

☐ Don't resist.

☐ Obey all instructions the robber gives you.

☐ Be alert—notice what's happening.

☐ Activate an alarm only if no one is endangered by doing so.

☐ Look for peculiar features—associate these with each of the robbers if there is more than one.

☐ Notice the weapon. If the robber has a gun, assume it is loaded.

☐ Notice the nose, eyes, ears, and other features that are immediately apparent.

☐ If time permits without arousing specific attention to what you are doing, try to notice and remember the following:

| | | | |
|---|---|---|---|
| Height | Sex | Complexion | Shirt or Tie |
| Weight | Hair | Voice | Belt |
| Build | Nose | Accent | Trousers |
| Age | Eyes | Name | Sox and Shoes |
| Race | Ears | Hat | Coat or Sweater |

☐ When the robber leaves, try and see how he gets away without exposing yourself to any danger. Note the color, make, and license number of the car. Note how many others are in the car and their features. Note the time and direction of escape.

- [ ] Call the police immediately. Report that you have been held up, give your name and current location, and give a description of the getaway car (if any) and the robber. Stay on the telephone. After the first call goes out to police cars in the area, the police dispatcher will come back on the line to obtain additional details.
- [ ] While awaiting the arrival of the police, lock the doors if you are inside. Don't touch anything and keep everyone away from the holdup area. Preserve anything that may have been touched by the robbers.
- [ ] Remember that the information you give the police will be all they have to work with, so be precise and accurate. Save anything left behind or dropped by the robbers, but don't touch it.
- [ ] While awaiting the police, don't discuss the crime with other witnesses. All those involved should make notes of the information they have while it is fresh in their minds.

Be available for answering questions immediately after the crime and also into the near future. Answer questions truthfully, if you don't know or can't be sure of the answer to a question, say so. Don't try to give an answer that is made only to appease the individual asking the question. Don't exaggerate or guess; specifics are required as much as possible. Finally, be willing to make statements and identify suspected robbers after they have been apprehended.

## FRAUD

*Fraud and bunco games* are crimes against persons and are perpetrated daily. Many people become victims to such crimes, but don't report them because of publicity or they feel foolish at having been duped. In not reporting such crimes, these people actually help the criminal to continue his illegal activities.

## Consumer Fraud

Are you planning to have repairs or improvements made to your home? If so, you may save a lot of headaches by following these tips:

- [ ] Shop around. Get estimates from at least three contractors. Check with people who have had work done by the contractor. Check with your local Better Business Bureau to determine if complaints have been filed.
- [ ] Check to see if the contractor is properly licensed to do business in your city/county.
- [ ] Be sure you understand the contract in its entirety. Do not sign it unless you do.
- [ ] Does your contact describe the service to be performed and the types of materials to be used along with a starting and completion date for the work?
- [ ] Is there a specific warranty with your contract?
- [ ] Be cautious of companies that require advanced payments.
- [ ] Be sure the entire cost of the work is always specified.
- [ ] The cheapest bid may not always be the best.

Local codes and ordinances usually require home improvement contractors to be licensed and to show prospective customers an identification card (issued by the municipality in which they are doing business) on request.

The most effective weapon against consumer fraud is an alert and informed consumer. Remember the following when making purchases from door-to-door salesmen or at a store:

- [ ] Beware of the smooth talking salesman who comes to your home unannounced. Also, be on guard for the phone call in advance to set up an appointment to come to your home to give you something or to ask you to participate in a survey.

- Be alert for the operator who poses as an inspector. If you are approached in this way, ask the person to produce credentials and call the agency represented.
- Watch out for bait and switch sales tactics. This is a scheme whereby the merchant will advertise a product at a certain price or as possessing certain qualities. When the customer attempts to buy it, he will be switched to a higher priced or off-brand product.
- Fight the temptation of referral selling. This scheme offers the consumer the chance to make a quick killing by simply supplying the names of friends and relatives as prospective customers.
- Carefully investigate free or "bargain" offers. There is often a hidden trick or condition attached to the offer meaning that the customer must pay much more.
- Don't be rushed into signing any papers. Carefully read, examine, and understand all conditions of any contract or agreements. Never sign a blank contract or a contract with blank spaces.
- Do not rely on verbal representations. Be sure that such promises can be found in the terms and conditions.
- Ask questions. Know exactly what you are buying. Find out what the product or service will cost.
- Know with whom you are dealing. Beware of the fly-by-night operator or the company without a local address. It's safer to deal with a local merchant whom you know.
- Don't hesitate to shop around. You may find a better price for the same product elsewhere.

### Charitable Solicitations

The generosity of Americans in helping those in need has made charity rackets profitable operations for swindlers. What appeals are legitimate? It is often difficult to tell. Many appeals are to raise funds for nonexistent causes.

To be safe, follow these three practices:

- Demand to see proper identification from any solicitor making an appeal.
- Restrict donations to causes and organizations with which you are familiar.
- If you have any doubts, ask for a certified financial statement from the charitable organization. Do not donate to any organizations that do not furnish this information on request.

### Door-to-Door Sales

Salemen peddle magazines, encyclopedias, cookware, club memberships, and other items door-to-door. Many salespeople are honest, but look for those who are not.

Here are a few pointers to help you:

- Be suspicious of a seller who says, "I'm taking a survey," or, "You have been selected . . ."
- Ask to see the seller's identification and company credentials. If you doubt the person, check with the local Better Business Bureau.
- Buy only if you need the item—not because you may feel sorry for the seller.
- Insist on a written guarantee.
- Take ample time to consider the purchase. Avoid any high-pressure tactics.
- Never sign a contract unless you completely understand it and know the total cost.

Court laws provide that a buyer of most consumer goods and services has three days after the purchase in which to cancel a home solicitation sale. If a "buyer's right to cancel" clause is not included in the contract and the company will not accept a written cancellation, contact your local or state consumer protection office.

Be cautious with door-to-door solicitors. Ask to see their solicitor's license. If they can't show you one, don't talk with them and call the police department. Get a specific guarantee in writing if the work is guaranteed.

A salesperson's job is to sell. If he is good, he can sell you almost anything. Some "good" salespeople are not reliable. A reliable salesperson will let you take time to think things over and will want you to fully understand what you sign.

### Contracts

Have you signed a contract with a health spa, a car dealership, or real estate firm and really did not read what you were signing? Sometimes what salespeople say and what is written in the contract are completely different. Contracts can sometimes be terminated by mutual consent of both parties or by a court of law if there is sufficient proof of fraud or misrepresentation. Many contracts are legal and binding to all parties concerned. Keep in mind:

- ☐ When signing a contract, you are agreeing to the terms in print—not to verbal representations.
- ☐ Keep a copy of what you sign.
- ☐ Have all blanks filled in.
- ☐ Understand what you sign.

Don't sign anything until you have read it and understand it. Get help in understanding it if necessary. Be suspicious of anyone who will not let you take a copy of a proposed contract or agreement to someone you trust before you sign. Call your Office of Consumer Affairs for suggestions.

Do not accept the seller's word that any part of a contract does not apply to you (unless that part is crossed out on all copies and initialed) or that something not listed will be done unless it is written in before you sign. No matter what is said, what you sign is what you agree to. Keep a copy of everything you sign. If you don't understand it, don't sign it.

### OPERATION IDENTIFICATION

*Operation Identification* (ID) is a nationwide program designed to discourage burglary and theft of valuables from your home and other locations. It also provides a way for you to easily identify stolen property.

Operation ID has dramatically reduced crime in communities where most citizens have joined the program because it reduces the profit in crime. The crime "triangle" consists of the opportunity, the desire, and a victim. Through the use of Operation ID, these are reduced (Fig. 8-11). Burglars steal valuables for resale. If you mark all items with permanent identification numbers, the burglar will be unable to sell them to his "fence" or other underground sources. If a criminal knows all valuables in your home are marked, he will look for easier and more profitable victims.

Operation ID works even if your property is stolen or lost. It helps the police to contact you when the property is recovered and lets you identify it so it can be returned to you.

After marking your property, make a list of the valuables and keep a copy of the list in a safe place. If you should subsequently become a burglary victim, you will be able to quickly describe the stolen property from the list. This will

Fig. 8-11. Different jurisdictions have various Operation ID decals and will gladly help you qualify for the program.

Fig. 8-12. The Detroit, Michigan, police department has an excellent program with proven results in crime reduction.

☐ Identify your property as conspicuously as possible without defacing it. On some valuables, you should engrave a second number in an inconspicuous spot for added security.

☐ When engraving, hold the engraver straight up and down—not at a slant.

☐ The engraver has a depth adjuster. To adjust for hard surfaces such as metal, adjust the knob to the loudest position.

be of great help to the police in their attempts to recover the stolen possessions.

When property has been marked and a list made, display an Operation Identification sticker at doors and windows that might be used for entry. By advertising your participation in Operation ID, you are announcing that your valuable property has been marked and will be difficult for a burglar to resell. The presence of the sticker alone often is enough to deter a burglar.

Ensure that the checklist is kept up to date. Every six months (once a year at a minimum) review your copy of items that have been marked. Add new items to the list or delete as necessary. Finally, make sure that your warning decal has not been obliterated, torn, or destroyed. If so, obtain another Operation ID decal and affix it in the appropriate spot. Figure 8-12 illustrates one of the many decals available through local community Operation ID programs.

In addition to the stylus pen, electric engravers can be used to mark your valuables. Figure 8-13 illustrates an electric engraver and the specifics of the unit. Here are tips for using an electric engraver:

☐ Practice using the engraving tool before your property is marked.

☐ Be sure to engrave the complete Operation ID number.

## SAFETY FOR CYCLISTS AND JOGGERS

With the tremendous growth of cycling and jogging in recent years, safety is directed toward keeping motorists from hitting the cyclist or jogger during the early morning hours, at dusk, or during the night. Many people who bike or jog a lot prior to dawn or after dark believe, and rightly so, that they shouldn't have to be so defensive all the time. Bikers or joggers may use a *Belt Beacon.*

The Belt Beacon uses the same lamp as the highway barricade flasher, but it is very much smaller in size and weight. It is 3″ inches in

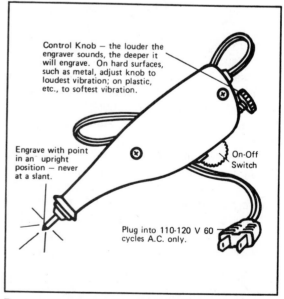

Control Knob — the louder the engraver sounds, the deeper it will engrave. On hard surfaces, such as metal, adjust knob to loudest vibration; on plastic, etc., to softest vibration.

Engrave with point in an upright position — never at a slant.

On-Off Switch

Plug into 110-120 V 60 cycles A.C. only.

Fig. 8-13. The electric engraver is only one of several items used for marking property.

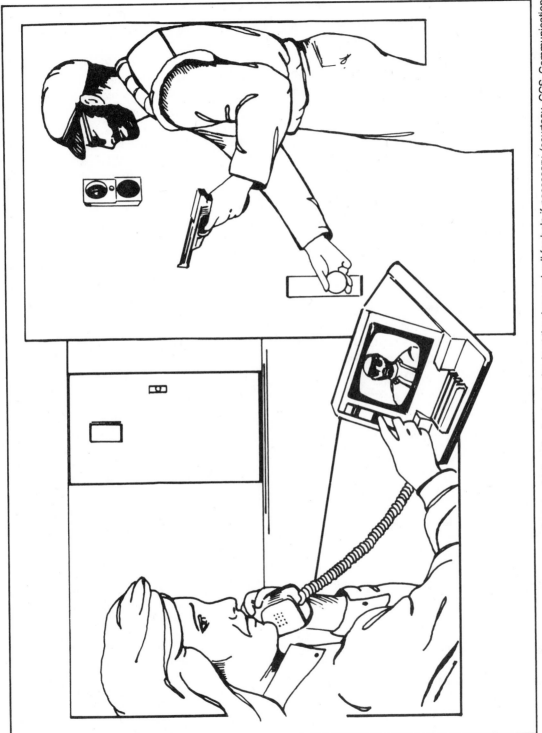

Fig. 8-14. The Electric Peephole is an excellent way to visually check out who is at the door and call for help if necessary (courtesy CCS Communication Control, Inc.).

diameter, weighs 4 ounces, flashes brightly for a very long time on a miniature 9-volt battery, and makes the cyclist or jogger exceptionally visible to approaching motorists. Early morning news delivery persons, hikers, and pedestrians also use it.

Advantages of a Belt Beacon over a common hand-held flashlight include:

- ☐ An intensely bright electronic beacon uses an optimized solid-state oscillator and a special signal lamp.
- ☐ Two-transistor control conserves the 9-volt battery. Battery life is many times longer.
- ☐ The Belt Beacon is substantially brighter, more visible, and visible at greater distances due to a light-gathering, semi-directional Fresnel lens.
- ☐ It is brightly visible through an angle of more than 180° for good side protection.
- ☐ The flash intensity is somewhat greater than that of most barricade flashers.
- ☐ Belt clip and hardware allow the Belt Beacon to be attached to your belt, bike, bag, pack, or clothing.

The Belt Beacon should be considered as a supplement to bicycle lights and reflectors and not as a replacement or substitute for them.

## ELECTRONIC PEEPHOLE

Figure 8-14 illustrates the theory behind the Electronic Peephole, a state-of-the-art device that allows you to determine who is at the door before answering it. Better than an alarm system, it allows the person to see, hear, and speak to the individual(s) at the door before these people are allowed to enter the premises. Their identity is verified through the use of a miniature viewing screen that lets you see by remote video. By use of the closed intercom, their identity and purpose can also be verified verbally.

The miniature television camera gives you a wide angle, distortion-free image that appears automatically on the desktop viewing monitor.

The condenser microphone and speaker are hidden behind an inconspicuous door panel.

## BULLETPROOF CLOTHING

The threat of a discharge weapon is frightening. Figure 8-15 shows a bulletproof vest.

A new synthetic fiber that is stronger than steel is woven into these body shields to provide the surest protection possible that you can have in bulletproof armor. A top-of-the-line body shield may have either 10- or 18-layer level protection woven into it. A 10-layer level will protect against .22, .38, and .45-caliber weapons, whereas the 18-layer level will protect against these as well as 9 mm and .357 Magnum weapons.

## RADIATION ALERT

The problems created by the Three Mile Island incident brought people's fears about nuclear

Fig. 8-15. This piece of clothing can stop bullets (courtesy CCS Communication Control, Inc.).

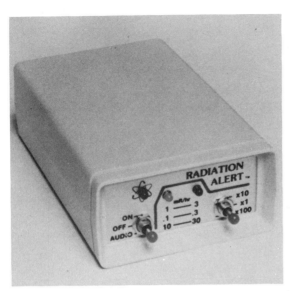

Fig. 8-16. The Radiation Alert, a pocket-sized unit, can forewarn you of potential danger (courtesy CCS Communication Control, Inc.).

radiation to the surface. Radiation is silent, invisible, and virtually undectable to humans, but that doesn't lessen its deadly effects.

Exposure to harmful radiation cannot be completely eliminated, but you can do something to protect yourself. The Radiation Alert (Fig. 8-16) can warn you instantly of increased radiation levels. Working on a Geiger counter principle, the audio alarm can actually lead you to (or away from) the radiation source. With the visual alarm lights, the radiation alert is virtually incapable of false alarms.

This miniature solid-state can fit in your pocket or be carried in the glove compartment of your car. It is so small (but still so effective) that it will fit into your jacket pocket and can also be carried in the palm of your hand. Wherever you go, you have immediate protection against the hidden danger of radiation.

## BULLETPROOF CARS

Imagine a corporate executive or even a treasurer for a major company who is transferring a lot of money, such as a company payroll, and the car is attacked. If you were in the car, could you survive? In the average car, the answer would be no. The bulletproof car (Fig. 8-17) is now available for optimum protection of its occupants. These cars are used by people to ensure their personal protection and privacy. A car can be refitted or custom-built to be virtually impenetrable to attack. The outward appearance remains completely unchanged and inconspicuous.

The car in Fig. 8-17 has the following protective features:

—Transparent bulletproof glass is inserted in all windows. It will protect against up to a .30-caliber carbine and even against hammers, bats, and hatchets.

—The entire car is installed with a revolutionary bulletproof fabric that's very light and stronger than old-fashioned steel reinforcement.

—Flip-down gun portholes allow the return of fire through the outer layer of the car for self-defense.

—An undercoating is added that will repel the effects of a land mine, grenade and other explosive charges to protect passengers.

—Steel-reinforced tires won't deflate even after being punctured by a bullet.

—A hidden tear gas system can be activated to immobilize attackers.

—An oil slick emission system will deter followers with a spill of 20 gallons of oil.

—The gas tank is enveloped with bulletproof fabric (as is the battery) to protect against explosion.

—An emergency oxygen unit is supplied for cases of smoke or gas inhalation.

—Reinforced ram bumpers aid when defensive driving techniques are put into use.

—A built-in tracking transmitter allows the car and its passengers to be found in cases of kidnapping.

—An ultrasensitive bomb sniffer can be used to investigate suspicious packages or other items.

—Remote start allows you to start the car from a safe distance to detonate any ignition-controlled explosives.

—Hand-free infrared goggles can be used

Fig. 8-17. The ultimate in protection for the person on the move (courtesy CCS Communication Control, Inc.).

Fig. 8-18. The Security Blanket flashlight can save you from kidnapping or a mugging. It can even save your life (courtesy SSC Communication Control, Inc.).

Fig. 8-19. Small enough to fit in your hand, the Bug Alert can alert you to bugging devices (courtesy CCS Communication Control, Inc.).

when driving to see clearly through smoke and gas or on unlit roads.

## SECURITY BLANKET FLASHLIGHT

Imagine you are walking down the street or to your car in an unlit or poorly lighted area, and you are approached by an attacker. By simply flashing the AL22 *Security Blanket* (Fig. 8-18) at an oncoming attacker, you instantly ensure that he is temporarily blinded by a beam that's 5 million lumens strong.

The Security Blanket looks like a flashlight and is a hand-held system that can be used anytime and anywhere for defense. It weighs only 1¾ pounds, is 12″ long and uses a 9-volt battery.

## PROTECTION AGAINST ELECTRONIC EAVESDROPPING

Telephone wiretaps and room bugs have become almost commonplace. They are easily obtained, inexpensive, and easily installed. Articles

about them now appear regularly in the daily press, so your suspicions of possible bugs on your premises may be well-founded. Wiretaps are not as common, though, as room bugs. Now there are transmitters tiny enough to fit in an olive, a pen, a tie clip and a ring. They are powerful enough to transmit your conversation up to a mile away.

A Bug Alert (Fig. 8-19) detects a transmitter using the sophistication of modern technology. This model detects a transmitter with the most sophisticated pocket-sized protection system in the world. You can take it wherever you go. Keep it in your pocket or hide it in your briefcase. You can even hold it in your hand. A tiny red alert light tells you when your conversation is being jeopardized by a transmitter. In its latch position, the alert light remains intact until you leave the room, check the warning, and reset the switch for future use. These Bug Alert systems can be neatly packaged into a zip-around leather notebook case or can be concealed in the base of a pen set.

# Chapter 9

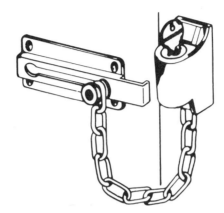

# Travel Protection

Nobody is immune from problems that can arise when traveling by car, airplane, bus, or boat. You should anticipate what problems may occur during travel and take appropriate measures beforehand to reduce the chance of you, or your family, becoming involved in a problem.

Some problems, like the unexpected flat tire in the middle of nowhere and a jack that suddenly doesn't want to work, cannot be foreseen. Other problems can be foreseen and actions taken to avoid or reduce the chance of the problem occurring.

Travel protection starts before you plan a trip. A trip may be for pleasure or business, one day or overnight, or for several weeks. In most instances, though, the planning for the trip and your protection during the trip involve the same steps.

Do you have a map that is up-to-date and not 10 or 15 years old? Have you planned the route? What are the best times for starting the trip so you don't get bogged down in rush hour traffic when going through another city? What should you take? How much money? What about credit cards?

Lock up the home to prevent burglaries while you are away. A vacant house, or one that appears to be vacant, is a very appealing target for a burglar.

## SECURITY MEASURES
## BEFORE LEAVING ON VACATION

At least one day before you leave on vacation, you should:

☐ Tell your newspaper carrier to discontinue the papers while you are away.
☐ Make sure that any broken windows, doors, and/or locks have been repaired and that the locks are in good working order.
☐ Have a neighbor or relative living close by watch your house while you are away. The neighbor or relative should have an

emergency address as to where to contact you. You should have the neighbor's or relative's telephone number with you.

☐ Your auto make, model, and license number should also be given to a close neighbor or friend.

☐ All lawn furniture, garden tools, ladders, etc., should be stored inside the home or the garage. Individual pieces of equipment that possess a higher than nominal value should be secured with a chain and locked to a standing post in the garage or home.

☐ Notify your local police of your impending departure. Let them know when you will go, when you will return, and who (name/address/telephone) has a key for access to your home.

☐ All valuables should be stored in a security closet (that is alarmed) or in a bank safe deposit box. Deposit extra cash into your savings or checking account.

☐ Have the post office hold all mail until you return or have a neighbor or close friend pick up the mail daily. (This can be the same person who checks your home and has a key).

Two or three days before your travel begins, you should start to do the following. Make sure all are accomplished prior to your leaving:

☐ Obtain recognized traveler's checks to use during the trip. If more than one person is in your party, some traveler's checks should be signed by each person. In case of an accident and one person is incapacitated, the other can still sign a portion of them. Otherwise, it might not be possible to cash any of them.

☐ Close the fireplace flue.

☐ Set the home thermostat so that your air conditioner or furnace will maintain a reasonable temperature of at least 50°-55°F. in the winter and 80°F. in the summer.

☐ Unplug all nonessential electrical appliances, lamps, television sets, radios, etc. Unhook the aerial from the television set.

☐ Close and lock all windows and doors.

☐ Test your home security alarm system, ensuring that all sensors are in proper working order. If you know or think that a sensor or other system component is bad, contact a security alarm company worker and have it repaired immediately.

☐ If you have a second car, lock it in the garage, then lock the garage. If you do not have a garage, leave the car in the driveway, but make sure it is locked.

☐ Leave a key with the neighbor. Provide the neighbor with information on where you will be.

☐ Turn down the volume control on the telephone, but not all the way down.

☐ If the trip will be for an extended period, turn off all gas pilot lights.

☐ Set electrical timers and lights. Test them out several days in advance. Have the lights adjusted so they all don't go on or off at the same time or at even times, such as on the quarter hour, half hour, or the hour. Random sequences of time are more realistic. Also, the time should coincide somewhat with your regular schedule within the home.

## TIPS FOR MOTORISTS

While driving on the road, you have to be concerned with where you are going, the road on which you are driving, the weather, other drivers, road conditions, and the hazards of driving long distances with minimal amounts of sleep.

People run red lights, drive while intoxicated, and go too fast. Pedestrians may creep into the streets, children may run out after a ball or pet, and bicyclists may ride carelessly. You must watch for these things while driving.

Defensive driving is important. It means thinking ahead, anticipating, and preparing to act should an emergency occur.

Fig. 9-1. The Sleeper Beeper is shown behind the driver's ear. A buzzer sounds when the driver's head nods below 22° (as depicted here), warning the driver that he is falling asleep. A miniature mercury switch from Micro Switch triggers the battery-powered circuitry. The ½-ounce unit fits comfortably over glasses or hearing aids, according to the manufacturer, Sleeper Beeper Corporation, of Richardson, Texas (courtesy Sleeper Beeper Corporation).

Your vehicle must be in the best condition possible. Check the oil and radiator coolant. Inspect the tires for bald or weak spots and for proper air pressure. Check the spare tire. The windshield wipers should be in good condition. If you have a windshield washer, it should be ready to use.

Check all lights; replace faulty or burned-out bulbs. The brakes should also be in top condition.

Make sure the seat belt is working properly and that you use it at all times when in the car. Seat belts keep you from getting thrown out of a car during an accident.

Curves, soft shoulders, bumps, hills, rolling rocks from the side, and sharp drop-offs may be encountered while driving. These road conditions may limit your visibility and impair your ability to properly control the car at medium and high speeds. Being prepared is being smart.

Weather conditions affect your ability and your reaction time. They also affect your car's performance. A slippery road in a rainstorm means slower speeds and continual and careful attention to the front, sides, and the rear of your car. It means observing other drivers and mentally preparing yourself for the worst. Use low-beam headlights in rainy weather.

When you look into the sun or the sun shines directly into your eyes, your reaction time to potential danger is slowed. Use your sun visor or sunglasses. High-beam lights of an oncoming car also are a problem. Avoid the temptation to turn your lights on bright. It doesn't help the other driver, and it certainly doesn't help you. You should slow down and look to the right edge of your lane. Use that as a guide until the other car is past you.

## SLEEPER BEEPER

One the prime causes of highways accidents is driver fatigue. A new driver alert system has been developed by Honeywell to sense head movement of the driver. The unit, which should be available nationwide by mid-1984, is called the *Sleeper Beeper* (Fig. 9-1). It is a ½-ounce elec-tronic warning unit that can be slipped over an ear. When the driver begins feeling tired, a buzzer warns the driver that he is falling asleep. Holding the head up in a normal driving position turns off the signal.

A miniature switch closes the circuit inside the warning unit when the driver's head tilts 22° from normal. Under normal conditions, the unit will give years of service.

The mercury switch is designed to resist inadvertent triggering of the unit on bumpy roads. The ergonomically molded plastic housing allows the unit to fit on either ear, and it may also be worn over glasses or hearing aids.

## DEALING WITH THE POLICE

Thieves prey on stranded motorists. Others force motorists—especially young pretty ones—to stop along back roads.

When driving from one place to another, try and make it nonstop. This doesn't mean driving all day and way into the night. We're referring to one-day trips under 350-400 miles. Driver fatigue starts to set in around 400 miles, you should look for a motel if you have to drive the next day.

The only person you should stop your car for is a uniformed police officer. Even in these instances, check identification and badge number. If you are still uncertain, you have a couple of possibilities. If you have a CB radio in your car, contact another driver on the road who will be coming to your location very soon. This person can also check the situation, take down the identification information and verify it, check out the police car, etc. The second possibility is to ask the officer to have a backup car come.

In both situations, the officers will realize that you are only being careful and trying to protect yourself. They should not hesitate to comply with your wishes.

If they are not police officers, the first thing they are going to do is get away from you and the area as fast as they can. Impersonating a police officer, especially for the commission of a crime, carries a heavy penalty. They cannot afford to be caught.

If the police officer in the first situation agrees to wait for another driver to come along, or to call a backup vehicle in the second situation, he is more than likely a police officer. If he refuses your wishes to wait for another driver or call a backup unit, be wary, but remember he may still be a police officer. Your situation will dictate what to do. In some instances, you may roll down your window only far enough to let him have your driver's license and registration, but still keep your doors locked. You might indicate that while you won't get out of the car on a lonely stretch of road, you will drive your car to the nearest police barracks or station where there are other policemen around.

## VEHICLE BREAKDOWNS

You want to get to your destination without experiencing a breakdown with your vehicle. No matter how much you inspect the car, you cannot guarantee that a nail won't cause a flat, that a stone kicked up by a car ahead of you won't fly back and break your windshield, or that running over a piece of metal or hitting a pothole won't damage your car.

Unusual noise, the lights going dim unexpectedly, or the engine sounding funny are potential breakdown signs. Perhaps the steering wheel fights when you attempt to drive the car down a straight road, or the car wants to move to either the left or right. Your car probably has a tire with low air pressure, and the pressure is going down fast. Pull over and replace the tire with your spare. On the other hand, you may make it to a service station before the tire goes completely flat.

Don't leave your broken-down car at the side of the road and go on foot for help. Put on your flasher lights, if possible, and exit from the passenger side of the car. Put up warning triangles or flares a short distance to the rear of your

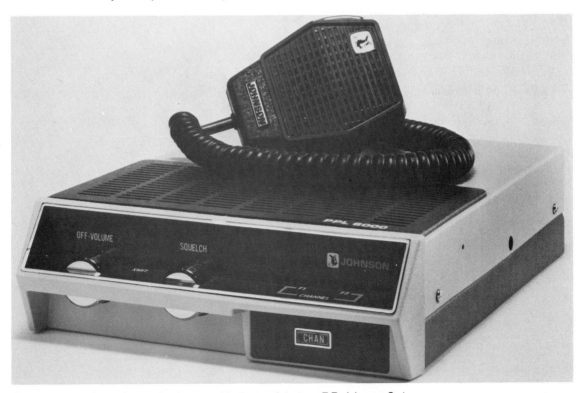

Fig. 9-2. The radio can be used at home and in the car (courtesy E.F. Johnson Co.).

car. You want to warn oncoming cars of your problem.

Tie a white rag to the car door on the driver's side and a rag on the antenna. Get back into the car.

If you have a CB or other portable radio in your car, use it to contact another driver or turn to channel nine of the CB. In most localities, the police monitor channel nine for possible distress and assistance messages.

Figure 9-2 shows one that can be used at home and in the car for obtaining assistance.

### SECURITY WITHIN A HOTEL OR MOTEL

When you arrive at your destination, you may consider yourself safe. If your destination is a hotel or motel, there are security procedures you can take for your personal and property protection.

Place money and jewelry in the hotel/motel safe if available. If the items are held overnight, be sure to get a receipt for them. Only let the items be stored if the management and accommodations are reputable. Cheap motels may offer a safety deposit box, but the level of security may be questionable. These motel owners may carry no insurance or else require you to sign a waiver holding them harmless from the possible loss of your valuables. Even well-known and reputable hotels may require a waiver, but they usually have the security protection available, and the chances of a robbery or burglary there are very low.

If you must take cash and valuables on a trip,

check your insurance company. Jewelry, cameras, and other valuables may be covered under the policy, or you can obtain special insurance for the trip. Policies, though, usually have an exclusion—sometimes up to $100 deductible.

Whether your room is in a well-known national or international hotel/motel chain or in a seedy-looking establishment, you can use portable alarm devices to warn you of a possible intruder into your room. For locking your door, consider a locking bar, plate, and lock like those used to secure sliding windows in stores (Fig. 9-3).

The all-purpose lock provides key control for hotel and motel doors, and it can even protect drawers. To use it on a door, open the door slightly, insert the locking bar, and put the hooked end into the door catch. Close the door, slide the locking plate on so that it is flush with the door, then slide the lock up tight against the locking plate. Keep the key with you. The same method

Fig. 9-4. The Portable Emergency Alarm can be used as a door alarm or as a personal alarm when out walking (courtesy Majima Co., Ltd.).

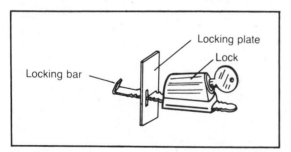

Fig. 9-3. The all-purpose door lock will help keep your hotel/motel room secure.

Fig. 9-5. This compact portable smoke/fire alarm gives the traveler an edge against potential danger in hotels and motels (courtesy Travel Commander, Inc.).

cooking area. The Travel Sentry can also be used in your own home as a smoke detector.

## LIFEGARD II

The *LifeGard II* (Fig. 9-6) is not the average personal distress unit. Worn on a belt or in a harness, it emits a piercing 98-decibel noise if the wearer is immobilized for more than 25 seconds. This distinctive sound can't be confused with smoke detectors and will sound continuously for hours.

The unit can also be triggered manually if the wearer becomes disoriented, lost, or

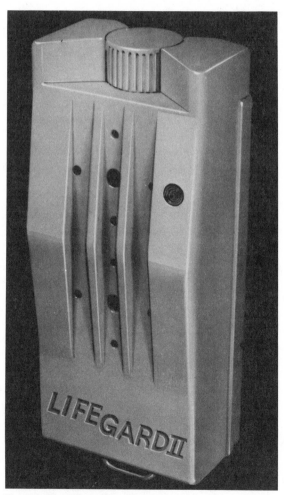

Fig. 9-6. The Lifegard II personal distress device (courtesy The Antenna Specialists Co.).

would apply to a bureau dresser drawer. The locking bar would be hooked upward, with the hook resting against the inside wooden bar above the drawer top edge. The locking plate and lock would then be slid into place.

A portable emergency alarm, designed especially for the ladies, is shown in Fig. 9-4. While it can be used for use in emergencies while walking, it can also be used to alert you to an intruder attempting entry into a motel room. It is propped up against the door in an upright position, and the pin is pulled from the end. If the door is opened slightly, the unit tips over and the alarm sounds. The 90-decibel emergency alarm is very loud in a small room. It will alert you, let an intruder know that his presence is known, and also alert people in nearby rooms of the situation.

The *Travel Sentry* is a portable smoke alarm that was designed especially for travelers. The portable detector can be easily mounted on the door with the bracket provided (Fig. 9-5). Should the alarm be sounded, you will be able to tell exactly where the door is in the dark. The smoke detector is designed to minimize false alarms. Smoking in the room will not normally set off the alarm unless the smoke is blown directly into the detector. Combustion particles from cooking (if allowed in the motel room) may set off the alarm if the detector is located close to the trapped, or has another situation that requires emergency assistance. There is no need to yell; the unit will yell louder than a human can.

The LifeGard II emits a short beep when armed to indicate operational readiness and, again, 5 seconds before its motion sensor sets off the urgent sound. The LifeGard II meets or exceeds OSHA specifications. It is rugged, waterproof, and engineered for reliability. For individuals that have problems walking, are elderly, or are concerned about the possibility of getting mugged, this unit is extremely helpful.

# Chapter 10

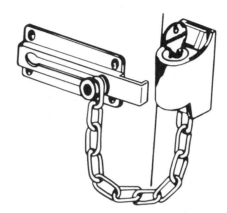

# Property Protection

Property protection can be as simple as a lock and key or as specialized as a closed-circuit, television-intercom system.

### THE HOME EMERGENCY PLAN

*Fyrnetics*, a company specializing in home fire and security protection and warning devices, has spent many years developing products and information for the consumer on fire prevention. The company has come up with some ideas and procedures for your home in emergencies. Further information on fire safety can be obtained in a pamphlet titled *In a Fire Seconds Count*, published by the National Fire Protection Association, Battery March Park, Quincy, MA 02269.

### Home Escape Plan

☐ Make a floor plan indicating all doors and windows and at least two escape routes from each room. Second-story windows may need a rope or chain ladder.

☐ Have a family meeting and discuss your escape plan, showing everyone what to do in case of fire.

☐ Determine a place outside your home where everyone can meet if a fire occurs.

☐ Familiarize everyone with the sound of the smoke alarm and/or other detectors in the home. Train your family members to leave your home when they hear the alarm.

☐ Identify children's bedrooms with red stickers placed in the upper left corner of the windows. They are usually obtainable from your local fire department. (If the fire department does not have any, you can make your own; the best material to use is one that is luminescent or fluorescent and easily reflects light.)

☐ Practice a fire drill at least every six months. Practice allows you to test your plan before an emergency. You may not be able to reach your children. It is vitally important that they know what to do.

## What to Do When the Alarm Sounds

☐ Leave immediately by your plan of escape. Every second counts, so don't waste time getting dressed or picking up valuables. Your life is more important.

☐ Don't open any inside door without first feeling its surface. If the door is hot or if you see smoke seeping through cracks, don't open it. Instead, use your alternate exit. If the inside door is cool, place your shoulder against it, open it slightly, and be ready to slam it shut if heat and/or smoke rush in.

☐ Stay close to the floor if the air is smoky. Breathe through a cloth; wet it if possible.

☐ Once outside, go to your selected meeting place and make sure everyone is there.

☐ Call the fire department from your neighbor's home—not from yours.

☐ Don't return to your home until fire officials tell you.

You may feel safe at home with your smoke detectors, but are you really protected from fire when traveling? There are more than 10,000 hotel and motel fires per year in the United States. There were 11,500 such fires in 1979. They resulted in 140 deaths and 1225 injuries. The statistics have risen more than 10 percent since 1979.

Smoke and panic often cause death. Smoke is extremely irritating to the eyes. Your eyes will take only so much irritation, then they will close and you won't be able to open them. Panic can make you do things that could kill you. You should take a portable smoke detector with you for added protection in your hotel or motel room. In addition, light is needed to cut through the smoke to determine where an emergency exit may be.

Here are some procedures to follow when you are confronted with a fire:

☐ If you smell smoke, call the fire department and prepare to leave. Get dressed if time allows.

☐ Don't panic. If you smell smoke or your fire alarm rings while asleep, don't sit up in bed. Roll out of bed into a crouched position or onto your hands and knees. Keep your head 2' or 3' above the floor as you move. Lethal gases from plastics can collect at floor level.

☐ Find your room key. You may need it later to retreat to your room.

☐ Leave your belongings. You can get them later.

☐ Feel the door with your hand. If it is cool, open it only a tiny crack and look outside to see if there is any smoke.

☐ If the door is hot, do not open it or flame or smoke may enter the room.

If you must stay in your room:

☐ Hotel doors lock automatically. If you must remain inside your room, unlock the door for firemen.

☐ Keep the water running in the bathroom, shower, and sink. Wet down the walls, doors, and furniture to slow the spread of fire.

☐ Take wet towels or clothing and drape them along the floor at the door to block the crack between the floor and the door.

☐ Open the window, but don't break it. If there is smoke outside, leave the window closed.

☐ Hang a sheet outside your window so firemen will know where you are.

If you leave your room:

☐ If you encounter smoke or fire and a second exit is not readily available, go back to your room. You may be trapped.

☐ When trying to move in a smoke-filled room or hall, stay near the floor where there is less smoke and more visibility. Try to stay about 12" off the floor, as deadly gases often sink to floor level.

☐ If you are in a high-rise hotel, full evacuation may not be necessary.

☐ If you are not on the fire floor, you may want to stay put. You may be safer than trying to move.

☐ If the fire is on your floor, try to move one or two floors below. Use the stairs. Elevators should always be avoided in a fire because of malfunctioning risks. When a fire alarm is sounded, some elevators automatically move to the lower level.

When you are staying at a hotel or motel:

☐ Ask about a fire and evacuation plan. If one is available get a copy and read it.

☐ Check for smoke detectors. (Bring your own just in case.)

☐ Find the closest exits to the outside (other than elevators).

☐ Study the floor plan leading to the exits from your room.

☐ Make sure the fire exit is not locked or blocked.

☐ Notice the location of the fire alarm box nearest your room.

☐ Write down the fire department phone number and keep it near your telephone.

☐ Know where your room key is in case you must leave in a hurry.

While these are only general guidelines for

Fig. 10-1. Point protection for windows and doors. These units are very easy to install (courtesy Fyrnetics, Inc.).

fire safety, the hotel/motel management should provide instructions and safeguards for their guests.

### SECURITY ALARMS: POINT PROTECTION

Micro-sensor security alarms that are easy to install in minutes without special tools can also be used as point protection within the home (Fig. 10-1). These units can be used for door protection, window alarm protection, sump pump, and heat alarm protection.

The door alarm has an exclusive three-way switch that will provide a 15-second delay for entrance/exiting and an instant alarm. The unit can be set in the off position when you are not using it. The window alarm has a 9″ adjustable slide to allow the window to be partially opened for ventilation without activating the alarm. The sump pump alarm will detect abnormally high water levels or sump pump failure in the home. If you reside in an area where flooding is possible, one of these units should be in the home at the lower level. The heat alarm will sound an alarm when the temperature at the detector reaches

approximately 135° F.

Each unit has a built-in local electronic horn that is so loud it can actually cause pain (85-110 decibels). You will be alerted by the actuation of the alarm horn. The units have digital integrated circuits to provide trouble-free operation.

In providing individual perimeter point coverage, the alarms are designed to repel intruders at the point of attempted entry into the home. Because the units have a full system capability, they can be installed singly, or at multiple entry points to provide complete home perimeter protection.

The electronic timing will sustain the alarm even though the door or window may be re-closed. The unit will automatically shut off and rearm itself for continued protection. The units, being self-contained, can be used on doors or windows.

The *Lifesaver travel alarm* with a detachable escape light (Fig. 10-2) should be taken with you on every trip you make—whether it is only overnight or a full vacation. The smoke alarm is approved for wall and door bracket

Fig. 10-2. The LifeSaver travel alarm has a detachable escape light (courtesy Fyrnetics, Inc.).

mounting only. When the unit detects fire and/or smoke, it immediately sounds a loud alarm and automatically activates the attached escape light. The escape light is removable so you can find your way to safety or signal for help.

Features of the Lifesaver travel alarm include:

☐ Dual ionization chambers to sense and alarm early. It resists false alarms.
☐ Solid-state circuitry for stability and low power consumption.
☐ A test button to allow you to test the circuitry, horn, battery, and the escape light.
☐ Uses a low-cost 9-volt battery—the light uses two AA batteries.
☐ A powerful alarm (85 decibels).
☐ An alarm low battery indicator, which "chirps" every 30 seconds for a minimum of seven days to signal a low battery.
☐ The escape light is detachable.
☐ The Lifesaver travel alarm is UL listed.

For travel use, you would mount the travel alarm on the door (Fig. 10-3). When traveling, you slide the smoke alarm off the standard wall mounting bracket and take it with you. When you are staying overnight at a motel, slide the door mounting bracket onto the smoke alarm. Mount the smoke alarm to the door by turning the locking lever. By rotating the metal door clip into position, you place it over the top of the entrance

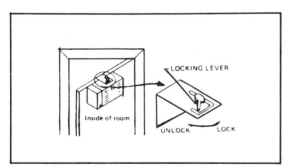

Fig. 10-3. Little time is needed to mount and activate your personal smoke alarm (courtesy Fyrnetics, Inc.).

door, with the smoke alarm on the inside of the room, and lock it in place by turning the locking lever. Close the door and test the smoke alarm.

## NATIONAL FIRE PROTECTION ASSOCIATION'S REQUIRED PROTECTION

The National Fire Protection Association's Standard 74, Section 2-4, provides information regarding the smoke detection equipment required within the family living unit. Section 2-4, 1.1, reads as follows:

"Smoke detectors shall be installed outside of each separate sleeping area in the immediate vicinity of the bedrooms and on each additional story of the family living unit including basements and excluding crawl spaces and unfinished attics. The provisions of 2-4, 1.1, represent the minimum number of detectors required by this standard. It is recommended that the householder consider the use of additional smoke or heat detectors for increased protection for those areas separated by a door from the areas protected by the required smoke detectors under 2-4, 1.1 above. The recommended additional areas are the living room, dining room, bedroom(s), kitchen, attic (finished or unfinished), furnace room, utility room, basement, integral or attached garage, and hallways not included in 2-4, 1.1, above. However, the use of additional detectors remains the option of the householder."

The equipment should be installed in accordance with the NFPA's Standard 74. While not all cities require basic protection in individual homes, your city manager or council should be made aware of the NFPA Standard. A local ordinance requiring detectors helps you and your neighbors.

Smoke alarms are an integral part of home security, whether they are part of an overall fire and security system or self-contained units. Figure 10-4 shows a battery-operated smoke alarm that has been approved by many states' fire marshals and is UL lited. Utilizing a low-cost, 9-volt battery, the alarm can be mounted on the wall or ceiling. Using a dual ionization chamber

Fig. 10-4. Battery-operated smoke alarms can be placed in any location in the home (courtesy Fyrnetics, Inc.).

and solid-state electronic circuitry, the unit is designed to alarm early when smoke is detected. It is specifically designed to resist false alarms.

## LOCATING SMOKE DETECTORS

We will assume you are installing more than one detector in your home. Locate the first detector in the immediate area of the bedrooms. Try to protect the exit path as the bedrooms are usually farthest from an exit. If more than one sleeping area exists, locate additional detectors in each sleeping area. You should locate at least one detector on every floor level (Fig. 10-5). A detec-

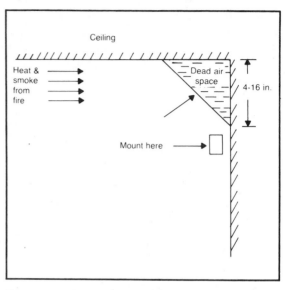

Fig. 10-6. Never mount a detector in a "dead" space; the alarm will not work properly (courtesy Fyrnetics, Inc.).

tor should be located in any area where a smoker sleeps or where electrical appliances are operated in sleeping areas. When you mount a detector on a wall, use an inside wall with the detector a minimum of 4″ and a maximum of 16″ below the ceiling and at least 2′ from any corner (Fig. 10-6).

Figure 10-7 illustrates locations of smoke detectors in a single-floor residence. If you have

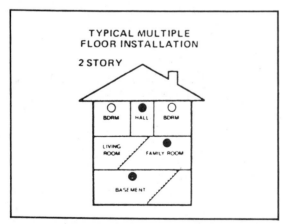

Fig. 10-5. Detectors should be located on every floor of the home (courtesy Fyrnetics, Inc.).

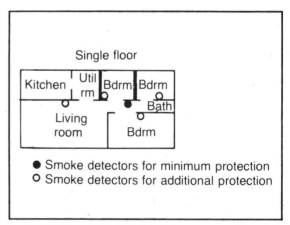

Fig. 10-7. Even single-floor homes require detectors for minimum protection, but consider providing additional protection (courtesy Fyrnetics, Inc.).

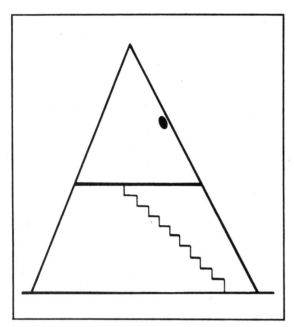

Fig. 10-8. Never attach a detector at the top; the dead space will make it very unreliable.

Fig. 10-9. The ac-wired alarms attach directly into the electrical mounting box (courtesy Fyrnetics, Inc.).

a mobile home, you should mount a detector only on interior walls.

There are locations to avoid in mounting smoke detectors. These include:

- ☐ The kitchen—smoke from cooking might cause an unwanted alarm.
- ☐ The garage—products of combustion are present when you start your automobile.
- ☐ In front of forced air ducts used for heating and air conditioning.
- ☐ In the peak of an A-frame type of ceiling (Fig. 10-8).
- ☐ In areas where temperatures may fall below 40° F. or above 100° F regularly.

There are ac-wired smoke alarms (Fig. 10-9) that operate off your standard household electrical circuits. They have a battery backup that operates the unit in case of a power failure. Like the previous unit, this smoke alarm also has dual ionization chambers for detection of smoke and is not disturbed by general household

smoking. Easy installation and access through a special mounting base makes the installation quick and also allows you to remove the alarm for easy access to the unit and battery replacement.

Both units have a test button and light for testing of the power supply of the entire alarm circuitry, including calibrated sensitivity (for the actual level of detection desired) and the alarm signaling horn.

### SECURITY LIGHTING

Every home should have security lighting of

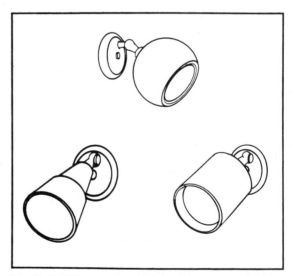

Fig. 10-10. Different styles of lighting fixtures are available to mount on your roof corner (courtesy Remcraft Lighting Products).

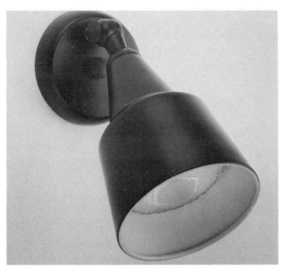

some type to highlight the exterior of the home and the lawn at night. Lights should be affixed to the home at the corners and upper levels (Fig. 10-10) to provide maximum visibility of the home and lawn area.

You can have single lights or twin fixtures mounted. Figure 10-11 illustrates a single fixture that might be mounted at the corner of the home, pointing in one direction. At another corner or at the side, a double light fixture (Fig. 10-12) may be used to provide a much wider coverage area.

You may have a fixture with a photoelectric control built into the unit. This means your security protection with the lights is automatic. Your exterior lighting is at work from dusk to dawn. Without such photoelectric sensors built into a lighting fixture, someone has to be home to turn them on.

Fig. 10-11. A single light fixture (courtesy Remcraft Lighting Products)

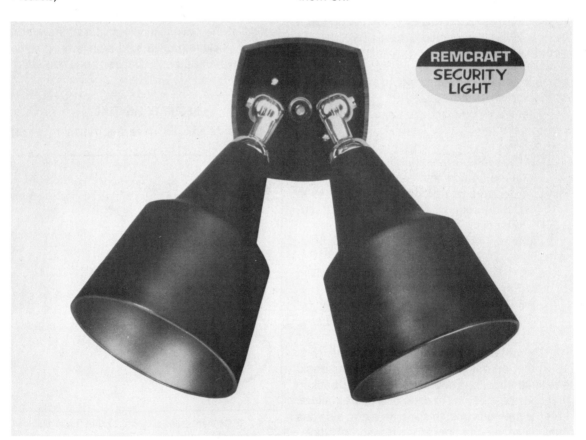

Fig. 10-12. A double light fixture (courtesy Remcraft Lighting Products).

If you have standard exterior lights that are switch-operated, at least consider the more positive aspects of automatic lighting. A photoelectric sensor in a lighting unit is ideal.

Security lights:

- [ ] Should be made of heavy-gauge aluminum.
- [ ] The reflectors should protect the lamps from accidental or intentional damage.
- [ ] The lights should be completely adjustable, putting light where it is needed, while not disturbing neighbors or flooding your bedrooms with sidelight splash.

- [ ] Should be capable of mounting to a standard outlet electrical box.
- [ ] Have fast and simple electrical wiring, with easy-to-follow instructions with the unit when purchased.
- [ ] Lamps should be at least 150-watt PAR spot or flood type (this is standard with most quality security lights).
- [ ] Optional, but highly recommended, is a photoelectric sensor built into the unit for automatic lighting.

A single lamp may be used to protect detached garages or other outbuildings. You may

Fig. 10-13. This light may be placed near a patio (courtesy Remcraft Lighting Products).

not want to have a standard "bullet" type security light placed near a patio for aesthetic reasons, so Fig. 10-13 is an optional type. The lamp unit, although considered more for interior accent lighting, can easily fit into this situation.

These lamps also have on-off switches in some models that make them portable. They can be used within the home for accent lighting. You may tie a lamp like this into your interior light timers for periods that you are away from home. An additional light in a room of the home going on and off for a short period at night may confuse a potential burglar that someone is home.

## AUTOMATIC TIMING LIGHTS

Timing light switches can be used for outdoor

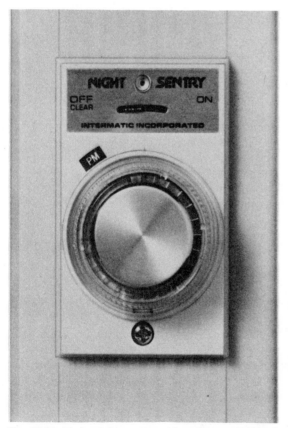

Fig. 10-14. Timing lights can provide numerous "hidden" functions, like security and energy savings (courtesy Intermatic, Inc.).

protection and safety lighting. A 24-hour time switch can be used to control outdoor protection and safety lighting, thus eliminating the need to manually perform this operation every evening. A time switch can also be used to control garden lighting.

Other uses include the home swimming pool. At night, an individual may venture outside and fall into the pool. Automatic timing switches ensure that the pool is properly lighted at night.

Hallway safety lighting is another feature of timing light switches that should not be overlooked. While you may have a hallway light switch, greater safety is assured when the lights automatically turn on at night.

Various timing light switches are available. The electronic in-wall timer (Fig. 10-14) can provide security, energy savings, and the convenience of silent solid-state microprocessor technology. These timers can provide up to 48 easily programmed on-off selections.

This Intermatic 24-hour dial can be used as an ordinary light switch for 24 hours to program the automatic repeat memory. After this period, the electronic wall timer will automatically turn on and off the lights. Even with the present programs that may be set, the unit still functions as an ordinary light switch.

In the event of power interruptions, the memory of the unit will retain the preset program for 15 minutes. To confuse the potential intruder, the electric timer's computer varies the program slightly each day to eliminate specific patterns of when lights are turned on and off.

Another model uses microprocessor technology in a contemporary style as an electronic clock-time (Fig. 10-15). This 24-hour clock-time with accurate to-the-minute setting, besides giving you the time, can control your stereo, recorder, television, radio, and more. It has an easily understood keyboard entry system with two present on/off programs daily.

Suppose your timing light has several settings on it, because you will be away for three or four days. By using the clock-timer also, in addition to the lights being turned on and off au-

Fig. 10-15. This timer will provide control over a lamp, radio, or stereo (courtesy Intermatic, Inc.).

tomatically at different times of the day or night, you can have the television turned on in the early evening and off shortly before the room lights are extinguished. Further, you could have the radio playing for short periods during the day. A potential intruder can not take the chance that someone is not home.

A photoelectric automatic toggle switch may fit your needs (Fig. 10-16). This unit can save energy by turning lights, particularly exterior ones, on and off automatically. It is constructed for outdoor installation to resist rust, rain, sleet, snow, dust, and oxidation. A light level adjustment slide allows for many applications.

Another unit with photoelectric control is shown in Fig. 10-17. This particular model also has an inherent delay action that will eliminate the lights turning on due to light flashes, such as those from passing automobiles that may momentarily contact the photoelectric control unit.

Home security can also be tied in with landscaping illumination. Perhaps you have considered exterior lighting to silhouette the home or maybe the trees, flowers, and walls. Figure 10-18 illustrates the Malibu lighting system. It provides

Fig. 10-16. Exterior units with photoelectric control provide light and security for the home at night (courtesy Intermatic, Inc.).

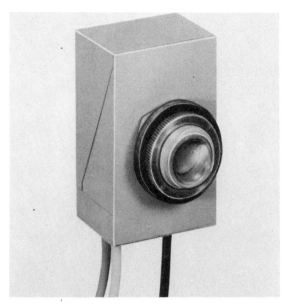

Fig. 10-17. Another unit with photoelectric control (courtesy Intermatic, Inc.).

an automatic timer unit and five light units. Figure 10-19 shows the four basic steps, as outlined below, that are performed once you have surveyed your property and have determined where to place your lighting.

**Step One.** Hang the transformer within 3' of a standard outlet. When mounted outdoors, install the transfer not less than 1' above the ground with the cable opening downward (Fig. 10-19A).

**Step Two.** Slit one end of the low-voltage power cable (the lights operate off 12 volts) approximately 4". Strip the insulation from both cable ends exposing the wire. Feed the cable through the cable opening at the bottom of the transformer case and attach it to the screw terminals. (Fig. 10-19B).

**Step Three.** Plug the transformer power cord into the outlet and turn it on. With an automatic timer, turn the manual switch to on or rotate the dial so the on tripper passes the time line indi-

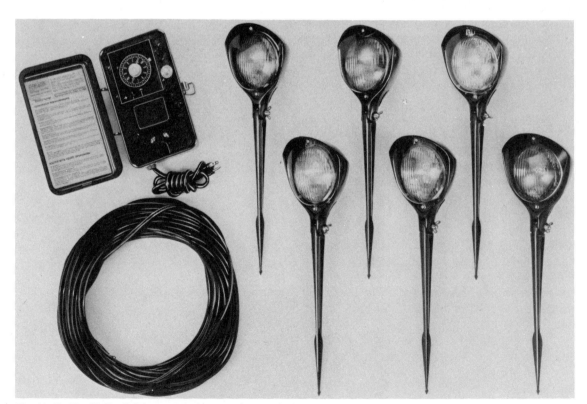

Fig. 10-18. The Malibu lighting system (courtesy Intermatic, Inc.).

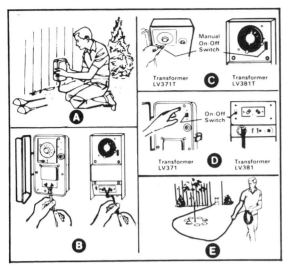

Fig. 10-19. Four easy steps for installing the Malibu system (courtesy Intermatic, Inc.).

cator (Fig. 10-19C). For a manually-operated mode, use the on-off switch (Fig. 10-19D).

**Step Four.** Stretch the power cable to its full length. Route the power cable where lights are desired and attach the cable to the Pierce terminals in the lamp fixture (Fig. 10-19E).

Programmable timers come in many forms and have different timing capabilities. Designed for multifunction control to help reduce danger and deter burglary attempts, every home should have at least one, if not more, for protection.

### FIRE-RESISTANT BOXES AND SAFES

Fire-resistant boxes and safes in the home protect valuables against attempted theft and fires that may occur (Figs. 10-20 and 10-21). Imagine the problems you would have if a fire were to break out in the home and you lost your insurance policies, family photos that had been handed down several generations, medical and dental records, receipts, and inventories of valuables.

Safes and storage boxes that are of high quality and carry the Underwriters Laboratories' fire rating test label are your best bet. Not all home safes can earn this label. Another advantage of having a safe in the home is that you are

Fig. 10-20. The Sentry fire-resistant safe (courtesy John D. Brush & Co.).

Fig. 10-21. Two different sizes of fire-resistant boxes (courtesy John D. Brush & Co.).

free from the restrictions of a bank safety deposit box.

Your selection of a safe will be based on what you are willing to pay to provide an adequate level of protection against theft and fire. More importantly, your selection must be based on what it may also cost you in time and money to replace the items lost.

The *Survivor fire-resistant boxes* (Fig. 10-21) have been fire-tested by Underwriters Laboratories' 1-hour fire test at up to 1700° F. Both are heavily insulated and have a removable key lock, providing convenient top opening. These boxes are easy to carry out of the home in case of a fire.

Figure 10-20 shows a larger model fire safe. In the Underwriters Laboratories' test, the material inside the safe remained below 350° F.—well below the 420° F. charring point of paper. The three-number combination lock provides further protection for the materials stored inside the minisafe. The minisafe, while small, is strong and can be concealed within a security cube (Fig. 10-22) so that it can be placed with other furniture within the home and not stand out conspicuously.

Figure 10-23 shows the Sentry 200 series fire-resistant safe with Underwriters Laboratories' 2-hour fire rating. To earn this rating, the safe had to withstand a fire test at temperatures up to 1850° F for 2 hours. The safe also passed tough tests that proved its protection against explosion and impact. These safes, while designed for businesses, churches, schools, and other organizations with rigorous fire protection requirements, are built with quality control and attention to detail. Records are kept clean and

Fig. 10-22. When placed inside a security cube, your safe can fit in with other home furniture (courtesy John D. Brush & Co.).

Fig. 10-23. Reliability, privacy, and convenience for home and business records are all combined in one safe (courtesy John D. Brush & Co.).

Fig. 10-24. In-floor safes can be used to store your better valuables and jewelry when not being used (courtesy John D. Brush & Co.).

undamaged after exposure to very high or prolonged heat.

The safe has a 3″ thick Pyronox insulation, a recessed three-number combination lock, a tamper-resistant bolt control handle, and an adjustable interior shelf. Concealed hinges and a hard plate protected locking mechanism give greater protection against illegal entry. There are four locking bolts—two on each side of the door. The wrap-around door design, interlocking body, and doorjambs are for greater fire protection.

Figure 10-24 illustrates an in-floor safe that can be installed in a concrete floor or on a wood floor. You can keep your valuables in the garage, the cellar, or a closet. Conceal the safe with a rug or any common household item. When properly

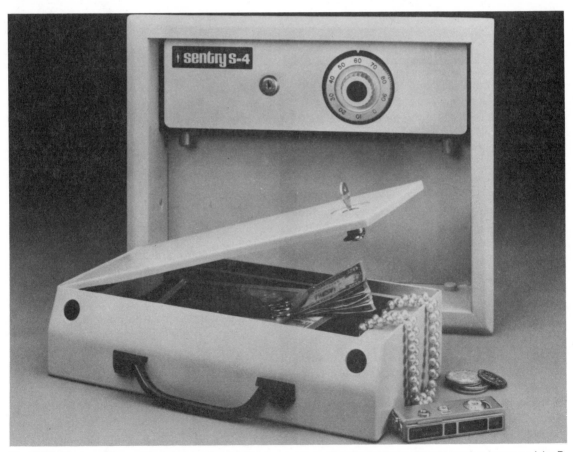

Fig. 10-25. The in-wall deposit box also can be used for transporting valuables from one place to another (courtesy John D. Brush & Co.).

Table 10-1. Guide for Storing Important Papers.

| | Home Fire Safe | Safe Deposit Box |
|---|---|---|
| Home/apartment lease | X | |
| Appraisals of furs and jewelry | | X |
| Auto title/bill of sale | | X |
| Birth certificates | | X |
| Canceled checks | X | |
| Contribution records/tax records | X | |
| Credit card numbers and company points of contacts | X | |
| Military discharge records | | X |
| U.S. government bonds | | X |
| Home improvement records | X | |
| Insurance policies | X | |
| Marriage certificate | | X |
| Medical records | X | |
| Receipts | X | |
| Savings passbooks | X | |
| Social security information | X | |
| Stocks | | X |
| Wills | | X |
| Wills (duplicate) | X | |

concealed in concrete, the in-floor safe also provides a degree of fire protection.

The safe features a three-number changeable combination lock, double-locking bolts, ½" thick hot-rolled steel door, heavy-gauge steel body, 9" square steel anchoring base plate, and a protective steel door cover. When the door cover is in place, any throw rug or other item virtually conceals the in-floor safe, because the top will be level with the floor.

The *Stowaway* (Fig. 10-25) is a heavyweight, steel in-wall home deposit box that can afford unmatched security with its four-bolt double-locking system and changeable three-number combination with key lock. (Both the key and the combination lock must be used to remove the deposit box within.) The cabinet is easily flush-mounted into a wall between the studs and may be concealed by a mirror or a picture. The cabinet measures 14¼" wide (plus a 1" flange) by 11¼" high (plus a 1" flange) by 3⅝" deep. The flanges directly assist in letting you easily flush-mount the wall safe between the studs.

The deposit box, kept within the wall safe,

has its own key lock. It is portable for easy carrying when transporting valuables from one place to another. See Table 10-1.

## PADLOCKS

There are misconceptions about padlocks that you should be aware of when looking for a lock. You would certainly want a better lock and high-security hasp on a garage used for storing many tools and other equipment than you would want on a small outdoor shed that has your hoe, rake, and a few garden implements.

Allen Vancura, of the American Lock Company, wrote an article in 1982 discussing the six major misconceptions about padlocks. With his permission, we are including the majority of this article below.

### Six Misconceptions about Padlocks

We have all encountered situations where a security system or product is used without any real knowledge of the product or its limitations. Padlocks frequently fall into this category.

While many security specialists take time to

read and learn about the newest electronic security devices, they frequently assume padlocks can be judged at face value because they are so common. Padlocks represent a sizable market, with a retail value of more than $300 million worldwide, according to the U.S. Department of Commerce. Despite their frequent use, however, security professionals often admit they are not sufficiently informed about the various padlocks. Consequently, misconceptions persist.

**Misconception Number One.** All padlocks of the same size will perform in the same way. This is not true. A padlock consists of four different components that, like links of a chain, all affect the overall performance of the lock. The four parts are the lock body, the cylinder, the shackle, and the locking mechanism. Table 10-2 summarizes the security performance that can be expected from each of these components.

**Misconception Number Two.** All I need to do is purchase the most expensive padlock, and I've solved all my problems. Not all applications require high or top security. Frequently, a lock is used simply to indicate to others that the object being locked is out-of-bounds. In these cases, a padlock with a low to intermediate level of security will suffice (and cost much less).

**Misconception Number Three.** Padlocks are old-fashioned. They aren't compatible with other security devices currently available.

**Table 10-2. Determining the Security Potential of a Padlock (courtesy American Lock Company).**

| | Security Level | | |
| --- | :---: | :---: | :---: |
| | High | Intermediate | Low |
| **Body Construction** | | | |
| Hardened Solid Steel | X | | |
| Laminated Steel Plates | | X | |
| Solid Brass | | X | |
| Die Cast | | X | |
| Formed Metal | | | X |
| **Cylinder Type** | | | |
| 4 Pin or less | | X | |
| 5-7 Pin | X | | |
| Blade | | X | |
| Warded | | | X |
| Combination | | | X |
| Tubular | X | | |
| **Shackle Material and Diameter** | | | |
| Hardened Steel | | | |
| 7/16" and over | X | | |
| 1/4" to 7/16" | | X | |
| Under 1/4" | | | X |
| Brass | | | X |
| Steel (not hardened) | | | X |
| Exotic Materials (Kryptonite) | X | | |
| **Locking Mechanism** | | | |
| Shingle Locking Lever | | | X |
| Double Locking Lever | | X | |
| Double Ball Locking* | X | | |

*The National Crime Prevention Institute recommends that padlocks used for higher security applications have shackles which lock at the heel and toe with hardened steel ball bearings.

Table 10-3. Guide to Padlock Selection Based on Application (courtesy American Lock Company).

| Type of Lock | High Security | Adverse Environment* | Machine Lockouts | Marine (Waterfront) | Trucks | Inside Warehouse | Cleaning Maint. | Employee Lockers |
|---|---|---|---|---|---|---|---|---|
| Solid Steel—Pin Tumbler | X | | X | | X | X | | |
| Solid Steel—Blade Tumbler | | X | | X | X | | | |
| Solid Steel—Tubular Cylinder | X | | | | | | | |
| Laminated Steel—Pin Tumbler | | | X | | | X | X | X |
| Laminated Steel—Warded | | | | | | | X | X |
| Diecast Body—Pin Tumbler | | | X | | | | X | X |
| Diecast Body—Blade Tumbler | | X | | | | | X | X |
| Solid Brass—Pin Tumbler | | X | X | X | | | | X |
| Fabricated Steel—Warded | | | | | | | X | X |
| Fabricated Steel—Lever Type | | | | | | | | X |
| Combination Type | | | | | | | X | X |

It's true that padlocks were used hundreds of years ago. Upgraded types, such as those listed below, can be obtained.

□ Keyed alike—many locks responding to one key. Only one key is required to open all the locks, as each lock would use the same key.

□ Master keyed—available with a keying system that allows one key to open all the padlocks in one location, even though individual locks may be keyed differently or keyed alike in groups.

□ Grand master keyed—a system that allows one key to control all the padlocks at different locations, even though a different master key system controls all the padlocks at each separate location. You may have a summer cottage or a mountain hideaway at different locations. Masterkeying allows you to have access to all padlocks with one key, while a friend or relative using one of the locations could have a master key that would work all the padlocks only at that location. If you have a small business, you could also have the padlocks at the business on the same master key system, with an individual local master for those locks at the business. You carry only one key for several locations. Table 10-3 lists appropriate padlocks for specific applications.

Some padlocking systems can accommodate a cylinder that matches the door hardware in use. Because this option is usually much more expensive, 100 to 200 percent above a standard keyed-alike padlock system, having people carry one additional key for the padlock is usually acceptable. This is particularly true when these padlocks are also available with high-security (pick-resistant) cylinders and restricted keyways.

**Misconception Number Four.** Since I can purchase a high-security padlock in the hardware store, I don't need a reference chart. While it's true padlocks offering high security can be purchased in hardware stores, not all padlocks marked high or top security are of that quality.

Some manufacturers mark their padlock packaging good, high, top, and super security to show the relative performance (and price) differences within their padlock lines. One company's top-security padlock may be equivalent to another company's high-security model. Both may only be intermediate-security padlocks, because they have a solid brass body and a four-pin cylinder.

**Misconception Number Five.** There are too many types and styles of padlocks. The manufacturers of padlocks have developed products to meet the specific security needs of their customers. They don't dream up styles to confuse the buyer. Each type of padlock generally fulfills a need (Table 10-2).

Common sense dictates that low-security locks should not be used in places where theft is occurring. A better padlock is needed and should be provided.

Long shackles are especially useful when securing special hardware. Long shackles, however, are more vulnerable to cutting and pry bars. A short shackle padlock is always recommended.

Padlocks are also available with chains and cables instead of the traditional shackle. This padlock is especially popular with bicycle owners, even though the flexible cable or chain is not as strong as a hardened steel shackle. Consequently, these special locks are not recommended—even for bicycles.

**Misconception Number Six.** Padlocks always get rusty and then don't work. When an application requiring a padlock is outdoors or in an environment unfriendly to ferrous metals, a solid brass body padlock can be used. When ordered with a brass shackle, these padlocks do not rust. They will operate well and look presentable for a long time. With a wafer cylinder, these locks will provide intermediate security and operate well under freezing, dirty, and corrosive conditions.

Pin tumbler locks, which provide higher levels of security, tend to be adversely affected by dirty, caustic, and freezing conditions. They can be used, however, when additional security is needed, provided they are covered and lubricated periodically with dry graphite or silicone spray. Petroleum-based lubricants are not recommended because they attract dirt, dust, and moisture.

Any padlock's performance is limited or enhanced by the form and quality of its companion hardware. The hasp or locking bolt must be equal to the job if the padlock is to perform as expected. An inexpensive bolt or hasp, or a worthy one attached to a rotted wood or thin sheet metal door, can be a major security problem that ultimately will affect the performance of the padlock. Hardened steel components and hidden fasteners, preferably through-bolts, are recommended.

Other features usually available on higher security padlocks are:

☐ *Changeable (removable) cylinders.* These allow the keys to be changed periodically merely by replacing the current cylinder. This renews the security in a system for a very modest cost per lock— several dollars rather than $10 to $30 each if the lock was replaced. This precaution is usually required when keys are lost or stolen or when an employee quits.

☐ *Restricted Keyways.* In this system, duplicate keys cannot be made except with the user's authority and through the original manufacturer. The key shape and blanks are not available except from the lock manufacturer.

☐ *Key retention.* This feature eliminates the problem of padlocks being left unlocked because the key cannot be removed unless the padlock is relocked. Key retention usually offered at no charge, is especially good for gate and door applications.

Some important intermediate and low-security padlocks are available with magnetic tumblers that work on the theory of magnetic attraction and repulsion or with push buttons that operate a combination mechanism. Other new padlocks employ special shapes or new designs to achieve their higher security status.

Although the padlock has served man for centuries, it can still be an important partner in any security system. Successful use of padlocks is possible if they are chosen carefully and serviced regularly.

### Shell Padlocks

The following information is provided courtesy of the *Master Lock Company*, the other major manufacturer and supplier of padlocks. This section discusses the Master Lock Company's line, but the information also can be applied to any other manufacturer's line of padlocks.

Locks vary tremendously in the amount of protection provided. Important differences may be hard for you to spot.

Remember that wrought steel or shell padlocks are the lowest priced locks you can buy. They are a great buy if you understand they're intended mainly for nuisance protection— keeping the kids out of your toolbox, locking power tools against tampering, restricting access to a mailbox, storeroom, cage, etc. These inexpensive padlocks can prevent injury from hazardous household and industrial items.

Laminated construction results in a lock far sturdier than shell types. A multispring, warded mechanism operates a strong shackle-locking lever. Design permits more key variations than offered by shell locks and less chance of duplication.

### Warded Locks

Costing more than shell types but less than those with a pin tumbler mechanism, warded locks offer dependable protection. Use them to secure oil tank caps, well covers, beach lockers, duffel bags, barn doors, etc.

Because of the relatively large clearances between internal moving parts, warded locks are frequently chosen for applications where sand, water, ice, or other contaminants are a problem. While they look almost the same as Master pin tumbler padlocks at first glance, there's a de-cided difference in the security provided. The most visible difference with a warded lock is seen in the type of key employed.

Because warded locks cost about half as much and pin tumbler and warded locks outwardly look so much alike, many unknowing consumers make the wrong buying decision where high security is essential. When locked property has substantial value, the pin tumbler lock with its many hidden strengths is infinitely superior and well worth the additional money.

Controlled by precision mechanisms, these locks can offer premium protection and thousands of key changes. Compared to a warded lock mechanism with only four working parts, master pin tumbler locks use 19 precision parts to assure top security. A patented double-locking feature multiplies this protection by independently locking each shackle leg. The result is a lock extremely difficult to open by forcing, shimming, or rapping.

For added security, look for the legend "HARDENED" on the shackle. Case hardening provides a very hard outer layer to resist cutting or sawing and a tough, inner core to keep the shackle from becoming brittle.

The key numbers of better locks are temporarily *inked* onto the casing. When you record the key number in a safe place, you can erase the number from the lock so no one can obtain copy by subterfuge.

### Brass Padlocks

Hard-wrought brass versions of Master high-security laminated padlocks are designed to withstand severe corrosion problems encountered along seacoasts, aboard boats, at refineries, and in areas of high humidity and atmospheric pollution. For theft deterrence, the shackle typically will be chrome-plated hardened steel. For extreme conditions, even the shackle can be brass. Expect the price of maximum-security brass padlocks to run substantially higher than for steel.

A lower cost medium-security alternative for the average user is the *solid brass* padlock.

Again, look for pin tumbler locking and a case-hardened shackle to protect valued property. Priced substantially less than heavy-duty laminated brass padlocks, solid brass locks are ideal for boats, outdoor lockers, gates, and similar applications. In addition, the sleek styling and golden luster of Master solid brass padlocks lend to their indoor use on gun cases, display cabinets, and other places where fashion is important.

## Combination Padlocks

Combination padlocks provide keyless convenience, particularly with children, where lost keys may be a problem. Protection features include reinforced double-wall construction—a tough stainless steel outer case over a sturdy wrought steel inner case—and a hardened steel shackle for added resistance against cutting and sawing. Combination locks are classed as medium security, with strength equivalent to a quality warded padlock.

The "resettable" combination padlock has four control wheels that can be set for any four-digit combination—10,000 choices! Master resettables make remembering your combination easy. Just program a familiar number, such as your phone number or address. Commercial users can give temporary access to employees, then change the combination to restore private control. Multiple padlock users also can set whole groups "combination alike" for personal convenience.

You should consider more than just the strength of the padlock. The finest lock affords little protection if burglars find it hung from an undersized or unhardened hasp that they can cut with ease. Get a hasp that matches the quality of the lock. Look for adequate size, a pinless hinge, concealed screws, case-hardened staple (the metal loop the lock passes through), and steel ribbing for added strength. A combination padlock should have:

- ☐ A stainless steel outer case and a heavy inner case.
- ☐ Specifically designed locking mech-

Fig. 10-26. Combination locks have many different uses within a household—especially for school-age children who need a lock, but might lose a key (courtesy American Lock Co.).

anism to withstand extreme abuse.
- ☐ A dial "scrambler" security feature that automatically spins the dial away from the last number when the lock is snapped shut.
- ☐ An anti-manipulation feature—built-in sound effect to prevent picking.
- ☐ At least 64,000 possible combinations.
- ☐ A three-number combination and a rotation dial having at least 40 numbers on it.
- ☐ A pry-resistant dial for more security against vandalism.
- ☐ The padlock casing should have a diameter of at least 2″, a shackle at least 9/32″ diameter, and a shackle clearance of 7/8″.

Figure 10-26 shows a combination padlock that would meet the above criteria.

## Hasp Locks

An evolutionary step beyond the hasp is the *hasp lock*. Instead of using a separate padlock, the lock and hasp are permanently joined so the lock can't be misplaced or stolen. Hasp locks give built-in convenience akin to the deadbolt door lock and offer much easier installation. This accounts for their popularity with builders, contractors, farmers, and do-it-yourselfers. Their uses range from garage doors and sheds to boat houses, warehouses, and other places.

### Chain and Cable

Another weak link in security may be the wrong choice of chain or cable. When it comes to movable property, a strong padlock with a properly matched chain or steel cable is the way to go. Owners of bicycles, boats, motorcycles, and other easily stolen items can secure them to a post, tree, dock, or other immovable object. Common chain available in hardware stores should be passed over in favor of chain specifically designed for locking applications. Be sure the chain is case-hardened for resistance to cutters, saws, and files. Individual links should be welded, not just twisted, to resist being pried apart. Multistranded security cable is available for equivlent protection, with the added benefit of light weight. The thicker the chain or cable, the greater the protection. Some manufacturers add a thick coating of vinyl to make a small steel strand look bigger.

For greatest protection, position the lock and cable (or chain) as high above the ground as possible. This makes it difficult for thieves to gain extra leverage by bracing one leg of a bolt cutter against the ground.

When in doubt about a lock, the best place to turn with questions of security is your local police department. Most enforcement agencies have experts to help you and may have displays of security locks. When in doubt and unable to get expert advice, buy the best padlock protection you can afford (strength and cost generally coincide). When possible, avoid leaving locked items in out-of-the-way places where thieves have time to work on the lock unseen. Back up your locks with some insurance.

### Other Padlocks

Solid extruded brass padlocks with 10-blade tumblers have hardened steel shackles (Fig. 10-27). In applications where rust, corrosion, or moisture would overpower other types of padlocks, these locks will stand up. The solid brass body lock is especially well-suited to marine or outdoor uses and is widely used by the military, utilities, refineries, and transportation industries.

Fig. 10-27. The solid padlocks can have different shackle lengths to meet different needs (courtesy American Lock Co.).

In the 5500 series, solid steel cover plates are available that offer additional protection for this pin tumbler cylinder. This padlock is available with a solid brass shackle or in various shackle lengths in case-hardened steel.

A hardened solid steel padlock with five-pin tumbler, the *Super Hercules* has a 2½" solid hardened steel case, is 1 3/32" thick, and has a triple satin chrome finish (Fig. 10-28). It has re-

Fig. 10-28. The padlocks have rekeyable, changeable cylinders (courtesy American Lock Co.).

Fig. 10-29. The tubular cylinder provides an extra measure of security in an already high-security padlock (courtesy of American Lock Co.).

movable brass cylinders for fast servicing and a hardened steel cover plate for additional cylinder protection. A hardened 7/16″ diameter alloy steel shackle, is chrome-plated. These cylinders can be changed and rekeyed.

The hardened solid steel padlock, with a hardened solid steel triple chrome-plated body and hardened steel shackles with hardened steel cover plates on some models to provide the cylinder with extra protection, is excellent. Unique features include:

☐ Hardened steel shackle that fights sawing and prying.
☐ Solid steel bodies give maximum protection against ordinary abuse from hand tools.
☐ Double locking with solid steel balls resists forcing of the shackle.
☐ Special shaped pins provide extra protection against picking.

☐ Hardened steel cover plate protects the cylinder.

These solid hardened steel padlocks have five-pin tumblers and provide security in many home applications. The seven-pin tumbler padlocks with a tubular cylinder (Fig. 10-29) has a 2″ solid hardened steel case, a 7/16″ hardened alloy steel shackle, and is triple chrome-plated.

The shrouded shackle padlock is virtually indestructible (Fig. 10-30). It is a solid one-piece hardened steel case, 2½″ wide by 4″ high, and the 7/16″ hardened alloy steel shackle is enclosed by the case design to make it practically invulnerable to physical attack.

A patented shackless hasp lock invulnerable to bolt cutters, hacksaws, hammers, or pry bars is the *Superlock*. It gives rekeyable, high security with a six-pin tumbler cylinder using mushroom pins to provide topnotch security.

### Armorlock Padlocks

Figure 10-31 illustrates an Armorlock padlock. It has been designed with three specific uses in mind: protection against removal of a trailer hitch (Fig. 10-32), as a secure lock on a hasp, and for a chain and cable for bicycles.

The Armorlock can be used in one of two heavy-duty systems for protecting mopeds. When combined with a double-locking cable

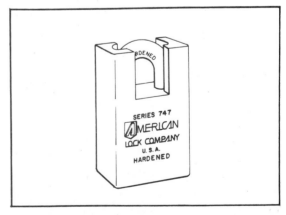

Fig. 10-30. The shrouded shackle is virtually indestructible and practically invulnerable to physical attack (courtesy American Lock Co.).

Fig. 10-31. The Armorlock padlock (courtesy Master Lock Co.).

(Fig. 10-33), the Armorlock enables you to lock the cable twice and secure a moped to a tree, post, or other immovable object. The padlock design offers extreme resistance to cutting and features a unique shackle too thick to fit in the jaws of most bolt cutters. The rugged cable locks the moped and guards against trucking it away.

A medium-weight chain has 3/16" welded steel, which is case-hardened and zinc-plated. A heavyweight chain should be 9/32" welded steel that is case-hardened and zinc-plated. The super-security chain must have the extra strength of alloy steel. In this case, the links will be 9/32" welded alloy steel that is case-hardened and zinc-plated. For more heavy-duty applications, a ⅜" welded alloy steel chain should be used. All of these chains should have a flexible vinyl protective cover to protect various objects from small dents, scrapes, and scratches that can occur when the chains are looped over,

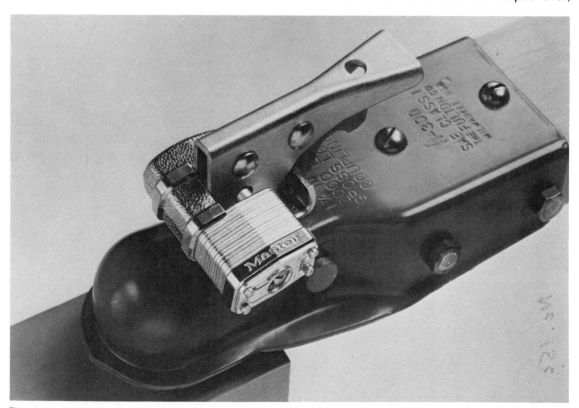

Fig. 10-32. The Armorlock provides high security to prevent trailer removal from an auto or truck (courtesy Master Lock Co.).

314

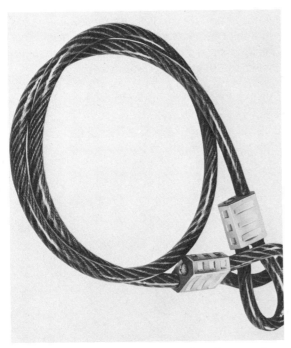

Fig. 10-33. Long heavy-duty cable allows items such as mopeds to be secured against immovable objects (courtesy Master Lock Co.).

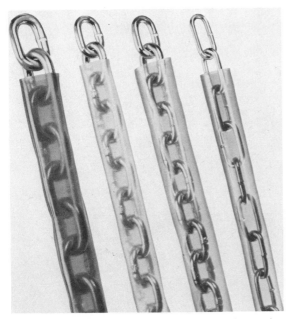

Fig. 10-34. These chains provide different levels of protection (courtesy Master Lock Co.).

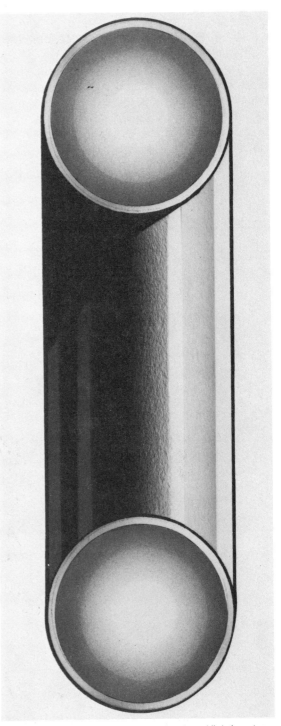

Fig. 10-35. Cutaway view of a case-hardened link (courtesy Master Lock Co.).

under, around, or through various objects to secure them. Figure 10-34 shows these four chain types.

The links must be welded to provide strong protection against prying. The chain must have a case-hardened steel surface (Fig. 10-35) to resist cutting. Finally, the link must have a tough malleable steel core to guard against breaking. Not all chains have all these features. If the package the chain is in doesn't specify these features you can't get an answer from the salesperson, look for a major manufacturer's product that you know does have these features.

### Cables and Cable and Locksets

Individual steel strands make up intertwined steel cable. Each steel strand contains many separate steel wires, all intertwined to make the

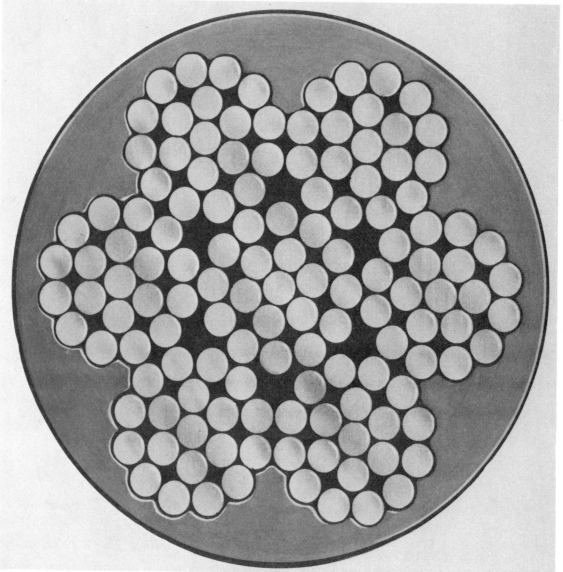

Fig. 10-36. Cutaway view of a steel cable (courtesy Master Lock Co.).

added security. Cable locks may have a combination type padlock instead of a keyed pin tumbler padlock. A barrel combination chain lock provides security with a chrome-plated welded steel chain (Fig. 10-39).

The combination padlock will provide you with keyless convenience, and thousands of available combinations make it extremely difficult

Fig. 10-37. Self-coiling cable (courtesy Master Lock Co.).

cutting of such a chain much more difficult (Fig. 10-36).

Cables can be heavy-duty, super heavy-duty, or self-coiling (Fig. 10-37). To protect the items themselves, ensure that the cable is vinyl-coated. For the standard cable, such as that in Fig. 10-33, ensure that it has multiwedged loop clamps at both ends designed for more than 5,000 pounds of pull strength.

A 3' flexible steel cable lock (Fig. 10-38) is vinyl-coated and permanently attached to a laminated steel padlock. It should have pin tumbler security, and the key change number stamped on the lock should be erasable for

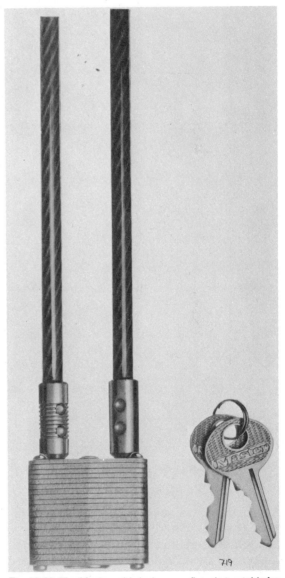

Fig. 10-38. The Master cable lock uses a five-pin turntable for extra security (courtesy Master Lock Co.).

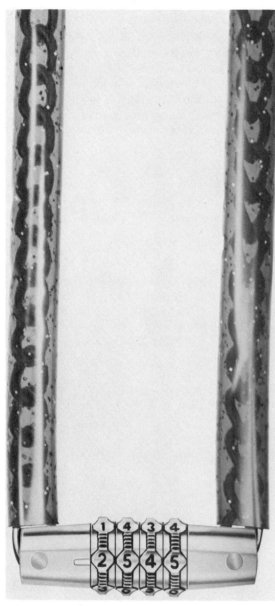

Fig. 10-39. Band combination chain lock (courtesy Master Lock Co.).

for a person to dial your combination. The combination padlock (Fig. 10-40) is built like the lock on a safe and incorporates many features. A combination padlock such as the one shown will have superior quality, durability, and trouble-free service.

When selecting the padlock, ensure that it has double-wall construction and a stainless steel outer case that can armor a heavy wrought steel inner case. The dial must be easy to read, and the grip knob used for turning must be large. The shackle should be case-hardened and the lock self-locking, automatically disarranging all the tumblers when it is closed.

Another combination padlock is a resettable combination lock (Fig. 10-41). You have the advantage of instantly resetting the combination at any time to your personally programmed four-digit combination. With such a lock, you have 10,000 possible settings. This is great for a lock user wishing to choose and control combination security at will. Like other padlocks, you can have more than one shackle length (Fig. 10-42).

Fig. 10-40. Like other quality keyed locks, a good combination lock will have a hardened shackle (courtesy Master Lock Co.).

318

Fig. 10-41. Numerous combinations are available, and you can change it as often as you please (courtesy Master Lock Co.).

Multipurpose padlocks can be either keyed or combination-operated. These locks can be used in many different situations.

### Outboard Motor Lock

Thousands of boat motors are stolen every year. Figure 10-43 illustrates the Master outboard motor lock that will fit the majority of motors secured to the transom by clamp screws. (Unfortunately, certain Chrysler outboards are excepted.) For added convenience in accessing two or more motors with the same key, keyed alike locks are readily available. These locks need no special installation, and they are quick to lock up. Secure the motor to the boat transom by tightening the clamp screws, then slip the motor-lock tube over the clamp screw handles and lock the padlock body in place with the shackle.

The outboard motor lock has a case-hardened steel tube, and it is vinyl clad to protect against weather and water. The lock is a precision marine brass model, using a pin tumbler mechanism. The padlock shackle is double-locked against prying and recessed in the tube, so the tube forms an added case-hardened shield against cutting.

### Ski Lock

This is the first lock designed to safeguard both skis and poles by securing them to a rack, tree, or post (Fig. 10-44). It can be used with almost any binding. The large dial makes opening easy even in the coldest weather with gloved hands.

The ski lock is complete with a security loop formed of multistranded steel cable and vinyl coated to a 3/16" diameter. A 40-number dial means that there are thousands of possible combinations. The extra ski loop (Fig. 10-44) means you can lock an additional set of skis and poles to the first set.

Fig. 10-42. Different shackle lengths allow you to meet varying home security needs (courtesy Master Lock Co.).

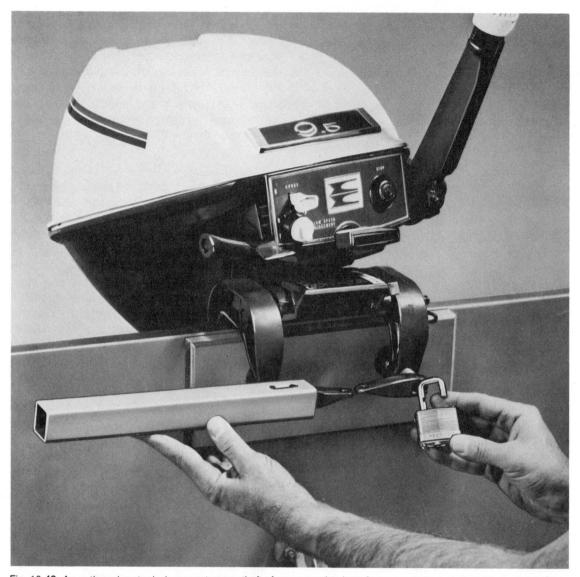

Fig. 10-**43**. An outboard motor lock prevents easy theft of an expensive item from your boat (courtesy Master Lock Co.).

### Gun Lock

The gun lock (Fig. 10-45) is designed to guard against tampering and dry firing of the weapon. It also deters theft by making stolen firearms difficult to use or sell. The gun lock is easy to use and is adjustable to fit most trigger guards. There is a positive locking action with this unit, and cushion pads on the gun lock protect the gun's finish.

Do not install the gun lock on a loaded gun. A loaded gun is dangerous. Remove the ammunition from the gun, then lock it up. Lock away the ammunition in a drawer, gun cabinet, or other area of the home.

### Safety Lockout

The safety lockout (Fig. 10-46) is a tamperproof device that can be used at home on switch and

320

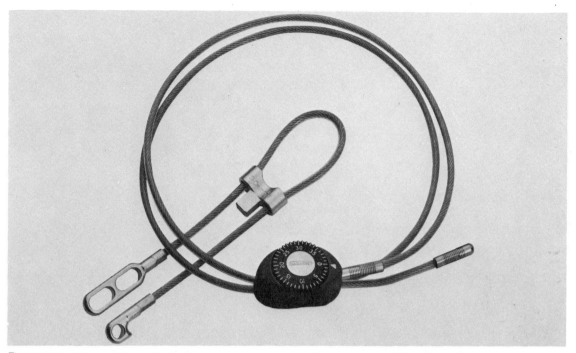

Fig. 10-44. A ski lock can be used to secure one or more sets of skis to an immovable object to prevent theft (courtesy Master Lock Co.).

fuse boxes (Fig. 10-47). Several padlocks can be put on the safety lockout to make it more difficult to enter.

### Hasp Locks

The hasp lock (Fig. 10-48) is a hasp with an integral padlock that can never be misplaced. It is installed as easily as a hasp and uses a high-security pinless hinge with rolled steel edges to enclose and protect the screws that are hidden from view when the hasp lock is locked.

### Bicycle Locks

Bicycle theft has risen dramatically over the past decade as more people have purchased bicycles either for a mode of transportation or just for physical fitness. The *Master Crimefighter* steel bike lock (Fig. 10-49) has a ½″ thick hardened shackle; a scuff guard body and shackle; a weather-resistant, solid brass, high-security pin tumbler lock cylinder; and precision ball-locking

action built into the lock. The wide jaws of the bike lock will solidly secure the frame and wheel to immovable anchored bike racks, anchor posts, and anything up to 4″ in diameter (Fig. 10-50).

Master lock even has theft protection guarantee. There is bike value built into each bike lock. If you purchased this lock through the owner's registration program, the value of the bike up to $350 would be paid if the lock was violated. Master would pay up to $200 value if its other model was violated. There is a registration form prepackaged with each lock.

### Hasps

Hasps may be a straight bar, 90° angle bar, flex-o-hasp, multipurpose top security, and vending machine types. Hasps can be low, good, medium, high, or top security in their relative levels of protection provided.

Figure 10-51 shows a heavy-duty straight bar hasp. The steel staple and locking bar are case-hardened and rustproof-plated.

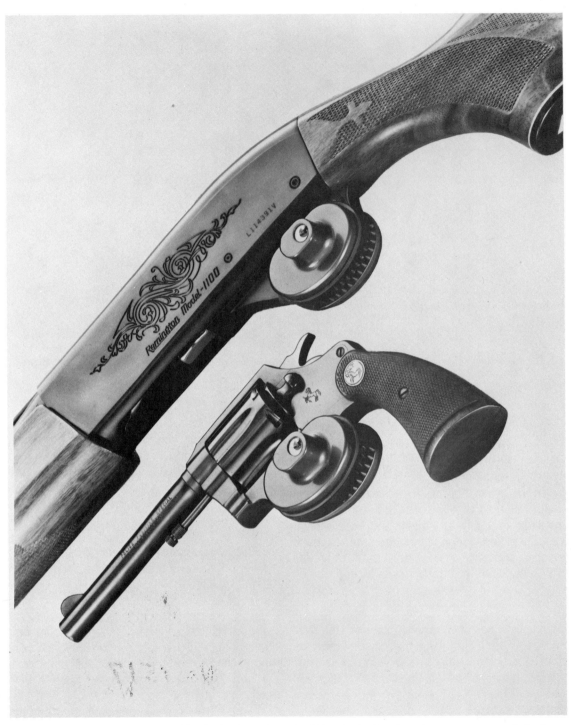

Fig. 10-45. The gun lock is for rifles and pistols. A gun lock should be obtained and used on every weapon in the home (courtesy Master Lock Co.).

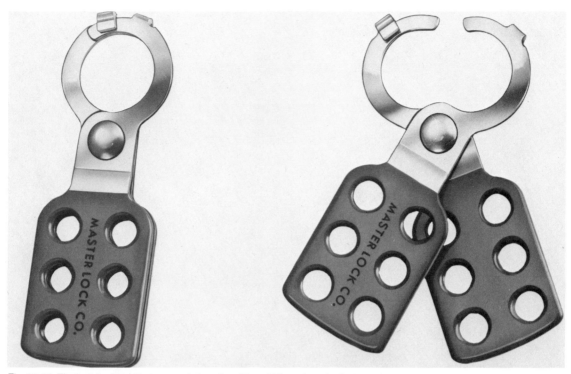

Fig. 10-46. The lock is shown in open and closed positions. When closed, a lock secures the unit, making tampering impossible (courtesy Master Lock Co.).

Fig. 10-47. One or more locks may be used to secure the switch box (courtesy Master Lock Co.).

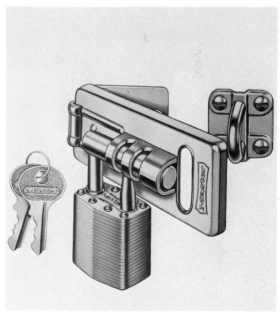

Fig. 10-48. The hasp lock is never lost or misplaced (courtesy Master Lock Co.).

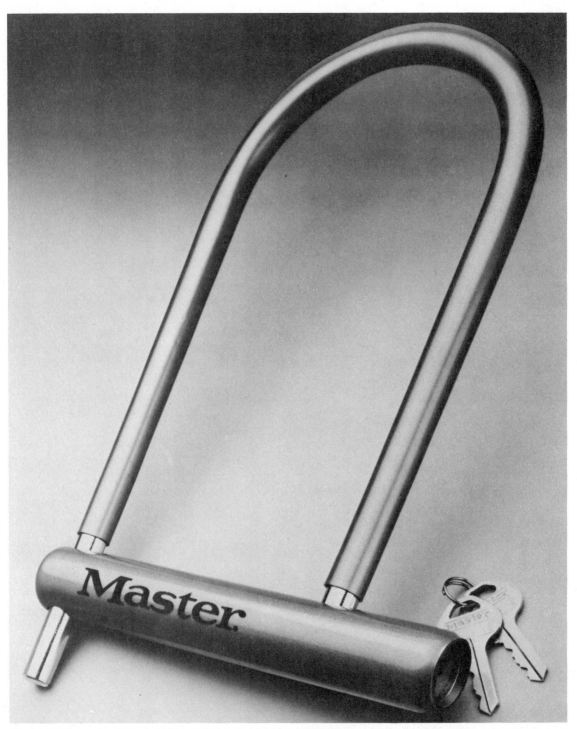

Fig. 10-49. High technology created this high-security bike lock. It's the best lock for bicycle protection (courtesy Master Lock Co.).

Fig. 10-50. The bike lock fits around poles and posts up to 4″ in diameter (courtesy Master Lock Co.).

Figure 10-52 is a 90° angle bar, heavy-duty hasp in which the steel staple and locking bars are case-hardened. The flex-o-hasp and multipurpose top-security hasp (Fig. 10-53) are both made of very heavy wrought steel designed for hard-to-fit applications where it is necessary to follow contours. The hinges and staples are hardened, and the entire unit is plated for protection against corrosion. All hinge pins are inaccessible, and the screws are concealed.

Specifically designed for vending machines, this hasp (Fig. 10-54) can sometimes be used

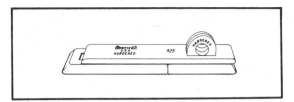

Fig. 10-51. Heavy-duty straight bar hasp (courtesy American Lock Co.).

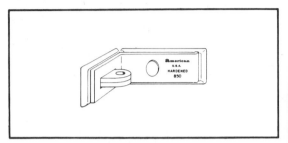

Fig. 10-52. Heavy-duty 90-degree angle hasp (courtesy American Lock Co.).

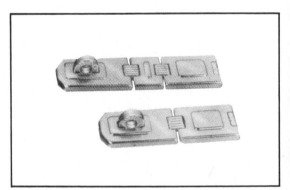

Fig. 10-53. The flex-o-hasp and multipurpose hinged hasps (courtesy American Lock Co.).

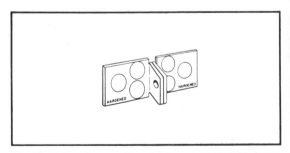

Fig. 10-54. Vending machine style hasps can provide home security for outbuilding and storage areas with double doors and some situations with inward swinging single doors (courtesy American Lock Co.).

when you need more than a lock and a regular hasp. Using a vending type machine hasp with bolts that go through your double doors may be the solution to your problem. The staple and locking bar on these hasps are case-hardened and rustproof-plated. Carriage bolts (⅜″) are used to secure the hasp. Backup plates are included with the hasp for use if needed.

## HOME LIGHTING

The *Sensor-Lite* (Fig. 10-55) turns on at dusk

Fig. 10-55. The Senor-Lite turns itself on, giving the impression that someone is home (courtesy Cable Electric Products, Inc.).

Fig. 10-56. The Night-Guard controls individual lamps. Every home should have at least one (courtesy Cable Electric Products, Inc.).

and increases in intensity to its maximum brightness as the level of darkness increases. The Sensor-Lite also turns off without a switch or timer. This inexpensive device plugs into your standard wall receptacle and is very convenient. Because there is no switch necessary, the unit lights and shuts off automatically. The Sensor-Lite can be used in homes or apartments for added safety and security of the occupants and belongings.

The *Night-Guard* (Fig. 10-56) has been developed by Cable Electric Products to increase security in homes and apartments. It plugs into the wall outlet, and the lamp plugs into the Night-Guard unit at the outlet. The unit provides a nice "lived-in" look when you are away because of the sensor built into it. As it grows dark, the unit electronically turns on the lamp in the evening. You can set the sensor on a window sill or on a tabletop by the lamp to allow for variations in when the lamp will light. Within the home, it will get darker earlier than outside, so you may want to keep the Night-Guard away from a window. In areas where it gets darker later in the evening, you may wish to keep it by a window. It is recommended, though, that you have more than one unit within your home.

## LIFESAVER III

The *Lifesaver III* intrusion security system

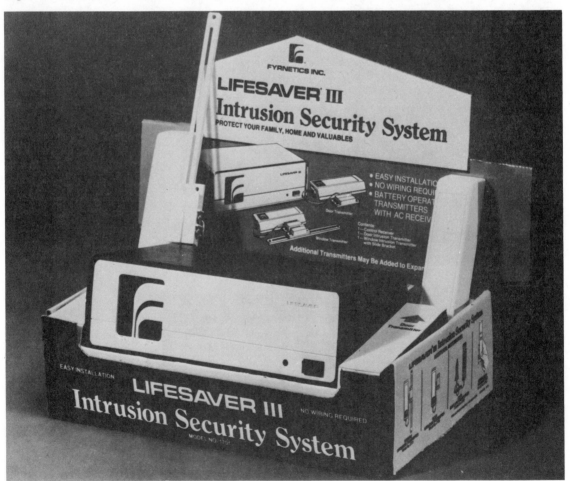

Fig. 10-57. You can install this system yourself in one evening (courtesy Fyrnetics, Inc.).

Fig. 10-58. Wireless transmitters for doors, windows, and the détection of smoke (courtesy Fyrnetics, Inc.).

(Fig. 10-57) is an easy self-installed system that has battery-operated individual transmitters reporting to a main control receiver. The receiver constantly monitors the intrusion detectors throughout the home. When a signal is received, a loud alarm will sound at the receiver. A triggering of a remote power switch turns on lights, radios, or sirens to scare away the intruder and alert your neighbors and you.

This complete wireless home security system is ideal for apartments and homes. The system features include:

Fig. 10-59. The Art Guard incorporates superior electronic technology to provide the highest security available today (courtesy Andra Systems, Inc.).

☐ An unlimited number of transmitters (Fig. 10-58) can be used with the control receiver.

☐ Each transmitter is battery-powered and provides continuous protection when in operation.

329

Fig. 10-60. The Saf-T-Space roll-up door turns a regular closet into a security room (courtesy Saf-T-Space).

- The ac control receiver has a standby battery backup capability to furnish power in the event of a power failure.
- Solid-state circuitry.
- The home security system is FCC-approved for use.

## ENTRY ALARM

The *Entry Alarm* unit can be used for local spot protection of a window or door. It provides the protection of a chain guard and an alarm system simultaneously for point protection. Using a 9-volt battery and simple instructions, the unit can easily and quickly be put in place and in use in a relatively short period.

## ART GUARD

The *Art Guard* (Fig. 10-59) is used in many museums and in many homes that have valuable works of art. The system is on 24 hours a day and is never turned off. It consists of a small wireless transmitter that is mounted behind the painting with a shock sensor mounted directly onto the rear of the frame. Any touch, movement, or cutting activates the transmitter. The signal is detected on a receiver that can decode up to 15 signals.

The Art Guard system transmitter is battery-operated. All wires of the Art Guard are supervised, meaning it will detect the cutting of a wire. Each transmitter has a sensitivity adjustment and possesses a Sonalert that "sounds" whenever the transmitter is activated.

## HOME SECURITY CLOSET

A home security closet can be used to store jewelry, cash, and other items. A *Safe-T-Space* is a steel security door that converts a standard closet into a walk-in security container for your valuables (Fig. 10-60).

# Chapter 11

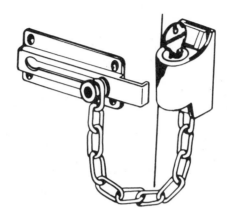

# Insurance

Our society could hardly function without insurance. There would be so much uncertainty that it would be difficult for anyone to plan confidently for the future. If you forego insurance, then you can cross off your overall security. We are indebted to the Insurance Information Institute for its invaluable assistance and permission to use extensive amounts of copyrighted information in this chapter.

### THE PURPOSE OF INSURANCE

The basic function of property/casualty insurance is described as a transfer of risk. Insurance reduces financial uncertainty and makes accidental loss manageable. Payment of a small, known fee—the insurance premium—is made to a professional insurer in exchange for the assumption of the risk of a large loss and a promise to pay in the event of such a loss.

### KINDS OF PROTECTION

The insurance policy legally binds the seller (the insurer) and the buyer (the policyholder) to certain obligations. Insurers are obligated to pay for losses if an event covered by the policy occurs. Policyholders are obligated to pay a premium for the financial protection that the policy provides.

Insurance companies offer many policies that cover:

☐ Losses of or damages to property resulting from fire, windstorm, theft, vandalism or other perils.

☐ The policyholder's legal liability to pay for injuries to other persons or damage to their property for which the policyholder is responsible.

☐ Costs arising from job-related injuries and illnesses.

☐ Protection for employers against losses caused by fraudulent or dishonest acts of employees (offered in the form of fidelity bonds).

☐ The failure of a contractor to perform

specified acts within a stated period (suretyship).

A major difference between a property/casualty insurance policy and other products is that the tangible benefits of the insurance policy are realized only after a loss has occurred. Insurance is a promise to pay in the event of a loss in the future. Remember that those policyholders who do not suffer a loss benefit from financial protection every minute of every day.

## MAJOR POLICY PROVISIONS

The insurance industry has many policies and coverages that are, in some respects, as individual as each policyholder. Nevertheless, there are characteristics common to most policies.

The typical insurance policy comprises four sections:

☐ *The declarations page*—names the policyholder, describes the property or the liability to be insured, and states the type of coverage and the maximum dollar limit that the insurer will pay in the event of a claim.

☐ *The insuring agreement*—describes the insurer's and the policyholder's responsibilities during the time the policy is in force.

☐ *The conditions of the policy*— spells out details regarding the coverage and what is required of the insured and the insurer in the event of a loss resulting in a claim.

☐ *The exclusions*—details the types of property and the types of losses that are not covered.

Included in the conditions section are provisions common to many property/casualty policies. Among them:

☐ *Concealment and fraud.* Should the policyholder in any way willfully conceal or misrepresent any facts or cir-

cumstances in applying for the policy or in the filing of a claim, the insurer may void the policy and refuse to pay any loss.

☐ *Perils not included.* Most property insurance policies exclude losses caused, directly or indirectly, by certain perils including enemy attack, rebellion, and civil war. Coverage of certain damages may be denied if the damages result from a policyholder's failure to use all reasonable means to save and preserve property during or after a loss.

☐ *Waiver provisions.* Essentially, any changes or modifications of the policy terms must be written and attached in the form of an endorsement to the policy. Oral or separately written changes cannot alter the policy terms.

☐ *Cancellation.* A policy usually may be canceled by the policyholder at any time or by the insurer under certain conditions. The remainder of the premium will be returned on a pro rata basis if the policy is canceled by the insurer. A charge for administrative costs will be made if the policy is canceled by the policyholder.

☐ *Mortgage interest and obligations.* Some property covered under the policy may be mortgaged, so the lender has a vested interest in the insurance on the property. Under this clause, the insurer recognizes the lender's interest.

☐ *Pro rata contribution.* This provides that if more than one policy is in force for the same property, each company will pay a share of any loss in proportion to the amount of coverage it agreed to provide. This effectively prevents an unscrupulous policyholder from overinsuring his or her property in order to profit from a loss.

☐ *Requirements in case of a loss.* Among the policyholder's responsibilities are: prompt notification to the company, protection of damaged property from further loss, submission of proof of loss, and making available all pertinent financial records at the request of the insurer.

☐ *Appraisal.* If the policyholder and the insurer disagree on the value or the amount of a loss, this provision outlines the procedures for selecting and paying independent, competent appraisers to arbitrate and determine a settlement.

☐ *Company's options.* The insurer may take all or part of the damaged property at an agreed value after payment; or repair, rebuild, or replace it with material or goods of a similar kind and quality; or settle in cash.

☐ *Subrogation.* The insurer, after paying a claim to a policyholder, has the right to recover the amount of the payment from a third party who either caused or was responsible for the loss. Consequently, the policyholder waives his right to collect twice—once from the insurer and once from the third party.

## DEDUCTIBLES

Many insurance policies—covering homes, automobiles, and businesses—include provisions for *deductibles.* Under these provisions, the policyholder agrees to absorb losses up to a certain amount—the deductible. By offering deductibles, insurance companies are able to reduce the cost of the policies because they are relieved of the obligation of handling many relatively small claims—those less than the deductible amount—that occur in great numbers and often cost just as much as large claims to process. Among commercial insureds, who often retain or self-insure substantial portions of their risks, deductibles are also commonly known as retentions. Where it is economically feasible, insurers urge policyholders to increase the size of their deductibles as a means of holding their premiums to a minimum.

## PROPERTY INSURANCE FOR YOUR HOME

Every nine seconds a fire breaks out somewhere in the United States. It may be a blaze in a downtown building, a house on fire in your neighborhood, or a brush fire nearby. Losses caused by fire total more than $3.75 billion. To protect themselves from such financial losses, homeowners purchase insurance. Each homeowner pays regularly a small amount of money to an insurance company. Thus, the company has enough funds to pay for the financial losses of the relatively few unfortunate families whose property is damaged. For a small sum of money, each homeowner is protected against the possibility of a large and unpredictable loss.

You can protect your property and your family by purchasing several different insurance policies, or you can buy the package policy. For example, you can purchase a standard fire policy that insures your home and contents against only fire and lightning. For an additional premium, you can have extended coverage that broadens the policy to include damage from wind, hail, smoke, explosion, riot, vehicles, and falling aircraft. Still another policy can be purchased for protection against burglary and theft, and another can be bought for injuries suffered by visitors on your property or damage you cause to the property of others. You can have separate policies for the perils just mentioned, or you can purchase a package policy—called the homeowner's policy—that includes all of them. Regardless of the type or number of policies you have, it is important to know just what property is covered and the specific perils you are insured against.

## HOMEOWNER'S POLICY: PROPERTY COVERAGES

You can purchase a homeowner's policy if you own and occupy a one- or a two-family residence. Advantages of such a policy are apparent. You have only one policy to be concerned about. Your property is insured against many perils, and you pay less than if you purchased these coverages separately.

If you are a farmer, you are not eligible for a

homeowner's policy, but a farmowner's policy is available in many farm states that includes many of the same features. Your insurance agent can tell you whether such a policy is available in the area where you live.

What properties are covered? Your house—or your dwelling as it is referred to in your policy—is covered under your homeowner's policy. This includes, in addition to the living quarters, such structures as an attached garage and other additions to your house.

Other structures on your property, such as a tool shed, a guest house, or a detached garage, are also covered. In your policy they may be referred to as *appurtenant structures* or *private structures*. Your homeowner's policy does not cover any building on your property that is used for commercial purposes or one that you rent or lease to others, except for garage purposes.

Your personal property is covered. This includes all household contents and other personal belongings used, owned, worn, or carried by you or your family. The protection applies whether the loss occurs at home or away. At your option, this coverage may also be written to apply to personal property of your guests while they are on your premises. Your pets are not included in this coverage.

An inventory of your personal property is quite important. In the event of loss or damage, it assists you in putting in a claim quickly and getting a prompt settlement. If your personal property includes antiques, such as a grandfather's clock that has been in the family for generations, have them appraised and keep a record of their values in a fireproof file or a safe deposit box. Otherwise, it will be difficult to prove the value of what has been lost or damaged.

Whether you own your home or rent an apartment or house, you should ask your insurance agent about insuring valuables such as antiques, jewelry, furs, and cameras separately. They may not be insured to full value under the limits set for personal property in your homeowner's policy.

Automobiles, although they are personal property, have their own special insurance. They are not protected under a homeowner's policy.

One of the features of a homeowner's policy is the coverage of additional living expense. The policy is designed to cover the increase in living expenses made necessary when your house cannot be occupied because of damage caused by an insured peril. For example, if your home is badly damaged by fire and you have to live in a hotel or motel and eat in restaurants, your insurance company will reimburse you for necessary increased living expenses up to the limits stated in your policy. The company will pay you the difference between living expenses you incur while your house is being repaired and what it would normally cost you for such living expenses.

If you set aside a portion of your residence for rental purposes and a loss covered under the policy makes that portion uninhabitable, your insurance company will pay the fair rental value for the time required to complete repairs.

A homeowner's policy covers your home and other structures on your property, household furnishings, personal belongings, and additional living expense. It also provides personal liability protection.

When you purchase a homeowner's policy, the number of perils your property is insured against depends on whether you choose the basic form (HO-1), the broad form (HO-2), or the comprehensive form (HO-5) of the policy. The widely purchased broad form (HO-2) insures your property against 18 different perils (Fig. 11-1). The basic form (HO-1) includes only the first 11 perils shown. The comprehensive form (HO-5) insures against all the perils shown in Fig. 11-1 and many more. It is sometimes referred to as an all-risks policy. The policy doesn't cover damage from every possible peril. An all-risks policy generally insures you against some perils and then lists exceptions.

## A POLICY FOR THE CONDOMINIUM UNIT-OWNER

If you own an apartment unit in a condominium, the condominium association normally buys the

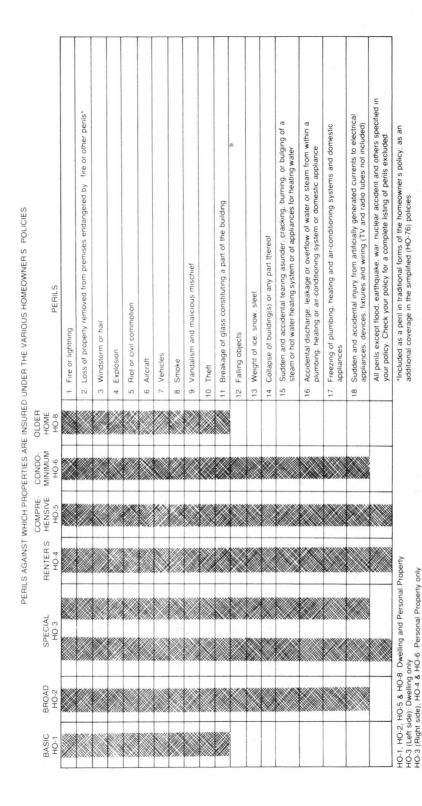

PERILS AGAINST WHICH PROPERTIES ARE INSURED UNDER THE VARIOUS HOMEOWNER'S POLICIES

HO-1, HO-2, HO-5 & HO-8: Dwelling and Personal Property
HO-3 (Left side): Dwelling only
HO-3 (Right side), HO-4 & HO-6: Personal Property only

Fig. 11-1. Depending on the policy, your perils against which property is insured may vary (courtesy Insurance Information Insititute).

insurance for the condominium property (building and structures) and liability. You may purchase a special condominium unit-owner's form HO-6 policy to insure your personal property and also any additions or alterations you make to the unit that are not insured by the association's policy. The coverage is basically the same as for the tenant's form HO-4, including personal liability protection.

## INSURANCE POLICIES FOR RENTERS

If you rent the apartment or house you occupy, there is a particular policy for you. It is the contents broad form or tenants form and is also referred to as form HO-4. It insures your household contents and personal belongings against virtually all of the perils included in the broad form (HO-2). Because you do not own the dwelling or appurtenant private structures when you rent, they are not insured under your contents broad form policy. Your policy does provide coverage for additional living expense.

## A SPECIAL FORM

Many homeowners want the broadest insurance coverage available for their dwelling and appurtenant private structures, but they do not want to pay for this same extensive coverage on their personal property. Their needs are satisfied by purchasing a special form (HO-3), which provides the same coverage for their dwelling and private structures as does the comprehensive form (HO-5), while covering their personal property for the same perils provided in the contents broad form (HO-4).

## A POLICY FOR THE MOBILE HOME OWNER

If you own and occupy a mobile home, that is at least 10' wide and 40' long, there is a special homeowner's type policy for you. The mobile home policy provides basically the same coverage you would receive if you purchased a homeowner's form HO-2 on a one- or two-family dwelling.

Premiums for a mobile home policy are sub-stantially higher than a similar policy for a conventional house because of the differences in construction and the greater susceptibility of mobile homes to wind damage.

## FLOOD INSURANCE

Until the late 1960s, flood insurance was not generally sold to homeowners. The only ones who wanted it were those who were almost certain to have losses. In 1969, however, the federal government and the private insurance business introduced a joint program to make flood insurance available in flood-prone areas at low cost. The program is now administered by the Federal Insurance Administration of the U.S. Department of Housing and Urban Development.

To qualify for flood insurance, your property must be located in a community that has told the U.S. Department of Housing and Urban Development that it will plan and carry out land use control measures to reduce future flooding.

As of mid-1978, flood insurance was available in more than 16,000 communities throughout the United States. Your agent or broker can tell you if it is available where you live.

## EARTHQUAKE INSURANCE

Earthquakes strike most often and usually most severely in the Pacific Coast area, and Californians buy about two-thirds of all the earthquake insurance purchased in the United States. Nevertheless, very few Californians were prepared when the devastating San Fernando Valley earthquake hit in February, 1971, causing property damage of more than $550 million. In other areas, a much higher percentage of property owners would be caught off guard, although every state is vulnerable to earthquakes and the insurance coverage is readily available.

Earthquake insurance usually is written as an addition to a fire or homeowner's insurance policy. Premiums in some states are as low as 3¢ per $100 for dwellings.

## ADDITIONAL COVERAGES

When a fire or other peril damages or destroys a

policy—items such as antique furniture, furs, house, there are expenses that go beyond the repair of the house itself. Insurers have added six of these after-the-fact expenses to the coverages for persons who own houses and have homeowner's policies. The sixth additional coverage applies also to renter's condominium, and mobile home policies.

- ☐ *Debris removal.* Insurers will pay the reasonable expense of taking damaged property away.
- ☐ *Reasonable repair.* Where temporary repairs are necesary to protect property from further damage, insurers will pay for the additional expense.
- ☐ *Trees, shrubs, and other plants.* Insurers will pay for certain insured perils (not including windstorm) up to $500 for any tree, shrub, or plant or an overall maximum of 5 percent of the limit of insurance for the dwelling. Lawns also are covered.
- ☐ *Fire department service charge.* In areas where property owners must pay for fire department services, insurers will reimburse policyholders up to $250.
- ☐ *Property removal.* When property is rescued from a dwelling, this coverage protects it for up to 30 days against direct loss from any cause.
- ☐ *Credit card, forgery, and counterfeit money.* Insurers will reimburse policyholders up to $500 if they lose their credit cards and others charge purchases to their accounts. The same limit applies to check forgery or a policyholder's loss resulting from acceptance in good faith of counterfeit money.

## PERSONAL ARTICLES COVERAGE

Certain property in the home may be more valuable than the limits set under the personal property coverage of a homeowner's or tenant's camera equipment, coin and stamp collections, jewelry, art pieces, and other expensive or unusual properties. These values may be insured by purchasing a personal articles "floater" as a separate coverage or by endorsement to the homeowner's policy. The term floater derives from the fact that the coverage applies wherever the property is located at the time of loss. The coverage, in effect, "floats" with the property.

Because the homeowner's policy provides only limited coverage of items that many people keep in safe deposit boxes, some companies offer a separate safe deposit box insurance policy to supplement that protection. Generally, such policies provide all-risk coverage for securities and burglary and robbery coverage for other valuables.

## INSURANCE AGAINST VOLCANIC ERUPTIONS

Damage from volcanos as a risk to be insured against did not readily come to most persons' minds until May 18, 1980, when Washington State's Mount St. Helens began a series of eruptions that resulted in millions of dollars in property damage. The volcanic activity at Mount St. Helens created confusion about insurance coverage. Traditional homeowner's policies specifically excluded volcanic eruptions, but the simplified homeowner's policies (HO-76 series) did not have this exclusion. Each type of policy, however, covers explosions. Insurers relied on that coverage in paying the vast majority of policyholders' property damage claims.

The months after the initial eruption saw the industry and regulators conferring on how to avoid confusion should such an event face them again. At the end of 1980, the Washington insurance commissioner issued a bulletin which began:

> "While the insurance industry responded well to losses resulting from the unprecedented eruptions of Mount St. Helens, it became evident that greater clarity was needed in the language of homeowner's and dwell-

ing fire insurance policies with respect to volcano coverage. Accordingly, representatives of a cross section of insurers have assisted my office in the development of a suitable endorsement.

The bulletin promulgated a rule, to be effective July 1, 1981, requiring homeowner's and dwelling fire insurance policies "that provide coverage for damage resulting from volcanic eruptions" to indicate precisely how the coverage applies.

## LIABILITY COVERAGES

All forms of the homeowner's policy include liability coverages that apply to the policyholder and to all family members who reside in the home. These coverages include liability, medical payments to others, and physical damage to the property of others.

### Personal Liability

The liability coverage is designed to provide protection against a claim or a lawsuit that could cripple a homeowner financially. Suppose, for example, that a visitor slips and falls on a policyholder's property, suffers a head injury that results in impaired vision, and eventually sues for $100,000 or more; or suppose that as a result of a policyholder's misjudgment in felling a tree in the backyard, the house next door is damaged extensively and the owner files a claim. If it is agreed by the parties involved or decided by a court that the policyholder is legally liable for the visitor's injury or the damage to the neighbor's property, the insurance company will pay the damages assessed up to the limits of the policy. Further, in case of a lawsuit, the insurance company will pay the legal costs of defense whether or not the policyholder ultimately is held to be legally responsible.

The minimum liability limit for each form of the homeowner's policy is $25,000, but larger amounts can be purchased. The two examples just mentioned deal with accidents occurring on or near the homeowner's property. Accidents occurring elsewhere (not including business-related accidents) are covered in the same way if they are caused by the policyholder, a family member, or a pet.

### Medical Payments

Accidents often result in minor injuries that are inexpensive to treat but which could become relatively burdensome in terms of both time and dollars if payment of the bills was dependent on establishing legal liability. The medical payments section of every homeowner's policy provides for payment of such bills without regard to fault in case of injuries to others on the policyholder's premises. It also applies elsewhere to injuries caused by the policyholder, a family member, or a pet. The basic amount of protection is $500 for each person injured, but larger amounts may be purchased.

While this coverage does not pay for injuries to the policyholder or family members, it does enable the policyholder to discharge what he or she may believe to be a moral obligation to pay for someone else's medical expenses under certain conditions.

The personal liability and medical payments coverages apply even to boats under certain conditions—and to golf carts when they are being used for golfing purposes. The homeowner's liability is covered if the boat he or she owns or rents is an inboard or inboard-outboard powered boat of 50 hp or less or a sailboat less than 26' long. Also, liability arising from the ownership of an outboard-powered boat with not more than 25 hp is covered.

## SUPPLEMENTARY COVERAGE

An important supplementary coverage in all homeowner's policies pays for minor damage that you or someone in your family might cause accidentally to another person's property, regardless of who is at fault or, as is sometimes the case, when no one is at fault. Damage caused intentionally by children under age 13 is covered because it is considered to be accidental. The maximum amount that an insurance company will agree to pay under supplementary coverage for any one incident is $250.

## WORKER'S COMPENSATION

Although worker's compensation insurance generally is regarded as a coverage for business and industry, it also is available to homeowners and renters to cover domestic employees—either part-time or full-time.

Two states, New Hampshire and New Jersey, now require that every policy issued to private individuals that affords comprehensive personal liability coverage—such as the homeowner's and renter's policies—includes worker's compensation coverage for household employees. In California, any homeowner who employs domestic workers on either full-time or part-time basis is required to have worker's compensation coverage.

## HOW MUCH COVERAGE?

To receive full replacement payment for any partial loss or damage under a homeowner's policy (with the exception of the special policies for older homes), the owner must insure the dwelling for at least 80 percent of its replacement value. For a home with a replacement value of $80,000, coverage in the amount of $64,000 (80 percent) meets the requirements of this provision. If a fire should result in $5,000 damage to the living room, the insurer would pay that amount, less the amount of the deductible, to cover the necessary repairs.

Should the same house be insured for less than $64,000, any payment for a partial loss would be reduced. The reduction is calculated in one of two possible ways. Assuming coverage of $40,000 (instead of the $64,000 of coverage the owner should have), the owner would stand to collect either 40/64 of the $5,000 loss ($3,150), or the actual cash value (replacement cost less depreciation), whichever is larger. In the event of a total loss, the insurer would pay no more than the amount of coverage ($40,000 in this example).

Insurers stress that the market value of a house is not a proper basis for determining the amount of coverage to buy. Homeowners should consult with their agent or broker for assistance in determining replacement value.

Table 11-1. Amounts of Coverages Under the Broad Form Homeowner's Policy (HO-2) (Assuming a House with an $80,000 Replacement Value Insured to Full Value and to 80 Percent of Value) (courtesy Insurance Information Institute).

| Property Coverages | Insured to Replacement Value | Insured to 80% of Replacement Value |
|---|---|---|
| Dwelling | $80,000 (full value) | $64,000 (80% of full value) |
| Other Structure on Property | 8,000 (10% of dwelling) | 6,400 (10% of dwelling) |
| Unscheduled Personal Property | 40,000 (50% of dwelling)** | 32,000 (50% of dwelling) |
| Additional Living Expenses | 16,000 (20% of dwelling) | 12,800 (20% of dwelling)** |
| Trees, Shrubs and Plants | 4,000 (5% of dwelling, subject to maximum of $500 per item) | 3,200 (5% of dwelling, subject to maximum of $500 per item) |
| **Liability Coverages** | | |
| Personal Liability | $25,000 (each occurrence)** | $25,000 (each occurrence)** |
| Medical payments to Others (regardless of fault) | 500 (each person)** | 500 (each person)** |
| Damage to Property of Others (regardless of fault) | 250 (each occurrence) | 250 (each occurrence) |

\* Amounts of coverages are the same under the basic form (HO-1), the special form (HO-3), and the comprehensive form (HO-5) except that additional living expenses under the basic form are covered only up to 10% of the amount of coverage on the dwelling.

\*\* Larger amounts are available.

With policies covering homes, the amount of coverage on the house becomes the basis for determining amounts of coverage that are automatically assigned to other structures on the property, personal property, and additional living expenses. The other structures are covered for 10 percent of the amount of coverage on the house, personal property for 50 percent, and additional living expenses for 20 percent (10 percent under the basic policy HO-1). For a detailed breakdown of the coverages, see Table 11-1.

Renter's policies provide a minimum of $4,000 coverage on personal property, with 10 percent of that amount to cover additions and alterations to the dwelling unit and 20 percent of the amount of personal property coverage for additional living expenses. Condominium policies cover personal property for a minimum of $4,000, 40 percent of the amount of that coverage for additional living expenses, and $1,000 for additions and alterations to the unit.

Table 11-1 summarizes the amounts of the principal coverages, under a homeowner's policy, on an $80,000 house insured to the full amount of its replacement cost and to 80 percent of its replacement value.

Insurers strongly recommend that policyholders make an inventory of all household furnishings and personal belongings for their own protection in deciding how much insurance to buy and for use in the event of a loss. The inventory, along with photographs of important items and receipts covering major purchases, should be stored in a safe place away from home.

## INSURANCE TO VALUE

Pointing to the sharp increase in home values during the 1970s and into the 1980s, insurers emphasize the importance to homeowners of reviewing regularly—at least once a year—the amount of insurance coverage on their property.

Studies have shown that thousands of homeowners are underinsured because they haven't kept pace with inflation by increasing the amount of their coverage, although most companies and their representatives regularly rec-ommend higher policy limits—if warranted— when policies are due for renewal. Some companies automatically increase coverage each year, in line with inflation, unless the policyholder objects.

An inflation guard endorsement is widely available to homeowners and periodically increases the amount of coverage under a homeowner's policy as protection against inflation. One endorsement provides for an automatic increase every three months in the amount of protection afforded by the policy at the rate of 1 percent of the original amount of coverage.

## PROPERTY INSURANCE PLANS

The insurance industry operates special property insurance plans in many states to assure the availability of insurance protection for high-risk properties or for properties in coastal areas vulnerable to severe windstorm damage, where insurance otherwise might be difficult to obtain.

About half of the states have property insurance plans known as FAIR plans, an acronym for *fair access to insurance requirements*. The plans as they operate today were established following passage by Congress of the *Housing and Urban Development Act of 1968*, which provided for federal riot reinsurance to those states that instituted such property insurance pools. In 1980, there were FAIR plans in 26 states, the District of Columbia, and Puerto Rico.

The FAIR plans are supported by the insurers that write insurance voluntarily on other properties in the state. Any plan, in order to qualify for riot reinsurance under current federal law, must offer insurance on inner city properties at rates no higher than those of the voluntary market, with the result that many of the plans consistently have sustained operating losses. New York and a few other states have elected to set rates at a level designed to make the plans more nearly self-sustaining rather than to continue federal riot reinsurance.

Following the riots in the middle and late 1960s, arson has developed as a more serious problem than riot in the inner city areas. Along with numerous other loss prevention activities, the insurance industry has supported vigorous anti-arson programs nationwide.

All of the FAIR plans offer fire and extended coverage (windstorm, vandalism, and certain additional coverages) on residences and commercial properties. Many plans now offer homeowner's commercial package policies and some miscellaneous coverages, too.

Counterparts to the FAIR plans are beach and windstorm insurance plans operated by property insurers in seven states along the Atlantic and Gulf Coasts to assure availability of insurance for both residences and commercial properties against damage from hurricanes or other windstorms.

## AUTOMOBILE INSURANCE

In the 1960s, the automobile insurance system in effect throughout the U.S. was the target for much public criticism. Dissatisfaction was expressed by those purchasing auto insurance, by companies and agencies marketing it, and by state officials regulating it.

Criticism and dissatisfaction with the system focused on the expensive and time-consuming process of determining who is at fault—legally liable—when accidents occur. This process frequently requires the services of lawyers both for the person suing and the one being sued. Because of so many cases in some areas, trials and settlements of claims are subject to long delay—as much as four or more years.

With the no-fault concept each person's financial losses, such as medical and hospital expenses and loss of income, would be paid by the policyholder's own insurance company without concern for who was at fault. For such a concept to be operative, legislatures must pass laws to that effect.

Massachusetts was the first state to enact a no-fault auto insurance law, effective January 1, 1971. Since then many other states have passed no-fault laws. For several years, federal no-fault legislation has been under consideration in Congress.

No fault laws vary from state to state. Variations include the following:

- [ ] The amount to be paid the insured person for medical expenses, which in some states is unlimited; or, in case of death, for funeral and burial expenses.
- [ ] Amount of loss of income to be paid an injured income producer.
- [ ] Amount to be paid a person hired to perform essential services that an injured nonincome-producing member of a family is unable to perform.
- [ ] Conditions governing the right to sue, which usually include death, permanent injury, or disfigurement; and a point at which medical expenses reach a stipulated amount, which is referred to as the threshold for suit.
- [ ] Inclusion or exclusion of property damage.

### Bodily Injury Liability

This coverage applies when your car injures or kills pedestrians, persons riding in other cars, or guests in your car. It is in force as long as your car is driven by you, members of your family who live with you, or others who drive it with your permission. You and all members of your family are covered even while driving someone else's car if you have the owner's permission.

When claims or suits are brought against you, bodily injury liability insurance provides protection in the form of legal defense. If it is agreed by the parties involved—or judged by a court—that you are legally liable for the injury, your insurance company will pay the damages assessed against you up to the limits stated in your policy.

Amounts of bodily injury coverage are written 10/20, 25/50, and 100/300. The first number refers to the maximum amount, in thousands of dollars, that the insurance company will pay for the injuries of any person in any one accident. The second number is the maximum amount, in thousands of dollars, it will pay for all of the in-

| Comparative Costs of Bodily Injury Liability Coverage | In an area where ...you can buy ...........and .............or | 10/20 costs 25/50 for 50/100 for 100/300 for | $ 55 a year $ 76 a year $ 90 a year $104 a year |
|---|---|---|---|
| Comparative Costs of Property Damage Liability Coverage | In an area where ................ ................ | $ 5,000 costs $10,000 costs $25,000 costs | $ 67 a year $ 70 a year $ 72 a year |

Fig. 11-2. Comparative costs of bodily injury liability coverage (courtesy Insurance Information Institute).

juries resulting from any one accident. In some cases, the maximum amount the insurance company will pay for all losses in one accident may be stated as a single figure.

You must know the minimum limits of coverage for bodily injury liability insurance under the financial responsibility laws in your state. In many states 10/20 is sufficient, but minimum limits are higher in a majority of the states. Comparative costs of different amounts of bodily injury liability coverage (along with those of property damage liability) are shown in Fig. 11-2.

### Property Damage Liability

This coverage applies when your car damages the property of others. More often than not the property damaged is another car, but you are also covered for damages to telephone poles and buildings. It does not cover damage to your car. Protection under property damage liability insurance is in force as long as your car is driven by you, members of your immediate family, or others who drive it with your permission.

When claims and suits are brought against you, property damage liability insurance provides protection in the form of legal defense and indemnification through the payment of damages for which you are legally liable. Your insurance company does not pay damages beyond the limits stated in your policy. You can purchase this coverage in amounts ranging from $5,000 to $50,000 or more.

Just as in the case of bodily injury liability insurance, you should check on minimum requirements for property damage liability insurance under the financial responsibility laws in your state.

When talking with your agent or broker about automobile insurance, you are certain to hear the abbreviations "BI" and "PD" (often written "BI/PD") for bodily injury and property damage liability coverages. When discussing amounts of BI and PD coverages, insurance agents refer to them as 10/20/5. The first two numbers refer to bodily injury (BI) and the last property damage (PD) in thousands of dollars.

Experienced drivers will tell you that the two liability coverages, bodily injury (BI) and property damage (PD), are an absolute must. To be without them is to run the risk of financial disaster for you and your family. If you have only 10/20/5 coverage and are judged legally liable for injuring a person to the extent, say, of $25,000, your insurance company would be obligated to pay only $10,000. The other $15,000 would have to come from you.

Most car owners are pleasantly surprised to learn how little it costs to increase bodily injury and property damage coverage from 10/20/5 to 50/100/10 and even to 100/300/25. The premiums vary widely from one area to another, so don't assume that the comparative costs presented in Fig. 11-2 are the same as those in your rating territory.

## Medical Payments

This coverage pertains to medical expenses resulting from injuries suffered by you and all family members who live with you while riding in your car or someone else's car or when struck by a car while walking. It also applies to guests occupying your car.

The insuring company agrees to pay all reasonable medical expenses incurred within one year from the date of the accident, including those for necessary medical and dental services, prosthetic devices, ambulance, hospital care, professional nursing, and funeral services.

Medical payments insurance differs from bodily injury liability coverage in that it applies to members of your family and guests in your car—not just to others. Payment is made without having to determine who is at fault. The maximum amount the insurance company will pay to any one person injured in any one accident is limited to the amount stated in the policy.

With the costs of medicine, a doctor's care, and hospital services increasing markedly over the past several years, many car owners are finding that the coverages they chose when they bought their policies are no longer adequate.

## Collision

If your car is damaged as a result of colliding with a vehicle or other object or turning over, your collision insurance will cover the damage to your car regardless of who was responsible. This coverage does not apply to personal injuries suffered in automobile accidents, nor to damage your car does to the property of others.

Because the year, make, and model of your car are major factors in determining what you pay for collision insurance, premiums are highest when a car is new and decrease as it gets older. There comes a time, however, in the life of a car when its value continues to decrease, but the cost of collision insurance does not.

A little understood advantage of having collision insurance is that even if the party you collide with is legally liable for damages to your car, you can collect from your insurance company and have your car repaired immediately. Without collision coverage, you have to wait for payment until you have completed negotiations with the other party or the insurance company that insures the other party.

## MOTORCYCLE INSURANCE

Although motorcycles are not classified as automobiles for insurance purposes, insurance for motorcycles—as well as for mopeds, snowmobiles, and other vehicles—is quite similar to auto insurance. Auto policies—with endorsements—are used to provide coverage for such vehicles. Most states that require car owners to have liability insurance require the same for motorcyclists.

A car owner who also has a motorcycle may insure the bike through an endorsement to the auto policy. The coverages available to motorcyclists are bodily injury and property damage liability, medical payments (usually limited to $500), uninsured motorist coverage, and physical damage coverage including collision. Some insurance companies offer six-month or nine-month policies to persons who live in colder climates and retire their motorcycles during winter.

# Chapter 12

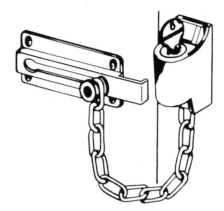

# Citizen Involvement in Fighting Crime

You can do something to fight crime within your community or neighborhood. Citizen involvement is community involvement; by working together with friends and neighbors, you can get criminals off the street.

### WHISTLESTOP PROGRAM

In some communities, the WhistleSTOP program is only one facet of crime deterrence. It is an action safety program that can provide residents of a community with a practical way to protect people on the street.

The WhistleSTOP program combines:

- ☐ Individual action—one can signal for help and get it.
- ☐ Collective action—one blow of a whistle can lead to another as witnesses react to a crime.
- ☐ Citizen and police action—citizens can assist police effectively by immediately reporting the distress signal and the incident.

This program does work. Countless purse snatchings, muggings, car thefts, and rapes have been averted just because the intended victim or a witness blew a whistle. Whistles also stop obscene telephone calls.

The key to the program's success lies in the cooperations of the police in responding to distress signal reports and the responsibility of citizens in the use of the whistle. Parents should never let children use whistles of the same tone of shrillness as toys. They should provide the children with a whistle for them to use in emergency situations only.

Whistles should be on a key chain or bracelet. Carry a whistle with you at all times. You could wear a lapel pin with a whistle on a retractable chain. Don't wear a whistle on a neck chain because it could be used to choke you.

If your community does not have a WhistleSTOP action safety program, talk to your local police department, neighborhood association, and other associations. WhistleSTOP could save your life.

Here are some tips on using a whistle:

When confronted on the street:

- ☐ Don't resist. Give up a handbag, for example.
- ☐ Blow your whistle when it is physically safe.
- ☐ Call the police as soon as possible.

If you fear trouble on the street:

- ☐ Run toward the street.
- ☐ Blow your whistle.
- ☐ Call the police as soon as possible.

If you observe trouble on the street:

- ☐ Blow your whistle to scare off the assailant and to attract attention to the trouble.
- ☐ Keep at a safe distance.
- ☐ Get to the nearest telephone and report details to the police.

If you hear a whistle or a cry for help:

- ☐ Call the police and report the trouble and location.
- ☐ Blow your whistle.
- ☐ Move toward the first whistle and keep blowing.

## TIPS FOR WOMEN

The following is a compilation of reminders specifically designed for the ladies who are reading this book. This information was developed through extensive research and put together by the Missouri Crusade Against Crime. It is provided here with that association's permission.

Safety rules:

- ☐ Know your home and family.
- ☐ Know your area within the community.
- ☐ Be cautious in your car.
- ☐ Be a reporter; the police need extra eyes.
- ☐ Carry a whistle; blow it when necessary.
- ☐ Be prudent.

Know your home and family:

- ☐ Responsible citizens do not steal and kill just because they fear the police, but because they believe such acts are morally wrong. Surveys show the major cause of crime is a lack of moral values.
- ☐ Uplift the moral tone of your home. Be a watchful mother and a better wife.
- ☐ Know where your children are and what they are doing. Warn them of the do's and don'ts on the streets and with strangers.
- ☐ Make clear-cut rules of behavior for your children and see that they are kept. Don't just find fault. Teach children that rights and privileges depend on responsibility.
- ☐ Obey the laws set up to protect you and your family. You employ the police with your tax money. Support them.

Know your neighbors:

- ☐ Acquaint yourself with the schools, churches, stores, and parks. Watch the trouble spots.
- ☐ Maintain your own property. This will be a good example for your neighbors to do likewise.
- ☐ Demand better lighting for your area. Leave on porch lights—front and back. Spend a few pennies a night for this protective light.
- ☐ Own a dog if possible and acceptable. Put up a "beware of dog" sign.
- ☐ Use the buddy system. Find yourself a partner on shopping tours. Two are safer than one and can be more fun.
- ☐ Join your neighborhood association. Joint action is more effective than a single voice.

Blow the whistle on crime:

- ☐ Carry a police whistle at all times—in your hand, on your key chain, or in your pocket. Be ready to blast the whistle or scream loudly.
- ☐ Be a block watcher. Act as a partner with the police by reporting crimes. You should know the local emergency and regular number for the police department. Keep the numbers posted on or near your telephone (Fig. 12-1). Many

```
Your Name _____
Your Address _____
    Police emergency number _____
    Police regular number _____
    Fire station _____
    Doctor (office) _____ home _____
    Dentist _____
    Hospital _____
    Emergency squad _____
    Local poison control center _____
    Baby-sitter _____
Neighbor (1) (name/tele/address) _____
         (2) _____
         (3) _____
Other important information:
    Telephone company (crank/obscene calls) _____
    Electric company _____
    Water company _____
    Gas company _____
Hospitalization insurance company _____ card nbr _____
Drugstore (pharmacy) _____
Taxi _____
Special medicine required in home _____ location _____
```

Fig. 12-1. Emergency telephone list.

police departments have a confidential reporting line. You do not have to give your name when using this line. (The most important aspect is reporting the crime to the police immediately so that the suspects may be apprehended as soon as possible.)

☐ Watch cars that don't belong in your area. If you are suspicious, take the description and license number.

☐ Do you suspect juvenile delinquency, truancy, drug pushing or abuse, or the trafficking of stolen goods? Report this information to the police—they welcome your help. They cannot be on every corner.

Abide by safe car rules:

☐ Keep your car in excellent shape. Always have plenty of gas and good tires.

☐ Make it a habit to lock the doors and roll up the windows before starting the motor. Travel well-lighted, busy streets. If threatened, hit the horn and drive away immediately—to the nearest open business or police station.

☐ Always lock your car and pocket the key. Put packages out of sight in the car trunk.

☐ Don't pick up hitchhikers.

☐ If the car becomes disabled, raise the hood; sit inside the locked car. Open the window slightly to talk to strangers. Do not go with them to seek aid. Ask them to call the nearest filling station. When alone, do not stop to assist a disabled motorist.

☐ Park your car in a well-lighted spot near your destination for greatest safety. Look for loiterers before leaving your car.

□ On arriving home, leave the headlights on until the garage is opened, the car is parked, and the house door is unlocked. (This provides you with light to see if anyone is lurking around near the garage or the door to the home.)

Home safeguards for safety:

□ Keep your doors and windows securely locked. Use chain and deadlocks on all doors.
□ Ask for identification of anyone seeking admittance. Do not allow a stranger to use your telephone. Make a call for him.
□ When leaving your home, turn on a few lights inside. After dark, turn on outside lights. Leave a light on all night.
□ Do not leave extra keys in obvious places. Separate your house keys and car keys so they cannot be duplicated.
□ Windows that are near fire escapes should have extra locks.
□ If you return home to find a door or window open, do not enter or call out. Use a neighbor's telephone to call the police.
□ Protect your valuables. Put jewelry and securities in your safe deposit box until needed.
□ Keep a record of your valuables.
□ Use Operation ID to properly mark your valuables.
□ Mark the items in the house with your driver's license number (usually the same as your social security number). Indicate the state also, such as 531-42-0319, VA. This provides a quick identification of stolen property by the police. Electric etching tools are normally available at local police departments and/or through local libraries for your use.
□ Put up decals on the front and back doors to show potential burglars that all your items are marked.
□ When going on vacation, notify the police of your plans. Cancel deliveries until you return. Put one or more lights on electric timers. Be sure your house is thoroughly secure. Ask a neighbor to keep an eye on the house.

Safety on the streets:

□ When walking, it is really best not to carry a purse. Most ladies must, though, so, carry a minimum amount of money and credit cards or use an inside pocket for storage.
□ When getting out of a car or bus, be wary of people nearby. If you see anyone suspicious, cross the street. If you are alarmed, walk out into the street. This will attract attention and scare the theif. Use your whistle if necessary.
□ If a thief wants your purse, it is better to throw it at him, then blow your whistle. The chances are you may well recover the purse as the thief flees at the sound of the whistle.
□ Don't thumb rides or accept rides from strangers.
□ Don't buy stolen goods. If you are approached on the street or elsewhere and offered goods at bargain prices, chances are the items are stolen. Buying or receiving stolen property is a felony under most state laws. Never buy unless the seller has the proper credentials and a bill of sale. Greed is a partner of the criminal. Don't be trapped.
□ Remember that shoplifting is stealing. The shoplifter may end up with a police record and ruin the chances of getting a job. The risk for the future is simply not worth it.

To family, friends, and neighbors:

□ Become involved.
□ Attack problems as part of a concerned group of citizens. You may be able to open channels to solve problems for

yourself and your neighbors.

☐ Be persistent in your efforts to search out crime in all its forms.

Other programs, such as McGruff "Take a Bite Out of Crime," Neighborhood Watch, Community Watch, Apartment Watch, etc., are only part of a national program to get citizens more involved in doing something about crime. Participate in any program that is offered within your community.

## BEING A GOOD WITNESS

We want to thank The Crusade Against Crime, St. Louis, Missouri, for their input in the development of this section. Justice is best served by those who are eyewitnesses to crime or those who learn specific facts relating to the crime. The problem that exists today is that many witnesses or those knowledgeable about criminal activity do not step forward. This pitfall enables criminals to continue to operate. Effective law enforcement and the criminal justice system become moot points in protecting society from the criminal.

People who are aware of crime, either before or after the fact, must take positive steps to assist those involved in the investigation and further the prosecution of those involved in the crime. Pertinent facts must be reported to the proper authorities. You should expect to see some of your own time consumed during the investigative process. Further, you should be willing to follow through once the facts have been turned over to law enforcement personnel—that is, to take the stand for justice. Without such cooperation, a witness is not a witness, but a middle-of-the-roader who cares not for society. This attitude allows the criminals involved to go free.

There are numerous publications and concepts on what an individual should do. Many different organizations concerned with crime and its impact on society have put together pamphlets to assist you. In some areas, cities and the local police also have programs to assist witness/victims of crime. Take advantage of

them; they are formulated to help you help society.

Being a witness is one thing. Being a *good* witness is another. For example, when asked to identify an offender, whether it be in a police lineup or in a courtroom, be specific and positive in your answer. Don't waver or attempt to clarify a noncommittal answer.

When asked to identify an offender in the courtroom, some witnesses may gaze all over the room, looking everywhere but directly at the defendant. A witness may act this way for a number of reasons: ignorance of the courtroom seating, doubts about his (the defendant's) identification, or a possible threat. Such action weakens the testimony and often undermines the prosecutor's case. On the other hand, a firm and positive identification, made with assurance, carries great weight with jurors.

## SUSPECT AND VEHICLE IDENTIFICATION

The following pointers on suspect and vehicle identifications will greatly help you to be a good witness if circumstances place you at the scene of a crime or accident. If you observe a crime, call the police and, as soon as possible thereafter, write down everything you can remember that would help to apprehend the criminal. Keep your notes and refresh your memory as necessary, especially just prior to taking the witness stand when the case comes to court.

### Suspects

Basic physical characteristics are critical to any identification (Figs. 12-2 and 12-3). Without them, police cannot initiate an effective search for the individual(s) involved. Further, the case and criminal may never come to court without them.

**Sex and Race.** Is the individual male or female? Is the person white, black, oriental, or hispanic.

**Age.** The age is usually approximate, unless you personally know the individual involved and know his actual age. The approximate age would be given as 15-18, 18-21, 21-24, etc.

**Height and Weight.** You might say that an

This checklist is used to assist in supplying police with pertinent information concerning an individual suspect or a car. You should be as accurate as possible; don't guess. Every bit of information provided may help the police in solving a crime.

1. Name (if known) _____
2. Race _____
3. Sex (male or female) _____
4. Approximate age _____
5. Height _____
6. Weight _____
7. Hair color _____ Hair style _____
8. Color eyes _____
9. Complexion _____
10. Build (slender, medium, heavy, etc.) _____
11. Scars visible (where and type) _____
12. Tattoos visible (where and type) _____
13. Clothing worn:
    Trousers (color) _____
    Shirt (long/short sleeve; color) _____
    T-shirt (color and imprint if any) _____
    Coat/Jacket (style and color) _____
        Missing buttons, tears, etc. _____
    Overcoat (style, material, color) _____
    Tie _____
    Socks _____
    Shoes _____
    Hat _____
    Glasses (and style or type of design) _____
    Mustache (type, color) _____
    Sideburns _____
    Abnormalities (if any) _____
    Other distinguishing characteristics noticeable _____

*Vehicle*

Make _____ Model _____ Nbr Doors _____
Year _____ Color _____ Nbr People _____
License Nbr _____ State _____
Characteristics that make it stand out (dents, missing parts, broken
    windows, etc.) _____
_____

Fig. 12-2. Description checklist.

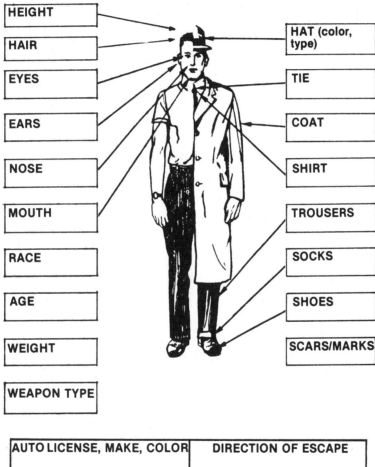

**ARLINGTON COUNTY, VIRGINIA**
POLICE DEPARTMENT
Arlington, Virginia 22201

# FILL IN ALL THE BLANKS

### GIVE TO THE FIRST POLICE OFFICER ON THE SCENE

| HEIGHT | | HAT (color, type) |
| HAIR | | TIE |
| EYES | | COAT |
| EARS | | SHIRT |
| NOSE | | TROUSERS |
| MOUTH | | SOCKS |
| RACE | | SHOES |
| AGE | | SCARS/MARKS |
| WEIGHT | | |
| WEAPON TYPE | | |

| AUTO LICENSE, MAKE, COLOR | DIRECTION OF ESCAPE |
|---|---|
| | |

## FOR CRIME RESISTANCE INFORMATION OR PROGRAMS CONTACT

### CRIME RESISTANCE SECTION
### ARLINGTON COUNTY POLICE DEPARTMENT

Fig. 12-3. Suspect identification guide (courtesy Arlington County, Virginia, Police Department).

individual was about 5'11" and 150-160 pounds. This is acceptable. But you may be wrong for a number of reasons. If you are 5' 10" and weigh about 160-170 pounds, the person is about your height and weight. Were you able to see the suspect's eyes on the same level? If so, then your statement would be accurate. If you have to look up or down, you should adjust your estimate accordingly.

Some suspects have taken this into account, either when the crime was committed or when in the courtroom. During a crime, perhaps the suspect wore cowboy boots and a large cowboy hat. His height was about 5'11". Take away the boots and the hat, and he may be anywhere from 5'5" to 5'8". If he comes into the courtroom without the boots and with his hair cut short, the difference would be noticeable and your testimony would not be as credible as before. In making the determination of height, take note of what else the suspect was wearing. This will have a direct bearing on your testimony and what the jury would believe.

If you hesitate to guess weight, you should use descriptive terms such as short, stocky, very muscular, thin, wiry, etc. You might also compare the person's stature with someone you know and get the particulars later.

**Hair.** Is it long or short? What color? Is there a particular hair style worn by the suspect? Did he wear a beard, sideburns, a mustache, or a goatee? Were the eyebrows bushy or thin? Did the hair color and the color of the eyebrows or mustache differ? If so and the difference was great, the person may have been wearing a wig to disguise his true hair color.

**Identifying Marks.** Were there scars or tattoos visible? Such things as a harelip, or a skin discoloration might also be evident.

**Other Characteristics.** Consider the complexion of the individual (light-skinned, swarthy, etc.) and the shape of the eyes. What about the teeth? Are some missing or does the person have gold or silver fillings? In many instances, the speech of a person is a partial form of identification. Is there a specific accent or does the person stutter? Does the person use words associated with a specific craft or trade, or does he talk with a lisp? Consider specific disabilities. Does the person favor his left or right leg when moving rapidly (may not be evident when walking slowly or normally)? What about a pronounced limp? Are all the fingers on each hand present or are some missing?

**Clothing.** The type and color of the subject's clothing is very pertinent if the police need to launch an immediate search. Articles include the hat, tie, shirt, coat/jacket, trousers, socks and shoes, and jewelry for male subjects. If the subject is a female, then note the slacks or skirt, the blouse, coat/jacket, socks/nylons, shoes, and jewelry.

Color descriptions on apparel can be troublesome because of the conditions under which it is viewed. You should cite the lighting conditions that were in effect at the time. Dark red or purple, for example, might appear brown under certain types of light; gold or yellow might very easily be perceived as tan.

**Behavior.** Was the subject excitable or emotionally disturbed or under the influence of drugs or alcohol? Could you smell alcohol? Was the person sweating profusely as is often the case when an addict is in need of a fix? Was the person armed? Which hand held the gun? Did he seem nervous? Did he threaten lives?

**Weapons.** It is important for the victim/witness involved to be able to identify the weapons used and to link them and the suspect together. When describing a weapon, make use of the following terms:

- [ ] Automatic—flat, no cylinders, "G-man" style, .45 caliber, etc.
- [ ] Revolver (a gun with a circular cylinder—cowboy style gun).
- [ ] Rifle/shotgun. Sawed-off, two-barrel, double trigger mechanism.

Whenever possible, attempt to estimate the length of the barrel. Was the weapon blue steel or silver-colored?

For knives, was it a kitchen knife, a Bowie

knife, a pocket knife, or a switchblade? Was the handle of wood? Perhaps there was no handle. Was the blade broken or the handle taped? Did the knife have a particular style that might identify its origin?

**Physical Evidence.** As an eyewitness to a criminal act, be sure to advise the police officers of any areas that the suspect may have touched. Don't touch these areas yourselves. Never touch anything at the scene of a crime. The police will have an evidence technician take fingerprints, photographs, and other technical types of information and evidence that is necessary.

Call attention to any notes, bits of paper, or other items that the suspect may have handled or accidentally dropped. In some cases, an item that was thrown (such as an ashtray) will provide physical evidence. Again, do not touch it. All these items will be marked as evidence and used when the suspect is caught and brought to trial.

## Vehicles

Most accidents and many crimes involve a vehicle of one type or another. Whether you are personally involved or even a witness to the incident, it is important to give the police as much information about the vehicle as possible. Again, it may be necessary to give the same information in court, be the case civil or criminal.

**Automobiles.** You can identify the automobile by the make, model, year, and color. Remember or write down the license number of the vehicle and the state in which the license was issued. Even if you cannot get all the letters and numbers, a partial identification may be enough to allow police to find the automobile. Maybe you cannot determine the state, then remember the color scheme of the license plate. If you can't remember the entire number on the plate, at least the first three characters will do. By not having all the letters and numbers of the plate, at least you have still provided valuable information.

Was the vehicle a two-door or a four-door model? Was it a station wagon, a camper, a van, or a jeep? Did it have particular markings, scratches, dents, or a multicolored design on it? These various painted motifs on the exterior are usually individually done, which makes the vehicle stand out from others of the same type. These are very excellent in vehicle identification. Along with scratches and dents, are there other visible defects, such as a broken window, a headlight missing, or perhaps a missing or partially damaged bumper? Were there dangling objects in the windows? At the rear window, did you observe various items, such as a stuffed animal or other object? Were there slogan bumper stickers?

**Tristate Buses.** By law, tristate buses carry an identification number on the front and rear. This usually is a four-digit number about 5″ high. The number also appears on the interior panel above the front window. Use it when making any type of complaint to the bus system or police or in court testimony. Report the direction that the bus was traveling at the time of the incident and the name of the bus line. For example, "Lindell Wydown, going east at approximately 3:45 P.M. The number was 3807. The incident took place at Olive and 14th Streets."

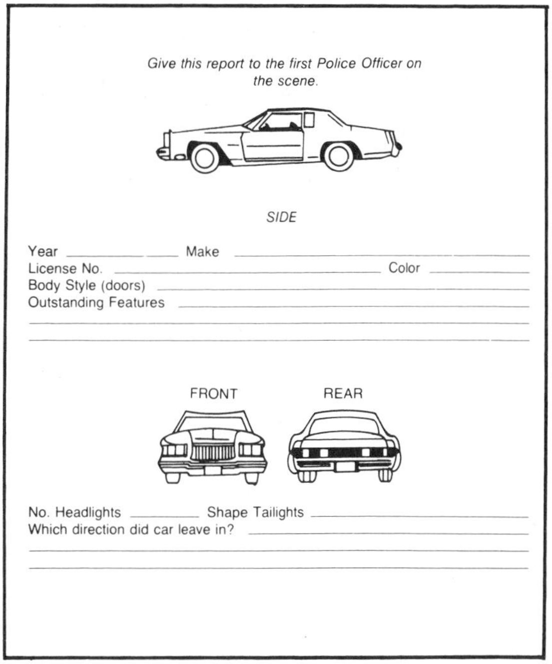
*Give this report to the first Police Officer on the scene.*

*SIDE*

Year ________ Make ________
License No. ________ Color ________
Body Style (doors) ________
Outstanding Features ________

FRONT REAR

No. Headlights ________ Shape Tailights ________
Which direction did car leave in? ________

Fig. 12-4. Automobile description guide.

You don't need the name of the driver. The above information would pinpoint him to the authorities.

**Taxicabs.** Identifying numbers also appear on the taxicab doors, along with the name of the taxi company. In some areas, taxicabs are owned and operated by independent drivers. In such cases, either the owner/operator name will appear or the name under which the taxi is registered. As with other automobiles, always note the vehicle color and license plate whenever possible.

**School Buses.** If you note a problem with a yellow school bus, get the identifying number on the rear or sides and the name of the school, school district, or county to which the bus belongs.

**Trucks.** Trucks may be identified as a 14′, 16′, diesel 18-wheeler, etc. On a tractor trailer, the key number should appear on the back and sides of the driver's cab as well as the left and right top front. The trailer may bear another number that is different from the cab. The name/owner of the cab and the trailer may be the same or different. Note these and report them.

The cab number is the important one. It can be fed into a truck company's computer to quickly determine the name of the driver, his destination, and the nature of his cargo. To report a crime or accident involving a truck, call the local emergency number—if one is in your area (usually 911)—or the city police or highway patrol (depending on where the crime or incident takes place). Note the weather and road conditions.

### TESTIFYING TIPS

As a witness or a victim to a crime or an accident, there is the very real possibility that you will be called to testify in court. If the responsibility of serving as a witness comes your way, here are some basics to remember.

☐ Use the word approximately when describing height, weight, time of day, etc.

☐ Dress conservatively and neatly.

☐ Be businesslike. Speak in a clear voice loud enough to be heard by the court stenographer, the jurors, and other courtroom personnel. Try to control any nervous mannerisms you may have. Let your gaze be direct.

☐ Keep you cool at all times, even though the attorney's questions might be hostile. If you let this disturb you, you'll be playing right into the hands of an attorney who wishes above all else to discredit your testimony for the sake of his client.

☐ If you fail to understand the meaning of a question or if you do not hear it clearly, it is perfectly proper to ask the attorney to repeat the question.

☐ Don't volunteer any information. Wait calmly for each question from the attorney. Then pause before your answer; don't let your tongue trip over your reply to the question. This pause allows for any challenges either attorney might wish to make as to the propriety of the question of you.

Remember that without you, the witness, justice cannot be served.

# Appendices

# Appendix A
# Security Checklist

This checklist should be reviewed at least yearly.

### DOORS AND WINDOWS

- [ ] Are exterior doors locked at all times?
- [ ] Are all exterior doors equipped with an operating deadbolt lock?
- [ ] Do exterior doors leading to a porch (even closed in) have a properly operating deadbolt lock?
- [ ] Does each lock have a deadbolt with a minimum ¾" throw? (A 1" deadbolt throw is preferred and more secure.)
- [ ] Is each exterior door sturdy?
- [ ] Is each exterior door of solid wood or reinforced hollow core?
- [ ] Has any exterior door containing glass or light wood panels been equipped with double-cylinder locks?
- [ ] If the door is not sturdy, has it been replaced or reinforced adequately?
- [ ] Do doors fit into their frames snugly?
- [ ] Is the door in excellent, good, fair, or poor condition? (Note dents, splinters, breaks, etc.)
- [ ] Is the door and/or door frame of steel? (Steel doors and frames are the best security possible.)
- [ ] Does the door have a peephole installed?
- [ ] Is the peephole viewed equipped with a wide-angle lens (160°-180°)?
- [ ] Is the door equipped with a chain door lock?
- [ ] Is the chain door lock used at all times or only occasionally?
- [ ] Is the key to the chain door lock kept on your person?
- [ ] Is the key to the chain door lock kept at least 3' away from the door opening and out of view from casual observation?
- [ ] Does the chain door lock have at least 1" screws holding it? If the door is metal, are metal screws used?
- [ ] Is the strike plate for the locking bolt

firmly affixed with screws of at least 1½″ length? Have you considered special steel screws?

☐ Is there any "play" in the door/frame when the door is pried away from the frame?

☐ Has the frame been checked to ensure that it is properly reinforced?

☐ Is the door frame loose or can it be easily pried away?

☐ Is there an identification tag (name/ address /telephone number) on the key ring that would identify your home to a potential burglar if the keys were lost or stolen?

☐ Are door keys kept on a separate ring from your automobile keys?

☐ Are door hinges interlocking or of the nonremovable type?

☐ Are the hinges properly secured into the frame/studs with long screws?

☐ Are the hinges of quality steel and in good condition?

☐ If the door swings outward, can the hinge pin be removed, or do you have a non-removable hinge pin?

☐ Are the doors properly locked at night?

☐ Are all family members aware that doors should be locked at night?

☐ If your doors have a double-cylinder lock, is the key left in or near the lock at night?

☐ Have your door locks been rekeyed within the last four years?

☐ If you have lost or had the house keys stolen, were the locks changed or rekeyed immediately by a qualified, bonded locksmith?

☐ If your doors have the same key for opening all of them, were *all* the locks changed or rekeyed?

☐ Do you have double doors leading to the exterior of the home?

☐ Do the double doors have a vertical deadbolt lock installed? Is it used all the time?

☐ Do the vertical deadbolt locks have a bolt

extension of at least 1″?

☐ Are there side glass windows surrounding the exterior door(s)?

☐ Can access be gained by breaking the glass window and opening the door by reaching through the opening?

☐ Do you keep doorstops near the doors and use them?

☐ Does your sliding glass patio door have impact-resistant glass installed?

☐ Does the sliding door have screws installed to prevent the door from being lifted out of the frame?

☐ Does the sliding door have a keyed lock? What about a second keyed lock?

☐ Does the sliding door have a Charlie Bar installed?

☐ Do you use a piece of dowel or a broomstick laid in the door track to stop the door from being opened? (This is a very poor security measure.)

☐ Are the patio doors secured with a vertical bolt lock at the point where the two doors meet when closed?

☐ Are the patio doors locked when not being used—especially at night?

☐ Do your windows have a sash catch or a sash lock?

☐ Is the key to the sash lock kept away from the window so it cannot be reached from the outside?

☐ Do you have another lock installed that allows the window to remain in a locked but partially open position for ventilation?

☐ Is the locking device suitable for the window?

☐ Is the opening for ventilation purposes less than 6″?

☐ Is the putty in the windows old? Is it adequate?

☐ Are windows generally locked at all times or merely closed?

☐ Are casement windows equipped with a locking handle?

☐ Have windows that are not opened been secured with screws or nails that are flush to prevent the window from being forced open?

☐ Are above-ground windows easily accessible from nearby trees or other objects?

☐ Have windows been protected with a grille or wire mesh?

☐ Have you considered or installed iron window guards?

☐ Are the window guards properly secured so they cannot be easily removed?

☐ Is there a window in each bedroom available for emergency exit? If bedrooms are on the second floor or higher, have provisions been made for an escape ladder or other emergency escape aid?

☐ Are sliding glass windows secured in the same fashion as sliding glass doors?

☐ Are window air conditioners properly secured and anchored to prevent their removal? Is the window used for unauthorized entry?

☐ Are the basement windows properly secured?

☐ Have you considered or installed glass brick in place of the basement windows?

☐ Are the basement windows properly secured at all times?

☐ Are the walls of an enclosed porch adequately strong to prevent entry through the wall?

☐ Is the door to the porch locked at all times with a deadbolt lock?

☐ Are other openings, such as ventilation holes, properly protected?

☐ Is the cellar door opening adequately protected?

☐ Is the hasp of steel or aluminum?

☐ Is the locking device at least a five-pin keyed lock?

☐ Have the serial numbers been removed (filed off) from the lock?

☐ Are the hinges in good shape and of steel?

☐ Can the hinge pins be removed?

☐ Are the screws one-way?

☐ Are the keys to your exterior doors and cellar kept on key rings?

☐ Are the keys kept hidden outside (under the mat or in the mailbox)?

☐ Are garage doors kept locked at all times?

☐ If the garage doors are of the double-door variety, do you have a vertical cane bolt to secure the inactive door?

☐ Are the doors locked with a padlock? Where is the key kept?

☐ If the garage door is vertical, do you keep an interior or exterior second locking device? Is it used at all times?

☐ Does the garage have a separate entrance door? Is it locked at all times?

☐ Are the windows properly secured?

## EXTERIOR SECURITY

☐ Is sufficient lighting provided for the yard areas near the main doors?

☐ Are the areas in shadows, such as trees and shrubs, properly lighted?

☐ Is the house number well-illuminated and easy to see/read from the street?

☐ Are the lights properly located?

☐ Are doors and windows that cannot be easily observed from the street properly illuminated?

☐ Is the area between your house and the alleyway properly illuminated?

☐ Do you have an automatic timer that turns on/off lights?

☐ Do you have minimum illumination for outbuildings, detached garages, etc.?

☐ Can valuable possessions be seen through windows, especially high value portable items?

☐ Can valuable possessions be seen through sliding glass doors?

☐ Does your mailbox have your full name or just the last name on it?

☐ Is the edge of your properly line properly delineated? Is it with a fence, hedge, a combination of both, or other type?

- [ ] Is the fence easily scaled (if it is a high fence)?
- [ ] If you have a hedge, is it low enough or trimmed so a passerby can easily see an intruder on the property?
- [ ] Are gates kept closed and locked when not in use?
- [ ] Are shrubs near the doors, windows, and garage areas kept well-trimmed?
- [ ] Can an individual easily hide behind your shrubs by a door or window?
- [ ] Is your parking area adequately lighted, and can it be seen from a room in the home by another family member?
- [ ] Do you have proper and adequate street lighting?
- [ ] Are the street lights working or inoperative? If inoperative, has the city been notified so it can be replaced/repaired?
- [ ] Do you and your neighbors participate in the neighborhood watch program?
- [ ] Are you aware of strange vehicles or people frequently in your neighborhood?
- [ ] Do you keep exterior lights on when away from home in the evening?
- [ ] Are tools, equipment, and small articles outside the home properly secured at night (in tool shed, garage, etc.)?
- [ ] Do you have a swimming pool? Do your neighbors or other people on your block also have a swimming pool?
- [ ] Do you call attention to the swimming pool unnecessarily?
- [ ] Do you keep items of a temporary or permanent nature (building supplies, firewood, etc.) by the house or stored away in an outbuilding?
- [ ] Do you use a neighborhood security patrol? Do your neighbors? Is it the same patrol?
- [ ] Does the patrol keep a regular schedule or is it frequently changed to maximize changing conditions?
- [ ] Do you live in a low, medium, or high crime area?
- [ ] Have you, a neighbor, or someone in your block been robbed recently?
- [ ] Do the police make patrols of your street?
- [ ] Are these patrols frequent, infrequent, day, night, or both?
- [ ] Do you know the police who patrol your area?
- [ ] Do you report suspicious vehicles, actions, or strangers to the police?
- [ ] Do you support your local police/private security patrol?

## INTERIOR SECURITY

- [ ] Does your door have a chain lock? Is it used at all times?
- [ ] Do you have and use a rubber doorstop when the door is completely closed or partially open?
- [ ] Do you check the identity of strangers prior to allowing them into your home?
- [ ] Do you have a wall safe or small floor safe for keeping small amounts of money and other valuables? Is it concealed or out of the way?
- [ ] Are your more valuable possessions, such as jewelry, cash, etc., stored in a bank safety deposit box?
- [ ] Do you keep large amounts of cash at home, even temporarily? Why not put it in the bank as soon as possible?
- [ ] Do you leave blank checks and your checkbook out, or are they put away in a drawer or other out-of-the-way place where they are not seen?
- [ ] Do you have a security closet in your home?
- [ ] Are all your household items inventoried, serial numbers noted, etc.?
- [ ] Is this inventory list kept in a separate location, such as the bank safety deposit box?
- [ ] Have you updated your property inventory list recently? Do you include new items on it immediately?
- [ ] Do you participate in Operation ID and have your property marked?

- [ ] Do you keep firearms in the home? Do you have a trigger lock for each weapon? Is the trigger lock used at all times?
- [ ] Do you have a telephone in your bedroom?
- [ ] Do you have the numbers of the police, fire department, hospital, and a neighbor affixed to the telephone?
- [ ] Do your children know the proper procedures on how to make an emergency telephone call?
- [ ] Do your interior doors, especially bedroom ones, have an interior lock?
- [ ] Can the lock be opened quickly in case of an emergency from the outside?
- [ ] Do you have a home burglar/fire alarm system?
- [ ] Does it have a backup (emergency) power supply so it will keep operating if the main power is disrupted?
- [ ] Does the alarm have connections to all doors and windows?
- [ ] Do you have panic buttons in the bedrooms and other areas for emergency activation of the alarm?
- [ ] Does your alarm require a key or a particular keypad number to arm and disarm the system? Where is the key kept?
- [ ] Do you have door or window decals indicating that the premises are alarmed?
- [ ] Does the decal reveal all details of the type of alarm system you have?
- [ ] Does the alarm have an automatic telephone dialer attached? (Check your local ordinances; it may be illegal to have a dialer to call the police department.)
- [ ] Do you have sensors for your alarm under the ground floor windows (floor mats)?
- [ ] Do you have a sensor nearby or attached to your safe?
- [ ] Do you have a sensor attached to your security closet?
- [ ] Do you have valuable art objects, silver, stamp or coin collections, guns, etc.?
- [ ] Are these valuables kept in cabinets or drawers that are equipped with alarm sensors?
- [ ] Where is your local alarm located? Is it by the attic vent or near the ground/first-floor level where it is easily accessible?
- [ ] Is the alarm device in a secure, tamper-proof steel box that is properly affixed to your home?
- [ ] Do you keep valuable items away from the windows and out of casual view from passersby?
- [ ] Do you have a checklist of all your credit cards and their numbers?
- [ ] Do you have the addresses/telephone numbers of all the credit card companies? Do you take action instantly when credit cards are lost or stolen?
- [ ] Do you avoid disclosing that you have a lot of credit cards and valuables?
- [ ] Do you let strangers into your home, assuming they are who they claim to be? Do you check them out with their company, Better Business Bureau, etc.?
- [ ] Are you wary of telephone calls that attempt to get you away from your home? What about individuals who come to the door and attempt the same thing?
- [ ] Do you have individual, self-contained, battery-operated fire/smoke/heat detectors in the home?
- [ ] When was the last time they were tested to ensure the batteries were not dead and that the alarm worked properly?
- [ ] Are they placed in hallways, stairwells, and individual bedrooms?
- [ ] Do you have alarms in the garage, work room, and basement?
- [ ] Do you have a water alarm in the basement?
- [ ] Do you have a gas alarm in the basement and kitchen or other areas where gas may be present?
- [ ] Do you have a fire extinguisher (hand-held model) in the kitchen? What about the basement, workroom, and other areas where a fire may start?

□ Does everyone know how to use the fire extinguishers?

□ Are the fire extinguishers the proper type for the types of fires that may start in a particular area? (It's best to have an A-B-C designated model fire extinguisher so it can be used on all classes of fires.)

□ Do you have an emergency plan for the home?

□ Is the plan tested with drills at least once every three or four months?

□ Do all rooms have more than one exit?

□ Are children or invalids on other than a main floor of the home? Can they easily escape? If not, what provisions have been made?

□ Do you have decals on main doors, windows, and individual rooms where an invalid sleeps indicating such?

□ Are the children capable of opening a window for emergency escape? Have they been tested to do this?

□ Do you have escape ladders or other aids for second-floor windows?

□ Have these devices been tested recently?

□ Can the children operate them safely and easily?

□ Are the devices kept near the windows and not stuck away in a cluttered closet somewhere?

□ In case of an emergency, does everyone know where to meet outside?

□ Are your neighbors aware of your emergency plan and have plans been made for mutual assistance in case of an emergency?

□ Do you feel safe in your home? If not, why not?

## HOME SECURITY DURING VACATIONS

□ Have you arranged for:
    —Plants to be watered?
    —Pet care, either by a neighbor or a kennel?
    —The lawn to be mowed and trimmed at least weekly?
    —The newspaper to be stopped or picked up by a neighbor?
    —The mail to be stopped, forwarded, or picked up by a neighbor?
    —The heating system to be maintained, if necessary?
    —The air conditioning to be running during day or evening if the weather is extremely hot? (Not running it during extremely hot weather is a pronounced sign that the residents are not at home.)

□ During the winter months, is the sidewalk and driveway shoveled when required?

□ Have the police, your apartment complex manager, and neighbors been made aware that you will be away?

□ Who has your alarm key if an emergency arises and access into the home is necessary?

□ Have your valuables been put in a safe deposit box or placed with a trusted friend, neighbor, or relative for safekeeping? (If the premises are alarmed, this may not be necessary unless the vacation will be for an extended period. You might also check with your insurance agent for his professional advice.)

□ Do you have automatic timer lights for evening installed? Do you have more than one? Is the timer a 24-hour or a seven-day one?

□ Does the whole neighborhood know about your vacation dates?

□ Has unnecessary electrically-operated equipment been unplugged (television, stereo, toaster, radio, washing machine, dryer, etc.)?

□ Has the refrigerator been turned down?

□ Are your shades and/or drapes in the position they would normally be if you were at home?

□ Does someone have a travel itinerary and telephone numbers to reach you in case of an emergency?

- [ ] Has your burglar/fire alarm been checked out recently and is it in excellent operating condition?
- [ ] Have your window and sliding door locks been checked to make sure they are properly locked?
- [ ] Have you checked the cellar, basement, and outbuildings to ensure they are properly locked?
- [ ] Does each exterior night-light have a new bulb?
- [ ] Are you leaving an automobile at home? If so, have a neighbor move it on a regular basis. If this is not possible, lock it in the garage. Keep the car locked at all times.
- [ ] Has the trash been put out? Ask a neighbor to do this chore.
- [ ] If you have gates, are they locked at night?
- [ ] Have bills been paid up that will become due during your absence?
- [ ] Do you pack the day before or just before you go? (You don't want the packed car sitting out overnight.)
- [ ] As you leave on vacation, walk through the house and again check all windows. Check the exterior doors from the outside, ensuring that all are properly locked.

## SECURITY ON VACATION AND BUSINESS TRIPS

- [ ] Do you carry large sums of cash?
- [ ] Do you utilize traveler's checks or credit cards?
- [ ] Do you take the minimum number of credit cards, ensuring that no one individual carries all of them? (If you are traveling alone, keep unnecessary or infrequently used credit cards locked up in a suitcase or trunk of your car.)
- [ ] Do you dress so you stand out or inconspicuously so you blend in with other people?
- [ ] Is your luggage locked in the car or the trunk and not carried on a rooftop carrier?
- [ ] If using public transportation (airplane, bus, train, travel tours), lock your luggage and don't overpack.
- [ ] At airports, use the skycap to transport luggage; strangers may be attempting to make off with your luggage. (This is another good reason to get to the airport early; if you are in a rush, help is always appreciated, even from strangers.)
- [ ] When staying in motels or hotels, use a travel alarm and a doorstop for increased room security.
- [ ] Guard all tickets; keep them on your inside pockets.
- [ ] During short stops at airports (layovers) and if you have hand baggage, find a coin-operated locker or check it with security personnel if you will be there several hours.
- [ ] Avoid strangers who strike up conversations, especially for a continued period. Definitely avoid strangers who are of questionable appearance or actions.
- [ ] Exercise caution when shopping in strange places. Carry only the amount of money necessary. Limit the number and type of credit cards on your person. (Many places will not cash checks for people unknown to them, even with proper identification.)
- [ ] Know the number of local police when you are in a strange town for a period. In large metropolitan areas (New York, Chicago, Los Angeles, etc., for example), even for a short period, get the number of the police and have it handy. (In large cities, tourists are a prime target for theft.)
- [ ] Do not carry weapons (especially aboard aircraft). If you are hunting, pack weapons in a carrying case and have it checked through to your destination.
- [ ] Keep your car locked at all times.
- [ ] Use AAA (American Automobile Associ-

ation) or an approved travel agency and seek information on the areas you will be traveling through or to. (Contact local Chambers of Commerce in areas where you will be staying for information.)

☐ When traveling out of the country:

—Are you familiar with foreign currency exchange laws and procedures?

—Can you ask for assistance/emergency help in the foreign language? If not, have local language phrases written out in advance.

—Are you aware of the various values of different denominations of foreign currency and their equivalent dollar value?

☐ Keep all luggage in your room at night. Do not use storage boxes, local storage rooms in hotels/motels, etc.

☐ If you go with a group/tour, do you stay with them? (There is safety in numbers.)

## AUTOMOBILE SECURITY

☐ Do you keep the car locked at all times when not in use?

☐ Do you always approach the car with the door key in your hand?

☐ Do you check around the car before approaching it?

☐ Do you check the interior of the car before opening it?

☐ On entering the car, do you immediately close the door and lock it, *then* fasten the seat belt and start the car?

☐ When driving, do you leave the windows all the way down or only open a few inches?

☐ Do you pick up unknown hitchhikers or other strangers, regardless of age or sex?

☐ If you have car problems, do you attempt to proceed to a safe place, a service station, or other area where there are many people around?

☐ Do you lock your car if it must be abandoned to go for help?

☐ Do you use prudence and judgment in

determing your route of travel for assistance?

☐ Do you use your car horn to alert people to your situation or signal for help?

☐ Do you make unnecessary stops along your travel route?

☐ Do you make stops in areas that are out of the way, remote, or have no other people nearby?

☐ Do you park the car in well-lighted areas only? Is the area isolated?

☐ If you encounter problems with the car at night, do you leave the car on foot for help?

☐ Do you flash lights and use the horn to signal for help?

☐ Do you keep the door locked and windows rolled up (except for a 1″ breathing space in the window)?

☐ Do you take offers of assistance that are unsolicited?

☐ Do you accept rides with strangers?

☐ If you are followed in a car, do you move to the inside lane? (This makes it difficult for the individual to force you off the road.)

☐ Do you drive to a populated area, to the nearest toll exit, or attract the attention of police via a CB for assistance? (Use CB channel 9.)

☐ Do you have a CB radio in your car? Is it operational?

☐ If you are involved in a *minor* accident at night, do you immediately get out of the car to talk with the other driver? (Some minor "accidents" are actually planned.)

☐ Do you wait for the other person to come up to your car?

☐ Do you remain in your car with the windows rolled up and the doors locked?

☐ Do you refuse to get out of the car until proper identification has been offered and you are sure that you will be safe?

☐ Do you use the CB radio to contact the assistance of police for the accident?

☐ If stopped by the police, do you stay in

the car with the windows up and the door locked until the officer has shown proper identification?

☐ Do you carry valuables in your car that have a high resale value or are untraceable?

☐ Is your car door equipped with pushbuttons that cannot be gripped easily with a coat hanger to open the door? (Use straight pushbuttons—not those with a flared top.)

☐ Is your car equipped with an alarm system?

☐ Is the alarm system easily deactivated by cutting a wire?

☐ Is the alarm system armed and disarmed by a key or a series of numbers required on a keypad?

☐ Do you leave your keys in the car when parking it in a lot? (Only the ignition key should be left with the car.)

☐ Do you have your identification attached to the key ring?

☐ If someone attempts to enter your car or smashes a window, are you prepared to drive off immediately?

☐ Do you lock your car, even when going into a convenience store for only a few minutes?

☐ Do you leave the engine running when you are not in the car for any length of time?

☐ Do you alarm the car when it is at home, either in the driveway, in front of the home, or in the garage?

☐ Do you have separate keys for the ignition, doors, and the trunk?

☐ Do you have a separate hood lock and chain to prevent the hood from being forced open and the engine parts removed or the car hot-wired?

☐ Do you have a trunk lock and chain?

☐ Can your spare tire be equipped with a locking device so it won't be stolen?

☐ Do you have a car stereo lock?

☐ Do you lock your tape deck or CB radio in the trunk when it is not in use?

☐ Do you use a removable CB antenna for the car? (The antenna mount also should be removable; otherwise, it identifies the car as having a CB installed.)

☐ Do you keep any extra keys in the car (ignition or trunk, for example)?

☐ Do you have a hidden electrical cutoff or gas cutoff switch? Are you the only person who knows where it is located?

## WALKING AND SHOPPING SECURITY

☐ When walking or shopping, do you carry more cash and/or other valuables than you can really afford to lose?

☐ Outside of busy pedestrian areas, do you normally walk against traffic?

☐ Do you normally carry your purse, briefcase, or other handbag on the side away from the curb?

☐ Do you take shortcuts through alleyways or other places where other pedestrians are not going?

☐ Do you carry your billfold in a pocket with a button or snap or else carry it on the inside of your coat where it cannot be easily removed by a pickpocket?

☐ Do you avoid carrying a gun, knife, or other weapon?

☐ If carrying valuables, are they all in one location on your body, or are they scattered throughout various pockets and bags? (You may lose some, but not necessarily all, to a thief this way.)

☐ Do you avoid strangers who attempt to stop you and start a quick conversation (asking questions, advice, etc.) in very busy and crowded situations?

☐ Do you hold your purse properly and securely *between* your arm and body?

☐ Do you make use of the strap (over the shoulder and not hanging loose)?

☐ Do you always carry a loud, shrill-sound whistle (in your hand—not in your purse)?

☐ Is the whistle carried loose or attached to

your wrist? (A loose whistle can be easily dropped when you are surprised or panicked.)

- ☐ Are your keys and identification carried in the same place?
- ☐ Are your keys labeled with your name, address, and/or phone number?
- ☐ Do you carry all your credit cards or only those you expect to use?
- ☐ Can you reduce the number of packages carried on a shopping trip by limiting the purchases made at separate stores? (Combine purchases at stores using the same card.)
- ☐ If attacked on the street, would you use the whistle or shout for help immediately?
- ☐ If attacked on the street, would you fight back knowing that your chances of winning were poor? What if your chances were about equal or quite good?
- ☐ If attacked on the street, would you look for the nearest U.S. Postal Service mailbox and go there? (If attacked, you could drop your purse or billfold into the mailbox for safekeeping and retrieve it later.)
- ☐ Do you always walk the same route?
- ☐ Do you plan your shopping trip, with an idea about where you will be at any given time?
- ☐ If you believe you are followed:

  —Would you take some form of evasive action (slow down, reverse direction of travel, speed up, or go to the nearest store for help)?

  —Would you make sudden moves that would unnerve your attacker? *Sometimes* an attacker may be more nervous than you.)

  —Would you avoid going in a direction or to a particular place if you thought there would be nobody there to assist you?

  —Would you move toward traffic and attempt to flag down a taxi, bus, or else attract the attention of other passing cars?

  —Would you take shortcuts through unfamiliar, darkened, or deserted areas in an attempt to lose your follower?

- ☐ Do you take your purse and all your identification, cash, etc., when you take strolls through parks and /or other playing areas?
- ☐ If pushing a baby carriage or stroller, do you put your purse in it or keep it on your person?
- ☐ When stopping to rest on a park bench or the like, do you set your purse down or continue to hold onto it?
- ☐ Do you observe people around you and what they are doing? (Anticipation of what a person might do is one measure of being forewarned of a possible action against you.)
- ☐ Do you avoid walking on dimly lighted streets at night?
- ☐ Do you avoid walking in unfamiliar areas/streets at night?
- ☐ Do you avoid walking through parks or deserted areas at night?
- ☐ Do you walk against traffic at night?
- ☐ If necessary, do you walk in the roadway at night to avoid a possible confrontation? (In such a situation, ensure the traffic is such that you will not be injured or cause a traffic accident.)
- ☐ On public transit, do you sit closest to the door? (Sitting in the middle or off to the side is best; by the door, a person departing could snatch your purse or bag and be gone in a moment.)
- ☐ If confronted directly by a robber, would you willingly give up your purse/bag without a fight?
- ☐ Would you antagonize your assailant if he had a weapon?
- ☐ Would you carry many bags or purchases from store to store or would you have them delivered to your home if possible?
- ☐ Do you keep your purchases locked in the trunk of the car and out of sight?
- ☐ Do you make the most expensive or

largest (volume or size) of purchases first or last?

☐ Do you park your car in a secure location (parking lot that has an attendant) or at a location where there are a number of people?

☐ Do you shop alone or with a friend?

☐ In a supermarket, do you carry your purse or put it in the shopping cart?

☐ Do you always keep your purse closed (buttoned, zippered, etc.) at all times? (An open purse is an invitation to casual theft of the contents.)

☐ When in the restroom, do you set your purse on the floor?

☐ Do you shop at night, especially for large or expensive items?

☐ During holiday seasons, do you always remove purchases from the store immediately, *lock them in your trunk,* and then proceed to the next store? (Holiday seasons are periods of highest theft of packages from shoppers. Don't carry very many with you.)

☐ For large shopping ventures, do you have children accompany you, who may provide unwitting distractions for potential package thieves?

☐ Do you take extra special precautions when shopping at night, carrying a large amount of cash, numerous packages, etc.?

☐ Do you use an electronic banking card to make cash withdrawals after normal banking hours?

☐ Do you draw out the maximum amount allowable or just a minimal amount? (It's better to draw out $20 a day instead of taking $200 for the week.)

☐ Do you conceal your hand when entering the access code into the machine?

☐ Do you have the access code written down and in your purse or on the card? (If your purse or card is stolen, you may well be out several hundred dollars within hours after the theft.)

☐ If a suspicious person is near the banking

area, do you enter the wrong access code or else cancel the transaction and leave the area without any cash?

☐ If you are approached after the withdrawal of money, especially if no one else is around, give the thief the money and then go for help.

☐ When out alone at night and you are accosted, do you have at least *some* money to hand over to a thief?

☐ If you encounter a crime in progress, do you report it immediately?

☐ Do you leave the scene of a crime after reporting it, or do you stay in the area to provide the local police with information that may help in their investigation?

## SECURITY FOR APARTMENT AND CONDOMINIUM DWELLERS

If you are an apartment or condominium dweller, ask yourself these questions:

☐ Is there a doorman or security guard to screen visitors?

☐ Are elevators attended? Is there a telephone with emergency numbers in the elevator?

☐ Is the garage attached to the building? Is it properly secured in terms of access? Are there lighting fixtures in the garage to provide adequate illumination?

☐ Can the building be entered from the garage through a door requiring a key to open?

☐ Is there adequate lighting inside the building and also around the building perimeter?

☐ Is there an intercom or closed-circuit television system tied to the main door system that is operated from each apartment? Is there a remote operation for opening the door to authorized visitors available from each apartment?

☐ Can alcoves or other blind spots within and outside the building be used as hiding places for burglars, thugs, vandals, etc.?

☐ Have the locks to your door been

changed since you moved in?

☐ Have spare keys been properly secured? Does management have an emergency access key?

☐ On your door and mailbox nameplate, are only your first initial and the last name indicated?

☐ Do you leave notes on your door?

☐ Do you walk hallways alone late at night?

☐ Do you warn management of unauthorized personnel in or lurking about your building?

☐ Are there adequate fire extinguishers in the hallway?

☐ Do you have a small A-B-C extinguisher in your apartment?

☐ Is there a central fire alarm or several on your floor?

☐ Are there possible exits in case of an emergency?

☐ Are your windows protected against entry from adjoining balconies, fire escapes, etc.?

☐ Are all windows protected with a locking device and not just a closure device?

☐ Is your door of solid wood or of metal?

☐ Does your door have a peephole for viewing visitors?

☐ Do you know your nieghbors? Do you have their telephone numbers? Do you have the telephone number of the manager and an emergency number for night calls to the manager?

☐ Does your door have an auxiliary lock installed?

☐ Does your building have emergency lights in the hallways in case of a power failure?

☐ Are there exit signs prominently located in the hallways?

# Appendix B
# Inventory of Valuables

This appendix is a checklist of items within the home that can be marked, registered, and identified to show lawful possession. You can mark serial numbers of various items within the home and mark individual pieces of property with your name, social security number, or driver's license number. Take photographs and keep the list up-to-date. You should be able to positively identify your property to the police and in court.

Protection of valuables can be done by using Operation ID with the completion of a home inventory listing. That listing should record all items of value in your home.

## ENGRAVING PROPERTY

Engravers are approved and recommended by police for protecting your valuables (Fig. B-1). Any engraver selected must be capable of engraving traceable identification symbols or numbers on any hard surface. The advantage of a nonelectric, portable engraver is that you can engrave items in areas where there is no electricity.

Your engraving tool should have a tungsten carbide or a diamond tip. The device can easily engrave your identification on hard surfaces, such as the metal on a CB radio, power tools, stereos, jewelry, office equipment, bicycles, appliances, etc.

Operation ID has been in existence for several years and has been very effective in helping people identify stolen property. Get your valuables marked. Determine what type of identification you will use. It is recommended that you use your state driver's license number. In many states this is the same as your social security number. If the item is one that you don't expect to sell or discard, you might consider putting your name and social security number on the item.

Record what identification you put on a specific item, where you marked the number, and the make, model, and serial number of the item. Your record book should be stored separately, away from the home, in a safe deposit box.

Many electrically-operated marking devices are on the market. To cut the cost of purchasing a

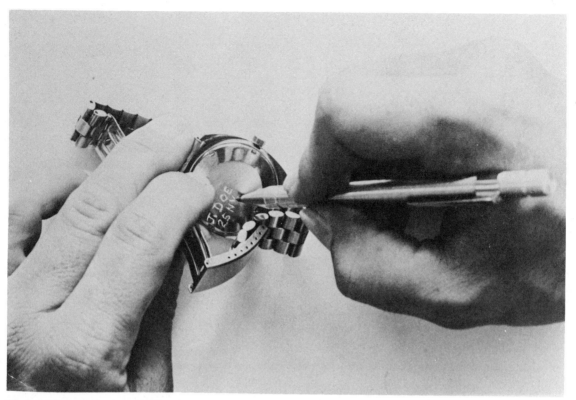

Fig. B-1. Use an engraver to make identifying marks on valuables (Home Safeguard Industries).

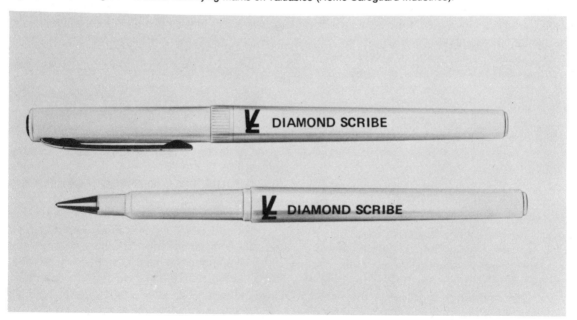

Fig. B-2. A diamond-tipped scriber is an effective tool (courtesy Lunzer Industrial Diamonds, Inc.).

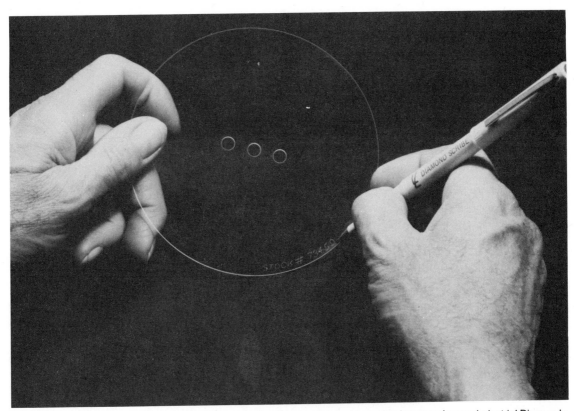

Fig. B-3. The diamond-tipped scriber can mark on plastic, glass, metal, and ceramics (courtesy Lunzer Industrial Diamonds, Inc.).

marking device, you might consider a pocket diamond-tipped scriber (Fig. B-2). This tool can engrave and mark on metal, glass, ceramics, and even plastic (Fig. B-3).

This scriber has an all-purpose polished natural diamond point. The scribe is in the shape of a standard writing pen. It is lightweight, easy to use, and has an easy grip.

## DESCRIBING PROPERTY

The following guidelines will help you describe property so that it can be identified and proven to be yours should it ever be lost or stolen. Note that the guidelines are not firm, but they should be followed wherever possible.

### Appliances and Commonly Found Items in the Home

Appliances include those items found within the kitchen and other common items such as stereos and their speakers, CB radios, televisions, radios, typewriters, etc.

☐ Name of object.
☐ Manufacturer's name (Panasonic, Simplicity—do not abbreviate).
☐ Model number/name (KM-4133, Hi-Liner).
☐ Size, color, weight (64″ high, 12″ wide, 14″ deep; brown walnut (light); solid metal base—total of 147 pounds).
☐ Style (riding lawn mower, electric typewriter, etc.).
☐ Identifying marks and where located.

### Furs and Clothing

☐ Name (full-length sable, jacket, stole, suit).

- [ ] Material (mink, leather, cashmere).
- [ ] Style (belted, straight stole, over the shoulder/wrap).
- [ ] Label (Christian dior, Brooks Brothers).
- [ ] Color (long white hairs, autumn brown).
- [ ] Size (small, 12, 42 long).

### Furniture, Mirrors, and Clocks

- [ ] Name of object/number (table and six chairs).
- [ ] Description (size, shape, color).
- [ ] Antique object? Country of origin? (circa 1823, United States).
- [ ] Manufacturer (Williamsburg Furniture Corp.).
- [ ] Where purchased.
- [ ] Construction material (maple, cherry, lacquered mahogony with maple veneer).

### Hand-Woven Rugs

- [ ] Country or origin (China, Pakistan, Turkey, India, France).
- [ ] Method of weave (hooked, hand-woven).
- [ ] General description (size, color).
- [ ] Pattern (Oriental motif, animals border).

### Guns

- [ ] Name of object (pistol, shotgun, rifle).
- [ ] Manufacturer (Remington, Browning).
- [ ] Model number or name (.38, .9mm Parabellum).
- [ ] Type of action (bolt, revolver, automatic).
- [ ] Barrel length (30", 2", 5").
- [ ] Caliber or gauge (12, 22, 38, 30-06).
- [ ] Color and material of grip or stock (walnut).
- [ ] Identifying marks (serial number, engraving) and where located (under grip side of stock, right side of barrel).

### Jewelry

- [ ] Name of object (ring, bracelet).
- [ ] Stones: color and kind (white diamond), cut or shape (round, pear, square, emerald), carat or size (.25 or ¼, millimeter), number (one diamond, two rubies).
- [ ] Metal: color (yellow, white, rose), material used (14 Karat, 18 Karat, gold-filled, sterling, platinum), finish (bright, textured, engraved).
- [ ] Mounting (Fig. B-4): setting of stones (prong, tiffany, fishtail), shank or band (narrow or wide), top of ring and shape (domed, flat, ballerina, oval, round, square, free form).
- [ ] Identifying marks (trade or jeweler's

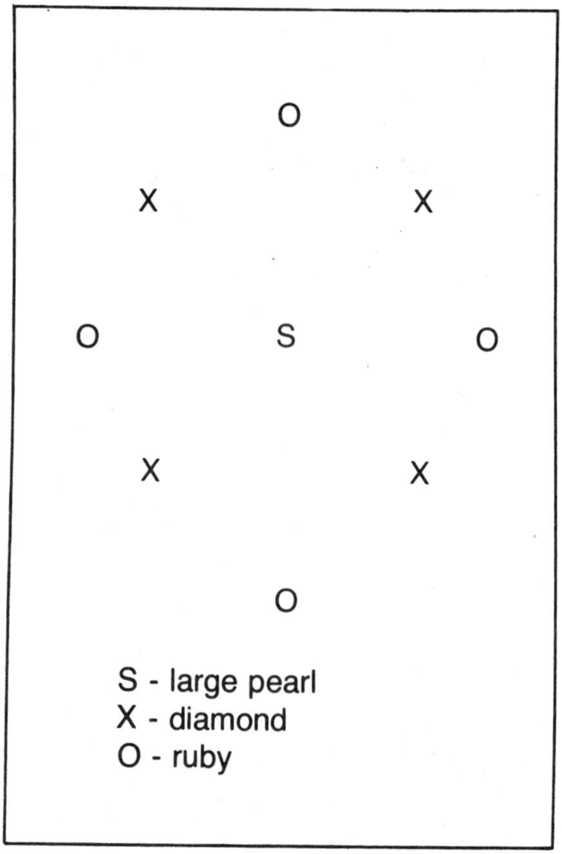

S - large pearl
X - diamond
O - ruby

Fig. B-4. Describe the mounting in as much detail as possible. Include a color photo with your inventory.

marks, scratch marks, engravings, ring size, monograms, missing stone, repaired place) and where located.

## HOME INVENTORY LIST

The list prepared should be as comprehensive as possible. List all valuable items. Include items that are physically located outside the home, such as your car, lawn mower, bicycle, etc. A list should also be prepared for articles kept in safety deposit boxs, at other locations, and on loan to your friends or relatives. Make at least one copy of the list. Keep a copy in a safe place at home, one in your safety deposit box, and another with your will (with the family lawyer or at a bank) or with a close friend or neighbor.

### Living Room

| Article | Manufacturer/ Brand Name | Model Nbr | Serial Number | Cost | Date Purchased | Other Identifying Marks |
|---|---|---|---|---|---|---|
| A/C | | | | | | |
| Clocks | | | | | | |
| Fireplace Equipment | | | | | | |
| Furniture: | | | | | | |
| Chairs | | | | | | |
| Table | | | | | | |
| Divan | | | | | | |
| Lamps | | | | | | |
| Mirrors | | | | | | |
| Paintings/ Pictures | | | | | | |
| Piano | | | | | | |
| Records | | | | | | |
| Rugs/Drapes | | | | | | |
| Stereo | | | | | | |
| Television | | | | | | |
| Video Player | | | | | | |
| Other: | | | | | | |

## Dining Room

| Article | Manufacturer/ Brand Name | Model Nbr | Serial Number | Cost | Date Purchased | Other Identifying Marks |
|---|---|---|---|---|---|---|
| Air Conditioner | | | | | | |
| Carpet/Drapes | | | | | | |
| Buffet/Hutch | | | | | | |
| China Service | | | | | | |
| Tea Service | | | | | | |
| Silverware | | | | | | |
| Other Silver | | | | | | |
| Crystal | | | | | | |
| Other Stemware | | | | | | |
| Dry Sink | | | | | | |
| Table/Chairs | | | | | | |
| Other: | | | | | | |

## Kitchen

| Article | Manufacturer/ Brand Name | Model Nbr | Serial Number | Cost | Date Purchased | Other Identifying Marks |
|---|---|---|---|---|---|---|
| Blender | | | | | | |
| Broiler | | | | | | |
| Clock | | | | | | |
| Can Opener | | | | | | |
| Coffee Maker | | | | | | |
| Electric Knife | | | | | | |
| Dishwasher | | | | | | |
| Mixer | | | | | | |
| Toaster | | | | | | |
| Waffle Iron | | | | | | |
| Freezer | | | | | | |
| Refrigerator | | | | | | |
| Stove | | | | | | |
| Table/Chairs | | | | | | |
| Silver | | | | | | |
| Fire Extinguisher | | | | | | |

## Den

| Article | Manufacturer/ Brand Name | Model Nbr | Serial Number | Cost | Date Purchased | Other Identifying Marks |
|---|---|---|---|---|---|---|
| A/C | | | | | | |
| Cameras | | | | | | |
| Calculator | | | | | | |
| Books | | | | | | |
| Chairs | | | | | | |
| Desk | | | | | | |
| File Cabinet | | | | | | |
| Lamps | | | | | | |
| Paintings/ Pictures | | | | | | |
| Projectors | | | | | | |
| Projection Screen | | | | | | |
| Tape Recorder | | | | | | |
| Television | | | | | | |
| Typewriter | | | | | | |
| Sports Equipment: Golf Bowling Firearms | | | | | | |
| Word Processor | | | | | | |
| W.P. Printer | | | | | | |
| Video Game | | | | | | |

## Recreation Room

| Article | Manufacturer/ Brand Name | Model Nbr | Serial Number | Cost | Date Purchased | Other Identifying Marks |
|---|---|---|---|---|---|---|
| A/C | | | | | | |
| Books | | | | | | |
| Clock | | | | | | |
| Pool Table | | | | | | |
| Video Games | | | | | | |
| Video Recorder | | | | | | |
| Furniture: Table Chairs Divan | | | | | | |
| Pictures | | | | | | |
| Other: | | | | | | |

## Master Bedroom

| Article | Manufacturer/ Brand Name | Model Nbr | Serial Number | Cost | Date Purchased | Other Identifying Marks |
|---|---|---|---|---|---|---|
| Air Conditioner | | | | | | |
| Bed | | | | | | |
| Chairs | | | | | | |
| Dresser (His) | | | | | | |
| Dresser (Hers) | | | | | | |
| Clothing | | | | | | |
| Furs | | | | | | |
| Jewelry | | | | | | |
| Watches | | | | | | |
| Sewing Machine | | | | | | |
| Fire Extinguisher | | | | | | |
| Tables | | | | | | |
| Paintings/ Pictures | | | | | | |
| Carpet/Drapes | | | | | | |
| Sporting Arms: Pistol Rifle | | | | | | |
| Television Set | | | | | | |
| Stereo | | | | | | |
| Video Player | | | | | | |
| Clock Radio | | | | | | |
| Other: | | | | | | |

## Children's Room #1

| Article | Manufacturer/ Brand Name | Model Nbr | Serial Number | Cost | Date Purchased | Other Identifying Marks |
|---|---|---|---|---|---|---|
| Air Conditioner | | | | | | |
| Bed | | | | | | |
| Chairs | | | | | | |
| Desk | | | | | | |
| Dresser | | | | | | |
| Records | | | | | | |
| Record Player | | | | | | |
| Musical Instruments | | | | | | |
| Radio | | | | | | |
| Video Games | | | | | | |
| Other: | | | | | | |

**Children's Room #2**

| Article | Manufacturer/ Brand Name | Model Nbr | Serial Number | Cost | Date Purchased | Other Identifying Marks |
|---|---|---|---|---|---|---|
| A/C | | | | | | |
| Bed | | | | | | |
| Chairs | | | | | | |
| Desk | | | | | | |
| Dresser | | | | | | |
| Musical Instruments | | | | | | |
| Radio | | | | | | |
| Records | | | | | | |
| Record Player | | | | | | |
| Video Games | | | | | | |
| Other: | | | | | | |

**Bathroom**

| Article | Manufacturer/ Brand Name | Model Nbr | Serial Number | Cost | Date Purchased | Other Identifying Marks |
|---|---|---|---|---|---|---|
| Electric Toothbrush | | | | | | |
| Electric Razors | | | | | | |
| Hair Dryer | | | | | | |
| Whirlpool | | | | | | |
| Scales | | | | | | |
| Medicine/ Drugs: | | | (Prescription Number) | | | (Doctor's Name) |

## Garage/Outbuilding

| Article | Manufacturer/ Brand Name | Model Nbr | Serial Number | Cost | Date Purchased | Other Identifying Marks |
|---------|--------------------------|-----------|---------------|------|----------------|------------------------|
| Bicycles | | | | | | |
| Automobile | | | | | | |
| Motorcycle | | | | | | |
| Moped | | | | | | |
| Go-Kart | | | | | | |
| Boat | | | | | | |
| Skis | | | | | | |
| Tent | | | | | | |
| Sleeping Bag | | | | | | |
| Fire Extinguisher | | | | | | |
| Snowmobile | | | | | | |
| Boat Motor | | | | | | |
| Fishing Equipment | | | | | | |
| Spare Tires | | | | | | |
| Battery Charger | | | | | | |
| Chain Saw | | | | | | |
| Garden Tools | | | | | | |
| Hedge Trimmer | | | | | | |
| Lawn Mower | | | | | | |
| Lawn Edger | | | | | | |
| Snow Blower | | | | | | |
| Leaf Blower | | | | | | |
| Ladders | | | | | | |
| Hand Tools | | | | | | |
| Electric Tools | | | | | | |

**Basement/Work Room**

| Article | Manufacturer/ Brand Name | Model Nbr | Serial Number | Cost | Date Purchased | Other Identifying Marks |
|---------|--------------------------|-----------|---------------|------|----------------|-------------------------|
| A/C | | | | | | |
| Bench Saw | | | | | | |
| Band Saw | | | | | | |
| Clock | | | | | | |
| Compressor | | | | | | |
| Fans | | | | | | |
| Fire Extinguisher | | | | | | |
| Hand Tools | | | | | | |
| Heaters | | | | | | |
| Power Tools | | | | | | |
| Tool Chest | | | | | | |
| Vise | | | | | | |
| Welding Equipment | | | | | | |
| Other: | | | | | | |

# Credit Card Inventory Listing

| Card Issuer | Card Number | Expiration Date | Who/Where to Notify in Case of Loss (Name/Address/Telephone Number) |
|---|---|---|---|
| | | | |

# Appendix C
# Manufacturers

**Abloy Security Locks**
5603 Howard St.
Niles, IL 60648

**Allen Manufacturing Co.**
4180 New Getwell Rd.
Memphis, TN 38118

**American Lock Company**
3400 West Exchange Rd.
Crete, IL 60417

**Andra Systems, Inc.**
84 West Broadway
New York, NY 10007

**The Antenna Specialists Co.**
12435 Euclid Ave.
Cleveland, OH 44106

**Ault, Inc.**
146 Amherst
St. Paul, MN 55105

**Automotive Security Systems**
9715 Miller Rd.
Suite 35
Dallas, TX 75238

**Bathurst, Inc.**
801 West 15th St.
P.O. Box 27
Tyrone, PA 16686

**Blue Grass Electronics, Inc.**
602 West Jefferson
LaGrange, KY 40031

**BRK Electronics**
780 McClure Rd.
Aurora, IL 60504

**Burbank Enterprises, Inc.**
155 Forrest Ave.
Palo Alto, CA 94301

**B-W Manufacturers, Inc.**
721 N. Webster St.
P.O. Box 739
Kokomo, IN

**Cable Electric Products, Inc.**
P.O. Box 6767
Providence, RI 02940

**C. A. M. Co., Inc.**
P.O. Box 94
Big Rock, IL 60511

**Campbell Chain Division**
**McGraw-Edison Company**
3990 E. Market St.
P.O. Box 3056
York, PA 17402

**Carpenter Emergency Lighting**
706 Forrest St.
Charlottesville, VA 22902

**C. C. S. Communication**
**Control, Inc.**
633 Third Ave.
New York, NY 10017

**Chamberlain Manufacturing**
**Corp.**
845 Larch Ave.
Elmhurst, IL 60126

**Christy Industries, Inc.**
1812 Bath Ave.
Brooklyn, NY 11214

**S. A. Clark & Associates**
P.O. Box 649
3545 Third Ave.
Marion, IA 52302

**Clark Manufacturing**
9156 Rose St.
Bellflower, CA 90706

**Colorado Electro-Optics, Inc.**
2200 Central Ave.
Boulder, CO 90301

**Controllor Systems Corporation**
21363 Gratiot Ave.
E. Detroit, MI 48021

**Cooper Industries, Inc.**
P.O. Box 188
250 Railroad St.
Canfield, OH 44406

**Corby Industries, Inc.**
2747 MacArthur Rd.
Whitehall, PA 18052

**Crest Electronics, Inc.**
4921 Exposition Blvd.
Los Angeles, CA 90016

**Datasonics, Inc.**
255 East 2nd St.
Mineola, NY 11501

**DTI Security**
1034 Keil Ct.
Sunnyvale, CA 94086

**Elbex America, Inc.**
20630 S. Leapwood Ave.
Suite "F"
Carson, CA. 90746

**Escape Tape Industries, Inc.**
P.O. Box 3435
Peabody, MA 01960

**Fichet, Inc.**
P.O. Box 92
Halesite, NY 11743

**Fyrnetics Inc.**
1021 David Rd.
Elgin, IL 60120

H.L.B. Security Electronics,
Ltd.
211 E. 43rd St.
New York, NY 10017

Home Safeguard
Industries, Inc.
29706 Baden Pl.
P.O. Box 4073
Malibu, CA 90265

Ideal Security Hardware Corp.
215 E. Ninth St.
St. Paul, MN 55101

IEC Interstate Engineering
522 E. Vermont Ave.
P.O. Box 431
Anaheim, CA 92805-0431

Imperial Screen Co., Inc.
5336 West 145th St.
Lawndale, CA 90260

Insurance Information Institute
1025 Vermont Ave, N.W.
Washington, DC 20005

Intermatic Inc.
Intermatic Plaza
Spring Grove, IL 60081

Interstate Engineering Co.
522 E. Vermont Ave.
P.O. Box 431
Anaheim, CA 92805

Jenser International
Distributors, Ltd.
P.O. Box 92
Halesite, NY 11743

E. F. Johnson Company
299 10th Ave., S.W.
Box 1249
Waseca, MN 56093

Kolin Industries, Inc.
P.O. Box 357
Bronxville, NY 10708

Koyo International Inc. of
America
1855 New Highway
Farmingdale, NY 11735

Kwikset Division
Emhart Hardware Group
516 E. Santa Ana St.
P.O. Box 4250
Anaheim, CA 92803

Lifeguard Products Co.
P.O. Box 106
Barnstable, MA 02630

Lightning Protection Institute
48 N. Ayer St.
P.O. Box 406
Harvard, IL 60033

Linear Corporation
374 S. Glasgow Ave.
P.O. Box 6019
Inglewood, CA 90301

Lock Technology Corp.
685 Main St.
New Rochelle, NY 10801

Lunzer Industrial
Diamonds, Inc.
48 West 48th St.
New York, NY 10036

Macurco, Inc.
3946 S. Mariposa
Englewood, CO 80110

Majima Company, Ltd.
44-2, 4-Chroma
Kita Karasuyama
Setagaya-Ku
Tokyo 157 Japan

Marlee Electronics Corp.
3965 Landmark St.
Culver City, CA 90230

Massa Products Corp.
280 Lincoln St.
Hingham, MA 02043

Master Lock Company
2600 N. 32nd St.
P.O. Box 10367
Milwaukee, WI 53210

Microtone, Inc.
P.O. Box 434
Morrow, GA 30260

Napco Security Systems, Inc.
6 Ditomas Ct.
Copiague, NY 11726

October Group Systems
Suite 481
5757 Wilshire Blvd.
Los Angeles, CA 90036

Ovenaire-Audio-Carpenter
Box 1528
706 Forrest St.
Charlottesville, VA 22901

PemAll Fire Extinguisher Corp.
39A Myrtle St.
Cranford, NJ 07016

The Peterzell Co.
951 N. Pennsylvania Ave.
P.O. Box 966
Winter Park, FL 32790

Pittsburgh Corning Corp.
800 Presque Isle Dr.
Pittsburgh, PA 15239

Preso-Matic Lock
Company, Inc.
3048 Industrial 33rd St.
Ft. Pierce, FL 33450

Pulnix America, Inc.
453F Ravendale Dr.
Mountain View, CA 94043

Recora Company, Inc.
Powis Rd.
St. Charles, IL 60174

Remcraft Lighting Products
P.O. Box 54-1487
12870 N.W., 45th Ave.
Miami, FL 33054

Rival Manufacturing Co.
36th & Bennington
Kansas City, MO 64129

Rofu International Corp.
230 Carson Mall
Carson, CA 90476

Rossin Corporation
1411 Firestone Rd.
Goleta, CA 93117

Sargent
Division of Kidde, Inc.
100 Sargent Dr.
New Haven, CT 06511

Se-Kure Controls, Inc.
5685 N. Lincoln Ave.
Chicago, IL 60659

Sendec Corp.
56 West Ave.
Fairport, NY 14450

Sentrol, Inc.
10831 W. Cascade Blvd.
Portland, OR 97223

Sentry
John D. Brush & Co., Inc.
900 Linden Ave.
Rochester, NY 14625

**Sescoa**
3621 Wells Fargo
Scottsdale, AZ 85251

**Silent Knight Security Systems**
1700 Freeway Blvd., North
Minneapolis, MN 55430-
1795

**Sleeper Beeper Corp.**
1701 N. Greenville Ave.
Suite 208
Richardson, TX 75081

**Stop Loss Security Systems**
1601 Mono Drive
Modesto, CA 95354

**Tapeswitch Corporation**
**of America**
100 Schmitt Blvd.
Farmingdale, NY 11735

**Thompson Lightning**
**Protection, Inc.**
901 Sibley Highway
St. Paul, MN 55118

**T.O.B., Inc.**
10821 Main St.
Clarence, NY 14031

**Travel Commander, Inc.**
3621 W. MacArthur Blvd.
Suite 109
Santa Ana, CA 92704

**Trigon Electronics, Inc.**
1220 N. Batavia
Orange, CA 92667

**Truth, Inc.**
700 W. Bridge St.
P.O. Box 427
Owatonna, MN 55080

**T-Track Systems, Inc.**
2301 Artesia Blvd.
Suite 7
Redondo Beach, CA 90728

# Index